GLASS PAPERWEIGHTS

of

THE BERGSTROM-MAHLER MUSEUM

Introduction and Cameo Incrustations
by Geraldine J. Casper

UNITED STATES HISTORICAL SOCIETY PRESS™
RICHMOND, VIRGINIA

DISTRIBUTED BY HARRY N. ABRAMS, INC.
NEW YORK

Library of Congress Catalog Card Number: 89-50485

ISBN   0-927997-00-2
ISBN   0-8109-3350-0 (Abrams)

Printed and bound in the United States of America

CONTENTS

FOREWORD

The following catalogue of the Paperweight Collection of the Bergstrom-Mahler Museum can only be described as a collaborative effort. We must first look to the work of Evangeline Bergstrom. Her acumen as a collector and research pioneer represent, even today, the backbone of the Paperweight Collection and this catalogue. To this we must add the long-standing efforts of Paperweight Collection Curators, Geraldine J. Casper and the late Evelyn Campbell Cloak. In addition to the donations of collectors which provide for the growth of the Paperweight Collection and the research of Curators which provide documentation, we must also acknowledge the many contributions of the Paperweight Collectors Association. It is through the support of its membership that the Bergstrom-Mahler Museum has become "Mecca" for collectors.

Special acknowledgment must be made to Bud Hjerstedt of Munroe Studios for his tireless work on the photography. I also want to recognize the work of Gracia Drew, Marlene Konsek and Norie Heckmann and many other volunteers without which this catalogue would not have been published.

Alex Vance
Executive Director

INTRODUCTION

Paperweights have been variously described as "jewels in glass," "bibelots," "novelties," or "lumps of glass." Like sorcerous crystal balls portraying a myriad of miniature worlds mysteriously imprisoned and magnified, glass paperweights beguile the eye and bewitch the mind. An aura of wonder surrounds the glass paperweight, its shimmering motif glorified by a lens-like dome and its optic appeal further enhanced, when faceted, by interaction of simultaneous magnification and miniaturization. Each is handmade, even those originated in factory environments. Only a glassmaker *wouldn't* ask, "How does the design get inside?"

If a paperweight appears as a magical miniature world, it reflects the maker's skill, a fusion of mind over matter, an alchemist's dream come true. A paperweight masterpiece masks the inherent manual dexterity and technical mastery that gave it birth.

Like small worlds, each paperweight mirrors a part of our history. During their classic period, 1845-55, glass paperweights offered multifaceted appeal: to actually hold down papers in drafty rooms or to simply decorate shelves, cabinets and étagères, and at the same time symbolize the colors and flower language so important to Victorians.

Paperweights saw royalty and all the distinguished members of their political and social circles. Paperweights traveled to collectors worldwide from the Cristalleries de Baccarat in the Vosges Mountains, from the Cristalleries de Saint Louis near Bitche, and from L. J. Maës, Clichy-la-Garenne, in France; from Venice, Bohemia, London and the Stourbridge area of England. United States visitors to the first World's Fair in 1851 at London's Great Crystal Palace returned with paperweights from the French makers, extending the vogue to Victorian America.

As in the old adage, beauty is, of course, in the eye of the beholder. Beauty may be in mid-19th century antique millefiori types reminiscent of Egyptian mosaics; or, it may be in lampwork flora and fauna descended from ancient whimseys and the elaborate scenic plateaus and figurines created by 17th century European glass artists "at-the-lamp"; or, early 19th century cameo incrustations (commonly called "sulphides") immortalizing the historically famous — both real and mythological.

One's interest may focus on souvenirs of historic places and events: popular Spas, World Fairs from 1851 to 20th century, centenaries and bicentenaries, or political campaigns. Beauty may be found, too, in paperweights inviting imagination: trapped air designs that reflect in multiples the world around them, or in illusionary flowers like bursts from fireworks.

The lure of the paperweight intensifies upon being handheld. Through its lens-like dome, its design is enhanced, revealing details intuitive to the practiced eye. The collector and student of glass become tuned to subtle variations in color, form, pattern and glass clarity — just as the scholar perceives nuances in poetry, literature, art and music. Evangeline Bergstrom observed that "interest and knowledge grow hand-in-hand."

I

Sheer coincidence attracted Evangeline Bergstrom (1872-1958), whose collection forms the nucleus of the Bergstrom-Mahler Museum's permanent display, to these almost overlooked objects of Victorian art. In the *unpublished* Foreword to her famous book, *Old Glass Paperweights,* Mrs. Bergstrom wrote:

"The love of a paperweight has been imbedded in my heart since childhood. As far back as I can remember, Grandmother had one which was not on the proverbial desk, but on the table in the parlor. I spent many summers in this small town in New York State, and I can remember my reward was to be allowed to play with this weight after I had played my piece on the piano or recited a poem for some caller.

"Many years later, when in Florida, my life companion and I were going to a stamp exhibition and across the street I saw the sign 'Antiques Show'. Never having been to one, I ventured forth and in one of the booths I spied 'Grandmother's' weight — a millefiori one similar to hers (**No. 3**) — and I could not separate myself from it and carried it away in much glee."

(Note: When interviewed by HOBBIES Magazine, October, 1941, for "Paperweight Collectors' Round-Up," Mrs. Bergstrom related: "As far back as I can remember my grandparents had one of the millefiori type … When the old house was dismantled, that was the one thing I wanted, but no trace of it could be found…")

"From that time on, whenever I saw a weight that took my fancy, I added it to the one nest egg, which has now increased 300-fold.

"They have been on display at the Chicago Art Institute, Milwaukee Art Institute, and Green Bay Museum. The vogue for weights has increased to such an extent that two overlays (in June, 1940, during the trying period of the War) sold in London for 57 pounds each — as much as a painting, and when brought to the United States would be increased by a 50% duty, plus the war risk insurance."

The exhibit of her paperweights at the Chicago Art Insitute in 1939 received considerable press. In Mrs. Bergstrom's scrapbook, a clipping from THE CHICAGO TRIBUNE's sophisticated column "Front Views and Profiles" describes the "enchanting Bergstrom paperweights" and backdrops other scenes in the limelight, including glimpses of opera and stage stars Lawrence Tibbett, Irene Castle, and Gertrude Lawrence on their way, after "Skylark" at the Harris Theatre, to the Pump Room.

A letter from a prominent New Yorker related that "the Chicago Art Institute exhibition is listed in all the art journals as well as the NEW YORK SUN."

The next year, 1940, the MILWAUKEE JOURNAL compared the Bergstrom paperweights to "bright verbena beds" and predicted that members of the City Hall Board of Estimates meeting at the Milwaukee Art Institute (to determine whether the City should continue its $20,000 annual support) would have to be "urged away from the glass cases" displaying the paperweights.

Evangeline Bergstrom enjoyed a challenge. Researching the "B" in her first weight, she eventually learned that it stood for the French factory of Baccarat. Information was, at best, sparse and scattered. Under the "B" was the year "1847" linking the weight to the European classic period, 1845-55, for three principal types — cameo incrustation ("sulphide"), millefiori, and lampwork — produced by three leading French factories — Baccarat, Clichy and Saint Louis — as well as makers in Venice, Bohemia and England.

To her library, Mrs. Bergstrom added a rare book whose title exactly described by that time her own passion: *Curiosities of Glassmaking,* published in 1849 by Apsley Pellatt, a London glassmaker best known for his ceramic cameo medallions incrusted in glass for desk and table. Mrs. Bergstrom's search for a fully signed object by Apsley Pellatt was not rewarded until 1941 (**No. 410**).

In 1940, a chance remark, overheard in a shop lamenting the lack of information on

paperweights, inspired Mrs. Bergstrom to remedy the void. Within the year, then age sixty-eight, she compiled and privately published the first comprehensive text appropriately titled, *Old Glass Paperweights,* Their Art, Construction and Distinguishing Features. Illustrated from her collection with twenty color plates and 81 half-tones, the book was an instant success. Although reprinted three times by Crown Publishers, it has been long out-of-print.

Again, insights from Mrs. Bergstrom's scrapbook: in the NEW YORK SUN, Antiques section, December 21, 1940: "At last, a paperweight book... paperweights will probably become still more popular...", and a letter from Harry

J. Owens who wrote the published Foreword: "Only a few months ago, I was completely unconscious that paperweights existed...you have made me feel about paperweights as Lorado Taft once made me feel about fine art when I had the privilege of visiting the Louvre with him." And, a prophetic note from Philadelphia: "...perhaps your work will prove to be the needed inspiration for the revival of paperweights."

During a WGN Chicago radio interview in 1945, Mrs. Bergstrom recalled, "...as a child, it amused me by the hour to try to find two similar florets...the beautiful color in the canes and flowers...have a sparkle and brilliancy resembling a precious jewel to me... the delicate and endlessly varied patterns of the designs...are brought out by the perfect workmanship...first displayed in the old French weights..."

Born 1872 in Ithaca, New York, the only child of Dr. (dentist) and Mrs. George W. Hoysradt (née Adelaide Gregg), Evangeline H. Bergstrom's name has become legend in paperweight literature. That Neenah, a papermaking center in the Fox River Valley of Wisconsin, should be the repository for one of the world's finest paperweight collections is pure happenstance. Evangeline Hoysradt and John Nelson Bergstrom were students when they met in

Ithaca, she at the Anna Brown School for Girls and he (born 1874 in Neenah) at Cornell University. Married in 1901, the young couple moved to Neenah in 1904 when Mr. Bergstrom joined his father, Dedric W. Bergstrom, in the manufacture of paper.

Childless, the Bergstroms' lifestyle focused

on their church, as well as historical, horticultural and educational pursuits. Mrs. Bergstrom's ancestry entitled her to memberships in the Mayflower Society of Massachusetts, Colonial Dames of Wisconsin, the Daughters of the American Revolution, and the Wisconsin Antiquarian and Historical Societies. She is included in *Wisconsin Women, A Gifted Heritage,* edited by Andrea Bletzinger and Anne Short, published by The American Association of University Women, Wisconsin; 1982.

That Mrs. Bergstrom's book, *Old Glass Paperweights,* provided the collecting world with a valuable resource was underscored by expert J. Percy Boore in "Bergstrom Reviewed," PAPERWEIGHT COLLECTORS' BULLETIN, June, 1963:

> "Little printed matter of a reliable nature preceded her effort. Small wonder, then, that the book contains some errors...the wonder is, not that there were errors, but that they were so few."

Mrs. Bergstrom herself recognized that in assigning certain items "the classification is often based upon nothing more substantial than a supposition." Since only about one-third of 19th century paperweights were signed, even more remarkable was her intuition in selecting rare and outstanding examples earning the collection worldwide status.

Between 1941 and 1945, Evangeline Bergstrom contributed four articles:
- "Steeple Weights," HOBBIES, October, 1941 (mantel ornaments with enclosed decoration)
- "B As In Baccarat," ANTIQUES Magazine, April 1943 (dated millefiori types, **Nos. 9, 123, 148, 447**)
- "Paperweights — Rare and Not So Rare," AMERICAN COLLECTOR, July, 1943 (authenticity of "antique" examples)
- "Pinchbeck But Precious," AMERICAN COLLECTOR, November, 1945 (**Nos. 493, 504, 506, 511**)

Still timely are comments from "Paperweights Rare and Not So Rare": "The entire field of modern imitations and outright counterfeits is far too great to cover in anything short of a bulky volume, but...certain facts...may be of help to collectors whose experience is still limited...who...stand in some danger of acquiring paperweights which...are...less valuable than they may appear...Allow me to say ...that collecting paperweights would not have quite its fascination if all the procedures were cut and dried — if there were not certain pitfalls along the way, if it were not necessary to exercise our wits at least a little..."

How did Evangeline Bergstrom in small midwestern Neenah, Wisconsin assemble a major paperweight collection? Contrary to popular assumption, she did not travel abroad during the 1930s and 1940s (the Depression and World War II years), but did visit the East coast and wintered in Florida. Most acquisitions came through C. W. Lyon, Inc., New York, and A. Starr Best and Arthur Ackermann & Sons, both of Chicago. Visualize the numerous insured packages from various dealers: "...in respect to the snake paperweight...this is definitely old...as fine as we have ever had...If, however, you are not satisfied...do not keep it for an instant." Fortunately, Mrs. Bergstrom bought this one (**No. 108**).

Paperweight purchases before 1935 and after 1944 were probably minor in number. Of eighty-nine items unrecorded in Mrs. Bergstrom's card file, most of these are numbered between 515 and 729 (Revised Edition). Her files indicate various sales from her collection, which probably occurred when she found other examples she preferred. That her acquisitions from certain dealers were considerable is recorded on invoices allowing her a "discount."

How did antique paperweights fare in the early twentieth century marketplace? During Mrs. Bergstrom's peak years of collecting, 1935 to 1944, 165 weights cost less than $50 and 111 examples ranged from $50 to $100. For the others, she paid from $200 to $2200, the latter amount only twice (**No. 393**, Saint Louis vase, 1941; **No. 502**, New England Glass Company faceted double overlay, 1943). (By contrast, Mrs. Applewhaite-Abbott, the quintessential early 20th century English collector, paid £1.50 ($3.00) in 1917 for her first paperweight. Note later references to the sales of the Applewhaite-Abbott collection in 1952 and 1953.)

The ambience of Mrs. Bergstrom's collection and preponderance of rare examples are extraordinary. Guided by her knowledge of art and inherent love for the beautiful, she selected not only superior paperweights but items related in technique, such as the Hellenistic glass beads, 3rd to 1st century, B.C. (**No. 227**).

Most of the antique examples she chose to illustrate *Old Glass Paperweights* are among the "rare" or "excessively rare" types shown in *Antique Glass Paperweights From France,* by Patricia K. McCawley, 1968. Among rare examples from Mrs. Bergstrom's collection included in Paul Jokelson's *One Hundred of the Most Important Paperweights,* 1966, are **Nos. 127, 128, 161, 228, 473, 485, 486** and **499**. In the Collection are examples similar to others illustrated by Jokelson: **Nos. 98, 105, 123, 136, 145, 179, 198, 204, 215, 236, 244, 299, 308, 337, 373, 424, 447, 467, 487, 498, 1145** and **1290**.

In "Conservatory in Crystal," 1976 PCA BULLETIN, Peter Nagel discussed classification of certain paperweights as "rare" or "uncommon." Webster defines rarity as "unusual excellence of workmanship, quality," which applies as well to glass art. Nagel stated, "Not all rarities are floral, but many are because lampwork techniques usually offer the greatest opportunity for variation and the artist can more easily express his individual taste and craftsmanship." Other designs (**No. 1281**) may be unique — perhaps a presentation piece, or were too complex (**No. 1112**) to perfect in number. On the other hand, Baccarat lampwork artists, ca. 1848-55, followed watercolor designs, as shown in T. H. Clarke's essay (**No. 782**). Details count in determining rarities. Note, for instance, the rare Saint Louis yellow ochre torsade in **No. 441** and its square center cane. **No. 450**, by Baccarat, has early pansy petal flowers in cruciform arrangement centered by a dark red camomile.

When provenance of rare paperweights is known, usually the anecdotes are worth retelling. The story of three weights from the Marquis de Bailleul Collection in France was "tucked in" an article entitled "How We Found The Oscar Wilde Collection of Paperweights" by Barbara Bastien Rowe, HOBBIES, October 1941. Mrs. Rowe, whose father was a buyer for A. Starr Best, Chicago, embellishes the provenance of **Nos. 234** and **236** purchased by Mrs. Bergstrom in 1939. They were part of a private sale by the Marquis at his Château d'Angerville.

"Our first glimpse of the grey stone château with high pointed roof was breathtaking. The interior was even lovelier, and to sit in the great hall hung with marvelous Gobelin tapestries and portraits done by Old Masters was an experience of a lifetime... The Marquis and his wife were most charming and gracious, and showed us around. In the game room, the billiard table had been converted into a showcase for a wonderful collection of "sulfures" containing many interesting items, such as a ring given by Napoleon to Josephine.

Finally, we went through the gardens to a small Normandy cottage...furnished with French provincial things. Here the collection of paperweights was kept. There were just under 200 weights in all ...a great deal of variety and many unusual examples, the *rarest* a magnificent yellow rose on cobalt background (**No. 236**). Its origin was French, but the specific factory that produced it, we were unable to determine..."

As one becomes more involved in the paperweight world, one discovers that the three main types exist in three sizes ranging from less than two inches to over four, called "miniature," "regular," and "magnum." Those with diameters of five or more inches are "doorstops." Others, in "egg" shape, are "handcoolers" made for fastidious Victorians when hand-kissing was in fashion and etiquette forbade offering a warm hand to a gentleman (symbol of passion!).

This paperweight world has its own confusing jargon: setups, upset muslin, torsade, basal ring, arrow and anchor canes, et cetera. One hears about "characteristics": profile, striae, "dings," carpet ground, basket, mushroom, piedouche. After one spends $200 for a $20 paperweight, these details become more critical in distinguishing the antique from the modern copy. Knowing original diameters of Classic period paperweights may also be helpful. Unless the motif is rare or exceptionally well executed, a cut-down (**No. 8**) altered weight is usually less valuable. One learns that, if a fine antique weight has been badly bruised (children have been known to use paperweights as playing balls or hammers), regrinding requires expert opinion before restoration. One's reward is enjoyment rather than disappointment.

The lure of the paperweight may be verging on addiction when the collector begins the intriguing area of research. One might paraphrase "The Funniest Thing Happened on the Way to The Forum" with "The Most Fascinating..." The extensive bibliography available in museums and public libraries can reveal enough new dizzying data to earn one a degree in glass history and paperweights or, at least, the thrill of discovery. Amusing tidbits are often tucked in with the scholarly. Paul Hollister uncovered THE NAMASKET GAZETTE, Middleboro, Massachusetts, for Friday, July 18, 1856. Under *Sandwich,* one finds references to the operation of the Boston & Sandwich Glass Works and its steamer, "Acorn," used for shipping to and from Boston. THE GAZETTE stated "the principal materials of which glass is made are silex and common lead..." Of special interest, however, to the writer (who adds to our appreciation of Cape Cod amenities at the time) was this observation: "But on the way to the Glass Works...one passes...a new building...found to be a Bathing House with four apartments (which) must constitute a luxury in the hot season...A person entering one of the rooms can supply himself with any amount of water and let it off with pleasure." The cost of the NAMASKET, published weekly, was "One Dollar per year in advance."

Sometime between 1820 and 1845, letter weights or "letter presses" (used mainly by the literate) became spherical and were renamed paperweights (presse-papiers in France, briefbeschwerer in Germanic-speaking countries). The palm-sized souvenir that really made paperweight history was simply a "hodge-podge" of odds and ends of glass slices from various design and silhouette rods. Its special appeal was the date "1845," commemorating the Exhibition of Austrian Industry meeting in Vienna, and the initials "POB." Attributed to the Venetian glassmaker, Pietro Bigaglia, the souvenirs were made in spherical, cylindrical, and cubical forms. Examples of the latter two, illustrated by Herbert W. L. Way, THE CONNOISSEUR, December, 1922, page 217, fig. 4, appeared in the sale of Mrs. Applewhaite-Abbott's Collection, Sotheby's Lot 149, July 1, 1952.

Widespread interest in the scientific excavations of Herculaneum and Pompeii, which began in 1737, set in motion a series of revivals of ancient decorative techniques to satisfy the tremendous market for cameo-carved gems, both intaglio and in relief, and for mosaic glass vessels and other artifacts. Details relating to these events, so significant in paperweight history, are discussed in the section on Cameo Incrustation.

By 1845, the Napoleonic wars and political turmoil in Europe that drastically diminished orders for luxury glass and elaborate chandeliers resulted in financial crises for glasshouses like Baccarat and Saint Louis. The story's happy ending is credited to the alertness of Professor Eugène Péligot of the Conservatoire des Arts et Métiers, who represented the Paris Chamber of Commerce at the 1845 Exhibition of Austrian Industry in Vienna. On his return to Paris, Prof. Péligot's perceptive appraisal of Pietro Bigaglia's small millefiori souvenirs was quickly translated into the novel yet inexpensive desk accessory that saved French glassmakers from bankruptcy.

Saint Louis was first to produce a millefiori paperweight signed and dated "SL 1845." Baccarat quickly followed with millefiori weights and tazzas dated "B1846." The year "1848" (sometimes with a "J") appears in Bohemian millefiori, and the same year appears in weights attributed to England. Incrusted cameo and enameled foil motifs of the 1820s-40s were soon outnumbered as millefiori and lampwork paperweights captured Victorian fancy.

The peak of the Classic period for glass paperweights, 1845-55, probably coincided with the first World's Fair in 1851. This unprecedented event to promote the arts and sciences, sponsored by Prince Albert and enthusiastically endorsed by Queen Victoria, attracted 6,000,000 visitors from around the world. Like a giant greenhouse in London's Hyde Park, the Great Crystal Palace was a marvel of iron framework sheathed with 300,000 sheets of glass. Its designer, Joseph Paxton, Chatsworth Conservatory botanist, was knighted for his creation. Not only was the visitor surrounded by glass, it was prominent among more than 100,000 exhibits. In the transept, a shimmering crystal fountain — twenty-seven feet tall — commanded immediate attention.

Elaborate glassware of numerous types included paperweights. Perhaps a unique commemorative is the Clichy spaced millefiori weight inscribed "V/A/LONDRES/1851" on its base, collection of The Corning Museum of Glass, gift of the Hon. Amory Houghton, Sr.; **No. 88**, The Corning Museum of Glass Exhibition Catalogue, 1978.

Quite possibly, a variety of Clichy paperweights were displayed. In *Encyclopedia of Glass Paperweights,* p. 41, Paul Hollister notes a faceted sulphide of Queen Victoria on black ground, its paper label stating "Exhibition, Hyde Park, London, 1851." Perhaps it was similar to **No. 342.**

Regrettably, only two other paperweights were specifically mentioned in Prof. Eugène Péligot's Jury Report on the Exhibition. One contains a sulphide cast by Allen & Moore from a medal of the Crystal Palace with the words "The Building for the International Exhibition/London/1851/"A & M" (**No. 261**).

Although Clichy received the Exhibition Council Medal for its superlative boracic optical glass, recent scientific tests by The Corning Museum reveal that Clichy continued using its lead glass formula for paperweights.

Baccarat and Saint Louis paperweights were conspicuously absent from the Exhibition. Sulphide letter weights were displayed by Apsley Pellatt, London glassmaker who patented ceramic incrustations in 1819 (**No. 1763**).

As the Classic period waned for European paperweights, the idea transcended the Atlantic to American glasshouses, quite likely via American visitors to London. Inspired perhaps by the Exhibition Council Medal, New England Glass Company, New Bedford, Massachusetts, pressed hexagonal flat colorless glass paperweights with conjoined intaglio profiles of Queen Victoria and Prince Albert and "1851" in Roman numerals; Hollister, *Encyclopedia of Glass Paperweights,* 1969; page 199. Among other similar "medallion" weights produced by New England Glass Company is **No. 799**, featuring Amos and Abbott Lawrence.

When the next World's Fair took place in 1853 at New York's Crystal Palace, Horace Greeley praised the Clichy paperweight display at great length in the NEW YORK TRIBUNE. It is not surprising that French prototypes were models for New England Glass Company and Boston & Sandwich Glass Company paperweights, 1852-80. Most American Victorian paperweights, in fact, reflect the English or Continental influence of immigrant glassmakers who were forced to seek jobs elsewhere because of political unrest in Europe and the English Excise Tax.

No. 134 typifies the exodus of foreign craftsmen looking for prosperity in America. William T. Gillinder (1823-1871), born near Newcastle-on-Tyne, England, made paperweights in the Birmingham area before immigrating in 1854. He eventually settled in Philadelphia, PA, where he founded "Gillinder & Sons" in 1867. William's grandson, James, wrote to Mrs. Bergstrom (letter dated June 30, 1948) complimenting her on *Old Glass Paperweights,* adding that "during the 1860s my grandfather made a great many different types of paperweights at the Gillinder factory. I had

an opportunity to visit the factory and found ...a box of rods that he had used...a great variety — stars, millefiore, figures, etc. Unfortunately, fire a short while later destroyed the room and its contents." The "figure" probably was the same Victoria silhouette used in **Nos. 399** and **132**. It is likely that the silhouette rod emigrated with Gillinder, who may or may not have used it at the Geo. Bacchus and Sons factory.

In 1878, a brief revival of classic-type paperweights was inspired by the Paris Exposition Universelle. Technology had advanced considerably. Impressionism was just gaining momentum. The "Golden Age" of 19th century glassmaking had produced an unparalleled panorama of colors and decorative techniques to satisfy the late Victorian market for "elegance." Three-dimensionality in glass was in vogue. In 1876, pressed, sculptural forms were popular souvenirs by glassmakers represented at the U.S. Centennial Exposition in Philadelphia. (**Nos. 1263, 1276**).

Several small French glasshouses of the 1870s may have produced encased designs in paperweight form. However, documentation is still nebulous, except for U.S. Commissioner Charles Colné's Report (U.S. Government Printing Office, Vol. 22, No. 42, part 3) on the 1878 Exposition. Among his brief descriptions of paperweights shown by Paris, London, and Austrian makers, most significant are the following:

"Paperweights of solid glass, containing glass snakes, lizards, squirrels, and flowers; air bubbles are distributed in the mass, looking like pearl drops...and... Paperweights in millefiori of roses, leaves, and fruit, embedded in lumps of clear glass ...A paperweight, containing a lizard of colored glass, which had been cut in several parts before being enclosed in the glass."

These items were displayed by Monot, père et fils, et Stumpf, Cristallerie de Pantin, Paris. In 1880, Pantin's gift of "a paperweight, flowers, and salamander" was recorded in the "Catalogue Officiel" of the Conservatoire National des Arts et Métiers. Unfortunately, the paperweight is no longer part of the Conservatoire's Collection. (Dwight P. Lanmon; "A Pantin Discovery," 1981 PCA BULLETIN). (No. 215).

The revolutionary idea of not just three but *four* major producers of 19th century classic French paperweights was first published by A. Christian Revi, "The Fourth Factory," 1965 PCA BULLETIN, and further discussed by subsequent authors, among them Paul Hollister, *Encyclopedia of Glass Paperweights,* 1969; pages 148-150.

In the Bergstrom-Mahler Collection are about twenty examples with certain characteristics attributable to Pantin. Yet, they vary in heft (use of lead versus non-lead glass formulas which, in turn, affects fluorescence tests). See "Pantin Paperweight Characteristics Compared," by this author, PCA BULLETIN 1985-86, pages 10-14.

The mystery of Pantin's paperweight production continues. Again, searching Museum files for clues, the subject appears in 1965 correspondence between Mrs. Cloak and the late Edouard Tabbagh, Paris dealer in "antiquités." Thanking her for a copy of A. C. Revi's article noted above, Monsieur Tabbagh wrote:

"It is very interesting...still many proofs to try to get...let us hope I will be able someday to give more details about Pantin ...I am sure many weights given as unknown are the product of Pantin but unless someone finds a weight bearing the name, it is impossible to prove it. I purchased a few years ago some weights from the son of a man who had been working at Pantin during 30 years...these weights were produced by his father and left at home as gifts to his wife, so I am sure they are Pantin products..."

Will Monsieur Tabbagh's research on Pantin be available to some French scholar for further study and publication? Concluding the Cloak-Tabbagh correspondence is a poignant touch to the spinning paperweight world: his New Year's greeting card illustrating an extremely rare Clichy bouquet of six roses, "avec ce bouquet" we wish you happiness "pour la Nouvelle Anné."

In Mrs. Bergstrom's files, certain correspondence is both tantalizing and frustrating, such as information concerning "two Bristol paperweights" in reply to a previous communication from W. Russell Button of Arthur Ackermann & Sons, Inc., Chicago.

The following was typed May 28, 1945, on U.S. Embassy stationery:

"...The V-E Day celebration really was something here, as I told you, and I am sending you some snaps that we took of the crowds.

"I was delighted to hear that Mrs. Bergstrom was as keen on those two Bristol weights as we were. I immediately got in touch with the family from whom I purchased them with a view to getting as much information as possible about them. Like most English people they were extremely reticent about giving their name ...I really don't think they would have sold them, but their home was rather badly done in by one of the buzz-bombs ...so many things were destroyed in the blast. The weights were a wedding gift to this chap's great-grandmother who was married in 1852...and have been in this house in London ever since...They were always in the drawing room on the bottom shelf of one of the cabinets that held their collection of porcelain and glass..."

Could these be weights **Nos. 508** and **509**? The mystery remains unsolved, as does the origin of these two unusual lampwork masterpieces, whose most common characteristic is each other and whose fluorescence test is inconclusive.

Another letter received by Mrs. Bergstrom had a happy follow-up nearly fifty years later. On August 27, 1939, Mr. C. A. Kilner wrote:

"My wife and I experienced today the pleasure of viewing at the Chicago Art Institute your collection of paperweights and enjoyed them very much. As we are also interested in paperweights...I am wondering if, in your searches...for those you collected, you ran across any of the Green Glass (type), particularly the ones with silvered flowers or pots and flowers made of minute bubbles...My father, before coming to America, was a member of a firm of Glass Makers...in the early days of the firm...a number of these weights were made by the workmen...we have three of them...just a few months ago, I discovered one of them with the name of the maker, my great-grandfather, in raised letters in glass on the bottom ...There is a very great lack of authentic information regarding methods and times of manufacture of these weights...I am endeavoring to gather all of it together that I can possibly secure..."

Mr. Kilner later authored "English Green Glass Paperweights," HOBBIES, October, 1941.

On October 17, 1987, his sons, Donald D. Kilner and Kenneth A. Kilner, presented to the Museum one of the marked Kilner bottle-glass paperweights together with a "Corrected History of Marked 'Kilner' Bottle-Glass Paperweights" dating them after 1865 when the company name was changed to J. Kilner & Sons, Makers, Wakefield, Yorkshire. Information was assembled from a "British Trade Journal" article of December 1, 1894, and from information gathered from Kilner descendants in England. The Museum is indeed grateful for this documented example (**No. 1784**).

Four previously unpublished essays by T. H. Clarke significantly enhance this Revised Catalogue. Mr. Clarke, author and connoisseur of art, was associated with Sotheby's, London, from 1946-1981. An expert on paperweights, Mr. Clarke has catalogued many prestigious collections: Mrs. Applewhaite-Abbott in 1952; Maurice Lindon, 1955; Robert Guggenheim, 1961; Maba, 1963; Olga Dahlgren, 1970; and many others.

"Baccarat Documentation" reproduces for the first time the watercolor drawings, ca. 1850, used for lampwork paperweight motifs. Baccarat's "Price List of Paperweights, dated March 1, 1850" includes seven sizes; Mr. Clarke adds an explanatory translation from the French.

The essay, "Conservatoire des Arts et Métiers," refers to paperweight gifts recorded in the Musée's "Catalogue Officiel," 1855-1908, and discusses French technical terms. Museum records sometimes represent the only documentation for unsigned objects.

"English Millefiori of the 1760s" suggests that experiments to revive the millefiori technique may have begun as early as 1760 in England, predating the work of the German, Brückmann, in 1786. Three objects attributed to English origin are illustrated: The pendant, Fig. 3, is now in the Bergstrom-Mahler Museum Collection (**No. 1629**). Mr. Clarke's "pièce de résistance," "The Indian Courtesan and The Yellow Overlay," illustrates the possibility that a Baccarat yellow double overlay exists! Might Providence someday bring it to the Bergstrom-Mahler to fulfill Mrs. Bergstrom's quest?

The Museum's first catalogue, *Glass Paperweights of the Bergstrom Art Center,*

1969, was not only an extension of the work begun by Evangeline H. Bergstrom but cognizance by the late curator, Evelyn Campbell Cloak, of the need for a reference offering a broad spectrum of paperweight types. Full-color illustration was important to Mrs. Cloak and also to interested collector, Ralph S. Johns, Wilmette, Illinois, who donated funds for the added photography cost. Like a pebble tossed into a pond, *Glass Paperweights of the Bergstrom Art Center* increased collector awareness of Mrs. Bergstrom's world-famous collection (then the only one of the top four on public display) and established the Museum as a paperweight "mecca."

For the past sixteen years, it has been my good fortune to continue Mrs. Cloak's work—both intriguing and challenging. Her enthusiasm broadened my initial interest in painting and sculpture to include glass paperweights. Holding up an exquisite double overlay type, she had only to focus my attention on a significant millefiori cane—and I found a new world, in miniature.

Thus, this author wishes to perpetuate Mrs. Bergstrom's request that the Collection be shared with the public and to emphasize its growth through gifts and purchases. The Revised Edition's purpose is three-fold: to provide a euphoric preview for the armchair (and potential) visitor, to serve as an encyclopedic reference, and to expand comparative examples for the collector and student of glass by juxtaposing the antique (100 years and older) with similar types produced during the current renaissance of paperweight making and collecting, which began in 1952.

Examples from the Bergstrom Bequest include the year in which she acquired them. Certain twentieth century weights, therefore, could not have been made later than this acquisition date.

Familiarity with leading museum collec-tions and study of contemporary paperweight characteristics are essential to building a satisfying collection. Unsigned modern paperweights are sometimes found in company with bona fide antiques of other types. Most leading contemporary paperweight makers sign their work with an initial cane, an etched logo, or a diamond-point pen. Hunting unusual examples of the art may be fascinating and rewarding, but it is usually wise to consult established paperweight dealers, specialists who take pride in helping their clients build a fine collection.

The collector need never be bored. A wealth of detailed data is available through extensive bibliography that has multiplied since 1948. The Bergstrom-Mahler Museum's Research Center and Library specifically relate to paperweights and glass.

Collectors may keep in touch with others who share their interests. The international Paperweight Collectors' Association publishes an annual BULLETIN and a quarterly Newsletter. Biennial conventions are held in cities near distinguished paperweight collections.

So, have a crystal ball with a past, present and future. Look beyond the mere visual impact of the motif. Explore not only the "small worlds" vignetted in spherical form but the forces that prompted them. Why immortalize the Count de Chambord, why one flower or certain combinations of flowers, fruit, insects, or reptiles? Might some millefiori designs have particular significance? Beyond aesthetics, is there subtle symbolism in the color palette?

Glass paperweights offer stimulation to the mind as well as to the eye. Perhaps it's not such a small world after all! Still relevant is Mrs. Bergstrom's conclusion to her book in 1940:

"It does not matter whether your collection of weights is large or small. You derive a certain amount of pleasure in possessing it, from learning the history of each piece, and from intimate contact with things that are beautiful. The interest grows with time, and the individual old (and new!) glass paperweights carry with them the mystery and magic inherited from days long gone."

CAMEO INCRUSTATIONS

Ceramic cameo incrustations (commonly called "sulphides") of the late 18th to mid-19th centuries, symbolize an historical period of tremendous growth in the humanities, sciences and arts, in spite of almost constant political turmoil. Like windows to the past, these portraits in miniature reflect prevailing interest in the excavations of Herculaneum and Pompeii and the revival of ancient cameo techniques for decorative elements. Made of an opaque white porcelaneous substance, cameo medallions most often immortalize the historically prominent, both real and mythological, in elegant glass tableware and other accessories. Although cameo incrustations in paperweights comprise the least number among the three principal Classic period types, their history is equally fascinating.

Since time began, perhaps with first glimpse of his image mirrored in a glassy pool, man has been concerned with preservation of his likeness. Portrayals of himself and others, in painting or in sculpture, have been highly favored subjects. Ancient Egyptian tomb paintings and statuettes, Greek and Roman art, architecture, and sculpture — including cameo-carved gems — spurred a growing demand for portraiture, particularly during the Renaissance. Patrons appear in 14th century religious scenes and in 15th century group paintings. Portrait medallions feature imperial rulers. A heightened awareness of the individual personality prompted a revival, in the 15th century, of the ancient custom of immortalizing ruling heads on coinage and the resumption in Italy of the art of cameo carving.

Gems, jewelry techniques, and glass, important elements in the history of the decorative arts, interact as symbols of prosperity providing, as well, a rich heritage of man's interpretations of himself and his environment.

Generic to the development of cameo incrustation are the ancient Egyptian, Greek and Roman lapidaries. For the elite society, cameos in ovals two inches or less were carved in chalcedony, jasper, onyx, sardonyx, turquoise and mollusk shell. The earliest Egyptian cameos were intaglios; later cameos "en relief" (requiring greater skill) were perfected by the Greeks.

Over the centuries since the reign of Alexander the Great, King of Macedon (336-323 B.C.), gem engravers have been privileged members of royal courts. When, more recently, the Emperor Rudolf II (1576-1611) restored Prague as capital and cultural center of the Bohemian Empire, he employed the most skilled artists in every medium, including Italian lapidaries. Bohemian aristocracy, impressed by the Italian Renaissance observed during their travels, had begun to emulate luxurious lifestyles seen elsewhere — a sort of "keeping up with the Baron von Joneses."

Rudolf II's passion for precious stones created a setting for elaborate personal adornment and initiated the carving in magnificent vessel forms (intaglio and in relief) of semiprecious stones mined in nearby mountains. Logically, it was suggested that these same techniques be applied to glass — cheaper and more plentiful. Thus began the most important period, ca. 1600-1750, of post-Roman glassmaking and decoration and the perfecting of glass-engraving techniques in Germanic countries.

Appropriately, Rudolf II is the subject of an early Bohemian masterpiece in the Kunsthistorisches Museum, Vienna. Engraved by Caspar Lehmann on a glass panel, ca. 1603, the Emperor appears in full regalia near a table bearing his crown and scepter. Portraiture "en relief" on glass vessels and plaques became a prestigious means of immortalizing one's likeness.

A factor in the successful development of incrusted cameos and enameled foil ornaments is Bohemian "Zwischengoldglas," which became the epitome of royal splendor about 1730. Court and hunting scenes engraved on foil were favored motifs. The ancient technique, Roman in origin, of sandwiching gold and/or silver foil between two layers of glass, is believed to have been revived in a Bohemian monastery. Production was limited due to difficulty in tightly fitting a foil-covered inner glass with an outer cylinder (or duplicate form), then sealing them together with natural resin. A similarly decorated sandwich glass disk was inserted in the basal aperture. Zwischengoldglas was never exactly duplicated after 1740, although a variation of the technique by Austrian J. J. Mildner appeared in 1788.

Another important factor — porcelain — emerges during the mid-18th century. The well-kept oriental secret for translucent hard-paste porcelain (kaolin clay), coveted by Europeans for centuries, was finally discovered about 1715 by the German chemist, Johann Böttger, who founded the Meissen factory near Dresden. Böttger's formula, however, became almost everybody's business after 1756, when the factory was seized and looted by the Prussians. Runaway craftsmen were welcomed in France and in Vienna, where the Empress Maria Theresa promptly sponsored the Vienna Porcelain Works.

Bohemian glassmakers — always competitive — produced "milchglas" in imitation of porcelain. Ceramic cameo incrustation in glass, a feasible spinoff of porcelain and attempted between 1760 and 1780 in Bohemia, was unsuccessful, however.

That cameos as a decorative element became a veritable vogue in Europe and England is not surprising. Stimulated by ancient prototypes discovered in the excavations, which began in the 1740s, of Herculaneum and Pompeii, reproductions to supply the demand were inevitable.

Scottish artist, James Tassie (1735-1799) and the English potter, Josiah Wedgwood I (1730-1795), enter the scene. Tassie, a stonemason before entering a Glasgow art academy, became skilled in modeling and sculpting and found employment in Dublin where he met Dr. Henry Quin. Together, they invented a vitreous (glass) paste for reproducing ancient gems. In 1766, urged by Dr. Quin, Tassie opened a shop in London. His classic and mythological subjects cast from ancient gems and his miniature relief portraits, both in wax and in enamel paste, soon attracted an affluent clientele. Social status seemed to hinge on whether one's gem collection had been reproduced in glass by Tassie. His spectrum expanded to imaginary 18th century portraits of medieval kings, emblems, and mottoes, as well as miniatures modeled from life and relief reproductions of well-known contemporary portraits.

In clear crystal or gem-like colors ranging in diameter from one-half to three inches and in depth from a thin sliver to almost an inch, "Tassies" were mounted in rings, seals and other adornments. Some reproductions bear the signatures of Giovanni Pichler, Nathaniel Marchant, and other 18th century miniaturists and glyptographers.

Greek and Roman signatures were sometimes spurious, however, according to Rudolph E. Raspé, German archeologist, connoisseur of art and author of "The Tales of Baron von Münchhausen." In 1783, Raspé catalogued Tassie's collection of 10,000 imitation gems and cameos for Russia's Catherine the Great, who ordered a complete set — many of them still displayed in green satinwood and gilt cabinets at The Hermitage in Leningrad. Among 500 collectors who allowed James Tassie to copy their gems were the British Museum and members of English and European nobility. Overall, 15,800 items appear in the two-volume catalogue compiled by Raspé in 1791. Tassie's work was continued by his nephew, William, until 1840.

Although Tassie's process was never completely revealed, the following procedure seems logical: (1) from the original intaglio gem a mold was cast of melted sulphur, which does not shrink as it solidifies; (2) from the sulphur cast now in relief, an intaglio cast in plaster of Paris was formed; (3) a mold in Tassie's enamel paste was then made for permanent use. For the signed and dated portrait medallions, the subject was modelled in wax — in relief — directly from life, and the same procedure followed.

In his "Biographical and Critical Sketch" (which included a catalogue) on the works of James and William Tassie, Curator John M. Gray, Scottish National Portrait Gallery, Edinburgh, wrote in 1894: "(Tassie's)... paste is virtually a form of lead potash glass... easily fusible... Casts made in the paste reproduced fine details with the greatest accuracy... yet were as resistant to damage as hard glass; their superiority over the plaster casts of Burch or the biscuit-clay medallions of Wedgwood was one principal reason for the popularity of Tassie's reproductions."

James Tassie's skill was not overlooked by Josiah Wedgwood, who saw the sales potential for his jasper and basalt wares decorated with classic and mythological reliefs. In 1768, Wedgwood built a new pottery at Etruria, Staffordshire, and employed Tassie to make various molds, including sixty casts of the original Barberini cameo glass vase in the British Museum. This famous antiquity, also known as The Portland Vase, was later copied by Wedgwood, Joseph Locke, and John Northwood I. Most of the reliefs shown on jasper and basalt wares in Wedgwood's 1773 catalogue had been made from Tassie molds. Josiah Wedgwood was the only Englishman renowned in Europe as a potter. Although he did not create style, his adaptations of classical medallions and figures influenced the evolution of other English and Continental porcelain and pottery.

Near the end of the 18th century, porcelain again interacts with glass — lead glass and medallions made of a china clay and supersilicate potash formula. Research by Paul Hollister, *Encyclopedia of Glass Paperweights,* page 255, reports: "the first known dated examples (cameo incrustations) from France are a goblet in the Ceramic Museum at Sèvres, made by Henri-Germain Boileau in 1790 or 1796, in the bottom of which is embedded a sulphide of Voltaire, and a pair of medallions from the Boileau factory...near Paris, whose sulphide profiles show, respectively, Benjamin Franklin and François Voltaire, who met in 1778." Franklin had traveled to the Academy of Sciences meeting in Paris to effect a treaty of commerce and friendship with France. The medallions, inscribed "PB 1798" (initials of Boileau) on the reverse, probably commemorate this historic event.

We are indebted to Paul Jokelson for the English translation of J. P. Emperauger's monograph, *Embedded Glass and Crystal (Embedded Cameos-Crystal Medals),* published in 1909, which appears in the 1958 and 1959 PAPERWEIGHT COLLECTORS' BULLETINS. Emperauger, collector of cameo incrustations and curious about their origins and process, undertook extensive research. Today's equally inquisitive collector will find Emperauger's detailed survey of considerable interest. From Ch. Laboulaye in "Dictionnaire des Arts et Manufactures," 1845-47: "...the glass surface is embedded, while it is being worked, with small figures made of white clay …then covered with a layer of transparent glass…(acquiring) the exact appearance of unpolished silver…"

Emperauger reported the cameo process studied by chemist Pelouze, who died in 1867. A relief model in "special silica-rich clay" was preliminary to obtaining an intaglio mold for producing the clay figures in relief. The intaglio mold was lightly oiled so that the clay figure, when half-dry and beginning to shrink, could be released "onto a piece of soft leather." When sufficiently dry, the entire figure was refined with "small precision tools," then fired. "This baking operation could be stopped as soon as the figure was hard enough to resist denting by nail." One can visualize the scene. Pure porcelain clay was unsuitable. If over fired, it became too glossy; if underdone, it cracked or split during the glass-embedding process. (No. 80).

Emperauger's perception and anecdotes enhance his narrative, not overlooking the political aspects of the early 19th century. He suggested that "white sulphides played the same public role as lithographs" to publicize leading players in opposing political parties. Medals of Louis XVIII (King of France, 1814-24) by Andrieu in 1817 were models for cameo incrustations produced by the Manufactory Royale de Mont-Cenis (Nos. 279, 586). Opposing this monarch was Napoleon I, whose image dominated medals and the ceramic incrustations often molded from them. Napoleon (No. 323) and the Empress Marie-Louise (No. 322) appear in matching plaques, both cameos probably after medals by Andrieu, but incrusted by the Creusot factory, ca. 1830.

One of the Museum's earliest sulphide paperweights portrays Mme. Marie-Rabutin de Sévigné (No. 258) from a medal dated 1816 by Gayrard, a medalist who in 1824 also engraved the image of Charles X (No. 1431).

The world of cameo incrustations became a competitive one. First to patent in 1818 an "improved process" was Pierre-Honoré Boudon de Saint-Amans (1774-1858), who that year joined Sèvres Porcelain Works after a period of studying porcelain manufacturing methods in England. Emperauger commented: "Although the original idea of embedding bas-reliefs was not Saint-Amans', he gave a new impetus and development to this magnificent industry, allowing it to produce marvelous works of art which the crowned heads of Europe were anxious to buy at any price…" In "Sulphides and Medals," 1966 PCA BULLETIN, pages 5-7, Ada Polak describes the various sulphide "trinkets" portraying King Carl Johann XIV of Sweden and Norway and members of his family (Royal Collections, Stockholm). During the 1820s, probably from a French source, the King ordered more than once small plaques, bottles and snuff boxes, which he frequently gave as gifts. A sulphide of King Carl Johann's son, Bernadotte, by the French medalist, J. J. Barré, is dated 1823. Another is signed "Desprez, rue de Récolets, No. 2 à Paris."

Barthélemy Desprez, employed by Sèvres Porcelain Works prior to founding in 1792 his own manufactory in Paris for making cameos and porcelain, may have begun incrusting cameos in glass before exhibiting them in 1806. Meticulously modeled and flawlessly encased, cameos were also produced by his son, Desprez, Jr. Directories of 1812-13 list the father as a maker of small cameos for necklaces. In 1819, his son advertised "fire-resistant porcelain, cameos…porcelain imitating Wedgwood…a variety of medals embedded in crystal" and, that year, received an award for cameo incrustations exhibited at the Louvre. After 1821 and until nearly 1830, cameo-embedded jewelry, flasks and "bonbonnières" by Desprez, Jr., signed "Desprez," immortalized "all the sovereigns and objects of piety." Identical portrayals of George Washington (1732-99), after a medal by Duvivier to commemorate the proclamation in 1776 of American independence from England, are signed "Desprez, rue de Récolets, No. 2 à Paris" (**Nos. 376, 413**).

Visualize chic couples strolling the rue de la Paix and Palais Royale (formerly rue de la Barillerie) — the same route daily traversed by the royal family enroute to the cathedral. In these areas of charming Parisian shops, imagine the delighted exclamations upon examining the latest in luxury wares displayed by dealers such as Acloque, Feuillet, J. B. Schmitt, and L'Escalier de Cristal: richly cut glass decanters (some incrusted with a ceramic cameo in both bottle and stopper), tumblers, goblets, plates, candelabrum, scent bottles, snuff and patch boxes, plaques to decorate one's apartment, and jewelry set with likenesses indicating one's literary acumen or political persuasion. From 1824-1830, classical figures, gods and goddesses of ancient Greece symbolized support for a crusade against the Turks.

During this period, other French manufacturers of cameos for incrustation included Martoret, also expert in glass-cutting and engraving, and Cristallerie de Creusot, who perfected the cameo incrustation process and was purchased jointly by the Cristalleries of Baccarat and Saint Louis in 1832. Cristallerie de Mont-Cenis, importers of English crystal-cutting equipment, were skilled as well in inlaid cameos, painting, and enamels.

Significant is the work of M. Joaillier Paris, noted by Roger Imbert and Yolande Amic in *Les Presse-Papiers Francaise* (France: Art et Industrie, 1948): "At the same time, Mr. Paris, jeweler at 13 rue Croix des Petits Champs, Paris, maker of medals and insignias... incrusted not only white paste reliefs but also flowers, insignias and little figures enamelled on gold; he thus adorned tumblers, decanters and all kinds of crystal caskets. In 1828, Mr. Paris founded the Bercy glass works. Some of his enamelled incrustations may have served as models for Baccarat weights." (**No. 283**, Legion of Honor replica enamelled on gold; see also **Nos. 313, 315, 420** and **575**.)

Meanwhile, across the Channel, the first English patent for cameo incrustation was issued in 1819 to Apsley Pellatt (1791-1863), Pellatt & Green, London. In *Memoir* on the Origin, Progress, and Improvement of Glass Manufactures: Including an Account of the PATENT Crystallo Ceramie (B. J. Holdsworth, London), pages 26-36, Pellatt acknowledged that "about forty years since" (1780), a Bohemian manufacturer had tried, with little success, to incrust small figures of greyish clay in glass, but that the idea "was caught" by some manufacturers in France, namely M. St. Amans, who "greatly improved the invention."

Pellatt remarked that the ancients, though knowledgeable, had not perfected the art. For successful incrustation, he advised, the cameo substance must be compatible with the encasing glass, yet be fusible at a higher temperature. "... The highly ornamental effect which by this means may be given to Glass, will recommend these Incrustations in the place of metallic ornaments for door-plates or handles, bell-pulls, and the inlaid work of tables, looking-glasses, and other sorts of furniture, besides plateaus, and the decorations of the table or sideboard... Nor will the invention be considered as wholly unimportant as connected with the progress of the arts. Whatever serves to connect more intimately the ornamental with the useful, has obviously a beneficial operation, more or less directly, on the Fine Arts..."

In *Memoir... Crystallo Ceramie,* Pellatt included twenty-four line drawings — among them a seal, a wafer stamp, and two "press papers or chimney ornaments," one with a cameo of "Buonaparte," the form similar to **No. 1763** portraying King George IV. Pellatt concluded: "These plates represent only one article of a kind, as it would occupy too much room to introduce a greater variety. These, it is hoped, will be sufficient to give a general idea of the invention, and the extent of its application."

In Pellatt's later book, *Curiosities of Glass Making,* London: 1849 (published after his glass manufactory had been established as "Falcon Glass Works," Holland Street, Southwark, and his 1819 patent had expired), details of his cameo incrustation process were revealed on pages 118-121. He took justifiable pride in having competed admirably with French products and repeated that his incrustation process was effective for encasing "ornaments of any description — arms, ciphers, portraits, and *landscapes* (**No. 536**) of any variety of colour, so as to become chemically imperishable... These ornaments (less fusible than glass) are introduced within the body of the Glass while the latter is hot... the air is effectually excluded ...the incrustation being thus actually incorporated in the Glass... The composition is of a white silvery appearance... when incrusted in richly cut Glass... Casts of medals and coins ...once incrusted in a solid block of crystal, like the fly in amber, will effectually resist for ages the destructive action of the atmosphere ...It is indeed an improvement of Mr. Tassie's mode of accurately transferring small bas-reliefs or intaglio pictures, from any material to solid Glass."

Information on Bohemian cameo incrustation is limited. Although illustrations appear in Gustav Pazaurek's *Glaser der Empire — und Biedermeierzeit;* Leipzig: 1923, Figs. 271, 272, 273, the technique was omitted by both Olga Drahotová and Jarmila Brozová in their essays on the "History of Czechoslovakian Glass" for The Corning Museum's 1981 exhibition cat-

alogue, *Czechoslovakian Glass,* 1350-1980. Pazaurek notes, however, that cameo incrustations can be dated to 1826 at Harrach Glass Works, Neuwelt (near Silesia) and that examples of the art were exhibited at the Prague Industrial Exhibition in 1829. The Bergstrom-Mahler Collection includes a letter weight, **No. 1519,** attributed to Harrach. A cameo of Tsar Nicholas I, reproduced from a Russian medallion, is incrusted in the faceted knob.

In *Sulphides,* Paul Jokelson comments that the poets Johann von Goethe (1749-1832) and Johann von Schiller (1759-1805), as well as Wolfgang Amadeus Mozart (1756-91), were favored Bohemian subjects for cameos incrusted in beakers and pokals, but adds, "Connecting Goethe with sweetness, or Mozart with spirits, must look as strange as the watering down of Schiller. In those days one wanted evidently to have, even during a drink, the company of one's favorite poet or composer and one believed that this strange 'honor' would not hurt them..."

It should be remembered that Bohemia's worldwide market for deeply engraved glass and its prominence in early 19th century development of an expanded palette of colored glass formulas very possibly took precedence over cameo incrustations. The cameos themselves may have been imported from France or Italy.

Although cameo incrusted glass paperweights were produced by all three leading mid-19th century French glasshouses, the fewest number is attributed to Cristalleries de Saint Louis. **No. 341** portrays Queen Victoria, rarely encircled by spaced millefiori canes, on amber flash base. Another rarity, **No. 125,** incrusts a small cameo of the Empress Josephine set in a transparent ruby cane centered on a paneled carpet ground.

Subjects by L. J. Maës, Clichy-la-Garenne, appear on colorless and superb translucent or opaque color grounds and may also be encircled by a distinctive pattern of florets alternated with Clichy roses (**No. 213**). The conjoined profiles of Napoleon III and the Empress Eugénie are further identified by the Imperial Eagle engraved on the paperweight's base. Another Clichy rarity incrusts a Queen Victoria cameo on dark amethyst ground, the weight's surface cut with four raised ovals and vertical flutes (**No. 342**).

No. 534, also attributed to Clichy, features Tsar Nicholas I encircled by a cane pattern characteristic of Clichy but paler in color. Perhaps unique is the cracked sulphide disk inscribed "1848" visible beneath the cobalt blue ground. Because it was not unusual for several factories to produce versions of the same cameo subject, accurate attribution can be difficult. The addition of millefiori canes to cameo incrusted paperweights, however, indicates a date after 1845.

Most prominent among 19th century producers of cameo incrustations is the Cristalleries de Baccarat. Its subjects are particularly attractive on turquoise grounds lined with white (**Nos. 197, 246**). Typical Baccarat faceting appears on **Nos. 178, 436, 460, 527**. Both clear and translucent color grounds — usually cobalt blue, ruby or rosaline, and green — enhance Baccarat incrustations such as the superb scenic Hunter and Dog and commemorative Joan of Arc found on all four grounds. In 1851, the Conservatoire National des Arts et Métiers accession catalogue noted three Baccarat gifts of cameo incrusted paperweights: "a crystal column surmounted by a crystal cross with a white clay Virgin embedded within the column; a crystal paper-weight with an embedded white clay hunting scene, green ground" (**No. 201**, on blue ground); and "another crystal paper-weight, with an embedded imaginary head, in white clay."

While Apsley Pellatt dominated cameo incrustation in England, 1819-40, he produced "letter weights" in geometric rather than spherical forms (**No. 1763**). In 1851, paperweight souvenirs by Allen & Moore, London, of the Great Crystal Palace Exhibition were signed "A. & M." A brief revival of finely conceived sulphides by John Ford & Co., Edinburgh, occurred in the 1870s.

Sulphide enclosures, perhaps molded from Staffordshire clay, decorate green bottle-glass weights that probably originated in the Castleford area of Yorkshire, 1860-1900. Although charming, they are more granular in quality (**Nos. 46, 437**).

Three cameo incrusted glass marbles, probably German, broadly date from 1840 to the 1920s (**Nos. 27, 32, 33**). Again, the subjects are intriguing, but the clay used does not compare with the best French and English incrustations.

A rare *polychromed* cameo by Val St. Lambert, Liège, Belgium, portrays Joan of Arc, who was beatified in 1909 and canonized in 1920 (**No. 1289**); gift of Paul Hollister in memory of Evangeline H. Bergstrom's niece, Alice Bergstrom Moore, 1976.

Significant new information about an early 19th century American producer of cameo incrustations surfaced in "American Heroes in Glass: The Bakewell Sulphide Portraits" by Arlene M. Palmer, THE AMERICAN ART JOURNAL, January, 1979, pages 4-26. As Associate Curator, Glass & Ceramics, at The Henry Francis du Pont Winterthur Museum, Wilmington, Delaware, she began researching a cut and engraved glass tumbler whose base encloses a Benjamin Franklin ceramic cameo. Common characteristics between this Winterthur tumbler and examples at several other museums led to the Bakewell, Page & Bakewell glasshouse, established 1808 in Pittsburgh, Pennsylvania.

A series of similar tumblers, produced by Bakewell, ca. 1825-26, commemorate the Marquis de Lafayette, George Washington,

DeWitt Clinton and Andrew Jackson, as well as Franklin. The Lafayette tumbler was made in anticipation of his visit to the United States in May, 1825. Arlene Palmer's observation of the name "Gobrecht" impressed in the shoulder edge of the Franklin cameo links the Bakewell tumbler to pairs of doorknobs and drawer-pulls, both in the Bergstrom-Mahler Collection (**Nos. 332/333** and **456/457**). Although the cameo portraying Lafayette does not show Gobrecht's mark, it appears on the truncations of all three Franklin cameos. Her further research reveals "Christian Gobrecht" as a Pittsburgh die-maker and, also, that the cameos could well have been molded by skilled potters in the Philadelphia area "using local fine white clays."

Thanks to Arlene Palmer, a diamond-cut mantel ornament incrusting a rare cameo of George Washington (**No. 377**) is now attributed to Bakewell, Page & Bakewell. Originally assumed to be French, perhaps the object's shield form, "acorn" finial, and greyish glass should have been "suspect." Her persistent research shows that the cameo was cast from a one-sided medal illustrated in the 1861 U.S. Mint catalogue. The mantel ornament dates, however, to about 1825 and compares with an identical cameo of Washington in a thick glass plaque at The Henry Francis du Pont Winterthur Museum.

The year 1845, when the first signed and dated millefiori types began their eclipse of the paperweight market, signaled a gradual decline in cameo incrustation which virtually disappeared in France during the 1850s and in England after the 1870s. The daguerrotype, invented in 1839 by the Frenchman, Louis Jacques Mandé Daguerre (1789-1851), and photography became increasingly popular as a means of preserving one's likeness.

The introduction of colorful millefiori patterns and lampwork, coinciding with a growing interest in botany, horticulture and flower symbolism, logically followed successful cameo and enameled foil incrustation. Although no longer in the limelight but just as enduring as Apsley Pellatt predicted, cameo incrustations continued to intrigue those with curious minds.

Almost one hundred years would pass before rediscovery of the technique and the revival of ceramic cameo incrustation in glass paperweights.

Geraldine J. Casper
Curator

ESSAYS

By T. H. Clarke

The Indian Courtesan and the Yellow Overlay

"Some day — who knows — a yellow overlay may turn up to startle collectors." So wrote Evangeline H. Bergstrom in prophetic vein in *Old Glass Paperweights,* the first book to be entirely devoted to this glass art form. This was in 1940; the English edition followed in 1948. But it was not until Corning's great exhibition in 1978 that the art of the paperweight in glass was given official status on a grand scale with the publication of Paul Hollister and Dwight Lanmon's catalogue: *Paperweights, "Flowers which clothe the meadows."* There had been earlier museum catalogues, such as that of the Bergstrom Collection in 1969; but the Corning exhibition was nevertheless a landmark in that paperweights were displayed as just a single facet of glass of all periods and techniques.

Amongst the highlights of the Corning exhibition was the only known yellow overlay, a double overlay from the St. Louis factory. This spectacular weight had turned up in London in the early post-war years, moving from dealer to dealer until it reached the hands of one of London's main experts, from whom it was acquired for a high price by that discerning and celebrated Parisian collector, the late Maurice Lindon. When Mr. Lindon decided to part with his collection of paperweights — his first collection, for he later formed another — it was sent for sale to Sotheby's in London. There it was included as the final number, lot 80, in the first of two sales into which the Lindon collection was divided. The catalogue of February 26,

1957, described this exceptional paperweight as "the celebrated St. Louis encased yellow overlay weight" and it made sale-room history as was only befitting. First, it was illustrated in colour together with five other distinguished weights as part of the frontispiece, the first occasion on which a paperweight had received such magisterial treatment; and secondly, it had the deserved and expected honour of fetching by far the highest price yet recorded for a French paperweight, namely, the princely sum for those days of £2,700.

The subsequent history of the Lindon weight is a matter of common knowledge, at least amongst paperweight enthusiasts. Purchased by the London dealer, Cecil Davis, on behalf of the Hon. Amory Houghton, the American Ambassador in Paris, it long remained the sun, or at least a bright star, in his private collection. For many years on loan to the Corning Museum of Glass, it finally found there its permanent home as a generous gift, one of many made by Ambassador Houghton as he was lovingly referred to by both friends and acquaintances.

But Mrs. Bergstrom's prophecy had not yet been completely fulfilled. Collectors had indeed been startled by the encased yellow overlay from the St. Louis factory. But in the context of Mrs. Bergstrom's words it was a Baccarat and not a St. Louis weight that had been foretold. The hunt was still on. Rumours were rife that another yellow overlay had been found in a Brazilian collection where, if true, it may yet reside, the secret pride of its owner. The paper-weight world began to lose heart, when after forty years there was still no sign of a Baccarat yellow overlay. However, patience has now been rewarded, even if only hypothetically.

Some reader may have been fortunate enough to have seen the enchanting exhibition of Indian paintings that travelled through certain American cities between April 1978 and February 1979. Called, "Room for Wonder: Indian  Painting during the British Period 1760-1880," it was organized and catalogued by Stuart Cary Welch. Item 65 is entitled *A Muslim Courtesan.* It was signed "the Work of Gopilal the Painter," and was painted in Rajasthan, North India, about 1875. I quote from the catalogue description: "Indian courtesans...tended to be well-covered and genteel, at least in public. This one is positively prim, sitting on an unaccustomed Victorian chair for her likeness. Unsmiling, eyes fixed straight ahead, she wears a portrait of her patron, the Maharajah...Glass and lacquered ivory bangles adorn her ankles and arms; and she wears rings on her toes as well as her fingers." But after one glance at the dusky beauty, it would be useless to prevent the reader from examining closely the objects on the draped table at her side. He would let his eyes rest for only a second on the framed portraits, the clock, the books or the vase of flowers; instead he would focus on the straw-yellow paperweight proudly set to the front of the other objects. It is no St. Louis weight, but a double overlay, cut with large windows on the top and on the

sides, a typical Baccarat form of cutting. Admittedly Clichy used the same form of cutting, but we must preserve at least the illusion that this is Mrs. Bergstrom's long-foretold Baccarat yellow overlay that has turned up "to startle collectors." Alas! it has only turned up in an Indian miniature; but that is enough to encourage the hardened collector to risk a journey to India.

But this imagined, or possibly real, traveller should be warned that others have been to India before him (or her). The export of French manufactured products, including glass paper-weights, to her colonial Empire has often been mentioned. France's last possession, Pondicherry, enjoyed a French way of life, which included the presence of paperweights of the "classic" period. It is a fact that during the last war an English officer, on leave from the Burmese front, used to visit Pondicherry regularly. Owning a little knowledge and considerable love of these ingenious glass baubles, he fell into the laudable habit of buying all of the good weights he saw for an average of one rupee (a few cents) each. On one occasion, he told me, he found a small garden with flower-beds edged in weights. Perhaps the Baccarat yellow overlay is still in Pondicherry. But unfortunately the value of these objects is now common knowledge. It has even been reported that the paper-weights framing a window embrasure in the palace of Udaipur (which once included flash overlays) have quite recently been replaced by modern millefiori weights said to be of Chinese manufacture.

Nonetheless, the miniature of the courtesan holds out hope that one day Mrs. Bergstrom will be wholly vindicated in her prophecy.

T. H. Clarke
April, 1983

Postscript.

Since writing the fantasy above, another Indian miniature of paperweight interest has appeared in London at The Great Rooms of Messrs. Christie, Manson & Woods, by whose courtesy it is here illustrated. Painted, as was the courtesan, in North India possibly

at Jaipur in about 1875, it is the portrait of a gentleman (perhaps a Raja or Maharaja) standing stiffly upright in black and gold as though facing a photographer in a studio filled with appropriate props.

There is a close resemblance in style and setting to the portrait of the Courtesan. Both have a wall with pilasters, heavy tasselled drapery, a patterned carpet (in this case perhaps influenced by the Clichy rose cane), and a table covered by a carpet and adorned with European objects. Even the objects are similar. A leather-bound book, a mother-of-pearl and cheap or-molu inkstand of Palais Royal type, an opaline vase of flowers, perhaps artificial; and, of course, a paperweight.

Was the man a collector of weights? Has he just unwrapped it from the towel or napkin held in both hands? The glass paperweight has the place of honour, perched a little dangerously near to the front edge of the table. Au-

thorities will surely argue as to the factory and type of weight represented. For me, it is a fine Baccarat flat bouquet weight, unfaceted, something hard to paint and therefore allowance must be given for artistic license.

The date of this second miniature must be close to the first, about 1875. It is stretching

the imagination too far, perhaps, to suggest that the man is the master of the Courtesan with the Yellow Overlay; it is too simple to equate his face with the miniature hung on a necklace four-square on her breast. As for the artist, it is very likely again the work of "Gopilal the Painter."

A final point. Since these two Rajasthani miniatures were proudly portrayed in about 1875, can it be that French paperweights of the finer sort were still being exported to India well after what is generally considered the "classic" period? Or, is it that they were already considered valuable heirlooms fifteen or less years after their purchase in Paris or from a Baccarat agent in India?

T. H. Clarke
January, 1987

English Millefiori of the 1760s

The glass technique of using slices of multi-coloured canes or rods embedded in clear glass has a long and distinguished history. This rather complicated decorative process, known especially to enthusiasts for paperweights as millefiori, has had three distinct periods of popularity: Roman Alexandria in the second and third centuries, Venice around 1500, and, of course, France in the mid-nineteenth century. But in between these three outstanding times of millefiori activity there have been other less publicized uses of this technique, particularly from the Renaissance onward. One such experimental attempt at a revival of the millefiori method of decoration, hardly if at all mentioned in glass literature, is the subject of this brief essay.

The three objects illustrated here are all English and all most likely made in Birmingham, described as "The Toyshop of Europe"; "toys" in this sense are not, of course, children's playthings but articles for personal adornment or use, the equivalent of the *Galanterie* of Germany at the same period. Such trifles were often of precious materials — hardstones, gold, silver — but in the early Industrial Revolution in which England led the way, these toys were also mass-produced in less expensive enamel and glass. It is of the latter that the snuff box (in part) (Fig. 1) and the two egg-shaped pendants (Fig. 2 & 3) were made in about the year 1760.

Figure 1 shows a snuff box in the Victoria and Albert Museum, London, given in memory of the Hon. Mrs. Nellie Ionides, who formed the most comprehensive collection of English enamels of the eighteenth century. The body of the box, not visible in the illustration, is of aventurine glass. In its natural state this is a stone of the quartz family, sometimes called mocha stone; it has brown inclusions that catch the light. Its counterfeit in glass had long been

Figure 1. Snuff box of aventurine glass, enamel on copper and fused mosaic glass, gilt-metal mounts, English, middle of 18th century. L: 2⅜ inches. Victoria and Albert Museum, from the Ionides Collection.

a Venetian monopoly, but its manufacture had only recently been successfully accomplished in England. R. Dossie in *The Handmaid to the Arts,* published in London in 1758, wrote that this "brown Venetian glass with gold spangles ... commonly called the Philosopher's Stone ... is used for a great variety of toys and ornaments with us." The lid of the box, on the other hand, is of enamel painted on copper, enriched, in the words of the museum description, with "fused mosaic glass." This added glass decoration in lilac, purple, light blue, green and opaque white seems in origin to be a multi-coloured cane that has been cunningly melted to enclose the enamel flowers with four cornucopia-like fingers or claws. The gilt-metal mounts are typical of Birmingham work.

These melted canes, then, may be the first step in aiming at fully developed millefiori canes. A second step may be seen on an egg-shaped pendant (Fig. 2) also in the Victoria and Albert Museum, and from an even more celebrated collection, that formed by Lady Charlotte Schreiber in the late nineteenth century. Such trinkets were usually of enamel and made for adding to the charms of a lady's châtelaine. Indeed, this pendant, referred to by its French name, bréloque, in the 1885 *Catalogue of the Schreiber Collection,* was even listed under the heading of Chelsea porcelain: to be corrected by Rackham in his 1924 catalogue as follows: "No. 444. BRELOQUE or pendant for watch-chain. Opaque white glass, inlaid with flower-like designs in crimson, blue and green. Probably VENETIAN; 19th century. Egg-shaped, mounted with a collar of gilt metal. Length, ¾ inch."

Figure 2. Opaque white glass pendant, English, about 1760. L: .75 cm. Victoria and Albert Museum, from the Schreiber Collection.

But there is no doubt that the pendant is English. The simple metal mounts are typical of thousands of enamel boxes made in the Birmingham and Stourbridge areas. The shape and small size (¾ of an inch) resemble countless enamel pendants. It is hard to tell whether the crimson rose is a wafer-thin slice of a cane or a "swirled-blob," as it has been rather unkindly called. Likewise the blue-and-white swirls seem to derive from a melted cane rather in the manner of Figure 1, the snuff box lid.

The third example (Fig. 3) shows a marked improvement in millefiori technique. But first let us look at the nature of the ground into which the canes are set. Its core is opaque white glass, overlaid back and front with a very thin layer of slightly marbled malachite-green enamel. Into this very rare colour are set the same crimson roses as in Figure 2, but also two very definite sections of cane, to my mind undoubtedly of millefiori type. The larger cane is in groups

of three, composed of pink and white stripes, foreshadowing the Clichy so-called "pudding-mould" canes. The smaller canes are of the same general formation, but in lilac and white; they are scattered rather haphazardly on the surface like satellites of the crimson roses. There are also lampwork stalks linking these diverse elements like umbilical cords. The size of the glass egg is .625 cm. As for the mounts,

Figure 3. Glass pendant of opaque white overlaid in green, with millefiori canes, English, about 1760. H: .625 cm. (glass only). Enlarged. (No. 1629).

this pendant retains its loop of gilt metal for attachment to the châtelaine. Further, the two halves are joined by gilt metal bands stamped with rows of relief dots.

A third pendant in another private collection has flecks of red, blue and purple embedded in opaque white. There must be many other such glass pendants, doubtless some with even more advanced millefiori decoration, masquerading as enamel, in museum and private collections.

The bald statement that the three objects here illustrated, two for the first time, are indeed English of around 1760 needs a little documentary backing. Quite apart from the obvious appearance of these objects to the trained eye, there is evidence enough in newspaper advertisements and Petitions of Patents to confirm both the making of glass and of glass trinkets in the Birmingham area in the third quarter of the eighteenth century. For example, it is known that Meyer Oppenheim, inventor of a kind of ruby glass (none of which has yet been identified with certainty), was manufacturing opaque white glass in 1762. There is also a firm record of the "glass-pinchers" of Birmingham who were making glass buttons in 1770. Solid white glass called "smooth enamel glass" was being made in Stourbridge, Staffordshire, in 1760. Perhaps more significant is the statement of that great entrepreneur and early industrialist, Matthew Boulton, in a letter of October 10, 1770, boasting that he had "seven or eight hundred persons employed in almost all those arts that are applicable to the manufacturing of all the metals . . . and various combinations of them, also Tortoise Shell, Stones, Glass, Enamel, etc." Boulton, reports a friend, Dr. Erasmus Darwin, in 1768, made "toys and utensils of various kinds," including those of "many vitreous and metallic compositions . . . wrought to the highest elegance of taste, and perfection of execution." He had been in control of the firm since his father's death in 1759.

There is, of course, no proof that Boulton or any other individual was responsible for any of the three pieces here published. Birmingham was a progressive town, an English counterpart of Augsburg, but more *nouveau riche*. It was teeming with ideas, of which this tentative millefiori production was an example. What a pity that it seems to have misjudged the potential market which the French in 1845 so brilliantly exploited with their paperweights.

T. H. Clarke

Bibliography

1) Robert Charleston and Bernard Watney. "Petitions for Patents concerning Porcelain, Glass and Enamels with special reference to Birmingham, 'The Great Toyshop of Europe,'" *Transactions of the English Ceramic Circle,* Vol. 6, Part 2, 1966.
2) R. Dossie. *The Handmaid of the Arts,* London 1758, two volumes.
3) Francis Buckley, "The Birmingham Glass Trade," *Transactions of the Society of Glass Technology* 11, 1927, pp. 347-86.
4) Paul Hollister. *The Encyclopedia of Glass Paperweights* by Crown Publishers, Inc., New York: Clarkson N. Potter, Inc. distributed 1969.
5) *Schreiber Collection. Catalogue of English Porcelain, Earthenware, Enamels, etc.,* 1885, No. 310.
6) Bernard Rackham and Herbert Read. *The Schreiber Collection, Vol. III, Enamels and Glass,* 1924, No. 444.

Musée du Conservatoire des Arts et Métiers.

For the serious study of French glass paperweights, in particular their precise date and provenance, one cannot afford to ignore the evidence provided by the Musée du Conservatoire des Arts et Métiers in Paris. It is a pity that their holdings of paperweights and millefiori objects, such as shot vases and other furnishings for the writing table, have never been published in illustrated form.

An undated catalogue of about 1855 lists 80 pieces of the finest products of the St. Louis factory as representative of their work in January 1851. The later *Catalogue Officiel* of 1908 increases this number to 130, adding that the gift, although still of the same date, that is, January 1851, was not registered until 1853. It is much the same with the Baccarat factory. Here there were 96 pieces representing their best products in April 1851, again not registered until 1853. Each gift included a number of paperweights, most of them still in the Musée.

Illustrated here are some of the St. Louis and Baccarat paperweights together with their descriptions, which help to explain the terminology of Baccarat's March 1850 Price List.

5986. Presse-papier, nielle (love-in-a-mist) sur fond quadrillé, émail

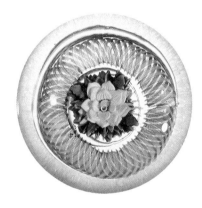

5987. Presse-papier, bouquet riche, cordon Venise

St. Louis
5926. Presse-papier lézard, triplé vert, taillé, huit pontils, décoré, (Entrée, 1853)

5997. Presse-papier pomme, sur socle

These descriptions are taken from the *Catalogue Officiel* of 1908; they differ from the earlier catalogue of circa 1855 in that the word "Presse-papier" has an additional 's', making the word "papier" into a plural.

Baccarat.
6074. Presse-papier á bouquet composé, uni

6075. Presse-papier à moquette, uni, dated 1848

6076. Presse-papier millefiori en plein, uni

6080. Presse-papier camée et guirlande, uni

Tarif des Verres à pieds.

Désignations	10°	9	8	7½	6½	5½	4½
Uni			2..	1.75	1.50	.90	.60
Mandarine guirlande sur fond uni	6..	4..	3..	1.50	1..	1.50	1.05
fleurs simples, roses &c			3.25	1.50	2..	1.60	1.40
fleurs compliquées, jaunis &c	7.75	5.50	2.75	3..	1.50	2..	1.75
Zooglyphites	7..	6..	4..	3.50	1.75	2.15	2..
Mille fiori plats			4.50	4..	3..	2.15	1..
gerbes mille fiori (un cordon 50.c en moins)	9..	7..	5..	4.50	3.75	3..	2.75
Millefiori en plein, rosaces au fond moquette	11..	8..	5.50	4.75	4..	3..	2.15
bouquets... élevés sans cordon ou couronne			4.75	4..	3.50	3..	2.75
& & avec & &			6..	5.25	4.75		
Vernis de fleurs —		1	4.15	3.50	3..	2.50	2.15

On ajoutera à ces prix pour

	10°	9	8	7½	6½	5½	4½
Une Couronne millefiori			.50	.50	.50	.15	.15
Un fond Doublé			.50	.50	.50	.15	.15
Doubl. en plein extérieurement (sur Agate ... couleur)			1.50	1.75	1..	.75	1.60
Un fond taillé gaspé ou quadrillé			.75	.75	.75	.50	.50
taillé en plein extérieurement			2..	2..	1.75	1.50	
Un fond filigrané vernis			1..	1..	1..	.75	.75
côtes à un ... couronné			.75	.75	.75	.50	.50
Un pied &c un cordon filigrané			1.50				
Un serpent			1..				
Étoile taillé			.15	.15	.15	.15	.15
Un rang de pontils ou un rosace taillé	.75	.75	.60	.40	.35	.30	.30
Deux rangs de pontils							
Deux rangs d'olives croisés							
Un rang de pontils &c côtes coupées	1.50	1.15	1..	.75	.50	.40	.40
facette tartrée & pontils							
Deux rangs d'olives & rameaux croisés							
facette tartrée en plein	2..	1.75	1.15	1..	.75	.60	.60
& décors			1..				

Unies
Macédoine, guirland, sur fond uni
Fleurs simples, roses, etc.
Fleurs compliqués, pensées, etc.
Zooglyphites
Millefiori plats
Gerbes millefiori (sans cordon 50.^{c} du moins)
Millefiori enplein, rosace sur fond moquette
Bouquet riche élévé sans cordon ou couronne
        do.   do.   avec   do.   do.
Semis de fleurs

Un ajoutera à ces prix pour

Une Couronne millefiori
Un fond doublé
Doub. enplein extérieurement (sur Agate 8.25 ensus)
Un fond triplé; jaspé ou quadrillé
Trip. enplein extérieurement
Un fond filigrane Venise
Pose d'un Camée
Un pied ou un cordon filigranne
Un serpent
Étoile taillée
Un rang de pontils ou une rosace taillée
Deux rangs de pontils
Deux rangs d'olives croisées
Un rang de pontils ou côtes coupées
Facettes lustrées et pontils
Deux rangs d'olives et diamans croisées
Facettes lustrées enplein
Décors

Notes on the French technical terms.

(A&M refers to the two catalogues of the *Musée du Conservatoire des Arts et Métiers* mentioned previously.)

Uni has the meaning of "plain." Presumably therefore the five categories of the Price List or Tarif from 8 cm. down to 4.5 cm. represent the cost of plain glass worked into paperweight shape. Maybe it has some more recondite meaning. If this interpretation is correct, they must have been considered as ephemera, since none has come to notice.

Macédoine. Happily this term is still occasionally used as an alternative to pell-mell or upset canes. Also known as "bons-bons anglais." Can still be found in all seven sizes.

Guirland sur fond uni. Presumably refers to another type of weight at the same price. (Guirland should be spelt guirlande.) From the evidence of the Baccarat cameo weight in the A&M, **No. 6080**, a garland is not a single ring of canes but a more complicated pattern, sometimes known as "patterned millefiori."

Fleurs simples. The French word "simple" has two separate meanings, either single or simple. In the present context the meaning is single.

Fleurs compliqués does not have the obvious meaning of complicated so much as elaborate, and refers to flat bouquets: as one can see from looking at the headings of the drawings for the 65 and 80 mm. ranges. Why a pansy or *pensée* should have been chosen to represent this group is strange.

Zooglyphites. No satisfactory explanation of this obscure term has been suggested.

Millefiori plats or flat millefiori would seem to mean scattered and perhaps, too, patterned millefiori. It is worth noting that the millefiori weights are more expensive than the lampwork flowers, the reverse of today's values.

Gerbes millefiori. Literally millefiori sheaves (as of wheat): perhaps a more suitable word than the usual mushroom or tuft. Note how very expensive this most common of the fine Baccarat millefiori weights was, even without adding 50 centimes for the cordon or torsade. The word cordon has the same meaning in English as in French, defined by the Shorter Oxford English Dictionary as "an ornamental cord or braid." A better word than torsade, which is not even included in the Shorter O.E.D.

Millefiori en plein. This is a close millefiori, as shown in the A&M Baccarat weight, No. 6076. The second most expensive weight made.

Rosace sur fond moquette. Sold at the same price as the former, this is a carpet-ground weight. The "rosaces" or rosettes may just mean the larger canes inserted regularly to give variety to the carpet. The phrase probably includes the panelled rosette type of carpet ground. It would be in order to call carpet grounds by this French designation, for the Shorter O.E.D. defines the English word moquette as "a fabric with a velvety pile, used for carpeting and upholstery."

Bouquet riche élevé, an upright bouquet of fine quality, rare in Baccarat, much commoner in St. Louis. Note the A&M description of **No. 5987,** "bouquet riche, cordon Venise."

Sans cordon ou couronne. The "bouquet riche" has or lacks one of these elements. The "cordon" is equivalent to today's torsade; see above. As for "couronne," this may be just a millefiori circlet. The pricing policy lacks consistency, for one of the optional extras mentioned later is "une couronne millefiori" at only 50 centimes; but an 8 cm. weight costs francs 4.75 without either of these extras, and 6 francs with one or the other. Why not francs 5.25?

Semis de fleurs. Literally a sowing of flowers. Quite clearly nothing to do with mille-fiori, but with lampwork flowers seemingly scattered around. Rare in Baccarat, less so at St. Louis.

Une couronne millefiori. Mention of the word millefiori suggests that this is a circlet of canes; see above.

Un fond doublé. Not, as one might think, a ground made of two layers, but a single layer, probably translucent. One meaning of the word "doubler" is to line, as of a coat.

Doubl. enplein extérieurement. Again the same meaning as the previous phrase, meaning a single, and therefore almost certainly a translucent overlay.

Sur agate. On an agate ground, that is, a flash overlay with agate ground. Rare, possibly none existing.

Un fond triplé. An opaque ground, coloured. Just as "doublé" means a single layer of glass, so "triplé" means a double layer, of which one would be opaque-white in all likelihood.

Jaspe. A jasper ground, uncommon at Baccarat.

Quadrillé. A ground of white filigree in a cross-over chequer pattern; see A&M, **No. 5986,** the love-in-a-mist St. Louis weight.

Trip. enplein extérieurement. A double or opaque overlay. See the A&M lizard weight **No. 5926,** a St. Louis weight.

Un fond filigrane Venise. Literally a Venetian filigree ground. Presumably a ground of short lengths of white and possibly other coloured strands, often wrongly called *latticinio.* The word Venetian doubtless springs from this old Venetian technique of the later 16th century and onwards. Filigree is an apt description, and should be used today.

Pose d'un Camée. For the inclusion of a cameo, see A&M, **No. 6080.** Incidentally, the description helps define the meaning of "guirlande" (see above).

Un pied ou un cordon filigranne. A filigree foot suggests a pedestal (or piedouche) weight. For a "cordon Venise," which should be the same as a "cordon filigranne," see A&M, **No. 5987**, a St. Louis specimen. The two "n's" in "filigrane" are an error in spelling.

Un serpent. How cheap was the inclusion of a snake at 2 francs. Made only to fit the 8 cm. size. So a snake inserted in a plain glass weight (unie) at 2 francs for the 8 cm. size would have cost only four francs; with the addition of a filigree ground, another franc. Total 5 francs.

Étoile taillée. A starcut on the base.

Un rang de pontils ou une rosace taillée. A row of pontils, that is, circular hollows, or a rosette cut possibly on the top surface.

Deux rangs de pontils. Two rows of punties, an ordinary type of cutting. This and the following kinds of cutting were all charged at the same price.

Deux rangs d'olives croisées. Literally, two rows of olives crossed over each other. In English a suitable name is pointed ovals, neither England nor the U.S.A. being so conscious of the olive, which in England cannot be grown any way.

Un rang de pontils ou côtes coupées. A single row of punties, occasionally in England called printies, and with the sides cut.

Facettes lustrées et pontils. Polished facets and punties.

Deux rangs d'olives et diamans croisées. A double row of pointed ovals and crossed diamonds. This more elaborate cutting was also more expensive, rightly 2 francs as against 1 franc 50 centimes.

Décors. Literally decoration, but apparently confined to added gilding, as for example in the St. Louis relief lizard already referred to under A&M, **No. 5926**. The word used there is "décoré," and in fact this superb weight is richly gilt.

T.H. Clarke, England, is a former director of Sotheby's, where he worked from 1946 to 1981. He early took a special interest in paperweights, and compiled the catalogues of many well-known collections, as well as acting as auctioneer. These collections included the Applewhaite-Abbott 1952, Maurice Lindon 1957, Guggenheim 1961, Maba 1963, Dahlgren 1970, and many others.

He has written numerous articles on glass and European porcelain in specialized journals and has recently published his first book on the Indian rhinoceros in European art: *THE RHINOCEROS from Durër to Stubbs • 1515-1799.*

Baccarat Documentation

The Compagnie des Cristalleries de Baccarat has generously given permission to publish here in full for the first time a series of watercolour drawings of flower paperweights preserved in the factory. Each sheet measures 34 cm. in height and 40 cm. in width. One has only a single flower weight; another has as many as eleven. There are two blank circles for the addition of further weights.

The volume containing these precise watercolours is unfortunately undated. But an approximate if not exact date can be surmised if these drawings are considered in relation with a Baccarat Price List of Paperweights (*Tarifs des Presse-Papiers*) dated March 1, 1850. The Price List does not concern itself only with flower and bouquet weights, but with the factory's entire paperweight production. However, what links the two, Price List and watercolour drawings, is the measurement of the weights. The Price List gives seven sizes, ranging from the miniature at 4.5 cm. in diameter to the magnums at 10 cm.; the drawings repeat these sizes except that they omit the largest.

As for the watercolours, it will be noticed that each page has not one but two measurements. The lesser would seem to be the diameter of the lampwork flower before it has received its clear glass dome. For example, the weight with an overall diameter of 52 mm. has a domeless diameter of only 30 mm. The other sizes vary in proportion.

Whether the drawings were intended as models for future manufacture or as records of those already in production is not clear. The latter is the more likely, for the condition of the drawings is such that they cannot have been in daily use in the heat of the kiln.

Fleurs diverses pour Presse-papiers
Fleurs pour Presse-papiers à 45 mm.
Fleurs simples à 20 mm.

1. blue primrose
2. double white clematis
3. stylized arrowheads
4. white wheatflower, blue spots

1504
Paperweight.
Baccarat (French), 1845-55.
Single flat primrose, 6 blue/white/blue petals, white stardust/red whorl cane center; 11 green leaves, 3 stems. Smooth slightly concave colorless base; basal ring.
D: 2-31/32″ (7.6 cm.)
Gift of Mr. and Mrs. William L. Liebman, 1983.

Fleurs pour Presse-papiers à 52 mm.
Fleurs simples de 30 mm.

1. red primrose
2. double white clematis
3. stylized arrowheads
4. wheatflower, blue spots
5. yellow wheatflower, black spots
6. red-on-white clematis type
7. red-on-yellow clematis type

Fleurs pour Presse-papiers à 65 mm.
Fleurs simples de 40 mm.

1. primrose type, red on yellow
2. clematis type, red on white
3. dark red rose
4. pansy, so-called early type
5. yellow wheatflower
6. primrose type, red yellow
7. white wheatflower
8. butterfly
9. rare double flower
10. bis. normal pansy (common)
11. pink rose

314

280

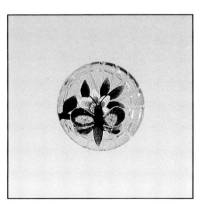

383

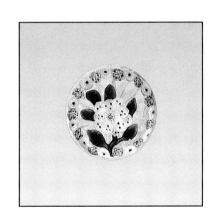

782

Fleurs pour Presse-papiers de 65 mm.
Fleurs compliqués de 40 mm.

1. bouquet of pink rose,
   pansy and blue-and-
   white primroses

Fleurs pour Presse-papiers de 80 mm.
Fleurs simples de 50 mm.

1. blue-and-white primrose
2. double white clematis
3. white wheatflower
4. primrose type,
   red on yellow
5. pansy, pouch petal
6. dark red rose
7. clematis type,
   red on yellow
8. yellow wheatflower
9. pale pink rose
10. pansy and bud, normal

1139

897

1117

Fleurs pour Presse-papiers de 80 mm.
Fleurs compliqués de 50 mm.

1. flat bouquet of yellow
   pom-pon, dahlia, flax
   and 2 stylized flowers
2. 'tricolore' of blue flax,
   red and white primrose,
   double white clematis

3. pink snake
4. striped purple dahlia

Plans pour Presse-papiers de 90 mm.
Fleurs compliqués de 55-60 mm.

1. flat bouquet of 2
   pansies, double clematis
   and pink bud
2. bouquet of pansy, pink
   rose and white narcissus
   (or double clematis)

3. cruciform flat bouquet of
   4 stylized arrowhead
   flowers surrounding a
   pink pom-pon
4. flat bouquet of yellow pom-
   pon, 2 pink and 1 blue
   flax, 3 stylized flowers

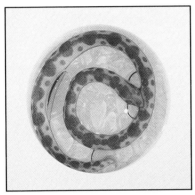

337

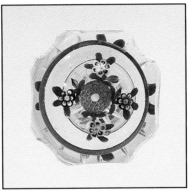

450

Paperweight.
Baccarat (French), ca. 1850.
Flat floral bouquet: central rust-red camomile (white star
cane center) surrounded by 4 blue/white/red arrow cane
flowers in cruciform arrangement, each with bud, leaves
and stem. Arrow canes in 2 of smaller "flowers" resemble
lower pansy petals of early Baccarat manufacture. 4 circular and 4 oval punties alternate on curve; large concave top
punty indicates possible use as wafer tray. Polished slightly
concave colorless base cut with 16-point star.
D: 3-3/8″ (8.6 cm.)
Bergstrom Bequest, 1958.
EHB acquisition: January, 1942.
No. 479, Pl. 2; Cloak Catalogue, 1969.

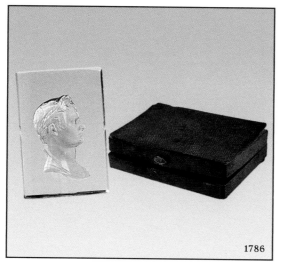

1786

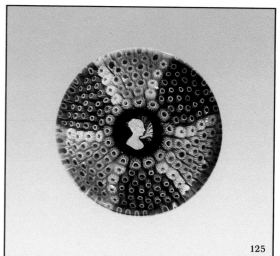

125

322

323

365

315, 420

1

313-A

324

536

313-B

279

415

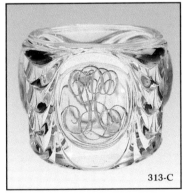

313-C

1133

1431

326

586

407

125

Saint Louis, 1840s. Paneled carpet ground. Large central ruby-cased colorless cane incrusts small ceramic portrait of the Empress Josephine (1763-1814), profile to sinister. 6 radially placed vertical lines of white/red star canes separate alternate panels of blue/white and white canes with translucent red centers. Peripheral canes converge at center of polished, concave, colorless base; basal ring.
D: 2¹³⁄₁₆″ (7.2 cm.)
Bergstrom Bequest, 1958.
Pl. X, Bergstrom book, 1940; later editions.
No. 134, Pl. 27; Cloak Catalogue, 1969.
Ref.: McCawley, Patricia K.: *Antique Glass Paperweights from France.* London: Spink & Son, Ltd., 1968.

315

Tumbler.
Baccarat, 19th century. Thick colorless glass cut in vertical and horizontal panels; near rim, incrusted medallion portrays, in colored enamel on gold leaf, a cupid emerging from pink rose, green stems, 4 leaves, pink bud. Polished base with 16 deep radial cuts.
H: 2⅜″ (6.1 cm.); D: 2⅞″(7.3 cm.)
Bergstrom Bequest, 1958.
EHB acquisition: May, 1940.
No. 336, Pl. 9; Cloak Catalogue, 1969.
Ref.: Lanmon, Dwight P.: "Glasses from The Strauss Collection at Corning," *PCA Bulletin,* 1980; pp. 2-12.
Jokelson, Paul: *Sulphides: The Art of Cameo Incrustation.* New York: Thomas Nelson & Sons, 1968; pp. 26-27.
Jokelson, Paul: "An Exceptional Baccarat Paperweight," *PCA Bulletin,* 1971; Fig. 1, p. 9.

322

Plaque.
Attributed to Creusot factory (French), 1810-1830. Beveled, octagonal colorless glass encases sulphide portrait, profile to sinister, of the Empress Marie-Louise (1791-1847), second wife of Napoléon I.
D: 3⅛″ x 2¾″ (7.9 cm. x 7.0 cm.)
Bergstrom Bequest, 1958.
EHB acquisition: June, 1940.
Illus. 41, Bergstrom book, 1940; Illus. 39, later editions.
No. 343, Pl. 10; Cloak Catalogue, 1969.
Ref.: Jokelson, Paul: *Antique French Paperweights,* 1955; pp. 226-227.
Jokelson, Paul: *Sulphides: The Art of Cameo Incrustation,* Fig 37, p. 47.

323

Plaque.
Attributed to Creusot factory (French), 1810-1830. Beveled, octagonal colorless glass encases sulphide portrait of Napoléon I, profile to dexter, probably after Andrieu, although sulphide is unsigned.
D: 3 x 2¼″ (7.6 x 5.7 cm.)
Bergstrom Bequest, 1958.
EHB acquisition: June, 1940.
Illus. 41, Bergstrom book, 1940; Illus. 39, later editions.
No. 344, Pl. 10; Cloak Catalogue, 1969.
Ref.: Jokelson, Paul: *Sulphides: The Art of Cameo Incrustation,* 1968; Fig. 36, p. 46.

365

Tumbler.
Baccarat, ca. 1820. Heavy cylindrical colorless glass encases, within chamfered cartouche, sulphide portrait, to sinister, of Napoléon I with crown, from a medal by Andrieu. Tumbler is cut to 10 gothic panels, circle of knobs at base edge. 12-point star in partially polished base extends to knobs.
H: 3⅞″ (9.9 cm.); D: 3⅛″ (8.0 cm.)
Bergstrom Bequest, 1958.
EHB acquisition: December, 1940.
No. 383, Pl. 11; Cloak Catalogue, 1969.
Ref.: Lanmon, Dwight P.: "Glasses from The Strauss Collection at Corning," *PCA Bulletin,* 1980; pp. 2-12.
Jokelson, Paul: *Sulphides: The Art of Cameo Incrustation,* pp. 26-27.

420

Patch Box, covered.
Baccarat, 1820-30. Cover: colorless glass; central medallion within 8-point cut star encloses basket of flowers painted with colored enamels on gold leaf. Fan cuts on curve extend to threaded gold-banded rim. Box: colorless glass; flat base faceted with square and radial cuts extending to threaded gold-banded rim.
D: 2⁹⁄₁₆″ (6.5 cm.)
Bergstrom Bequest, 1958.
EHB acquisition: September, 1941.
No. 442, Pl. 9; Cloak Catalogue, 1969.

1786

French, ca. 1804-10. Rectangular colorless glass, bevel edge plaque. Sulphide portrait, to sinister, of Napoléon I wearing laurel wreath. Fitted, green lizard-skin case lined with purple velvet.
D: 1½″ x 2⁹⁄₁₆″ (3.9 x 6.6 cm.)
Gift of Mrs. Virginia Bensley Trowbridge, 1987.
Ref.: Jokelson, Paul: *Sulphides: The Art of Cameo Incrustation,* p. 62.

*   *   *

279

Tumbler.
Baccarat, 1820-30. Heavy colorless glass incrusted with sulphide, profile to sinister, of Louis XVIII (1755-1824), signed, "Andrieu," and faceted in squares with strawberry-cut centers. Smooth, concave base, finely ray-cut edge.
H: 3⅜″ (8.6 cm.); D: 2⅞″ (7.3 cm.)
Bergstrom Bequest, 1958.
EHB acquisition: January, 1940.
No. 298, Pl. 9; Cloak Catalogue, 1969.
Ref.: Lanmon, Dwight P.: "Glasses From The Strauss Collection at Corning," *PCA Bulletin,* 1980; pp. 2-12.
Jokelson, Paul: *Sulphides: The Art of Cameo Incrustation,* pp. 26-27.

313
Glass Cylinder (part of tumbler).
Baccarat, mid-19th century. Heavy, molded colorless glass, relief "festoon" pattern between each of three incrusted medallions: (A) bust portrait of "Esculape"; (B) running black-spotted white dog with floral-decorated letter in its mouth; (both subjects painted with enamel on gold leaf); (C) gilt monogram. The tumbler mid-section was quite likely salvaged because of its rarity. Only one or two incrustations appear on most examples.
H: 2⅜" (6.1 cm.); D: 2⅞" (7.3 cm.)
Bergstrom Bequest, 1958.
EHB acquisition: May, 1940.
No. 334, Pl. 23; Cloak Catalogue, 1969.

324
Box, covered.
Origin unknown, possibly French, possibly Apsley Pellatt, 1830-40. Round, flat tortoise shell box, the cover mounted with oval medallion in narrow gold frame, incrusting ceramic cameo portrait, profile to dexter, of Pompey, (106-48 B.C.).
D: 3" (7.6 cm.); Cover: 3 1/16" (7.8 cm.)
Bergstrom Bequest, 1958.
EHB acquisition: June, 1940.
No. 345, Pl. 11; Cloak Catalogue, 1969.
Ref.: Jokelson, Paul: *Sulphides: The Art of Cameo Incrustations,* Fig. 70.
Jokelson, Paul; Tarshis, Dena K.: *Cameo Incrustation: The Great Sulphide Show,* The Corning Museum of Glass Exhibition Catalogue, 1988;
Pellatt, Apsley: *Memoir on the Origin, Progress, and Improvement of Glass Manufacturers,* London, 1821.

326
Bottle, stoppered.
French, early 19th century. Colorless glass, mallet form, 12 panels of square facets, each with sunburst cutting. Faceted raised collar circles neck, 12-sided flared rim. Polished flat base cut with 24-point star. Matching cut stopper encases sulphide bust portrait (facing upward) probably of Benjamin Franklin, profile to dexter; edge cut in 12 panels of square facets, each square cut with sunburst design; 12-sided panel-cut stem.
H: 7¼" (18.4 cm.); D: 2¾" (6.9 cm.)
Bottle H: 6⅛" (15.6 cm.)
Stopper L: 2¼" (5.8 cm.); D: 2 5/32" (5.5 cm.)
Bergstrom Bequest, 1958.
EHB acquisition: June, 1940.
No. 347, Pl. 11; Cloak Catalogue, 1969.

407
Patch Box, covered.
French, ca. 1820-45. Round, colorless glass box; base deeply cut with 8-point star extending to curve; threaded brass fitting. Cover encases octagonal medallion with front view sulphide bust portrait of William VI, Prince of Orange; edge inscribed "S K H de Prins van Oranje" in blue script. Gadroon-cut cover edge; threaded brass fitting.
D: 2⅜" (6.1 cm.)
Bergstrom Bequest, 1958.
EHB acquisition: August, 1941.
No. 427, Pl. 10; Cloak Catalogue, 1969.
Ref.: Jokelson, Paul: *Sulphides: The Art of Cameo Incrustation,* Fig. 47, p. 53.

415
Plaque.
French, possibly Baccarat, ca. 1810-33. Oval glass, framed in metal band, encloses cameo bust portrait, front view slightly to sinister, of Ferdinand VII (1784-1833), wearing Spanish Order of the Golden Fleece; translucent cobalt blue ground; edge beveled both sides.
D: 3 x 3¼" (7.6 x 8.3 cm.)
Bergstrom Bequest, 1958.
EHB acquisition: September, 1941.
No. 437, Pl. 4; Cloak Catalogue, 1969.
Ref.: Jokelson, Paul: *Sulphides: The Art of Cameo Incrustation,* 1972 *PCA Bulletin,* pp. 33-38.

536
Origin unknown, possibly Apsley Pellatt, London, ca. 1840. Thin white ceramic disk painted in color portrays figure of man. Tiny bubbles cover surface of disk. Polished concave colorless base; basal ring.
D: 2 13/16" (7.2 cm.)
Bergstrom Bequest, 1958.
EHB acquisition: Unrecorded.
No. 572, Pl. 34; Cloak Catalogue, 1969.
Ref.: Pellatt, Apsley: *Memoir on the Origin, Progress, and Improvement of Glass Manufactures,* 1821; p. 33.
King, C. Eileen: "Apsley Pellatt," *Antique Dealer & Collectors Guide,* March, 1978; pp. 63-65.

586
Plaque.
Manufactory Royale de Mont-Cenis (French), 1800-1832. Octagonal colorless glass lavaliere plaque, both sides bevel-edged, encases sulphide portrait, profile to sinister, of Louis XVIII (1755-1824). "Andrieu F." on shoulder edge; "Montcenis" impressed on reverse. Bronze acorn and oak leaf mount supports ring at top.
D: 2½" x 1⅞" (6.3 x 4.8 cm.)
Bergstrom Bequest, 1958.
EHB acquisition: Unrecorded.
No. 627, Pl. 10; Cloak Catalogue, 1969.
Ref.: Jokelson, Paul: *Sulphides: The Art of Cameo Incrustation,* p. 141.

1133
Origin unknown, French, ca. 1820. Sulphide bust portrait, profile to dexter, of Napoléon I in uniform of Colonel of the Guard; high in dome. Polished concave pontil area; basal ring.
D: 2 23/32" (6.9 cm.)
Gift of Mrs. Florence Gosselin Marsh in memory of her husband, Raymond Clark Marsh, 1976.
Ref.: Jokelson, Paul; Tarshis, Dena K.: *Cameo Incrustation, The Great Sulphide Show,* Fig. 80.

1431
Plaque.
French, probably Martoret, 1824-40. Pressed circular colorless glass plaque, scallop edge; sulphide portrait, to dexter, of Charles X (1757-1836); diamond pattern base. Top edge hole for hanging.
D: 3 11/32" (8.5 cm.)
Museum Purchase, 1981.
Ref.: Jokelson, Paul: *Sulphides: The Art of Cameo Incrustation,* Fig. 53, p. 60.

410

1763

411

413

1208

647

327

592

585

456, 457

649

332

637

376

377

327
Bottle, stoppered.
French, early 19th century. Flattened, ovoid form. Obverse: diamond-shaped medallion encloses sulphide portrait of Napoléon I in Colonel of the Guard uniform, profile to sinister. Reverse: faceted star motif with strawberry cuts on alternate rays, honeycomb facets along sides and across shoulders of bottle. Polished flat oval base cut with 32-point star. Flared neck rim, flat edge. Faceted flattened "lozenge" stopper.
H: 8″ (20.3 cm.); D: 3½″ (8.9 cm.)
Bottle H: 6½″ (16.6 cm.)
Stopper L: 2³⁄₁₆″ (5.7 cm.); W: 1¹⁄₁₆″ (2.7 cm.)
Bergstrom Bequest, 1958.
EHB acquisition: June, 1940.
No. 348, Pl. 11; Cloak Catalogue, 1969.

410
Scent Bottle, stoppered.
Apsley Pellatt (1791-1863), London, ca. 1819-40. Colorless cut glass bottle encloses, on obverse, rectangular medallion bearing sulphide male portrait, profile to sinister, signed "Apsley Pellatt." Reverse faceted in diagonal squares; sides in horizontal grooves; polished oval base; basal ring. Mushroom-shape stopper, faceted with deep radial cuts, strawberry cutting on alternate rays.
H: 3³⁄₃₂″ (7.8 cm.); W: 2½″ (6.3 cm.)
Stopper D: 1²³⁄₃₂″ (4.3 cm.); L: 1²³⁄₃₂″ (4.3 cm.)
Bergstrom Bequest, 1958.
EHB acquisition: August, 1941.
No. 430, Pl. 11; Cloak Catalogue, 1969.

411
Scent Bottle, stoppered.
Attributed to Apsley Pellatt (1791-1863), London, ca. 1820. Colorless cut glass, flattened form. Obverse encases sulphide bust, profile to dexter, of George III (1738-1820). Reverse diagonally cut; horizontal grooved cuts on sides and shoulders. Polished oval base; basal ring. Flat stopper top cut with deep radial facets; "#6" appears in bottom.
H: 3³⁄₃₂″ (7.9 cm.); W: 3⅞″ (9.9 cm.)
Stopper D: 1⅜″ (3.5 cm.); L: 1¹⁹⁄₃₂″ (4.1 cm.)
Bergstrom Bequest, 1958.
EHB acquisition: August, 1941.
No. 431, Pl. 11; Cloak Catalogue, 1969.

413
Plaque.
French, probably Desprez, 1780-1806. Round colorless glass plaque, faceted edge, encases sulphide portrait of George Washington (after Duvivier), profile to sinister. Plaque, encircled by gold ormolu rosebuds on blue background, is mounted in round recessed walnut frame. (Sulphide is identical to No. 376.)
D: 6¹⁄₁₆″ (15.4 cm.) including frame.
Bergstrom Bequest, 1958.
EHB acquisition: August, 1941.
No. 434, Pl. 11; Cloak Catalogue, 1969.
Ref.: Jokelson, Paul: Sulphides: The Art of Cameo Incrustation, Fig. XVII.

585
Mold.
Origin unknown, possibly Italian. Circular incised blue marble or soapstone mold (possibly used in making sulphides or medals) portrays bust profile of Angelus

Politianus, Italian poet (1454-94). Near periphery the name "Angelus Politianus" (in reverse) encircles portrait; "Ric." or "Nic. Cerbana V" appears below.
D: 1¾″ (4.5 cm.)
Bergstrom Bequest, 1958.
EHB acquisition: Unrecorded.
No. 625, Pl. 39; Cloak Catalogue, 1969.

592
Cup and saucer.
French, possibly Sévres, early 19th century. Porcelain cabinet cup. In the base, a bevel-edged colorless glass disk encloses sulphide bust portrait (profile to dexter) possibly of George Washington, facing upward. Cup sides lined with gold; applied gilt handle extends above rim. Glazed dark blue exterior (gilt bands below white rim and at base) decorated with gilt shield monogrammed "F.A." between cornucopias and leaves; 2 gilt designs portray music and art. White porcelain saucer: glazed dark blue rim, banded in gilt, decorated with 5 spaced symbols of the arts. Blue "F" appears under glaze underside of base.
Cup H: 2³⁄₁₆″ (5.5 cm.)
Saucer D: 3³⁄₁₆″ (8.1 cm.)
Bergstrom Bequest, 1958.
EHB acquisition: Unrecorded.
No. 634, Pl. 11; Cloak Catalogue, 1969.
Ref.: Jokelson, Paul: Sulphides: The Art of Cameo Incrustation. Scarsdale, NY: Paul Jokelson, 1955; Fig. XIV, p. 58. Martin, Mary: "The Crystal Cameos of France," House & Garden, December, 1926; pp. 68, 69, 132, 134, 138.

647
Baccarat, dated 1954. Sulphide bust portrait, front view slightly to dexter, of George Washington. "G.P. 1953" inscribed edge of sulphide resting on translucent cobalt blue base, beveled and etched "Baccarat 1954." Top, 6 side punties.
D: 2¾″ (7.0 cm.)
No. 663, Pl. 30; Cloak Catalogue, 1969.
Gift of Mr. and Mrs. Ralph S. Johns, 1962.

1208
Plaque.
French, possibly Desprez, ca. 1800-20. Circular colorless glass plaque, slightly convex upper surface, polished flat base, encases sulphide portrait, profile to sinister, of George Washington; unsigned. Narrow bronze frame with tooled shamrocks; small bronze ring at top.
D: 2²⁵⁄₃₂″ (7.0 cm.)
Gift of Mrs. Florence Gosselin Marsh in memory of her husband, Raymond Clark Marsh, 1976.

1763
Letter Weight.
Attributed to Apsley Pellatt, London, England, ca. 1820. Rectangular colorless glass panel, step-cut top and horizontal rib-cut reverse, encloses sulphide profile portrait, to sinister, of George IV (1762-1830). Short panel-cut stem, oval collar; bevel-edged oval base cut with 12-point oval star. Obverse of panel also bevel-edged.
H: 4³⁄₁₆″ (10.7 cm.); W: 2½ x ⁹⁄₁₆″ (6.4 x 1.5 cm.)
Base: 2⅞ x 1¹⁵⁄₁₆″ (7.5 x 5.0 cm.)
Museum Purchase, 1987.
Ref.: Hollister, Paul: Encyclopedia of Glass Paperweights, pp. 254-258.

332
Door Knob, one of pair.
Attributed to Bakewell, Page & Bakewell, Pittsburgh, PA, ca. 1826. Colorless glass encases sulphide portrait of the Marquis de Lafayette (1757-1834), profile to sinister; shoulder edge impressed with indistinguishable letters, probably "Gobrecht." Brass fitting. (Matching knob encases sulphide portrait of Benjamin Franklin.)
D: 2" (5.1 cm.)
Bergstrom Bequest, 1958.
EHB acquisition: July, 1940.
Illus. 57, Bergstrom book, 1940; Illus. 55, later editions.
No. 353, Pl. 10; Cloak Catalogue, 1969.
Ref.: Palmer, Arlene M.: "American Heroes in Glass: The Bakewell Sulphide Portraits," *The American Art Journal,* January, 1979; p. 4.
Jokelson, Paul: *Sulphides: The Art of Cameo Incrustation,* p. 140; Fig. 92, p. 91.

376
Plaque.
Desprez (French), ca. 1800. Round colorless glass (edge faceted both sides) encases sulphide portrait of George Washington, profile to sinister, probably after a medal by Duvivier. Back of sulphide impressed "Wasington" and "Desprez, Rue des Récolets, No. 2 à Paris." Note: Wasington is correct...the "h" was omitted.
D: 3¼" (8.3 cm.)
Bergstrom Bequest, 1958.
EHB acquisition: March, 1941.
No. 396, Pl. 10; Cloak Catalogue, 1969.

377
Mantel Ornament.
Attributed to Bakewell, Page & Bakewell, Pittsburgh, PA, ca. 1825. Greyish glass, shield form, encases oval medallion, the sulphide bust of George Washington, profile to dexter. Reverse is diamond-cut; shoulders cut in fine horizontal grooves; sides diamond and grid-cut. Waisted stem, cut to 8 panels, above flat circular foot cut with large 32-point star. Diamond-cut, acorn form finial; step-cut stem.
H: 8" (20.3 cm.); D: 4" (10.2 cm.) foot
Bergstrom Bequest, 1958.
EHB acquisition: March, 1941.
No. 397, Pl. 11; Cloak Catalogue, 1969.
Ref.: Palmer, Arlene M.: "American Heroes in Glass: The Bakewell Sulphide Portraits," *The American Art Journal,* January, 1979; pp. 5-26.
Innes, Lowell: *Pittsburgh Glass,* 1976; p. 132.

456, 457
Drawer Knob (pair).
Bakewell, Page & Bakewell, Pittsburgh, PA, ca. 1824-26. Colorless glass encases sulphide portrait, profile to dexter, of Benjamin Franklin; letters "BRECHT" (part of "Gobrecht") on shoulder edge. Brass fitting.
D: 1¾" (4.5 cm.)
Bergstrom Bequest, 1958.
EHB acquisition: March, 1942.
No. 485/485A, Pl. 10; Cloak Catalogue, 1969.
Ref.: Palmer, Arlene M: "American Heroes in Glass: The Bakewell Sulphide Portraits," *The American Art Journal,* January, 1979; p. 21.

637
Baccarat, 1955-59. Double overlay: pastel blue/opaque white. Sulphide bust portrait, slightly to dexter, of the Marquis de Lafayette (1757-1834); edge marked "B G.P. 1955" (French sculptor, Gilbert Poillerat). Top, 5 side punties; diamond-cut colorless base.
D: 3⅛" (7.9 cm.)
No. 653, Pl. 31; Cloak Catalogue, 1969.
Gift of Mr. and Mrs. Ralph S. Johns, 1962.

649
Baccarat, dated 1955. Sulphide bust portrait, profile to dexter, of Benjamin Franklin (edge marked "G.P. 1954" for French sculptor, Gilbert Poillerat) rests on translucent cobalt blue, flanged base. Top, 6 side punties. "B 1955" etched near base.
D: 2¹³⁄₁₆" (7.2 cm.)
No. 665, Pl. 32; Cloak Catalogue, 1969.
Gift of Mr. and Mrs. Ralph S. Johns, 1962.

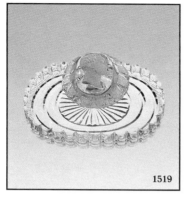

1519

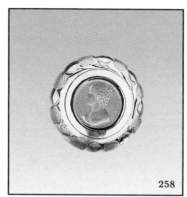

258

1209

534

283

496

534

325

368

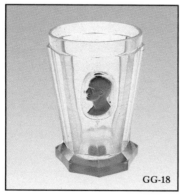

GG-18

311

744

460

544

CGM

246

197

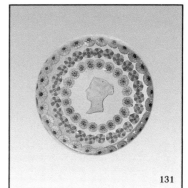

131

177

482

1134

234

1285

1286

GG-18
Footed beaker, Bohemian, 1830. Slightly tapered, 8-sided colorless glass. On obverse: encased ceramic cameo medallion portrays, profile to dexter, a male head. Recessed plain rim; conical, 8-sided foot.
H: 4¾″ (12.0 cm.)
Gift of Mr. and Mrs. Ernst Mahler, 1954.

258
Baccarat, 1820-40. Shallow form. Sulphide replica of medal portraying Mme. de Sévigné, profile to dexter, inscribed "Marie Rabutin de Sévigné," dated 1816, signed "Gayrard." Strawberry diamond cutting on curve alternates with raised swirl cuts. Polished concave translucent cobalt blue base; basal ring.
D: 2¹⁵⁄₁₆″ (7.4 cm.)
Bergstrom Bequest, 1958.
EHB acquisition: November, 1939.
Illus. 38, Bergstrom book, 1940; Illus. 36, later editions.
No. 275, Pl. 11; Cloak Catalogue, 1969.
Ref.: Hollister, Paul: *The Encyclopedia of Glass Paperweights,* 1969; p. 258.
Palmer, Arlene M.: *The American Art Journal,* January, 1979; pp. 24-25.
Kaminsky, Dena: "Sulphides," 1984 *PCA Bulletin.*

283
Baccarat, 1840-50. Solid colorless glass dome encases replica of French Legion of Honor medal in colored enamel on gold leaf. Medal shows white, 5-armed cross on green laurel wreath hanging from jeweled crown and translucent red enameled ribbon. Gilt male profile in dark blue cartouche at center of cross. Medal rests on incised circular colorless foot; polished concave base; basal ring.
D: 3³⁄₁₆″ (8.1 cm.)
Bergstrom Bequest, 1958.
EHB acquisition: February, 1940.
No. 302, Pl. 5; Cloak Catalogue, 1969.

311
French, possibly Clichy, 1830-50. Conjoined sulphide portraits of Frederik William VI, King of Denmark, and Queen Marie Sophie Fredrikke, profiles to dexter. Translucent cobalt blue ground. Wide top punty, triangular facets on curve. Polished concave colorless base; basal ring.
D: 3⅝″ (9.2 cm.)
Bergstrom Bequest, 1958.
EHB acquisition: May, 1940.
No. 332, Pl. 10; Cloak Catalogue, 1969.

325
Bottle Stopper or Seal.
Origin unknown, possibly Apsley Pellatt, ca. 1826-40. Step-cut, lozenge-shape, colorless glass encased in octagonal plaque the sulphide portrait, profile to sinister, of George IV, signed "P D & R" on shoulder edge; bluish green background outlined with red. On plaque reverse: small relief portrays reclining nude female figure. Hexagonally cut short stem; polished flat "wafer" base.
D: 2⅝″ x 2″ (6.6 x 5.1 cm.)
Bergstrom Bequest, 1958.
EHB acquisition: June, 1940.
No. 346, Pl. 10; Cloak Catalogue, 1969.

368
Attributed to Baccarat, 1845-55. Full-length sulphide figure of Madonna wearing crown holding child with bird; mitered translucent red ground. Wide flat top punty; geometric side facets. Polished flat base.
D: 3″ (7.6 cm.)
Bergstrom Bequest, 1958.
EHB acquisition: March, 1941.
No. 387, Pl. 1; Cloak Catalogue, 1969.

496
Baccarat, 1845-55. Full-length sulphide figure of Madonna wearing crown, cherub at her feet; translucent cobalt blue ground. Wide top punty, triangular and diamond shape cutting on curve; mitered polished flat base.
D: 3¼″ (8.3 cm.)
Bergstrom Bequest, 1958.
EHB acquisition: Unrecorded.
No. 526, Pl. 1; Cloak Catalogue, 1969.
Ref.: Jokelson, Paul: *Antique French Paperweights,* Scarsdale, New York, 1955; p. 212.

534
Attributed to Clichy, dated 1848. Sulphide portrait, profile to sinister, of Nicholas I; translucent cobalt blue ground; peripheral circle of pastel olive-green whorls and dark pink pastry mold canes. Underside of blue ground reveals large date "1848" in blue numerals on cracked white disk. Polished concave colorless base; basal ring. Slight circular depression on exterior at motif level.
D: 3¾″ (9.6 cm.)
Bergstrom Bequest, 1958.
EHB acquisition: Unrecorded.
No. 570, Pl. 16; Cloak Catalogue, 1969.

744
Baccarat, early 1960s. Standing sulphide figure, signed "GP" (Gilbert Poillerat) and "58," of Madonna of Lourdes on cobalt blue ground. Large top punty, 6 side punties. Flanged, polished flat base, etched with Baccarat insignia.
D: 2¹³⁄₁₆″ (6.5 cm.)
Gift of Mrs. W. H. Nicholson, 1969.

1209
Letter Seal.
Attributed to Baccarat, 1835-55. Step-faceted, lozenge shape, colorless glass encases 2-sided sulphide bust portrait, to dexter, of female angel; images are dissimilar. Faceted collar, 8-sided stem, diamond-cut knop, extends to oval seal end engraved "HB" within garland of roses and leaves.
H: 3⁹⁄₁₆″ (9.1 cm.); W: 2²⁵⁄₃₂″ (7.0 cm.)
Gift of Mrs. Florence Gosselin Marsh in memory of her husband, Raymond Clark Marsh, 1976.

1519
Letter Weight, Harrach Glass House, Neuwelt, North Bohemia, 1821-30. Shallow oval colorless glass base, polished flat top, scallop-cut edge; miter-cut underside edge, 32-point star-cut oval within double-grooved cartouche. Circular knop encased in raised oval cartouche sulphide portrait reproduced from Russian medallion, profile to sinister, of Nicholas I. Shoulder edge inscribed: "R 123." Sturdy colorless stem between knop and base.
H: 2¹³⁄₁₆″ (7.2 cm.)
D: 2⁹⁄₁₆″ (6.2 cm.) knop
D: 5½ x 3⁷⁄₁₆″ (14.0 x 8.8 cm.) base
Museum Purchase, 1984.
Ref.: Kovacek, Michael: *Glass From Four Centuries.* Glass Art Gallery, Wien, 1982; p. 74.

Ceramic Cameo.
Queen Victoria; mid-19th century. On loan from The Corning Museum of Glass, Corning, New York. This cameo is similar, but not identical, to that incrusted in No. 131.

131
Baccarat, 1845-55. Concentric millefiori: 3 circles of pastel canes (not contiguous) surround center sulphide of Queen Victoria, profile to dexter. Polished concave colorless base.
Ex collection: Oscar Wilde.
D: 2¹⁵⁄₁₆″ (7.4 cm.)
Bergstrom Bequest, 1958.
EHB acquisition: October, 1938.
Illus. 40, 1940 Bergstrom book; Illus. 38, later editions.
No. 140, Pl. 6; Cloak Catalogue, 1969.

177
Attributed to Clichy, 1830-48. Sulphide portrait, profile to dexter, of Louis Phillippe (1773-1850); translucent cobalt blue ground. Top punty, 6 on curve. Wide polished concave base.
D: 2¹⁵⁄₁₆″ (7.4 cm.)
Bergstrom Bequest, 1958.
EHB acquisition: January, 1939.
No. 190, Pl. 10; Cloak Catalogue, 1969.

197
Clichy, 1840s. Sulphide portrait, profile to dexter, of George Washington (1732-99). Opaque white cased with turquoise-blue ground (or disk). Polished concave colorless base; basal ring.
D: 3¹⁄₁₆″ (7.8 cm.)
Bergstrom Bequest, 1958.
EHB acquisition: February, 1939.
No. 212, Pl. 12; Cloak Catalogue, 1969.

234
Possibly Baccarat or Bohemian, 1830s-40s. Sulphide bust portrait, profile to sinister, of Louis Philippe; translucent cranberry ground. Wide shallow form; mitered top punty; circle of white enamel/gilt dots; gilt leaves, vines and berries between narrow gilt bands. 48 radial cuts extend to periphery of polished concave mitered base.
Ex collection: Marquis de Bailleul.
D: 3½″ (8.9 cm.)
Bergstrom Bequest, 1958.
EHB acquisition: September, 1939.
Illus, 35. Bergstrom book, 1940; Illus. 33, later editions.
No. 250, Pl. 39; Cloak Catalogue, 1969.
Ref.: No. 81, *The Corning Museum of Glass Exhibition Catalogue,* 1978.
Jokelson, Paul: *Sulphides: The Art of Cameo Incrustation,* New York, 1968, p. 83.

246
Probably Clichy, 1840-50. Sulphide portrait, profile to sinister, Romanesque head of Napoléon I (1769-1821); star near periphery. Sulphide signed "Andrieu" (1761-1822); opaque white cased with turquoise-blue ground (or disk). Polished concave colorless base; basal ring.
D: 3⅛″ (8.0 cm.)
Bergstrom Bequest, 1958.
EHB acquisition: September, 1939.
Illus. 34, 1940 Bergstrom book; Illus. 32, later editions.
No. 263, Pl. 12; Cloak Catalogue, 1969.

460
Baccarat, 1845-51. Sulphide portrait of Victoria as a young Queen (1819-1901) (head and bare shoulders in profile to dexter) encircled by "Victoria I Reine de la Grande Bretagne" on thin translucent ruby ground. Exterior groove between colorless base and crown of weight. Wide top punty; allover geometric faceting on curve. Polished flat base.
D: 3¼″ (8.3 cm.)
Bergstrom Bequest, 1958.
EHB acquisition: March, 1942.
No. 488, Pl. 12; Cloak Catalogue, 1969.
Ref.: No. 83, *The Corning Museum of Glass Exhibition Catalogue,* 1978.
Hollister, Paul: *Encyclopedia of Glass Paperweights,* 1969; p. 260.

482
Attributed to Clichy, 1846-50. Incrusted ceramic portrait, profile to dexter, of Pope Pius IX (1792-1878), on amber-flashed polished concave base; wide basal ring.
D: 2¹⁵⁄₁₆″ (7.4 cm.)
Bergstrom Bequest, 1958.
EHB acquisition: November, 1942.
No. 512, Pl. 10; Cloak Catalogue, 1969.
Ref.: McCawley, Patricia K.: *Antique Glass Paperweights from France,* 1968; p. 37.

544
Attributed to Clichy, 1840s. Greyish glass encases sulphide portraying death mask of Napoléon I on cushion, profile to dexter; from medal by Depaulis. Polished base, pontil concavity.
D: 3⅝″ (9.2 cm.)
Bergstrom Bequest, 1958.
EHB acquisition: Unrecorded.
No. 580, Pl. 12; Cloak Catalogue, 1969.
Ref.: Jokelson, Paul: *Sulphides: The Art of Cameo Incrustation,* 1968; p. 94.

1134
Origin unknown, European, 1845-55. Sulphide portrait, profile to dexter, of Pope Pius IX; polished pontil area. 2 extant depressions in wide basal ring.
D: 2½″ (6.4 cm.)
Gift of Mrs. Florence Gosselin Marsh in memory of her husband, Raymond Clark Marsh, 1976.

1285
Origin unknown, possibly Bohemian, mid-19th century. Sulphide bust portrait, to sinister, of Louis Philippe; translucent cobalt blue; polished concave base; trace of pontil mark; basal ring.
D: 3⁷⁄₁₆″ (8.7 cm.)
Gift of Mrs. Florence Gosselin Marsh in memory of her husband, Raymond Clark Marsh, 1977.
Ref.: Jokelson, Paul: *Sulphides: The Art of Cameo Incrustation,* 1968; Fig. 78.

1286
Possibly Bohemian, 1845-48. Magnum, shallow dome. Large sulphide of Zeus, bust portrait to dexter; translucent rosaline-red, mitered polished flat base.
D: 3¹¹⁄₁₆″ (9.3 cm.)
Gift of Mrs. Florence Gosselin Marsh in memory of her husband, Raymond Clark Marsh, 1977.
Ref.: Jokelson, Paul: "A Superb French Collection of Antique Sulphides," *PCA Bulletin,* 1984; pp. 45-54.

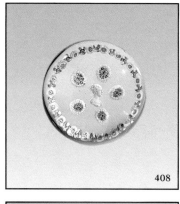

408

342

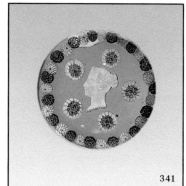

341

173

261

80

559

465

154

201

106

451

166

213

1123

436

57

178

1186

174

1289

527

705

746

80

Origin unknown, 1840s. Sulphide bust portrait, profile to dexter, of Lord Melbourne (1779-1848). Right front edge of sulphide initialed "C.S.K." Polished concave colorless base.
D: 3½″ (8.9 cm.)   Bergstrom Bequest, 1958.
EHB acquisition: October, 1937.
No. 85, Pl. 12; Cloak Catalogue, 1969.

106

Saint Louis, 1837-51. Small sulphide portrait of Victoria (1819-1901); profile to dexter; "Victoria" inscribed on shoulder. Half-wreath of leaves/rose below sulphide. Small top punty, 3 rows of punties on curve, concave colorless base; basal ring.
D: 2⁹⁄₁₆″ (6.5 cm.)   Bergstrom Bequest, 1958.
EHB acquisition: February, 1938.
No. 113, Pl. 9; Cloak Catalogue, 1969.

154

Clichy, 1845-55. Sulphide of Napoléon I (1769-1821). Circle of 6 pastry mold canes set alternately with 5 pink florets; translucent cobalt blue ground lined with opaque white. Large flat top punty, 5 punties on curve. Polished concave colorless base; basal ring.
D: 3¼″ (8.3 cm.)   Bergstrom Bequest, 1958.
EHB acquisition: October, 1938.
Pl. VIII, Bergstrom book, 1940; later editions.
No. 163, Pl. 18; Cloak Catalogue, 1969.
Ref.: No. 160, *The Corning Museum of Glass Exhibition Catalogue,* 1978.

173

Origin unknown, possibly Clichy, 1840-51. Greyish glass encases, sulphide double profile to dexter, of Queen Victoria and Prince Albert. Polished concave colorless base.
D: 2¹¹⁄₁₆″ (6.8 cm.)   Bergstrom Bequest, 1958.
EHB acquisition: December, 1938.
Illus. 63, Bergstrom book, 1940; Illus. 61, later editions.
No. 185, Pl. 43; Cloak Catalogue, 1969.

201

Baccarat, 1845-55. "Hunter and dog" sulphide; translucent blue ground. Wide top punty; diamond faceting on curve. Polished flat base.
D: 3¼″ (8.3 cm.)   Bergstrom Bequest, 1958.
EHB acquisition: February, 1939.
Illus. 39, Bergstrom book, 1940; Illus. 37, later editions.
No. 216, Pl. 1; Cloak Catalogue, 1969.
Ref.: No. 85, *The Corning Museum of Glass Exhibition Catalogue,* 1978.

261

Origin unknown, English, ca. 1851. Circular sulphide disk commemorates the 1851 London Crystal Palace Exhibition. Words "The Building for the International Exhibition" appear near top perimeter of medallion; below: "A & M" (Allen & Moore) and "London 1851." Cobalt blue ground. Concave colorless base; basal ring.
D: 2¹⁄₁₆″ (5.3 cm.)   Bergstrom Bequest, 1958.
EHB acquisition: November, 1939.
No. 279, Pl. 10; Cloak Catalogue, 1969.

341

Saint Louis, 1845-55. Sulphide portrait, profile to dexter, of Queen Victoria, shoulder edge inscribed "Victoria." 5 spaced large canes surround portrait. Peripheral circle of canes. Polished, amber-flashed concave base; basal ring.
D: 2⁹⁄₁₆″ (6.5 cm.)   Bergstrom Bequest, 1958.
EHB acquisition: August, 1940.
No. 361, Pl. 6; Cloak Catalogue, 1969.
Ref.: No. 236, *The Corning Museum of Glass Exhibition Catalogue,* 1978.

342

Attributed to Clichy, 1845-55. Sulphide portrait, profile to dexter, of the young Queen Victoria on amethyst cushion lined with opaque white. On curve, 4 oval bosses, vertical flutes between each. Cut, domed top; concave colorless base.
D: 2¹³⁄₁₆″ (7.2 cm.)   Bergstrom Bequest, 1958.
EHB acquisition: August, 1940.
No. 362, Pl. 10; Cloak Catalogue, 1969.
Ref.: No. 158, *The Corning Museum of Glass Exhibition Catalogue,* 1978.

408

Saint Louis, 1845-55. Sulphide portrait of the Empress Josephine, profile to sinister, encircled by 5 spaced large identical canes; peripheral circle of canes. Polished concave colorless base; basal ring.
D: 2⁷⁄₁₆″ (6.2 cm.)   Bergstrom Bequest, 1958.
EHB acquisition: August, 1941.
No. 428, Pl. 2; Cloak Catalogue, 1969.

451

Baccarat, 1845-55. Sulphide figure of Joan of Arc (1412-31) holding sword, helmet on stump, flanked by oak and laurel branches forming wreath; green base. Flat top, diamond-shaped faceting on curve extends to form 10-sided polished flat base.
D: 3⁵⁄₁₆″ (8.4 cm.)   Bergstrom Bequest, 1958.
EHB acquisition: January, 1942.
No. 480, Pl. 12; Cloak Catalogue, 1969.
Ref.: No. 84, *The Corning Museum of Glass Exhibition Catalogue,* 1978.

465

Clichy, 1845-55. Sulphide bust portrait, profile to sinister, of a Madonna on bordered green oval plaque, centered on cobalt blue ground lined with opaque white. Peripheral circle of 5 florets between each of 6 pastry mold canes. Polished concave colorless base; basal ring.
D: 3″ (7.6 cm.)   Bergstrom Bequest, 1958.
EHB acquisition: May, 1942.
No. 493, Pl. 14; Cloak Catalogue, 1969.

559

Baccarat, 1953. Sulphide double portrait, profiles to dexter, of Queen Elizabeth II and Prince Philip; "G Poillerat" impressed edge of sulphide. Top and 5 side punties. Polished, diamond-cut colorless base.
D: 2⅝″ (6.6 cm.)   Bergstrom Bequest, 1958.
EHB acquisition: Unrecorded.
No. 595, Pl. 30; Cloak Catalogue, 1969.

57
Origin unknown, possibly Clichy, 1851-60. Greyish glass encases, near dome, sulphide bust portrait, front view slightly to sinister, of Lajos Kossuth; sulphide edge marked "Kossuth." Circular depression on weight's exterior surface at cameo level. Polished concave colorless base; basal ring.
D: 2⁹⁄₁₆″ (6.5 cm.)
Bergstrom Bequest, 1958.
EHB acquisition: August, 1937.
No. 58, Pl. 12; Cloak Catalogue, 1969.
Ref.: Martin, Mary: "The Crystal Cameos of France." *House & Garden,* December, 1926; p. 138.

166
Clichy, 1848-52. Sulphide portrait, profile to sinister, of the Comte de Chambord (1820-83); translucent green ground. Peripheral circle of 5 white star canes/green centers interspersed with 6 larger white edelweiss canes, yellow stamen centers. Polished concave colorless base; basal ring.
D: 3¹⁄₁₆″ (7.8 cm.)
Bergstrom Bequest, 1958.
EHB acquisition: November, 1938.
No. 175, Pl. 14; Cloak Catalogue, 1969.
Ref.: Jokelson, Paul: *Sulphides: The Art of Cameo Incrustation,* 1968; p. 137.

174
Saint Louis, 1848-50. Colorless glass encases close to crown 3-dimensional sulphide carp fish, tiny red fish in its bite; predominantly blue, green, white and red jasper ground. Polished concave colorless base; basal ring.
D: 2¾″ (7.0 cm.)
Bergstrom Bequest, 1958.
EHB acquisition: January, 1939.
Illus. 37, Bergstrom book, 1940; Illus. 35, later editions.
No. 186, Pl. 3; Cloak Catalogue, 1969.

178
French, possibly Baccarat, 1848-52. Small sulphide portrait, profile to dexter, of Naploéon III (1808-73); flanged transparent green base. Top punty, geometric facets on curve. Polished concave base; basal ring.
D: 2⅜″ (6.1 cm.)
Bergstrom Bequest, 1958.
EHB acquisition: January, 1939.
No. 191, Pl. 12; Cloak Catalogue, 1969.

213
Clichy, 1852. Sulphide profiles to dexter of Napoléon III and Empress Eugénie (possibly by Apsley Pellatt) encircled by 6 large pink/green Clichy roses set alternately with 5 smaller white rose canes/red centers. Cobalt blue ground lined with opaque white. Polished concave colorless base engraved with the Imperial Eagle.
D: 3″ (7.6 cm.)
Bergstrom Bequest, 1958.
EHB acquisition: May, 1939.
Pl. IX and Illus. 36, Bergstrom book, 1940; Pl. IX, Illus. 34, later editions.
No. 228, Pl. 14; Cloak Catalogue, 1969.

436
Attributed to Baccarat, 1852-60. Sulphide portrait, profile to sinister, of Louis Napoléon, shoulder edge inscribed "L'n Bonaparte" in blue script. Alternating white star and red/white canes encircle portrait. Wide top punty, 3 rows of geometric facets on curve. Polished concave colorless base; fine basal ring.
D: 2¼″ (5.7 cm.)
Bergstrom Bequest, 1958.
EHB acquisition: October, 1941.
No. 464, Pl. 12; Cloak Catalogue, 1969.

527
Baccarat, 1845-55. Sulphide bust portrait of Saint Augustine (354-430 A.D.), foreground with "St. Augustin" in blue script. Peripheral circle of red/white/green arrow canes alternate with white/red canes just below portrait. Wide top punty, 3 rows of diamond cutting on curve. Polished base alternately cut with 12 miters and 12 flutes.
D: 2⅝″ (6.7 cm.)
Bergstrom Bequest, 1958.
EHB acquisition: Unrecorded.
No. 561, Pl. 12; Cloak Catalogue, 1969.

705
Baccarat, 1966. Sulphide bust portrait, profile to dexter, of Pope John XXIII (1881-1963), truncation signed "A. David Paris 1964"; flanged flat translucent amber base etched with Baccarat insignia. Top, 5 side punties.
D: 2¹³⁄₁₆″ (7.2 cm.)
Museum Purchase, 1966.
No. 725, Pl. 32; Cloak Catalogue, 1969.

746
Saint Louis, 1967. Sulphide portrait, profile to dexter, of King Saint Louis IX (1215-70). Circle of small serrated, rose-colored canes/pale green centers. Sulphide, signed "Coëffin," floats ½ inch above polished colorless base. Underside of sulphide inscribed in blue: "1767/SL/1967." Top, 5 side punties. 1158/2,000.
D: 2½″ (6.4 cm.)
Gift of M. Gérard Ingold, 1969.

1123
Attributed to Saint Louis, 1845-55. Sulphide portrait, profile to dexter, of Queen Victoria; truncation signed "Victoria" in blue script. Peripheral circle of pink/white/green canes. Amber-flashed concave base.
D: 2⁷⁄₁₆″ (6.2 cm.)
Gift of Mrs. Florence Gosselin Marsh in memory of her husband, Raymond Clark Marsh, 1976.

1186
Origin unknown, probably Saint Louis, 1848-55. Colorless glass encases 3-dimensional sulphide carp within peripheral circle of salmon/green millefiori canes. Polished concave colorless base; basal ring.
D: 3⅛″ (7.9 cm.)
Gift of Mrs. Florence Gosselin Marsh in memory of her husband, Raymond Clark Marsh, 1976.

1289
Val St. Lambert (Belgian), 1850-1920. Small polychromed sulphide cameo, to sinister, of Joan d'Arc on horseback, holding a green/red banner; surrounded by hexagon of counter-clockwise barberpole canes alternately red/white and green/white; translucent deep blue ground. Large top punty, double row of oval side punties; polished flat colorless base.
D: 3⅜″ (8.7 cm.)
Given in memory of Mrs. Alice Bergstrom Moore by Paul Hollister, 1976.

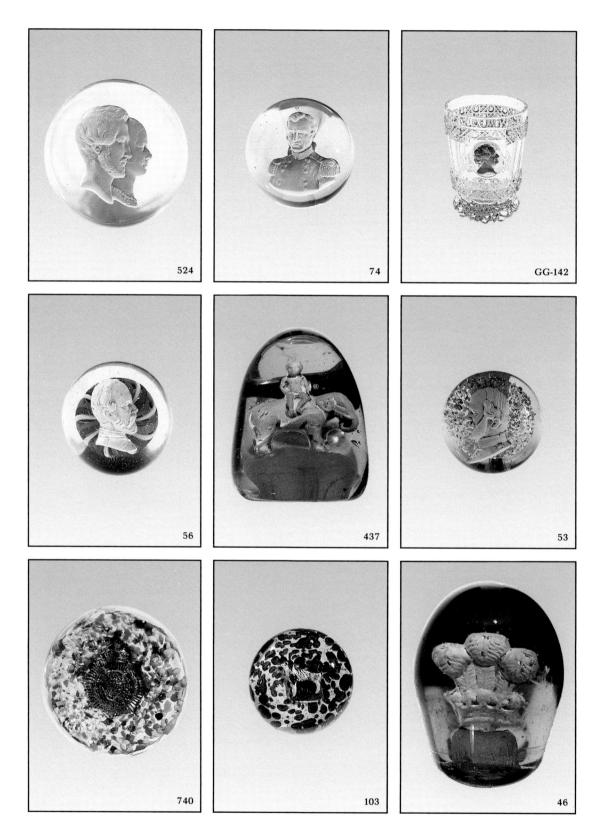

524

74

GG-142

56

437

53

740

103

46

9

3

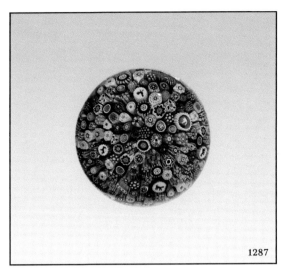

1287

142, 691

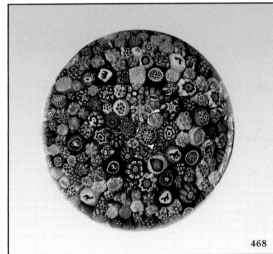

468

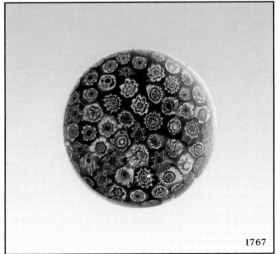

1767

1767

46

Yorkshire, England, 1850-90. Ovoid green bottle glass encases ceramic "Prince of Wales Feather" on translucent "pedestal" drawn to smooth concave base, pontil mark. (Less common than "flower pot" motif.)
H: 3⁹⁄₁₆" (9.1 cm.); D: 2¹⁵⁄₁₆" (7.4 cm.)
Bergstrom Bequest, 1958.
EHB acquisition: August, 1937.
No. 46, Pl. 33, Cloak Catalogue, 1969.

53

Origin unknown, probably Bohemian, 1860-70. Sulphide male bust portrait, profile to dexter; mica-flaked colorless cushion. Smooth base.
D: 2¼" (5.7 cm.)
Bergstrom Bequest, 1958.
EHB acquisition: August, 1937.
No. 53, Pl. 43; Cloak Catalogue, 1969.

56

Origin unknown, probably Bohemian, 1860-70. Sulphide male bust portrait, profile to sinister; red/white/blue "pinwheel" cushion. Smooth flat colorless base.
D: 2⁵⁄₁₆" (5.8 cm.)
Bergstrom Bequest, 1958.
EHB acquisition: August, 1937.
Illus. 66, Bergstrom book, 1940; Illus. 64, later editions.
No. 57, Pl. 43; Cloak Catalogue, 1969.

74

Origin unknown, possibly Clichy, 1849-50. Greyish, bubbly glass encases, midway in weight, sulphide bust portrait of Zachary Taylor (1784-1850); "Taylor" in blue script on reverse. Faintly perceptible depression on weight's exterior surface at cameo level. Concave colorless base.
D: 2¾" (7.0 cm.)
Bergstrom Bequest, 1958.
EHB acquisition: September, 1937.
No. 79, Pl. 12; Cloak Catalogue, 1969.

103

Origin unknown, American (possibly Pittsburgh area) or Central European, ca. 1870. Colorless glass encases black/white sulphide dog standing on green "grass"; opaque white ground with green/blue spatter.
D: 2⁵⁄₁₆" (5.8 cm.)
Bergstrom Bequest, 1958.
EHB acquisition: May, 1938.
No. 110, Pl. 60; Cloak Catalogue, 1969.
Ref.: Baumann, Paul: *Collecting Antique Marbles.* Iowa: Prairie Winds Press, 1970; p. 76, p. 84.

GG-142

Footed beaker, Bohemian, 1840. Faceted, colorless glass encloses, on obverse, ceramic cameo portrait, profile to sinister, of Johann Wolfgang von Goethe (1749-1832). Flanged, scalloped foot.
H: 4¹⁷⁄₃₂" (11.5 cm.); D: 3⁵⁄₁₆" (8.4 cm.)
Gift of Mrs. Marjorie W. Seybold, 1979.

437

Doorstop.
Northern England, late 19th century. Ovoid green bottle glass encases ceramic figure of child sitting sidewise on elephant standing on translucent, rock-like mound that rises from flat base; pontil mark.
H: 4⁹⁄₁₆" (11.6 cm.); D: 3⅝" (9.2 cm.)
Bergstrom Bequest, 1958.
EHB acquisition: October, 1941.
No. 465, Pl. 33; Cloak Catalogue, 1969.

524

Origin unknown, possibly Clichy, 1864. Greyish glass encases ceramic cameo portraits, profiles to sinister, of the Emperor Maximilian of Mexico and Empress Carlota. Polished base, slight concavity. An almost imperceptible depression on exterior surface at cameo level.
D: 3³⁄₁₆" (8.1 cm.)
Bergstrom Bequest, 1958.
EHB acquisition: Unrecorded.
No. 559, Pl. 12; Cloak Catalogue, 1969.

740

Origin unknown, possibly American; probably early 1900s. Colorless glass encases replica of gold medal, sunburst form, royal crown at top, and inscription "Honi soit qui mal y pense" which translates "Evil is he who evil thinks." Thin multicolor spatter cushion, colorless ground; flat polished base. Flat oval cut on curve.
D: 2⅞" (7.3 cm.)
Gift of Mr. and Mrs. George Cowan, 1969.

3

Baccarat, dated, 1847. Close millefiori canes include dog, kangaroo and devil silhouettes and date "B 1847." Polished colorless base; basal ring. (This weight is believed to be Mrs. Bergstrom's first purchase and the one that inspired her collection.)
D: 2%6″ (6.5 cm.)
Bergstrom Bequest, 1958.
EHB acquisition: March, 1935.
No. 2, Pl. 5; Cloak Catalogue, 1969.

142

Baccarat, dated 1846. Close millefiori; date "B 1846"; star, honeycomb, whorl and various arrow canes; flower and white pheasant silhouettes on upset white filigree. Polished concave colorless base etched with number "28"; wide basal ring.
D: 3″ (7.6 cm.)
Bergstrom Bequest, 1958.
EHB acquisition: October, 1938.
No. 151, Pl. 5; Cloak Catalogue, 1969.

468

Baccarat, dated 1848. Magnum, close millefiori: date cane "B 1848"; various colors of arrow, quatrefoil, trefoil, honeycomb, etc., as well as 9 silhouettes: deer, goat, pigeon, dog, horse, stork, rooster, butterfly, and elephant. Canes are laid on ground of red, white and blue filigree twist segments. Crisscrossed miter cuts encircle periphery of polished concave colorless base.
D: 4″ (10.2 cm.)
Bergstrom Bequest, 1958.
EHB acquisition: May, 1942.
No. 497, Pl. 9; Cloak Catalogue, 1969.

691

Baccarat, 1958-63. Close millefiori canes, the colors more pastel than in antique Baccarat examples. Canes include Zodiac series silhouettes and number "8." Polished flat colorless base etched with Baccarat insignia.
D: 2⅞″ (7.3 cm.)
No. 710, Pl. 32; Cloak Catalogue, 1969.
Gift of Mr. and Mrs. Ralph S. Johns, 1963.

1287

Baccarat, dated 1849. Close millefiori; 1 cane dated "1849," 5 silhouettes: dog, goat, horse, squirrel, rooster; arrow canes; numerous varicolored honeycomb canes. Polished concave colorless base; basal ring.
D: 2½″ (6.5 cm.)
Gift of Mrs. Florence Gosselin Marsh in memory of her husband, Raymond Clark Marsh, 1977.

1767

Origin unknown, possibly American or Italian, 1960s-70s. Magnum. Greyish glass encases Italian multicolor close millefiori canes; multicolor spatter ground. Wide, polished flat colorless base, center etched with fake Baccarat logo (goblet/decanter/tumbler, encircled by "Baccarat France"). Note: This weight, although using Italian canes, may have originated in the United States. Various paperweights with fake Baccarat signatures were reported in the 1970s.
D: 3³¹/₃₂″ (10.1 cm.)
Museum Purchase, 1987.

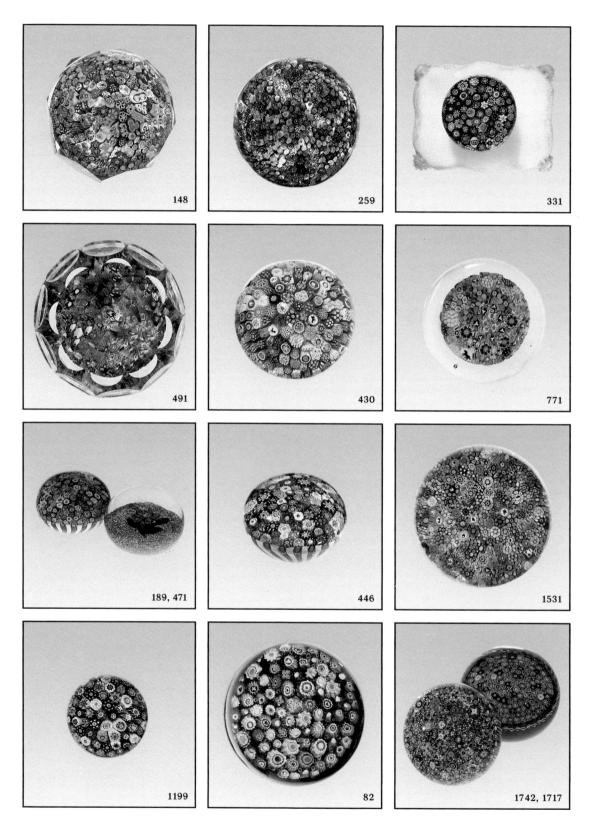

148

259

331

491

430

771

189, 471

446

1531

1199

82

1742, 1717

11

1190

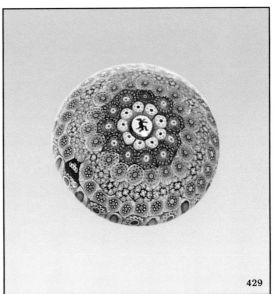

429

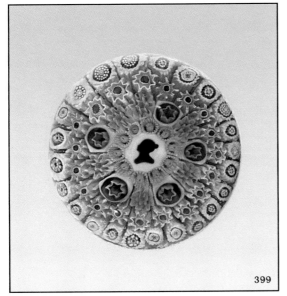

399

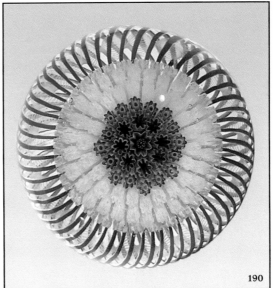

190

12

82
Bohemian, 1909. Close millefiori canes, one with bright orange center; tiny bubbles; translucent dark green ground flecked with mica; smooth flat base.
D: 3" (7.6 cm.)
Bergstrom Bequest, 1958.
EHB acquisition: October, 1937.
No. 87, Pl. 63; Cloak Catalogue, 1969.

148
Baccarat, dated 1847. Close millefiori motif includes unusual canes: pigeon with 2 shamrocks; pigeon surrounded by shamrocks; double squirrel; arrow, flower and whorl canes; 2 "B 1847"canes. Allover geometric faceting. Polished flat colorless base; pontil mark.
D: 2¹⁵⁄₁₆" (7.4 cm.)
Bergstrom Bequest, 1958.
EHB acquisition: October, 1938.
Illus. 15, Bergstrom book, 1940; Illus. 16, later editions.
No. 157, Pl. 4; Cloak Catalogue, 1969.

189
Clichy, 1845-55. Outstanding variety of close millefiori canes include 4 Clichy roses: 2 pink/green, 1 white/green, 1 all white; Clichy "C" serif signature cane surrounded by 8 green/white rods within serrated opaque white casing. At periphery, alternating green and white staves form basket drawn almost to center of polished concave colorless base; basal ring.
D: 3³⁄₁₆" (8.1 cm.)
Bergstrom Bequest, 1958.
EHB acquisition: February, 1939.
No. 202, Pl. 18; Cloak Catalogue, 1969.

259
Clichy, 1845. Probably one of the early weights. Small close millefiori canes, include approximately 25 Clichy roses in various shades of pink/green, also white with pink center. Top punty, 2 circles of punties on curve. Polished concave colorless base reveals uneven ends of canes; basal ring.
D: 3¼" (8.3 cm.)
Bergstrom Bequest, 1958.
EHB acquisition: November, 1939.
Illus. 26, Bergstrom book, 1940; later editions.
No. 277, Pl. 18; Cloak Catalogue, 1969.

331
Clichy, 1845-55. Miniature. Close millefiori canes include 3 pink Clichy roses. Peripheral circle of alternating turquoise-blue and opaque white stave canes drawn to base form basket. Weight is affixed to rectangular marble base relief carved at edges and corners.
D: 1¾" (4.5 cm.) sphere; D: 3½ x 2½" (8.9 x 6.3 cm.) marble base.
Bergstrom Bequest, 1958.
EHB acquisition: June, 1940.
No. 352, Pl. 15; Cloak Catalogue, 1969.

430
Baccarat, dated 1849. Close millefiori motif; "1849" date cane and 6 silhouettes: horse, pony, rooster, goat, pigeon, squirrel; 2 colored flowers; also arrow, trefoil, quatrefoil, shamrock, honeycomb, and other typical Baccarat canes. Polished concave colorless base; basal ring.
D: 2⅞" (7.3 cm.)
Bergstrom Bequest, 1958.
EHB acquisition: October, 1941.
No. 457, Pl. 6; Cloak Catalogue, 1969.

446
Clichy, 1845-55. Close millefiori. Exceptional variety of compound canes include central small pink Clichy rose; "C" serif signature cane; 2 turquoise-blue Clichy roses; 3 purple Clichy roses; one pastel yellow Clichy rose with green moss/pink-white whorl cane center. At periphery, alternating opaque white and turquoise-blue staves form basket. Polished concave colorless base; basal ring.
D: 2⁷⁄₁₆" (6.2 cm.)
Bergstrom Bequest, 1958.
EHB acquisition: January, 1942.
No. 475, Pl. 17; Cloak Catalogue, 1969.

471
Saint Louis, 1845-60. Coral-pink clematis with 10 striped pointed petals, blue/white center cane; 3 leaves and pointed stem; fine green and white jasper ground. Polished concave colorless base.
D: 3¹⁄₁₆" (7.8 cm.)
Bergstrom Bequest, 1958.
EHB acquisition: July, 1942.
No. 500, Pl. 24; Cloak Catalogue, 1969.

491
Saint Louis, 1845-55. Magnum. Macedoine motif includes 7 silhouette canes, one with white dog in center surrounded by 6 distorted images (2 resembling devil silhouettes); random millefiori, white and colored filigree and ribbon twist segments. Top punty encircled by 3 rows of punties increasing in size toward polished concave colorless base; basal ring.
D: 3¾" (9.6 cm.)
Bergstrom Bequest, 1958.
EHB acquisition: April, 1943.
No. 521, Pl. 24; Cloak Catalogue, 1969.

771
Islington Glass Works, Birmingham, England, 1849. Close millefiori; small canes include arrow, star, whorl, and "propellor"; silhouette of black draft horse and black initials "IGW," each in opaque white canes. Polished basal concavity; basal ring.
D: 2¹¹⁄₁₆" (6.8 cm.)
Gift of Friends of Bergstrom, 1970.

1199
Baccarat, 1845-55. Miniature. Close millefiori includes arrow and 4 flower canes of which 3 are miniature camomiles. Polished concave colorless base; basal ring.
D: 1¹³⁄₁₆" (4.5 cm.)
Gift of Mrs. Florence Gosselin Marsh in memory of her husband, Raymond Clark Marsh, 1976.

1531

Baccarat, dated 1968. Close millefiori canes, one dated 1968, with zodiac silhouettes. Polished flat colorless base, etched Baccarat signature in pontil area.
D: 3¹⁄₁₆″ (7.8 cm.)
Bequest of J. Howard Gilroy, 1986.

1717

Perthshire Paperweights, Ltd., Crieff, Scotland; dated 1983. Close millefiori. Grey/white/green/orange ribbon twist torsade at periphery. Translucent dark cobalt blue ground. Polished basal concavity; "P 1983" cane; basal ring.
D: 3¹⁄₁₆″ (7.8 cm.)
Gift of Mr. and Mrs. F. John Barlow, 1986.

1742

Perthshire Paperweights, Ltd., Crieff, Scotland; dated 1986. Close millefiori includes date "P 1986," arrow, flower, and multicolor compound canes; white filigree ground. Polished colorless basal concavity; basal ring.
D: 2⅝″ (6.7 cm.)
Gift of Mr. and Mrs. F. John Barlow, 1986.

*   *   *

190

George Bacchus & Sons, Birmingham, England, 1845-55. Millefiori tuft: central ruffled red/white cane; 5 concentric rings of blue, green, white, and pink ruffled canes. Peripheral torsade spirals to right: flattened narrow cobalt blue/opaque white rod encloses single twisted white filigree. Concave polished base; basal ring. Note: Bacchus torsades twist clockwise.
D: 3⁷⁄₁₆″ (8.7 cm.)
Bergstrom Bequest, 1958.
EHB acquisition: February, 1939.
No. 203, Pl. 34; Cloak Catalogue, 1969.
Ref.: No. 241, *The Corning Museum of Glass Exhibition Catalogue,* 1978.

399

George Bacchus & Sons, Birmingham, England, 1845-55. Shallow domed, colorless glass encases concentric millefiori motif: central opaque white cane bears dark blue female silhouette, to dexter, encircled by minute white star rods with same silhouette center. 4 additional concentric circles of ruffled and serrated pink, blue, and white canes include 3 compound canes with silhouette centers. Peripheral circle of blue-lined, serrated white canes drawn to center of base. Polished flat colorless base; trace of pontil mark. Silhouette and tiny canes visible underside. Identical silhouette appears in weight by Gillinder & Sons, Philadelphia, PA. 132.
D: 2⅞″ (7.3 cm.)
Bergstrom Bequest, 1958.
EHB acquisition: June, 1941.
No. 419, Pl. 34; Cloak Catalogue, 1969.
Ref.: *Glass Club Bulletin,* No. 91/92, September-December, 1969; Fig. 4, p. 5.

429

Saint Louis, dated 1848. Concentric millefiori motif: 6 circles of closely packed predominantly blue, pastel-colored canes; central "devil" silhouette cane. "SL 1848" in black cane near peripheral circle of finely serrated white/red/cornflower blue canes alternated with white/red/white green canes all drawn to center of base following contour of weight. Polished concave colorless base; basal ring.
D: 2⅝″ (6.6 cm.)
Bergstrom Bequest, 1958.
EHB acquisition: October, 1941.
No. 456, Pl. 27; Cloak Catalogue, 1969.

1190

Clichy, 1845-55. Concentric millefiori motif: central blue floret encircled by white stardust canes and ring of 5 each, alternately spaced, pink/white Clichy roses and moss canes. Other circles include purple/white, white/red, green/pink, white/pink/red, blue and white star canes, white/green florets; outer circle of alternating green and white stave canes drawn down to pedestal foot. Polished concave colorless base; basal ring.
D: 3¹⁄₁₆″ (7.8 cm.)
Gift of Mrs. Florence Gosselin Marsh in memory of her husband, Raymond Clark Marsh, 1976.

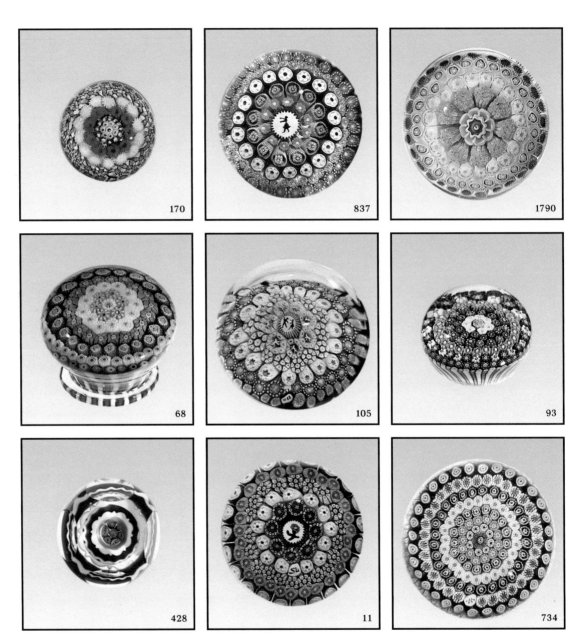

170   837   1790

68   105   93

428   11   734

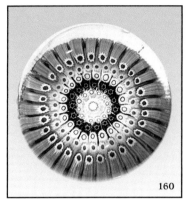

160

151

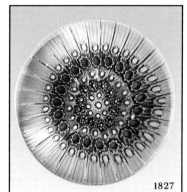

1827

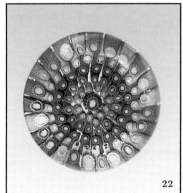

22

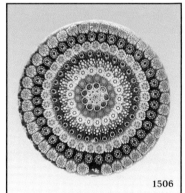

1506

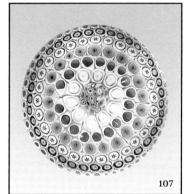

107

1082

484

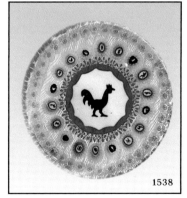

1538

14

11
Saint Louis, 1845-55. Concentric millefiori: 5 circles of predominantly blue, white, green, pink, and dark green canes; central cluster surrounds blue silhouette flower/ stem/ leaves in white cane. White floret circle includes "SL" signature. Peripheral green/white canes drawn to center of polished concave colorless base; basal ring.
D: 3³⁄₁₆″ (8.1 cm.)
Bergstrom Bequest, 1958.
EHB acquisition: May, 1936.
Illus. 5, Bergstrom book, 1940; later editions.
No. 11, Pl. 24; Cloak Catalogue, 1969.

68
Clichy, 1845-55. Concentric, piedouche. 7 circles of blue, white, green, purple, and red millefiori canes; central cane of white stars and stamens. Peripheral circle of alternate cobalt blue and opaque white staves extends to base forming pedestal, colorless round flat foot.
D: 2¾″ (7.0 cm.)
Bergstrom Bequest, 1958.
EHB acquisition: September, 1937.
No. 73, Pl. 15; Cloak Catalogue, 1969.

93
Clichy, 1845-55. 7 concentric circles of varicolored canes surround pink/green Clichy rose. At periphery, alternating opaque white and pink canes, drawn to base, form stave basket. Polished concave colorless base; basal ring.
D: 2³⁄₁₆″ (5.5 cm.)
Bergstrom Bequest, 1958.
EHB acquisition: November, 1937.
No. 98, Pl. 15; Cloak Catalogue, 1969.

105
Saint Louis, dated 1848. 6 concentric millefiori cane circles surround central "dancing couple," silhouette cane; inner circle encloses 7 white devil silhouettes in translucent green bordered by white/pink rods. "SL" and date "1848" appear near periphery. Outer circle of flattened cobalt blue canes/white centers drawn, following contour of weight, to center of polished concave colorless base; basal ring.
D: 3⅛″ (8.0 cm.)
Bergstrom Bequest, 1958.
EHB acquisition: February, 1939.
Illus.: Pl. III, Bergstrom book, 1940; later editions.
No. 112, Pl. 27; Cloak Catalogue, 1969.
Ref.: McCawley, Patricia K.: *Antique Glass Paperweights from France,* 1968; 76(a).

170
Saint Louis, dated 1848. Concentric millefiori: 4 circles of blue, white and varicolored canes surround central cluster of small red/white rods. Peripheral circle of chartreuse/blue canes and "SL 1848" in white/black extend to center of polished concave colorless base; basal ring.
D: 2¹⁄₁₆″ (5.3 cm.)
Bergstrom Bequest, 1958.
EHB acquisition: December, 1938.
No. 182, Pl. 28; Cloak Catalogue, 1969.

428
Clichy, 1845-55. Colorless glass encases single compound cane, unreduced in size, resting on base. Cluster of 4 small blue/white and 3 green/white whorl canes within a scalloped opaque white circle surrounded by peripheral serrated dark ruby-red/white circle. Polished concave base.
D: 2⅛″ (5.4 cm.)
Bergstrom Bequest, 1958.
EHB acquisition: October, 1941.
No. 455, Pl. 28; Cloak Catalogue, 1969.
Ref.: Hollister, Paul: *The Encyclopedia of Glass Paperweights,* 1969; p. 127.

734
Saint Louis, dated 1953. Concentric piedouche. 8 millefiori circles of predominantly green, white, and red star canes. Double torsade of flattened white filigree twists edged with red, border white latticinio pedestal. "SL 1953" green/white signature cane near periphery. Polished concave colorless base.
D: 2¹⁵⁄₁₆″ (7.4 cm.)
Gift of Mr. and Mrs. Ralph S. Johns, 1968.

837
Saint Louis, dated 1847. Concentric millefiori. Large central "dancing girl" silhouette cane within 6 circles of millefiori canes: chartreuse, deep blue, green, pink (square), white (floret), pastel blue, red; "SL 1847" in white cane. Polished concave colorless base; basal ring.
Note: "Square" canes in second row.
D: 3½″ (8.3 cm.)
Museum Purchase, 1972.

1790
George Bacchus & Sons, Birmingham, England, 1848-55. Concentric millefiori: large central ruffled white/transparent red cane encircled by 9 pastel pink/white/green compound canes, circle of white/colorless canes, circle of white/pink canes. Outer circle of crimped white/transparent green canes drawn down to center of polished concave colorless base; fine basal ring.
D: 3½″ (8.9 cm.)
Gift of Mrs. Virginia Bensley Trowbridge, 1987.

22

Whitefriars Glass Works, London, England, dated 1848. Shallow form. 5 concentric circles of amber/white, pink/white, and blue/white canes surround large serrated blue/white center cane. Date "1848" appears in crudely formed blue numerals in white canes next to outer circle. Polished concave colorless base, "jelly glass" rim.
D: 3¼″ (8.3 cm.)
Bergstrom Bequest, 1958.
EHB acquisition: June, 1937.
Illus. 50, Bergstrom book, 1940; Illus. 48, later editions.
No. 24, Pl. 35, Cloak Catalogue, 1969.
Ref.: *PCA Bulletin,* 1987; "The Myth of Whitefriars." The attributions for 1 and 22 have been researched by John Smith, London, and were found to be false. These bear fake dates and were produced during the 1930's by John Walsh-Walsh, Ltd., Birmingham, England.

107

George Bacchus & Sons, Birmingham, England, 1848-55. 6 concentric circles of predominantly white rods surround central cluster of small pastel millefiori canes; 1 white circle with translucent red lining, another with translucent blue. Peripheral circle of serrated white canes/translucent pink centers drawn, following curve, to center of polished concave colorless base; basal ring.
D: 3⅝″ (9.2 cm.)
Bergstrom Bequest, 1958.
EHB acquisition: February, 1938.
Illus. 48, Bergstrom book, 1940; Illus. 46, later editions.
No. 114, Pl. 34; Cloak Catalogue, 1969.

151

Clichy, 1845-55. Concentric millefiori. Large compound center cane surrounded by 7 successive circles: green/pink/white Clichy roses; pink/white/yellow stamen Clichy roses; pink/white/yellow stamen florets; blue/white/yellow stamen florets; alternating white star/yellow stamen florets and green/pink/white Clichy roses; peripheral circle of green/white moss canes. Polished concave colorless base.
D: 2⅝″ (6.7 cm.)
Bergstrom Bequest, 1958.
EHB acquisition: October, 1938.
No. 160, Pl. 17; Cloak Catalogue, 1969.

160

Attributed to Whitefriars Glass, Ltd., London, 1848-55. Magnum. Low in weight: 5 concentric circles of blue/white, green/red, white/amber, and white/translucent green canes; large opaque white/red pastry mold center cane. Outer circle: ochre/white/red center canes extend to base following curve of weight. Peripheral exterior groove between colorless base and high crown. Polished wide flat basal ring, trace of pontil mark in basal concavity. (Canes similar to other Whitefriars concentrics dated 1848. See No. 22.)
D: 4⅛″ (10.5 cm.)
Bergstrom Bequest, 1958.
EHB acquisition: November, 1938.
No. 169, Pl. 34; Cloak Catalogue, 1969.

484

Clichy, 1845-55. 7 concentric circles of white, red, green, purple, pink and blue canes; outer circle of amethyst and opaque white stave rods drawn down form basket. Polished concave colorless base.
D: 2⁹⁄₁₆″ (6.5 cm.)
Bergstrom Bequest, 1958.
EHB acquisition: April, 1943.
No. 514, Pl. 13, Cloak Catalogue, 1969.

1082

Origin unknown. Early 19th century. Possibly Bohemian, 1840-45. 4 concentric circles of millefiori canes: striped blue/white, pink/green florets; pink/white with scallop edge; white/pink stars; cobalt blue/white florets; white/red/green center cane. Closely twisted red/white/blue torsade. Smooth colorless base, trace of pontil mark; basal ring.
D: 3⅛″ (7.9 cm.)
Museum Purchase, 1975.

1506

Saint Louis, dated 1972. Concentric millefiori canes, predominantly blue, white, red, and green; black "SL 1972" signature cane. Opaque white filigree and latticinio piedouche; polished concave colorless base; basal ring.
H: 2³¹⁄₃₂″ (7.6 cm.); D: 2²⁷⁄₃₂″ (7.2 cm.)
Gift of Mr. and Mrs. William L. Liebman, 1983.

1538

Baccarat, dated 1971. Concentric millefiori canes include all 18 of the 19th century Gridel animal silhouettes. Large central "rooster" silhouette, first of the 20th century Gridel Series. "B 1971" date cane. Blue, pink and yellow canes predominate; fine white filigree rods (laid parallel) form ground. Polished flat colorless base etched with Baccarat insignia and "No. 1089."
D: 3⁵⁄₃₂″ (8.1 cm.)
Bequest of J. Howard Gilroy, 1986.

1827

Attributed to Stourbridge area, England, 1850. Magnum. High dome. Crimped opaque white/yellow cane centers 5 concentric circles: white/blue/white; red/white/dark blue/colorless; white/blue/colorless/ white; orange/white/red; outer circle matches central cane drawn to flanged colorless base. Pontil mark.
D: 3²¹⁄₃₂″ (9.3 cm.)
Gift of Mrs. Virginia Bensley Trowbridge, 1987.

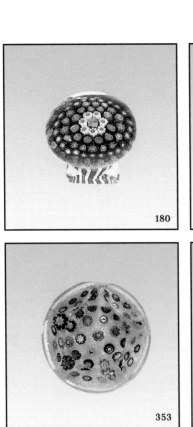

180

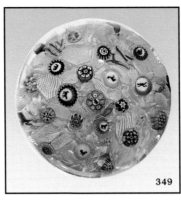

349

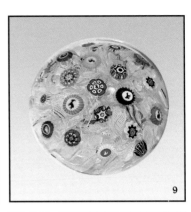

9

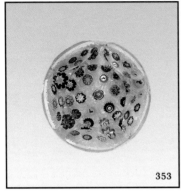

353

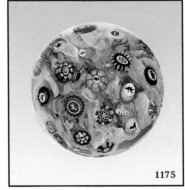

1175

513

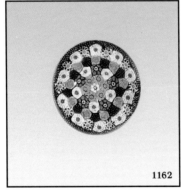

1162

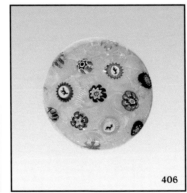

406

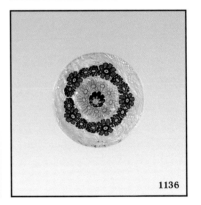

1136

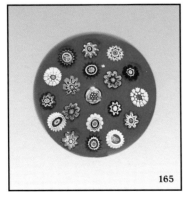

165

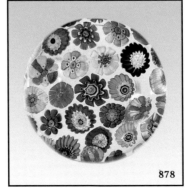

878

149

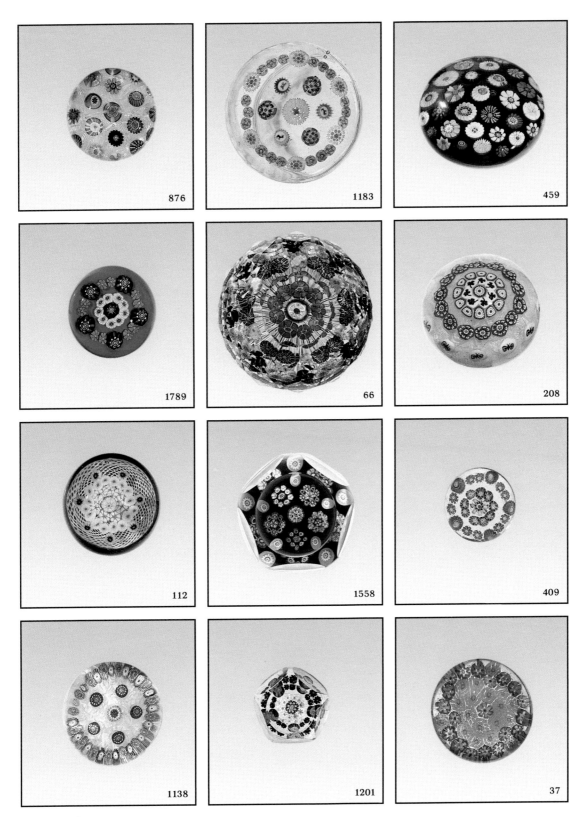

876

1183

459

1789

66

208

112

1558

409

1138

1201

37

9
Baccarat, 1848. Spaced millefiori canes on upset white filigree ground. 3 arrow-cane color combinations: red/white/blue, blue/white/red, and white/green/white; 8 silhouettes; deer, goat, dog, horse, hunter, pelican, squirrel, pigeons (lovebirds); "B 1848" date cane. Polished concave colorless base; basal ring.
D: 3³⁄₁₆″ (8.1 cm.)
Bergstrom Bequest, 1958.
EHB acquisition: May, 1936.
Illus. 14, Bergstrom book, 1940; Illus. 15, later editions.
No. 9, Pl. 1, Cloak Catalogue, 1969.

149
Clichy, 1845-55. Spaced millefiori: 19 canes include 1 white/green Clichy rose; a green/white moss cane, star flower center; 2 "C" signatures (serif in blue, red "horseshoe"). Royal blue ground lined with opaque white. Polished nearly flat colorless base; basal ring.
D: 2⅝″ (6.7 cm.)
Bergstrom Bequest, 1958.
EHB acquisition: October, 1938.
Pl. VII, Bergstrom book, 1940; later editions.
No. 158, Pl. 17; Cloak Catalogue, 1969.
Ref.: *Hobbies* (cover), October, 1941.

165
Baccarat, 1845-55. Spaced millefiori: 19 canes encircle pink/white/green "Clichy-type" rose (6 tiny star stamens). Near periphery, minute unusual "Clichy-type" rose on green stem/leaves in crimped white casing. Translucent cobalt blue ground lined with opaque white. Polished concave colorless base; basal ring.
D: 2¹³⁄₁₆″ (7.2 cm.)
Bergstrom Bequest, 1958.
EHB acquisition: November, 1938.
No. 174, Pl. 14; Cloak Catalogue, 1969.

180
Clichy, 1845-55. Concentric piedouche. 7 circles of white, pink, green, red, amethyst millefiori and floret canes (1 green "moss" type circle) surround green/pink Clichy rose. Peripheral circle of alternating opaque blue and white stave rods form pedestal; beveled square colorless foot.
D: 2½″ (6.3 cm.)
Bergstrom Bequest, 1958.
EHB acquisition: January, 1939.
Illus. 31, Bergstrom book, 1940; later editions.
No. 193, Pl. 15; Cloak Catalogue, 1969.

349
Baccarat, dated 1848. Magnum. Spaced millefiori canes on scrambled white filigree ground, scattered ribbon twists. 1 cane dated "B 1848"; 9 silhouette canes (rooster, horse, monkey, deer, pelican, goat, crane, shamrocks, pigeon/2 shamrocks); white/green, blue/red, floret center arrow cane; blue/white/red, star center arrow cane; 6-point star with green/white arrow cane rods in alternate interstices. Polished concave colorless base; basal ring.
D: 3¹⁵⁄₁₆″ (8.4 cm.)
Bergstrom Bequest, 1958.
EHB acquisition: October, 1940.
No. 368, Pl. 1; Cloak Catalogue, 1969.

353
Baccarat, 1845-55. Spaced millefiori canes, upset white filigree. An unusual weight with "Clichy-type" canes (including a pink "Clichy-like" rose) and Baccarat animal silhouettes (goat, deer, and rooster). Top punty, 10 smaller side punties; polished concave colorless base; basal ring.
D: 2⁹⁄₁₆″ (6.5 cm.)
Bergstrom Bequest, 1958.
EHB acquisition: November, 1940.
No. 372, Pl. 8; Cloak Catalogue, 1969.

406
Baccarat, dated 1849. Spaced millefiori canes: date "1849", arrow, and compound millefiori; dog, goat, and deer silhouettes; upset white filigree ground. Polished concave colorless base; basal ring.
D: 2⁹⁄₁₆″ (6.5 cm.)
Bergstrom Bequest, 1958.
EHB acquisition: August, 1941.
No. 426, Pl. 8; Cloak Catalogue, 1969.

513
Clichy, 1845-55. 2 concentric circles of spaced varicolored millefiori canes; central pink Clichy rose; white filigree rods fill interstices; ground of white filigree rods laid parallel; polished concave colorless base. Top punty, 2 circles (5 in each) side punties.
D: 3″ (7.6 cm.)
Bergstrom Bequest, 1958.
EHB acquisition: Unrecorded.
No. 547, Pl. 18; Cloak Catalogue, 1969.

878
Clichy, 1845-55. Spaced millefiori canes include 3 Clichy roses: yellow; pink/white; white/pink. Central and other large pastry mold canes. Polished concave colorless base; basal ring.
D: 3¹⁄₁₆″ (7.9 cm.)
Bequest of Mrs. L. E. Kaumheimer, 1973.

1136
Clichy, 1845-55. Concentric millefiori canes (compound purple center cane ringed by pink/white florets and outer circle of 5 blue and 10 green compound canes); white filigree cushion laid over parallel filigree rods. Polished concave colorless base; basal ring.
D: 2¼″ (5.7 cm.)
Gift of Mrs. Florence Gosselin Marsh in memory of her husband, Raymond Clark Marsh, 1976.

1162
Clichy, 1845-55. Concentric millefiori: pink, green and white Clichy rose canes; dark purple and green moss canes; green/white stave peripheral canes. Polished concave colorless base; basal ring.
D: 2⁷⁄₃₂″ (5.6 cm.)
Gift of Mrs. Florence Gosselin Marsh in memory of her husband, Raymond Clark Marsh, 1976.

1175
Baccarat, 1845-55. Spaced millefiori canes include arrow and cockerel, monkey, elephant, devil, horse, goat and moth silhouettes, date cane "B 1847", and also 2 unusual gingham-patterned strips: blue/white and orange/white; on upset white filigree, some with salmon-pink coils. Polished concave colorless base; basal ring.
D: 3⁵⁄₃₂″ (8.0 cm.)
Gift of Mrs. Florence Gosselin Marsh in memory of her husband, Raymond Clark Marsh, 1976.

37
Chinese, ca. 1930. Shallow, colorless glass. Patterned millefiori; loosely formed yellow canes with red centers, blue/white canes at periphery.
D: 2½″ (6.3 cm.)
Bergstrom Bequest, 1958.
EHB acquisition: March, 1935.
No. 37, Pl. 62, Cloak Catalogue, 1969.

66
Origin unknown, probably Bohemian, 1848-60. Magnum; heavy. Allover geometric faceting. Concentric motif (not contiguous); pink, blue/white, and red/white millefiori canes; 5-point star canes predominate. Large central "wagon-wheel" cane: green border, 8 opaque white spokes, green stamen center. Polished concave colorless base cut with 32-point star; basal ring.
D: 3⅞″ (9.9 cm.)
Bergstrom Bequest, 1958.
EHB acquisition: September, 1937.
No. 71, Pl. 2; Cloak Catalogue, 1969.

112
New England Glass Co., East Cambridge, MA, 1852-68. Patterned millefiori: rosette of pastel canes within circle of 7 spaced compound white canes with bumblebee silhouette centers, double-swirl white latticinio cushion; colorless base, smooth deep concavity. "Dimpled" dome.
D: 2¹⁵⁄₁₆″ (7.4 cm.)
Bergstrom Bequest, 1958.
EHB acquisition: May, 1938.
No. 120, Pl. 42; Cloak Catalogue, 1969.

208
Baccarat, 1845-55. Patterned millefiori: Central red/white cog cane encircled by 7 green/white shamrock canes, a circle of red/white cog canes, a circle of cobalt blue/red/white arrow canes; at periphery, spaced butterfly canes; scrambled white filigree ground. Motif close to glass surface. Polished concave colorless base.
D: 3″ (7.6 cm.)
Bergstrom Bequest, 1958.
EHB acquisition: February, 1939.
No. 223, Pl. 3; Cloak Catalogue, 1969.

409
Clichy, 1845-55. Miniature. Spaced concentric: cranberry/white/green star center pastry mold cane within circle of 9 green/yellow/white floret center canes; peripheral circle of 5 turquoise/pink/white canes spaced between 10 pink/honeycomb center canes. Polished concave colorless base.
D: 1¾″ (4.5 cm.)
Bergstrom Bequest, 1958.
EHB acquisition: August, 1941.
No. 429, Pl. 13; Cloak Catalogue, 1969.

459
Clichy, 1845-55. Spaced millefiori: 37 large (predominantly pastry mold) varicolored canes include: red "C" serif signature in white pastry mold ribbed cane (partially cased with dark red); tiny white star flower cane/white stamen center; tiny green star flower cane; 1 white Clichy rose. Transparent red ground. Polished concave colorless base; basal ring.
D: 3³⁄₁₆″ (8.1 cm.)
Bergstrom Bequest, 1958.
EHB acquisition: March, 1942.
No. 487, Pl. 18; Cloak Catalogue, 1969.

876
Clichy, 1845-55. Spaced millefiori canes on white filigree chequer laid over parallel filigree rods. 4 Clichy roses: green/white; green/pink; pink/white; and unusual blue with single circle of moss canes and one in center forming rose center. The pink/white rose has multiple moss-cane center. Polished concave colorless base; basal ring.
D: 2⅛″ (5.4 cm.)
Bequest of Mrs. L. E. Kaumheimer, 1973.

1138
Saint Louis, 1845-55. 5 spaced blue/white compound millefiori canes encircle center salmon/white/blue cane; peripheral circle of alternating salmon/blue/white and green/white/red canes; upset white filigree cushion. Polished concave colorless base; basal ring.
D: 2¹⁵⁄₃₂″ (6.2 cm.)
Gift of Mrs. Florence Gosselin Marsh in memory of her husband, Raymond Clark Marsh, 1976.

1183
Baccarat, 1845-55. Spaced millefiori motif: large central white stardust cane, white/red square center encircled by 3 blue/white/red arrow canes alternate with dog, goat, and deer silhouettes; peripheral circle of 3 small green/white/blue/red compound canes spaced between each of 6 larger white/red/blue star canes. Polished concave colorless base; basal ring. Note: Seen less often on colorless ground.
D: 3⅛″ (7.9 cm.)
Gift of Mrs. Florence Gosselin Marsh in memory of her husband, Raymond Clark Marsh, 1976.

1201
Clichy, 1845-55. Miniature. Spaced concentric millefiori motif; central blue/white/ochre pastry mold cane encircled by 10 white florets; 5 green/pink/white Clichy roses alternate with purple canes in peripheral circle. Top and 5 side punties. Polished concave colorless base; basal ring.
D: 1²⁷⁄₃₂″ (4.6 cm.)
Gift of Mrs. Florence Gosselin Marsh in memory of her husband, Raymond Clark Marsh, 1976.

1558
Paul Ysart, possibly at Caithness Glass, Wick, Scotland; 1950s-70s. Spaced millefiori canes: 5 opaque pink/white canes; central cluster of cobalt blue/white compound canes. Dark amethyst ground. Red "PY" cane in 1 circle. Wide polished flat base.
D: 2²⁹⁄₃₂″ (7.4 cm.)
Bequest of J. Howard Gilroy, 1986.

1789
Clichy, 1845-55. Patterned millefiori: 5 purple/white pastry mold canes, 2 pink/white florets between each. Central green/white pastry mold cane encircled by 9 white/red/blue canes; turquoise-blue ground lined with white. Polished concave colorless base; basal ring.
D: 2⅛″ (5.5 cm.)
Gift of Mrs. Virginia Bensley Trowbridge, 1987.

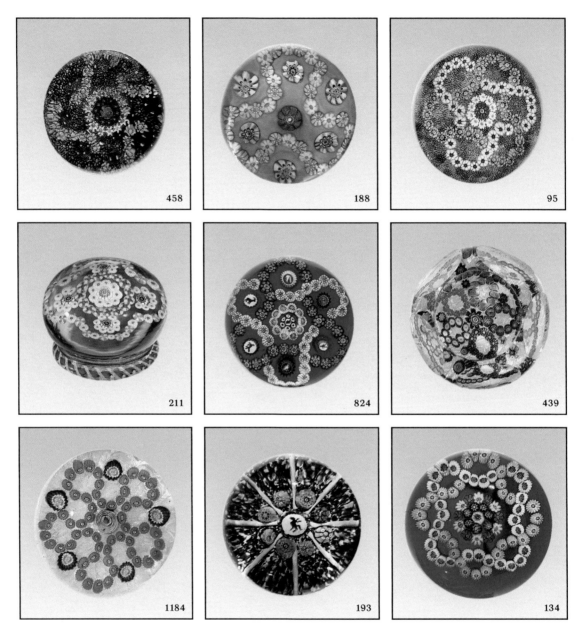

458

188

95

211

824

439

1184

193

134

17

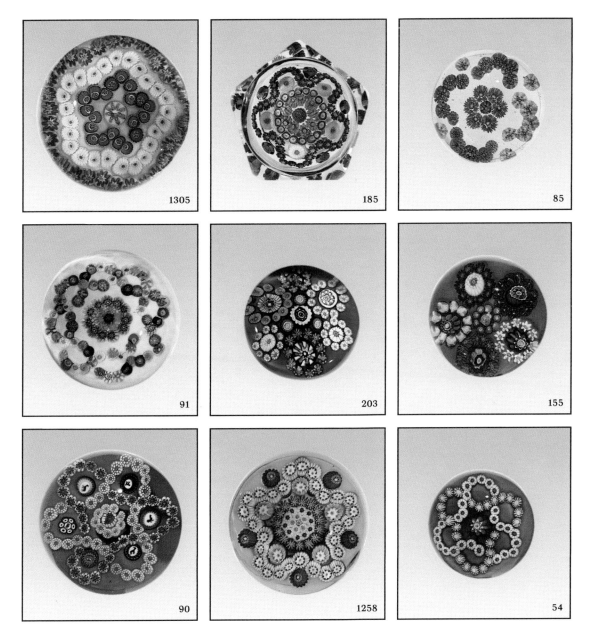

1305

185

85

91

203

155

90

1258

54

18

95
Clichy, 1845-55. Patterned millefiori. Interlaced garlands of pink and white/blue canes form double trefoil centered by white florets surrounding large blue pastry mold cane. Partially translucent moss cane ground resembles blades of grass. Polished concave colorless base; basal ring.
D: 3¹/₁₆″ (7.8 cm.)
Bergstrom Bequest, 1958.
EHB acquisition: November, 1937.
No. 100, Pl. 14; Cloak Catalogue, 1969.

134
Clichy, 1845-55. Patterned millefiori, double quatrefoil motif: 2 interlaced garlands of pink/green and white/green pastry mold canes centered by 2 concentric circles of red/white, green, and pink canes surrounding white stardust cane with "moss" cane core. Translucent cobalt blue ground; polished concave colorless base; basal ring.
D: 3³/₁₆″ (8.1 cm.)
Bergstrom Bequest, 1958.
EHB acquisition: October, 1938.
No. 143, Pl. 18; Cloak Catalogue, 1969.

188
Clichy, 1845-55. Patterned millefiori garland: pastel pastry mold canes set in transparent pink ground lined with opaque white. Trefoil design interspersed with larger individual canes; green whorl rods encircle pink/white center floret. Polished flat colorless base.
D: 3⅛″ (8.0 cm.)
Bergstrom Bequest, 1958.
EHB acquisition: February, 1939.
No. 201, Pl. 18; Cloak Catalogue, 1969.

193
Saint Louis, ca. 1850. Patterned millefiori: blue/white/green and red/white/green jasper in alternate panels separated by 8 opaque white rods, large central "dancing devil" silhouette cane (black on white edged with amethyst). Near center: large varicolored cane on each panel. Visible from side: peripheral white filigree/coral ribbon twist torsade. Green/white jasper ground. Polished concave colorless base; basal ring.
D: 3³/₁₆″ (8.1 cm.)
Bergstrom Bequest, 1958.
EHB acquisition: February, 1939.
No. 206, Pl. 25; Cloak Catalogue, 1969.
Ref.: McCawley, Patricia K.: *Antique Glass Paperweights from France,* 1968; pp. 30, 84.

211
Baccarat, 1845-55. Patterned millefiori: 2 concentric circles (white stardust/green and white/red canes) surround single white/red cane. Quatrefoil garland of alternating white/blue and white stardust/red canes contains group of 8 canes in each lobe. Colorless circular foot encases torsade of red ribbon twists coiled with white filigree. Polished concave underside; trace of pontil mark; basal ring. Torsade coils to right; indentation visible where ends meet.
D: 3⅛″ (8.0 cm.)
Bergstrom Bequest, 1958.
EHB acquisition: May, 1939.
No. 226, Pl. 4; Cloak Catalogue, 1969.

439
Clichy, 1845-55. Patterned millefiori motif, upset white filigree ground on various white filigree rods laid parallel. 5 looped garlands: pink Clichy roses; turquoise-blue florets; red/white/pastel blue canes; green/white/yellow florets; purple/white/red/green canes. 5 millefiori canes spaced between loops. Large burgundy-red/white/green/red pastry mold center cane. Large top punty, 2 circles of punties on curve. Polished concave colorless base; basal ring.
D: 3″ (7.6 cm.)
Bergstrom Bequest, 1958.
EHB acquisition: November, 1941.
No. 467, Pl. 13; Cloak Catalogue, 1969.

458
Clichy, 1845-55. Patterned millefiori: central pink/green Clichy rose surrounded by 2 concentric circles of blue florets and white star pastry mold canes; interlaced garlands of pink/white canes and purple/green canes form double quatrefoil; green moss cushion with tiny white spaced stars. Polished concave colorless base; basal ring.
D:3¼″ (8.3 cm.)
Bergstrom Bequest, 1958.
EHB acquisition: March, 1942.
No. 486, Pl. 17; Cloak Catalogue, 1969.
Ref.: No. 118, *The Corning Museum of Glass Exhibition Catalogue,* 1978.

824
Baccarat, 1845-55. Patterned millefiori: Double trefoil garland of white/green and red/white canes, each loop enclosing a single cane, among them a squirrel, deer, dog, bird, man, and pair of lovebirds. Butterfly cane centers circlet of white/red canes. Translucent cobalt blue ground. Polished concave base.
D: 2¹³/₁₆″ (7.2 cm.)
Gift of Mrs. Fred A. Nagel and family in memory of Fred A. Nagel, 1971.
Ref.: McCawley, Patricia K.: *Antique Glass Paperweights from France,* 1968; 7a.

1184
Clichy, 1845-55. Cinquefoil garland of small turquoise-blue/red/white canes, 5 large garnet-red/white/green canes alternated between loops. Large central pink/white Clichy rose. Upset white filigree cushion laid over parallel white filigree rods. Polished concave colorless base; basal ring.
D: 3⅛″ (7.9 cm.)
Gift of Mrs. Florence Gosselin Marsh in memory of her husband, Raymond Clark Marsh, 1976.

54
Clichy, 1845-55. Double trefoil garland: intertwined pink/white and white star/blue star canes, large red/white pastry mold center cane. Translucent emerald-green ground lined with white. Polished concave colorless base; basal ring.
D: 2¹¹⁄₁₆″ (6.8 cm.)
Bergstrom Bequest, 1958.
EHB acquisition: June, 1939.
No. 54, Pl. 16; Cloak Catalogue, 1969.

85
Clichy, 1845-55. Patterned millefiori; varicolored canes in 4 "C" patterns surround central pink/blue/white cane cluster. (Green "moss" canes form 1 "C.") Polished concave colorless base; basal ring.
D: 2¾″ (7.0 cm.)
Bergstrom Bequest, 1958.
EHB acquisition: November, 1937.
No. 90, Pl. 23; Cloak Catalogue, 1969.

90
Baccarat, 1845-55. Patterned millefiori; translucent ruby ground. Intertwining trefoil garlands: white stardust/white-red whorl centers and blue/white pastry mold canes, each loop studded with a silhouette cane: moth, deer, dog, rooster, goat, lovebirds. Center circlet of white stardust/green-white whorl center canes surrounds white/pink cane. Polished concave base; basal ring.
D: 3³⁄₁₆″ (8.1 cm.)
Bergstrom Bequest, 1958.
EHB acquisition: November, 1937.
No. 95, Pl. 4; Cloak Catalogue, 1969.

91
Clichy, 1845-55. Patterned millefiori set into opaque white ground. Interlaced garlands of varicolored canes form double quatrefoil motif. Dark blue center cane, encircled by 2 rings of green/white/pink canes, appears several times in the garlands. Polished concave colorless base; basal ring.
D: 3⅜″ (8.6 cm.)
Bergstrom Bequest, 1958.
EHB acquisition: November, 1937.
No. 96, Pl. 18; Cloak Catalogue, 1969.

155
Clichy, 1845-55. Patterned millefiori. Central green/pink/white Clichy rose, 9 small serrated green/white canes. 5 spaced varicolored cane circlets, one being green/white Clichy rose. Large single pastry mold cane centers each circlet. Unusual color ground: transparent tomato-red lined with white. Polished concave colorless base.
D: 2⅝″ (6.7 cm.)
Bergstrom Bequest, 1958.
EHB acquisition: October, 1938.
No. 164, Pl. 17; Cloak Catalogue, 1969.

185
Clichy, 1845-55. Convex patterned millefiori: cinquefoil garland of cobalt blue/white/yellow honeycomb-center pastry mold canes studded with 5 white star canes/moss and pink/white whorl centers; 5 pink/white/green Clichy roses between loops. 9 pink florets and 18 serrated green/white canes encircle central turquoise-blue/white/pink/green pastry mold cane. Wide flat top punty, 5 on side; polished flat colorless base cut alternately with 12 miters and 12 oval radials.
D: 3″ (7.6 cm.)
Bergstrom Bequest, 1958.
EHB acquisition: January, 1939.
No. 198, Pl. 14; Cloak Catalogue, 1969.
Ref.: Hollister, Paul: *The Encyclopedia of Glass Paperweights,* 1969; pp. 131-132.

203
Clichy, 1845-55. Patterned millefiori: 6 various millefiori cane circlets (each centered by large millefiori cane); large ribbed white/green/red pastry mold center cane surrounded by 3 spaced red/white canes. Translucent dark amethyst ground lined with opaque white. Polished concave colorless base; basal ring.
D: 2¹⁵⁄₁₆″ (7.5 cm.)
Bergstrom Bequest, 1958.
EHB acquisition: February, 1939.
No. 218, Pl. 17; Cloak Catalogue, 1969.

1258
Clichy, 1845-55. Patterned millefiori: white/blue/red canes in 5-point star; red and alternating pink florets at intersections. In star center: concentric circles of red/white star canes, white stardust/blue, and white stardust/green moss/pink canes. Translucent green ground. Polished concave base; basal ring.
D: 3¹⁄₁₆″ (7.8 cm.)
Museum Purchase, 1976.

1305
Clichy, 1845-55. Patterned millefiori. Red/white, white/pink, blue/white florets in star pattern on lettuce-green ground lined with white opaline. Polished concave colorless base; basal ring.
D: 3⅜″ (8.6 cm.)
Gift of Robert S. Sage and Jeanne Sage Groves in memory of their parents, Charles H. and Lyda P. Sage, 1978.
Ref.: Hollister, Paul: *The Encyclopedia of Glass Paperweights,* 1969; p. 128.

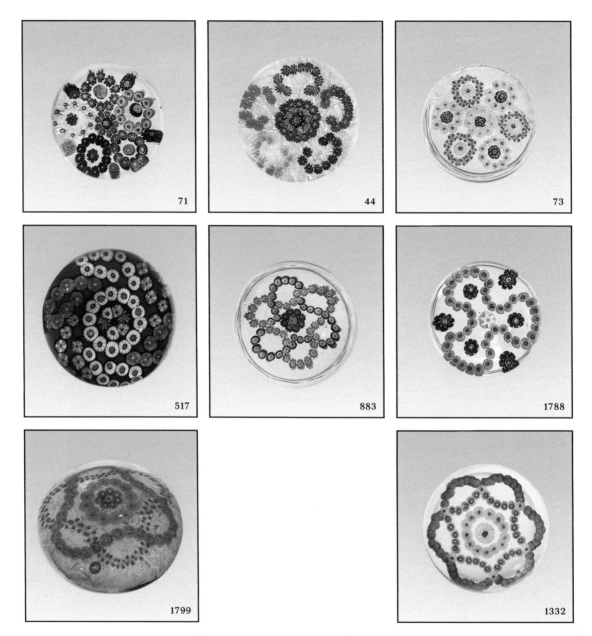

71

44

73

517

883

1788

1799

1332

19

1166

474

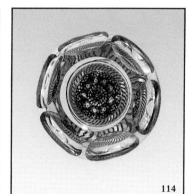

114

137

247

441

448

478

10

44
Clichy, 1845-55. Patterned millefiori. 2 concentric circles: pink/green Clichy roses and blue/white canes surround large red/white pastry mold cane; 5 varicolored peripheral groups of canes in "C" form. White upset filigree ground over segments of white filigree rods laid parallel. Polished concave colorless base (with traces of filigree); wide basal ring.
D: 2¹³⁄₁₆″ (7.2 cm.)
Bergstrom Bequest, 1958.
EHB acquisition: June, 1937.
No. 44, Pl. 14; Cloak Catalogue, 1969.

71
Clichy, 1845-55. Patterned millefiori: 6 circlets of varicolored canes; a single cane at periphery between circlets as well as within — one being a large pink/green Clichy rose cane. Polished concave colorless base.
D: 3″ (7.6 cm.)
Bergstrom Bequest, 1958.
EHB acquisition: September, 1937.
No. 76, Pl. 17; Cloak Catalogue, 1969.

73
Baccarat, 1845-55. Patterned millefiori: 7 circlets, each enclosing a single cane of which 4 are arrow canes. Predominant colors: red/white/blue; blue/white/green/red; salmon-red/white/green star canes; and white star/green whorls. Polished concave colorless base; basal ring.
D: 3″ (7.6 cm.)
Bergstrom Bequest, 1958.
EHB acquisition: September, 1937.
No. 78, Pl. 5; Cloak Catalogue, 1969.

517
Clichy, 1845-55. Patterned millefiori: swirled loops of green, white, and pink canes, all with star centers, surround 2 central concentric circles of similar canes (except for 2 green/pink pastry mold canes in center ring). Cobalt blue ground; polished concave colorless base; basal ring.
D: 3″ (7.6 cm.)
Bergstrom Bequest, 1958.
EHB acquisition: Unrecorded.
No. 551, Pl. 14; Cloak Catalogue, 1969.

883
Clichy, 1845-55. Central pink/white/green Clichy rose encircled by blue/pink/white canes within double trefoil garland of green/white and pink/white millefiori canes. Polished concave colorless base; basal ring.
D: 2¹³⁄₁₆″ (7.2 cm.)
Bequest of Mrs. L. E. Kaumheimer, 1973.

1332
Baccarat, 1907-early 1930s. Interlaced millefiori garland: green/red/white/yellow canes surround central white stardust floret with cobalt blue center. Polished concave colorless base; wide basal ring.
D: 2²⁷⁄₃₂″ (7.2 cm.)
Gift of Paul Hollister, 1978.
Ref.: Hollister, Paul: *Encyclopedia of Glass Paperweights,* 1969; pp. 48-49, 270.

1788
Clichy, 1845-55. Patterned millefiori: pink/white/green millefiori trefoil garland, white edelweiss cane center; 3 green/white/red canes in each loop, 3 cobalt blue/white/red canes outside each loop. Polished colorless basal concavity and basal ring.
D: 2¹⁵⁄₁₆″ (7.5 cm.)
Gift of Mrs. Virginia Bensley Trowbridge, 1987.

1799
Baccarat, dated 1971. Patterned millefiori. Double trefoil garland: pink/amber/pastel green canes interlace cobalt blue/white/pastel yellow canes; circle of pastel green/blue/pink canes surround central cluster of compound pink/yellow canes. Blue/white "B 1971" signature cane. Upset white filigree ground. Wide polished flat colorless base etched with Baccarat insignia and "312/1971."
D: 3⁹⁄₃₂″ (8.4 cm.)
Gift of Mrs. Virginia Bensley Trowbridge, 1987.

10

Baccarat, 1845-55. Close millefiori mushroom motif; peripheral torsade: tubular white filigree coiled with dark blue. Polished concave colorless base cut with small 32-point star; basal ring.
D: 3″ (7.6 cm.)
Bergstrom Bequest, 1958.
EHB acquisition: May, 1936.
No. 10, Pl. 6; Cloak Catalogue, 1969.
Ref.: Philippe, Joseph: *Le Val-Saint-Lambert*, 1974; p. 57.

114

Saint Louis, 1845-55. Concentric millefiori mushroom motif: Cobalt blue/white/green "anchor" canes surround central compound blue/white/salmon-red and white/blue star. Outer circle of white serrated canes, drawn to point at base, forms tuft. Dark blue/white filigree torsade (colorless core). Top punty, 6 on curve. Polished concave colorless base cut with small 24-point star.
D: 3″ (7.6 cm.)
Bergstrom Bequest, 1958.
EHB acquisition: May, 1938.
No. 122, Pl. 28; Cloak Catalogue, 1969.

137

Baccarat, 1845-55. Concentric millefiori mushroom motif: large central opaque white serrated cane/blue star center; 4 circles of salmon/red/green star rods, white/red center star rods, serrated dark red/white/pink camomile flower rods, and serrated white/red/white/green arrow canes — all drawn down to base. White filigree coiled with cobalt blue torsade low in weight. Polished concave colorless base cut with 16-point star; basal ring.
D: 3¼″ (8.3 cm.)
Bergstrom Bequest, 1958.
EHB acquisition: October, 1938.
No. 146, Pl. 4; Cloak Catalogue, 1969.
Ref.: McCawley, Patricia K.: *Antique Glass Paperweights from France*, 1968; 77(c).

247

Clichy, 1845-55. Concentric millefiori mushroom: 6 circles: 1 purple Clichy rose, another, white/green rose alternating with dark red/white canes. Peripheral circle of cobalt blue rods alternated with opaque white rods drawn to base form tuft. Wide flat top punty, 6 side punties. Polished flat colorless base cut with 32-point star.
D: 3³⁄₁₆″ (8.1 cm.)
Bergstrom Bequest, 1958.
EHB acquisition: September, 1939.
No. 264, Pl. 16; Cloak Catalogue, 1969.
Ref.: McCawley, Patricia K.: *Antique Glass Paperweights from France*, 1968; No. 78.

441

Saint Louis, 1845-55. Millefiori mushroom motif. Large serrated white central rod lined with translucent cobalt blue centered by 4 red/white canes that form a "square." 3 peripheral circles of canes: salmon-red/white/yellow star center; cobalt blue/white/red; and white/chartreuse star. Rare amber torsade coils twisted flat opaque white

filigree. "Mercury" ring. Polished concave colorless base; basal ring.
D: 2¹³⁄₁₆″ (7.2 cm.)
Bergstrom Bequest, 1958.
EHB acquisition: December, 1941.
No. 469, Pl. 28; Cloak Catalogue, 1969.

448

Saint Louis, 1845-55. Millefiori mushroom motif. 5 concentric circles of green, white, and varicolored canes surround central group of smaller rods. Peripheral circle of alternating chartreuse/white star/red center canes and white/red/white canes drawn down to point form tuft. Flat twist of thin opaque white rods coiled with cobalt blue forms torsade; "mercury" ring. Polished concave colorless base cut with small 24-point star; basal ring.
D: 2¹¹⁄₁₆″ (6.8 cm.)
Bergstrom Bequest, 1958.
EHB acquisition: January, 1942.
No. 477, Pl. 28; Cloak Catalogue, 1969.

474

Clichy, 1845-55. Concentric millefiori tuft: large central pink Clichy rose; 5 concentric circles of varicolored canes include edelweiss and moss canes; pink Clichy roses alternate with purple canes in one circle. Peripheral opaque white staves drawn to base form mushroom. Flat top punty, 6 side punties. Polished concave colorless base cut alternately with 12 petals and 12 miters.
D: 3⅜″ (8.6 cm.)
Bergstrom Bequest, 1958.
EHB acquisition: September, 1942.
No. 504, Pl. 16; Cloak Catalogue, 1969.
Ref.: No. 104, *The Corning Museum of Glass Exhibition Catalogue*, 1978.

478

Baccarat, 1845-55. White star carpet ground mushroom centered by compound red/white/blue arrow cane. Torsade: white filigree coiled with cobalt blue. Polished concave colorless base cut with small 32-point star. Note: also called "bouquet de mariage" type.
D: 3¼″ (8.3 cm.)
Bergstrom Bequest, 1958.
EHB acquisition: October, 1942.
No. 508, Pl. 4; Cloak Catalogue, 1969.
Ref.: McCawley, Patricia K.: *Antique Glass Paperweights from France*, 1968; 77(d).
No. 22, *The Corning Museum of Glass Exhibition Catalogue*, 1978.

1166

Clichy, 1845-55. Close millefiori mushroom motif includes typical Clichy florettes, an edelweiss and a green/white moss cane; pink and white stave rods alternate at mushroom periphery and are drawn to center of polished flat colorless base cut with 32-point star. Top and 6 side punties.
D: 3⁹⁄₃₂″ (8.3 cm.)
Gift of Mrs. Florence Gosselin Marsh in memory of her husband, Raymond Clark Marsh, 1976.

124

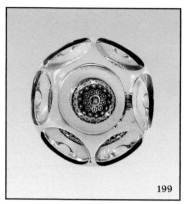

199

1281

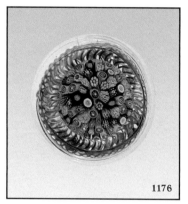

1176

144

248

781

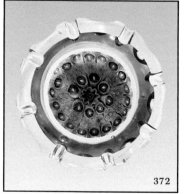

372

435

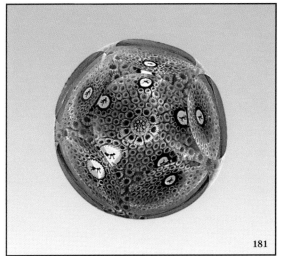

181

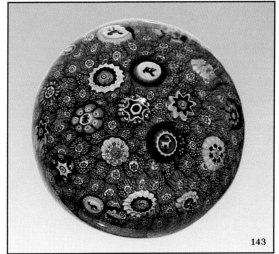

143

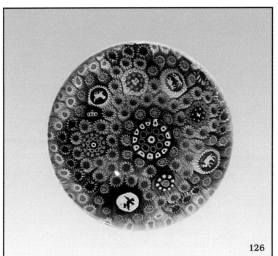

126

480

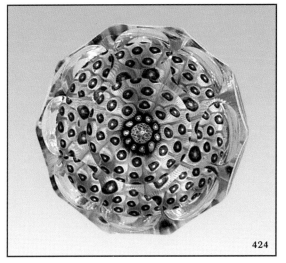

424

447

124

Saint Louis, dated 1848. Millefiori "mushroom" motif: 4 concentric circles of white, cobalt blue, green, and ochre canes surround central cluster of small blue/white rods, white star center. Outer circle of serrated white/red/black "bull's eye" canes (also "SL 1848" signature cane) drawn to point at base form tuft. Peripheral torsade of twisted flat white filigree within coiled dark blue rod. Polished concave colorless base cut with small, 24-point star; basal ring.
D: 2¹⁵⁄₁₆″ (7.4 cm.)
Bergstrom Bequest, 1958.
EHB acquisition: June, 1938.
No. 133, Pl. 27; Cloak Catalogue, 1969.
Ref.: McCawley, Patricia K.: *Antique Glass Paperweights from France,* 1968; 79(a).

144

Saint Louis, dated 1848. Millefiori mushroom motif: 6 concentric circles of white, blue, and green canes. Circle of white stardust canes, green/white whorl centers. Outer circle, drawn down to point at base, forms tuft; "SL 1848" in black cane at periphery. Torsade of twisted flat opaque white rods coiled with salmon-pink. Polished colorless base etched with No. 26 and cut with small 16-point star; basal ring.
D: 3¹⁄₁₆″ (7.8 cm.)
Bergstrom Bequest, 1958.
EHB acquisition: October, 1938.
No. 153, Pl. 27; Cloak Catalogue, 1969.
Ref.: McCawley, Patricia K.: *Antique Glass Paperweights from France,* 1968; 79(a).
PCA Bulletin, 1969; Fig. 5, p. 15.

199

Saint Louis, 1848-55. Millefiori mushroom: 4 concentric circles (salmon/pink/blue, blue/white, white stardust/blue, and green/white/red/white star canes) surround serrated white/green cane with rare white/salmon square rod center (square rod comprised of 4 square canes). In base, this compound central cane appears in miniature. Top punty, 6 side punties. Amber-flashed, polished concave base.
D: 2⅞″ (7.3 cm.)
Bergstrom Bequest, 1958.
EHB acquisition: February, 1939.
No. 214, Pl. 28; Cloak Catalogue, 1969.

248

Saint Louis, 1845-55. Concentric millefiori mushroom: 4 circles (cobalt blue/white/red cogs, chartreuse-green/salmon/pink canes, small salmon/white/blue canes, and white star, square cobalt blue/green/white canes) surround slightly swirled serrated white/salmon/green/white center cane. Outer circle forms tuft, drawn to polished, amber-flashed concave base; basal ring.
D: 3¼″ (8.3 cm.)
Bergstrom Bequest, 1958.
EHB acquisition: September, 1939.
No. 265, Pl. 28; Cloak Catalogue, 1969.

372

George Bacchus & Sons, Birmingham (English), 1845-55. Concentric millefiori mushroom motif: 4 circles of thinly cased pink, blue, amethyst and white canes surround central pink/white flower cane; outer circle drawn down forms tuft. 8 flute and 8 oval cuts alternate on curve. Wide, concave top punty suggests use as wafer tray. Polished concave colorless base; trace of pontil mark. Note: two circles of canes have solid stick-like opaque white centers.
D: 3½″ (8.9 cm.)
Bergstrom Bequest, 1958.
EHB acquisition: March, 1941.
No. 391, Pl. 34; Cloak Catalogue, 1969.
Ref.: Hollister, Paul: *The Encyclopedia of Glass Paperweights,* 1969; p. 160.

435

Origin unknown, possibly English, late 19th to early 20th century. Ovoid colorless glass. Slightly convex upright floral motif: crudely formed pink, cobalt blue, turquoise, and opaque white canes (distorted to form 5 petals) drawn downward form stem within opaque white bowl, spaced canes of similar colors impressed into its rim. Bowl rests on flat colorless base; pontil mark.
D: 3¹⁄₁₆″ (7.8 cm.)
Bergstrom Bequest, 1958.
EHB acquisition: October, 1941.
No. 463, Pl. 59; Cloak Catalogue, 1969.

781

Hand Cooler.
Baccarat, 1845-55. Ovoid colorless glass, cut to 8 vertical panels, base encircled by fan faceting. Concentric mushroom motif: red/white/blue arrow cane centers 3 circles of white stars/pink canes, serrated blue/white/pink canes, outer circle of white stars/pink square center canes drawn down to form mushroom.
D: 2⅝″ (6.6 cm.)
Museum Purchase, 1970.

1176

Saint Louis, 1845-55. Millefiori mushroom motif; pink/white coil torsade; mercury ring at periphery. Polished concave colorless base cut with 24-point star; basal ring.
D: 3⅛″ (7.9 cm.)
Gift of Mrs. Florence Gosselin Marsh in memory of her husband, Raymond Clark Marsh, 1976.

1281

Saint Louis, dated 1848. Concentric millefiori mushroom motif, 1 black cane in peripheral circle dated "SL 1848." 6-point *double* star cut in polished concave colorless base; basal ring.
D: 3¹⁄₃₂″ (7.7 cm.)
Gift of Mrs. Florence Gosselin Marsh in memory of her husband, Raymond Clark Marsh, 1977.

126

Saint Louis, dated 1848. Patterned millefiori canes on unusual "assorted" carpet ground. Compound center cane of small green/white overlaid colorless rods encircled by blue/white/red and salmon/white/opaque blue canes. 4 silhouettes (dog, camel, dancing figures, and devil) and 4 varicolored compound canes spaced in circle among closely set, serrated multicolor rods. "SL" above "1848" in black cane. Polished concave colorless base.
D: 2⁹/₁₆″ (6.8 cm.)
Bergstrom Bequest, 1958.
EHB acquisition: August, 1938.
No. 135, Pl. 28; Cloak Catalogue, 1969.
Ref.: McCawley, Patricia K.: *Antique Glass Paperweights from France,* 1968; 5(a).

143

Baccarat, dated 1848. Spaced millefiori canes set in carpet ground of blue/white star center canes; date cane "B 1848"; white/red/green and red/white/blue arrow canes; green shamrocks/floral center cane; silhouettes: deer, dog, goat, moth, pigeon with two shamrocks, cockerel. Polished concave colorless base.
D: 3″ (7.6 cm.)
Bergstrom Bequest, 1958.
EHB acquisition: October, 1938.
No. 152, Pl. 4; Cloak Catalogue, 1969.

181

Saint Louis, 1845-55. Ribbed pink cane carpet ground set with 5 spaced silhouette canes (dancing girl, 2 dogs, 2 devils), each encircled by ribbed white/green rods which also surround center cane formed of small pink/blue/white rods. Top punty, 5 punties on upper curve. Polished concave colorless base; basal ring.
D: 2⅝″ (6.6 cm.)
Bergstrom Bequest, 1958.
EHB acquisition: January, 1939.
No. 194, Pl. 28; Cloak Catalogue, 1969.
Ref.: No. 173, *The Corning Museum of Glass Exhibition Catalogue,* 1978.

424

Saint Louis, 1845-55. Convex carpet ground: red-lined, finely ribbed white canes, blue/white flower centers; large central pink/white/blue compound cane encircled by pink-lined green rods with white star centers. Top punty, 3 circles of smaller punties on curve. Polished concave colorless base; basal ring.
D; 2¹¹/₁₆″ (6.8 cm.)
Bergstrom Bequest, 1958.
EHB acquisition: September, 1941.
No. 448, Pl. 25; Cloak Catalogue, 1969.
Ref.: McCawley, Patricia K.: *Antique Glass Paperweights from France,* 1968; 5(b).
No. 164, *The Corning Museum of Glass Exhibition Catalogue,* 1978.

447

Baccarat, dated 1848. Spaced millefiori on white stardust/red center carpet ground lined with white filigree. Arrow and 9 silhouette canes: elephant, squirrel, rooster, monkey, horse, dog, deer, butterfly, and swan. Date cane: "B 1848." Top punty, 2 circles of punties on curve. Polished concave colorless base; basal ring.
D: 2¹¹/₁₆″ (6.8 cm.)
Bergstrom Bequest, 1958.
EHB acquisition: January, 1942.
No. 476, Pl. 2; Cloak Catalogue, 1969.
Ref.: *Antiques,* April, 1943; p. 178.

480

Baccarat, 1845-55. Patterned millefiori on carpet ground: cobalt blue/white/red arrow canes alternate with salmon-white whorl/blue-white star canes in "6-petal" motif outlined by serrated white/blue canes. White and salmon canes surround concentric circles of the arrow and whorl canes forming center of "flower." Close-pack carpet ground of cobalt blue/white star canes. Polished concave colorless base cut with small 32-point star; basal ring.
D: 3¹/₁₆″ (7.8 cm.)
Bergstrom Bequest, 1958.
EHB acquisition: October, 1942.
No. 510, Pl. 9; Cloak Catalogue, 1969.
Ref.: McCawley, Patricia K.: *Antique Glass Paperweights from France,* 1968; 4(d).

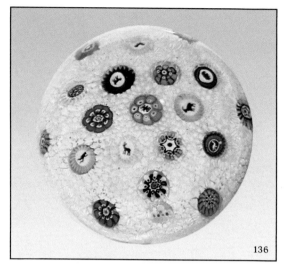

136

132

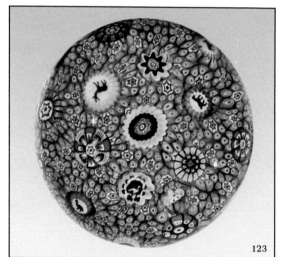

123

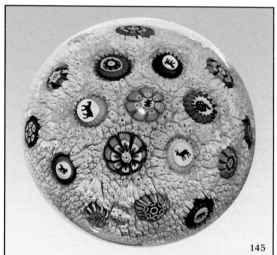

145

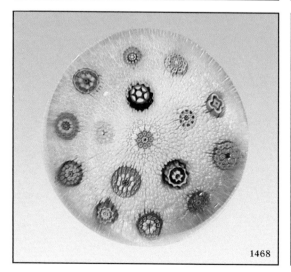

1468

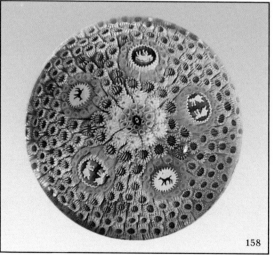

158

8

98

340

219

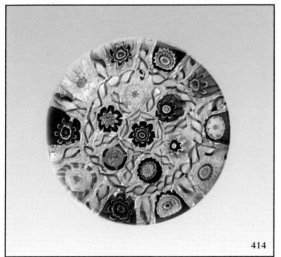

414

494

123

Baccarat, dated 1848. Spaced millefiori canes set in unusual carpet ground (red/white canes, blue star centers). "B 1848" date cane. 8 silhouettes: elephant, moth, pelican, rooster, goat, deer, horse, and pigeon with two green shamrocks. 3 arrow cane types: green/white; blue/white/red/green/white; white/blue/red. Almost flat, polished colorless base, trace of pontil mark; basal ring.
D: 3" (7.6 cm.)
Bergstrom Bequest, 1958.
EHB acquisition: June, 1938.
No. 132, Pl. 1; Cloak Catalogue, 1969.
Ref.: *Antiques,* April, 1943; p. 178.

132

Gillinder & Sons, Philadelphia, PA, 1861-71. Probably William T. Gillinder; possibly Charles Challinor (after 1867). Carpet ground, tuft motif. Female profile silhouetted in black, to dexter, in opaque white cane encircled by ruffled transparent pale yellow rods and carpet of white/colorless cog canes. Peripheral circle of serrated white rods (lined with transparent pink) drawn to center of colorless base reveal the tiny silhouette. Polished concave colorless base. Top punty, 6 vertical oval punties on curve.
Ex collection: Oscar Wilde.
D: 3³⁄₁₆" (8.1 cm.)
Bergstrom Bequest, 1958.
EHB acquisition: October, 1938.
No. 141, Pl. 45; Cloak Catalogue, 1969.
Ref.: Hollister, Paul: *The Encyclopedia of Glass Paperweights,* 1969; p. 225.

136

Baccarat, dated 1848. White stardust carpet ground studded with spaced millefiori canes; butterfly, elephant, monkey, dove, and swan silhouettes; "B 1848" signature cane. Polished concave colorless base; basal ring.
D: 2⅞" (7.3 cm.)
Bergstrom Bequest, 1958.
EHB acquisition: October, 1938.
No. 145, Pl. 1; Cloak Catalogue, 1969.

145

Baccarat, dated 1848. Millefiori canes spaced on white stardust (red dot center) carpet ground: green/white arrow cane; orange/white/blue arrow cane; 7 silhouettes: 2 dogs, horse, cockerel, goat, elephant, moth, flower, and "B 1848" signature cane. Polished concave colorless base; basal ring.
D: 3³⁄₁₆" (8.1 cm.)
Bergstrom Bequest, 1958.
EHB acquisition: October, 1938.
No. 154, Pl. 1; Cloak Catalogue, 1969.

158

Saint Louis, 1845-55. Patterned millefiori on carpet ground of serrated white canes lined with transparent green. Large compound cane encircled by white/pastel blue florets form central cluster surrounded by 5 spaced silhouette canes (each ringed by pastel pink/white rods): camel, 2 dancing figures, 2 horses. Polished concave colorless base; trace of pontil mark.
D: 3" (7.6 cm.)
Bergstrom Bequest, 1958.
EHB acquisition: November, 1938.
No. 167, Pl. 24; Cloak Catalogue, 1969.

1468

Saint Louis, 1982. 16 spaced millefiori canes in white stardust carpet ground. Polished concave colorless base reveals yellow "SL 1982" signature cane; basal ring.
3/200.
D: 3" (7.7 cm.)
Gift of William L. Liebman, 1982.

98
Baccarat, dated 1848. Spaced millefiori canes, one dated "B 1848," set in green/red/white star-cane carpet ground. Salmon/white arrow cane segments surround large central black/white star cane. Silhouette canes: goat, horse, cockerel, dog, deer, and pigeon with 2 green shamrocks; 2 unusual flower canes: blue/white border with arrow-cane flower, green stem, and a salmon-pink trefoil flower, 2 green leaves, stem in colorless glass with white stardust border. 3 arrow canes: blue/white/red; salmon/white/blue; white/red/green. Polished concave colorless base; trace of pontil.
D: 3¼″ (8.3 cm.)
Bergstrom Bequest, 1958.
EHB acquisition: December, 1937.
No. 104, Pl. 1; Cloak Catalogue, 1969.

219
Clichy, 1845-55. Chequer motif: cobalt blue/opaque white ribbon twists (coiled by white filigree) laid between spaced millefiori canes. White filigree cushion over parallel white filigree rods. Pastry mold and compound canes include white/green Clichy rose and "C" serif signature cane. Polished concave colorless base; basal ring.
D: 2⁹⁄₁₆″ (6.5 cm.)
Bergstrom Bequest, 1958.
EHB acquisition: June, 1939.
No. 234, Pl. 13; Cloak Catalogue, 1969.

340
Clichy, 1845-55. Chequer pattern: 2 concentric circles of spaced millefiori canes surround center cane (white stars/yellow stamens/red whorl). Between canes, segments of tubular fine pink/white filigree rods form chequer pattern over ground of parallel white filigree rods. Polished concave colorless base encloses unusual white latticinio swirl in pinwheel design.
D: 3³⁄₁₆″ (8.1 cm.)
Bergstrom Bequest, 1958.
EHB acquisition: August, 1940.
No. 360, Pl. 18; Cloak Catalogue, 1969.

414
Clichy, 1845-55. Chequer motif: spaced millefiori canes (including a pink/green Clichy rose and a white/red Clichy rose) stud chequer pattern of white filigree-spiraled opaque white/green ribbon twists. Tiny bubbles and white filigree rods laid parallel form ground over polished concave colorless base; basal ring.
D: 2⅝″ (6.7 cm.)
Bergstrom Bequest, 1958.
EHB acquisition: September, 1941.
No. 436, Pl. 17; Cloak Catalogue, 1969.
Ref.: *PCA Bulletin*, 1970; Pl. 3, p. 8.

494
Baccarat, dated 1847. Close millefiori canes include signature "B 1847" and 5 silhouettes (pigeon, 2 pigeons with 2 shamrocks, 2 monkeys) spaced among white and colored filigree segments, opaque colored rods, cane fragments, and occasional goldstone. Polished concave colorless base; basal ring.
D: 3⅛″ (7.9 cm.)
Bergstrom Bequest, 1958.
EHB acquisition: Unrecorded.
No. 524, Pl. 9; Cloak Catalogue, 1969.

477

882

1787

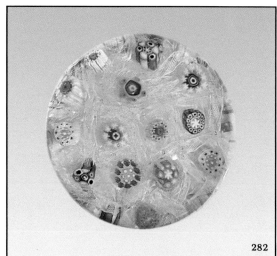

282

1181

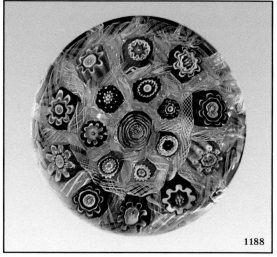

1188

25

503

363

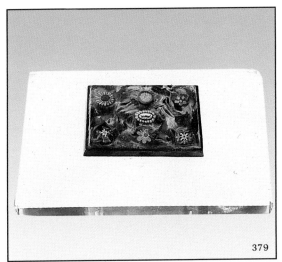

379

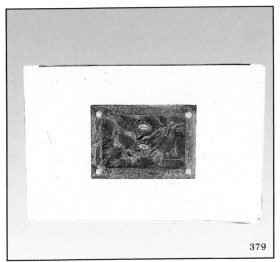

379

518

1272

282
Clichy, 1845-55. Spaced millefiori canes (predominantly pastel) and "C" signature cane set in fine white filigree with tiny bubbles in chequer pattern. White filigree ground. Polished concave colorless base; basal ring.
D: 2⅞″ (7.3 cm.)
Bergstrom Bequest, 1958.
EHB acquisition: February, 1940.
Illus. 25, Bergstrom book, 1940; later editions.
No. 301, Pl. 17; Cloak Catalogue, 1969.

477
Clichy, 1845-55. Chequer motif: large millefiori canes (including white Clichy rose and a "C" signature cane) spaced on white filigree rods laid parallel. Opaque red/white ribbon twists and white filigree form chequer pattern. Polished concave colorless base; basal ring.
D: 3″ (7.6 cm.)
Bergstrom Bequest, 1958.
EHB acquisition: October, 1942.
No. 507, Pl. 16; Cloak Catalogue, 1969.

882
Clichy, 1845-55. Chequer type. Spaced millefiori canes (1 each: green/pink Clichy rose; white/pink Clichy rose centered by 7 red/white rods; edelweiss; moss cane, center circle of stars; unusual translucent amber cane); blue/white filigree rods in chequer motif over ground of white filigree rods laid parallel. Polished concave colorless base; basal ring.
D: 2⁹⁄₁₆″ (6.5 cm.)
Bequest of Mrs. L. E. Kaumheimer, 1973.

1181
Clichy, 1845-55. Spaced concentric millefiori canes set in chequer pattern; short white filigree rods form a convex cushion over tubular white filigree laid parallel. Canes include Clichy roses: deep pink/green/white with pale yellow stamen center; purple/white with center of 2 concentric circles of green/white tubes, pink/white whorl centers; green/white with single circle of pale yellow stamen rods with pink/white/green whorl centers. These represent the three basic types of Clichy rose centers. Top and 10 side punties. Polished concave colorless base; basal ring.
D: 3⁵⁄₃₂″ (8.0 cm.)
Gift of Mrs. Florence Gosselin Marsh in memory of her husband, Raymond Clark Marsh, 1976.

1188
Clichy, 1845-55. Magnum. Spaced millefiori canes set in white filigree chequer ground. Large central pink/green/white Clichy rose, another at periphery. Thumbprint facets surround polished concave colorless base.
D: 3⁷⁄₁₆″ (8.7 cm.)
Gift of Mrs. Florence Gosselin Marsh in memory of her husband, Raymond Clark Marsh, 1976.

1787
Clichy, 1845-55. Turquoise-blue/white filigree "barber pole" chequer pattern studded by 17 various millefiori canes; 1 pink Clichy rose, green sepals. Parallel white filigree rod ground. Polished concave colorless base; basal ring.
D: 3³⁄₃₂″ (7.9 cm.)
Gift of Mrs. Virginia Bensley Trowbridge, 1987.

363
Italian, 1860s. Near surface: scrambled segments of fili-gree twists, ribbons, opaque colored rods, a male bust portrait cane (probably Italian patriot General Giuseppi Garibaldi, 1807-82) and 2 pansy florets. Polished base, pontil mark. Light in heft.
D: 2⁷⁄₁₆″ (6.2 cm.)
Bergstrom Bequest, 1958.
EHB acquisition: November, 1940.
No. 381, Pl. 38; Cloak Catalogue, 1969.
Ref.: *Antiques,* August, 1945; p. 110.

379
Plaque.
Venetian, dated 1846, but mounted perhaps at a later date. Rectangular millefiori plaque, possibly made origi-nally as a box lid, framed in silver, mounted on beveled rectangular colorless glass base. 7 separate millefiori canes spaced among segments of varicolored opaque canes and goldstone; center silhouette cane with gondola and blue waves on opaque white encircled by tiny white stars. Underside reveals 2 canes: "1846" and "GBF" (presumably for Giambatista Franchini).
Plaque: 1¼ x 1⅞″ (3.2 x 4.8 cm.); Base: 2¾ x 4⁷⁄₁₆″ (7.0 x 11.1 cm.)
Bergstrom Bequest, 1958.
EHB acquisition: March, 1941.
No. 399, Pl. 38; Cloak Catalogue, 1969.
Ref.: Hollister, Paul: *Encyclopedia of Glass Paper-weights,* 1969; pp. 18-21.
Antiques, August, 1945; p. 110.
Dorigato, Gasparetto, Mentasti, and Toninato: *Mille Anni di Arte del Vetro a Venezia,* 1982; Fig. 387, p. 214.

503
Venetian, attributed to Pietro Bigaglia, dated 1847. Scram-bled motif extends to encasing glass; variety of millefiori canes, white filigree twists, goldstone, and individual canes: date "1847," initial "R," birds, checkerboard, lyre, and Italian inscription "IX Congreso degli Scienziati in Venezia 47" (9th Scientific Congress in Venice '47). Slightly frosted colorless base, trace of pontil mark; basal ring.
D: 2⅞″ (7.3 cm.)
Bergstrom Bequest, 1958.
EHB acquisition: May, 1944.
No. 535, Pl. 38; Cloak Catalogue, 1969.
Ref.: *PCA Bulletin,* 1978; pp. 44-47, Fig. 1.
Antiques, August, 1945; p. 110.
PCA Bulletin, 1985-86.

518
Portrait Rods/Silhouette Rod
Venetian, attributed to Giambatista and Jacopo Franchini, 1840-70.
— Double overlay: deep amethyst/opaque white rod por-trays Count di Cavour, Italian statesman (1810-61).
— White overlay rod portrays, possibly, Victor Emanuel II.
— Triple overlay: white/dark amethyst/white rod por-trays, possibly, General Garibaldi.
— Translucent amethyst/white rod with tiny red/white/blue stars, black gondola silhouette in center.
D: ¼″ (.6 cm.)
Bergstrom Bequest, 1958.
EHB acquisition: Unrecorded.
No. 552, Pl. 38; Cloak Catalogue, 1969.
Ref.: *Antiques,* August, 1945; p. 110.

1272
Scent Bottle, covered.
Attributed to G. B. Franchini, Venice, Italy, 1845-64. Flattened, ovoid form; marbled red, yellow, blue and green glass with aventurine inclusions and silhouette portrait of mustachioed gentleman. Hinged metal cover with band of tooled floral design; metal chain with ring.
D: 2½″ (6.4 cm.)
Museum Purchase, 1977.
Ref.: Hollister, Paul: *Encyclopedia of Glass Paper-weights,* 1969; pp. 15, 19, 21.
PCA Bulletin, 1958; pp. 23-26.
PCA Bulletin, 1956; pp. 11-14.

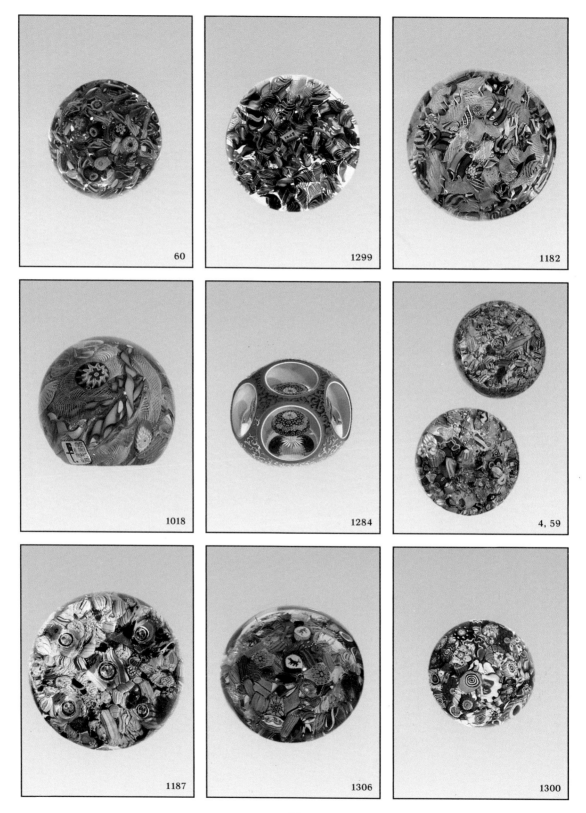

60

1299

1182

1018

1284

4, 59

1187

1306

1300

27

204

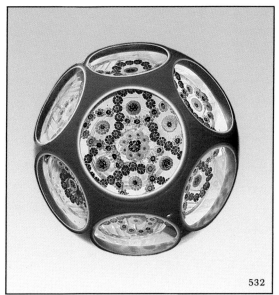

532

533

475

28

4
Boston & Sandwich Glass Co., Sandwich, MA, 1852-80.
Scrambled millefiori canes include 4 eagle and 2 running
rabbit silhouettes, opaque ribbon twists, white filigree
segments and spaced small bubbles. Concave base.
D: 2⅞" (7.3 cm.)
Bergstrom Bequest, 1958.
EHB acquisition: June, 1936.
No. 3, Pl. 45; Cloak Catalogue, 1969.

59
Boston & Sandwich Glass Co., Sandwich, MA, 1852-80.
Scrambled. 2 layers of varicolored and opaque millefiori
cane segments and bits of goldstone; top layer punctu-
ated near periphery by 7 spaced small bubbles and large
central bubble. Smooth almost flat colorless base.
D: 2⁹⁄₁₆" (6.8 cm.)
Bergstrom Bequest, 1958.
EHB acquisition: September, 1939.
No. 63, Pl. 45; Cloak Catalogue, 1969.

60
Chinese, ca. 1930. Scrambled multicolor (predominantly
pink, mauve and blue) millefiori canes with filigree and
ribbon twist rods high in dome. Flat colorless base.
D: 2⁵⁄₁₆" (5.8 cm.)
Bergstrom Bequest, 1958.
EHB acquisition: September, 1937.
No. 64, Pl. 62; Cloak Catalogue, 1969.

1018
Murano, Italy, 1960-70. Scrambled pastel pink/green/
blue/white filigree, blue/pink/goldstone ribbon twists,
and large spaced millefiori canes. Polished flat colorless
base. Paper label: "F. Made in Italy Murano Glass."
D: 3¹⁄₁₆" (7.8 cm.)
Gift of Dr. M. J. Caldwell, 1974.

1182
Saint Louis, 1845-55. Multicolored millefiori and filigree
rods (including some aventurine and cane slices) set somewhat haphazardly on convex cushion just above polished
concave colorless base; basal ring.
D: 3⅛" (7.9 cm.)
Gift of Mrs. Florence Gosselin Marsh in memory of her
husband, Raymond Clark Marsh, 1976.

1187
Attributed to Boston & Sandwich Glass Co., Sandwich,
MA, 1852-80. Scrambled pastel millefiori canes and rods,
punctuated by tiny bubbles, and goldstone. Elongated
central bubble, 4 surrounding spaced smaller bubbles
drawn down between canes. Smooth, flat colorless base.
D: 3¹⁄₁₆" (7.8 cm.)
Gift of Mrs. Florence Gosselin Marsh in memory of her
husband, Raymond Clark Marsh, 1976.

1284
Baccarat, 1845-55. Double overlay: turquoise-blue/
white, scroll-gilded. Millefiori tuft: white star-center
canes encircle quatrefoil/red dot, surrounded by 7 arrow-
cane florets, white honeycomb canes and ochre/green/
white florets at periphery, pulled down to colorless base
cut with small 24-point star.
D: 3⅛" (8.0 cm.)
Gift of Florence Gosselin Marsh in memory of her husband, Raymond Clark Marsh, 1977.
Ref.: No. 24, *The Corning Museum of Glass Exhibition
Catalogue,* 1978.

1299
Dupont-Baccarat, 1920s. Loosely arranged chequer
motif; multicolor filigree canes include fake date, "1847"
in blue and red numerals on white. Polished concave
colorless base; wide basal ring.
D: 2¾" (7.0 cm.)
Gift of Robert S. Sage and Jeanne Sage Groves in memory of their parents, Charles H. and Lyda P. Sage, 1978.

1300
Clichy, 1845-60. Scrambled millefiori canes include one
with "Clichy" in reverse, except for the "C" (YHCIL);
pink/white Clichy rose. Polished concave colorless base;
basal ring.
D: 2¼" (5.8 cm.)
Gift of Robert S. Sage and Jeanne Sage Groves in memory of their parents, Charles H. and Lyda P. Sage, 1978.

1306
Saint Louis, 1845-55. Scrambled millefiori and filigree
canes; dog and dancing devil silhouettes; goldstone.
Polished concave colorless base; basal ring.
D: 3⅛" (8.0 cm.)
Gift of Robert S. Sage and Jeanne Sage Groves in mem-
ory of their parents, Charles H. and Lyda P. Sage, 1978.

204
Saint Louis, 1848-55. Encased double overlay: cobalt blue over opaque white, the blue partially cut away to create 8 alternating white and blue vertical panels cut with circles and stars. Large top punty reveals small upright bouquet (centered by 5-petal amber-cased white flower) of blue, red, white and amber flowers; polished concave colorless base cut with 24-point star; basal ring.
D: 3″ (7.6 cm.)
Bergstrom Bequest, 1958.
EHB acquisition: February, 1939.
Pl. XV, Bergstrom book, 1940; later editions.
No. 219, Pl. 20; Cloak Catalogue, 1969.
Ref.: No. 216, *The Corning Museum of Glass Exhibition Catalogue*, 1978.
McCawley, Patricia K.: *Antique Glass Paperweights from France*, 1968; No. 82.

475
Clichy, 1845-55. Double overlay: dark emerald-green over opaque white. Large pink Clichy rose centers 6 concentric circles of millefiori canes including 1 circle of alternating purple and white Clichy roses, another of green moss/white star/red dot center canes. Peripheral opaque white stave rods drawn to base form mushroom. Flat top punty; 5 punties on curve. Fine strawberry-cut, polished concave colorless base.
D: 3¹⁄₁₆″ (7.8 cm.)
Bergstrom Bequest, 1958.
EHB acquisition: October, 1942.
No. 505, Pl. 14; Cloak Catalogue, 1969.
Ref.: McCawley, Patricia K.: *Antique Glass Paperweights from France*, 1968; Nos. 81, 78.
No. 106, *The Corning Museum of Glass Exhibition Catalogue*, 1978.

532
Baccarat, 1845-55. Double overlay: translucent rose-red/opaque white. Patterned millefiori: double trefoil garland of small blue/white star canes interlaced with white/red florets; white/red arrow and white stardust/green whorl canes alternate in the lobes. In center: white star canes surround red/white/green arrow cane. Top punty, 5 punties on curve; 12 oval cuts near polished concave colorless base.
D: 3³⁄₁₆″ (8.1 cm.)
Bergstrom Bequest, 1958.
EHB acquisition: Unrecorded.
No. 568, Pl. 8; Cloak Catalogue, 1969.
Ref.: No. 32, *The Corning Museum of Glass Exhibition Catalogue*, 1978.
McCawley, Patricia K.: *Antique Glass Paperweights from France*, 1968; 80(a).

533
Saint Louis, 1845-55. Encased double overlay: coral-pink/white. Upright bouquet: central rose-colored flower, furrowed petals, bubble and cane center; 2 blue, 2 white (rust-colored centers), and 2 yellow ochre flowers each with bubble center. Bouquet is studded with green foliage. Overlay, cut with top punty and 6 on curve, is further encased in colorless glass. Polished concave base cut with small 24-point star; basal ring.
D: 3⅛″ (8.0 cm.)
Bergstrom Bequest, 1958.
EHB acquisition: Unrecorded.
No. 569, Pl. 25; Cloak Catalogue, 1969.
Ref.: McCawley, Patricia K.: *Antique Glass Paperweights from France*, 1968; No. 82.

502

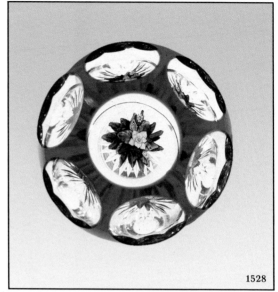

1528

184

476

29

159

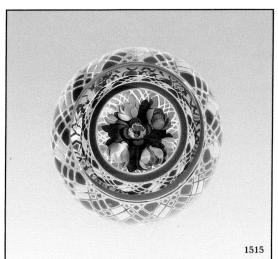

1515

470

1491

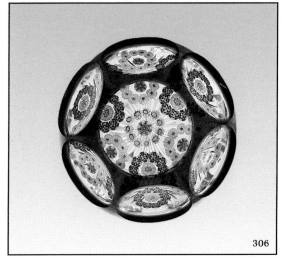

306

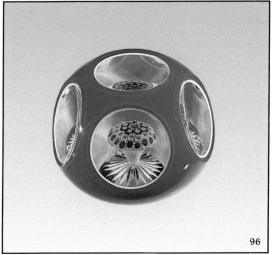

96

184

Clichy, 1845-55. Thin double overlay, deep rose/opaque white. Millefiori tuft motif: 6 concentric circles of blue/white, green/white, pink/white, green/pink/white, pink/red, and white/green florets surround central red/white/pink floret. Outer circle of opaque white staves drawn to base, form mushroom. Flat top punty, 5 on side. Strawberry-cut, polished concave colorless base.
D: 3⅟₁₆″ (7.8 cm.)
Bergstrom Bequest, 1958.
EHB acquisition: January, 1939.
Pl. I, Bergstrom book, 1940; later editions.
No. 197, Pl. 14; Cloak Catalogue, 1969.
Ref.: McCawley, Patricia K.: *Antique Glass Paperweights from France,* 1968.

476

Clichy, 1845-55. Double overlay: cobalt blue over opaque white. Mushroom-shaped, close millefiori bouquet, outer circle of alternating opaque pink and opaque white stave rods drawn to point at base. Circular flat cut on top; 5 punties on curve. Green and purple moss pastry mold canes and compound whorls. Concave colorless base cut with 12 radial ovals alternated with 12 small miters.
D: 2⁹⁄₁₆″ (6.5 cm.)
Bergstrom Bequest, 1958.
EHB acquisition: October, 1942.
No. 506, Pl. 13; Cloak Catalogue, 1969.
Ref.: McCawley, Patricia K.: *Antique Glass Paperweights from France,* 1968.

502

American, probably New England Glass Co., East Cambridge, MA, 1852-80. Double overlay: dark red over opaque white. Upright bouquet: red, blue, and 2 opaque white flowers, 4 millefiori canes, and 6 green leaves; opaque white cushion. Circular top facet; round and oblong cuttings on curve; grooved cut encircles weight above level of motif. Diagonal thumbprint cuts near polished concave colorless base.
D: 2⁷⁄₁₆″ (6.2 cm.)
Bergstrom Bequest, 1958.
EHB acquisition: November, 1943.
No. 534, Pl. 41; Cloak Catalogue, 1969.

1528

Baccarat, 1845-55. Faceted translucent overlay; top and 6 punties on curve, 12 thumbprint cuts surround colorless base cut with 24-point star. Upright bouquet with central white clematis flower, 2 red/blue buds, 4 colored florets, numerous green leaves. Baccarat upright bouquets are rare and usually enclosed within a torsade. This appears to be the only recorded example without a torsade and in a ruby flash overlay.
Ex collection: Roy Moore.
D: 3⁷⁄₃₂″ (8.2 cm.)
Museum Purchase, 1986.
Ref.: No. 69, *The Corning Museum of Glass Exhibition Catalogue,* 1978.
PCA Bulletin, 1983; Fig. 20.
Exhibited: Spink's, London (for Paperweight Tour), June, 1982, No. 161.

96
Baccarat, 1845-55. Double overlay: turquoise/opaque white. Millefiori mushroom motif: center cane and those in peripheral circle somewhat resemble Clichy roses; outer circle of white/blue canes (drawn down to base) form tuft. Top and 5 side punties. Polished concave colorless base cut with 24-point star.
D: 3³⁄₁₆″ (8.1 cm.)
Bergstrom Bequest, 1958.
EHB acquisition: December, 1937.
No. 102, Pl. 1; Cloak Catalogue, 1969.

159
New England Glass Co., E. Cambridge, MA, 1852-80. Opaque white single overlay; circular, quatrefoil and trefoil facets; 2 circles of diagonal and trefoil cuts near slightly concave colorless base. Spaced pastel millefiori canes set into interior white overlay mushroom crown; translucent spaces between canes appear frosted.
D: 3¼″ (8.3 cm.)
Bergstrom Bequest, 1958.
EHB acquisition: November, 1938.
Illus. 78, Bergstrom book, 1940; Illus. 76, later editions.
No. 168, Pl. 42; Cloak Catalogue, 1969.
Ref.: No. 248, *The Corning Museum of Glass Exhibition Catalogue,* 1978.

306
Baccarat, 1845-55. Translucent red overlay. Patterned millefiori: 7 circlets (3 of blue/green/red arrow canes), single center cane. Top punty, 6 on curve, 12 thumbprint cuts near base. Polished concave colorless base cut with 24-point star.
D: 3⅛″ (8.0 cm.)
Bergstrom Bequest, 1958.
EHB acquisition: May, 1940.
Pl. IV, Bergstrom book, 1940; later editions.
No. 326, Pl. 8; Cloak Catalogue, 1969.
Ref.: *Hobbies,* October, 1941; Cover.

470
Baccarat, 1845-55. Double overlay: turquoise-blue/opaque white; gilt scroll tracery. Millefiori tuft motif: white star center cane, 3 concentric circles of blue/white/green/red arrow, white star/red dot, and rust/green/white whorl center canes. Peripheral white star canes pulled down to base form mushroom. Top punty, 5 punties on curve. Polished concave colorless base cut with small 24-point star.
D: 3⅛″ (7.9 cm.)
Bergstrom Bequest, 1958.
EHB acquisition: July, 1942.
No. 499, Pl. 8; Cloak Catalogue, 1969.

1491
Saint Louis, 1983. Magnum. Encased faceted triple overlay: red lined with white on medium blue. 3-dimensional upright bouquet: 3 flowers, white stardust cane centers, others with tiny bubbles. Green stems drawn to polished concave colorless base; signature cane invisible.
D: 3¹¹⁄₁₆″ (9.4 cm.)
Gift of Mr. and Mrs. William L. Liebman, 1983.

1515
Perthshire Paperweights, Ltd., Crieff, Scotland, 1983. Magnum. Encased "gingham"-cut dark rose/white double overlay. Stylized flat nosegay of 5 partly open flowers: pink, white/pink, pale green/white, shaded pale orange (1 bud), 1 white bud; 4 green stems, flat leaves. Wide top punty; polished deep basal concavity; basal ring. Edition limited to 20.
D: 3¹³⁄₁₆″ (10.0 cm.)
Gift of Mr. and Mrs. William L. Liebman, 1984.

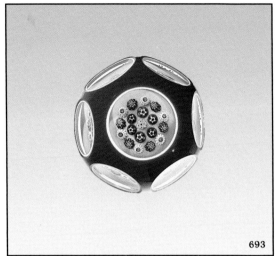

693

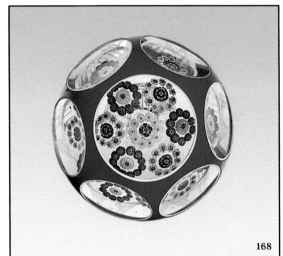

168

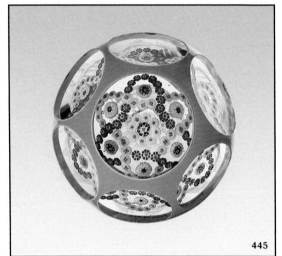

445

194

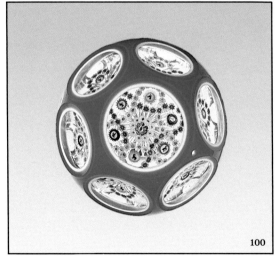

100

419

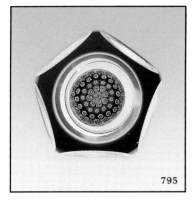

795

70

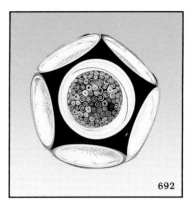

692

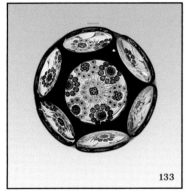

133

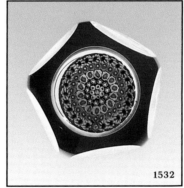

1532

1544

1004

1291

1829

233

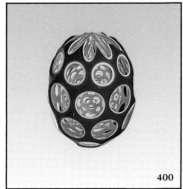

400

1115

32

100

Baccarat, 1845-55. Double overlay: turquoise-blue/opaque white. Patterned millefiori; double trefoil encloses silhouette canes: pelican, rooster, goat, dog, deer, horse. Center circlet of white star and red canes surround moth silhouette. Top and 6 side punties; 12 oval cuts near polished concave colorless base cut with 24-point star.
D: 3⅛" (8.0 cm.)
Bergstrom Bequest, 1958.
EHB acquisition: December, 1937.
No. 106, Pl. 1; Cloak Catalogue, 1969.

168

Baccarat, 1845-55. Double overlay: cobalt blue/opaque white. Patterned millefiori: 7 circlets of varicolored canes, each centered by single cane (4 arrow, 3 white stardust/green whorl center). Top punty, 6 on curve, 12 oval cuts near polished concave colorless base.
D: 3¹⁄₁₆" (7.8 cm.)
Bergstrom Bequest, 1958.
EHB acquisition: December, 1938.
No. 178, Pl. 1; Cloak Catalogue, 1969.

194

Saint Louis, 1848-55. Encased faceted opaque white single overlay, top and 6 side punties. Small upright floral bouquet, coral-red central flower (bubble center) surrounded by green leaves. Polished concave colorless base cut with 24-point star.
D: 2⅝" (6.6 cm.)
Bergstrom Bequest, 1958.
EHB acquisition: February, 1939.
No. 207, Pl. 20; Cloak Catalogue, 1969.

419

New England Glass Co., E. Cambridge, MA, 1852-80. Dark red/opaque white double overlay; top cut with concave hexafoil design, punties and leaf-like cuts on curve. Near crown: patterned millefiori motif (pastel pink/blue/white canes) on opaque white latticinio cushion. Polished colorless concave base.
D: 2⅞" (7.3 cm.)
Bergstrom Bequest, 1958.
EHB acquisition: September, 1941.
No. 441, Pl. 42; Cloak Catalogue, 1969.

445

Baccarat, 1845-55. Double overlay, pink/opaque white; unusually thin layers produce delicate effect. Patterned millefiori, double trefoil garland: blue/white star canes, white stardust/green-white whorl canes; white/blue/red arrow cane in each loop. Top, 6 side punties; 12 oval cuts near polished concave colorless base.
D: 3¹⁄₁₆" (7.8 cm.)
Bergstrom Bequest, 1958.
EHB acquisition: January, 1942.
No. 474, Pl. 8; Cloak Catalogue, 1969.

693

Charles Kaziun, Brockton, MA, early 1960s. Red over white double overlay, cut with top and 6 side punties, reveals 19 spaced millefiori (red, green, and white) canes on opaque light blue cushion. Polished flat colorless base shows "K" with red hearts signature cane beneath cushion.
D: 2⁵⁄₁₆" (5.8 cm.)
No. 712, Pl. 54; Cloak Catalogue, 1969.
Gift of Mr. and Mrs. Ralph S. Johns, 1963.

70
Attributed to Bohemia, 1845-55. Cobalt blue single overlay, top punty, 3 rows of circular facets on curve. 13 spaced millefiori canes on upset white filigree cushion drawn to polished concave colorless base; basal ring.
D: 2⁵⁄₁₆″ (5.9 cm.)
Bergstrom Bequest, 1958.
EHB acquisition: September, 1937.
No. 75, Pl. 58; Cloak Catalogue, 1969.

133
Baccarat, 1845-55. Single overlay: transparent emerald green; top punty, 6 side punties, 12 thumbprint cuts near polished slightly concave colorless base. Patterned millefiori: 7 circlets of canes, each circlet enclosing arrow cane. Polished colorless base cut with small 24-point star and etched with number "386."
D: 2⁷⁄₈″ (7.3 cm.)
Bergstrom Bequest, 1958.
EHB acquisition: October, 1938.
No. 142, Pl. 8; Cloak Catalogue, 1969.

233
Val St. Lambert, Liège, Belgium, 1890-1900. Cobalt blue overlay. Radial notches frame circular top punty; 4 oval side punties with star and spray cuts between them. Motif: 4 loops of white filigree with central floret; spaced bubbles encircled by opaque white ribbon twist coiled with red, white, blue and yellow; rose-red cushion lined with opaque white. Polished flat colorless base.
D: 3⁵⁄₈″ (9.2 cm.)
Bergstrom Bequest, 1958.
EHB acquisition: August, 1939.
Pl. XIV, Bergstrom book, 1940; later editions.
No. 249, Pl. 39; Cloak Catalogue, 1969.
Ref.: Philippe, Joseph: *Le Val St. Lambert Ses Cristalleries et l'Art du Verre en Belgique,* 1974; Pl. 19a.

400
Hand Cooler.
Baccarat, 1845-55. Double overlay, Hollow-blown egg-shaped colorless glass overlaid with cobalt blue on opaque white; 4 side circles of punties, an 8-lobed medallion cut on top; polished concave colorless base. Note: Also found in emerald green/white double overlay.
H: 2⁵⁄₈″ (6.6 cm.); D: 2″ (5.1 cm.)
Bergstrom Bequest, 1958.
EHB acquisition: July, 1941.
No. 420, Pl. 8; Cloak Catalogue, 1969.
Ref.: Jokelson, Paul: *Antique French Paperweights,* 1955; B. 138, 252.

692
Saint Louis, dated 1953. Double overlay: dark green/opaque white. Millefiori tuft, varicolored canes (many with star centers); and black signature cane "SL 1953." Top, 5 side punties. Small 24-point star cut in polished concave colorless base.
D: 3⅛″ (8.0 cm.)
No. 711, Pl. 32; Cloak Catalogue, 1969.
Gift of Mr. and Mrs. Ralph S. Johns, 1963.

795
Saint Louis, 1970. Red/white double overlay: concentric mushroom motif. "SL 1970" center cane surrounded by chartreuse green stars. Mauve, green, and white canes predominate and are drawn down to center of polished concave colorless base. Large top punty, 5 side punties.
D: 3⅛″ (7.9 cm.)
Gift of Cristalleries de Saint Louis, 1970.

1004
Murano (Italian), 1960s. Thin translucent cobalt blue overlay. Patterned millefiori: 7 clustered cane circles: white, yellow, orange, green, blue, amethyst. Wide flat top punty, 5 flat side punties between smaller oval cuts and miters. Cross-hatched wide flat colorless base.
D: 3⁹⁄₁₆″ (9.0 cm.)
Gift of Dr. M. J. Caldwell, 1974.

1115
Val St. Lambert, 1920s. Translucent cobalt blue single overlay; top and 4 side punties, miter-cut edges; 3 flute cuts between each punty above and beneath the 4 junctures; multi-faceted, star-cut colorless base.
D: 3¼″ (8.2 cm.)
Gift of Mrs. Florence Gosselin Marsh in memory of her husband, Raymond Clark Marsh, 1976.

1291
Perthshire Paperweights, Ltd., Crieff, Scotland, 1977. Faceted translucent blue overlay laid over encased faceted double overlay (pink/opaque white); multipetaled blue flower/green leaves, stem.
D: 2¾″ (7.1 cm.)
Purchased by the City of Neenah Municipal Museum Foundation members and Board of Directors in memory of Alice Bergstrom Moore, November, 1977.

1532
Baccarat, dated 1974. Cobalt blue/white double overlay; concentric millefiori tuft motif, 1 cane dated "1974." Wide top and 5 side punties. Polished flat colorless base etched with Baccarat insignia and No. 46/1974.
D: 3³⁄₃₂″ (7.9 cm.)
Bequest of J. Howard Gilroy, 1986.

1544
Saint Louis, dated 1975. Cerulean blue/white double overlay. Flat floral bouquet: 1 pastel blue flower, star cane center; 1 coral-colored flower, "SL 1975" signature cane center. 8 pastel green leaves, 2 stems. Wide top punty, 5 side punties. Polished concave colorless base; basal ring.
D: 3¹⁄₁₆″ (7.8 cm.)
Bequest of J. Howard Gilroy, 1986.

1829
Perthshire Paperweights, Ltd., Crieff, Scotland; dated 1978. Faceted encased faceted double overlay (translucent cerise red/opaque white). Miniature dragonfly (white filigree wings, 2 black eyes and black dot on each lower wing; gold aventurine body) above miniature bouquet: a blue/white, a yellow ochre, and a pink flower, each with 5 petals and white honeycomb cane center; 8 green leaves, 3 stems. Wide top punty; double overlay with 8 ovals and small flute cuts between. 16-point star cut in polished concave colorless base signed "P/P 1978." One of a kind.
D: 2¹³⁄₁₆″ (7.2 cm.)
Gift of Mrs. Virginia Bensley Trowbridge, 1987.

885, 196, 1095, 546, 147, 886, 370

33

467

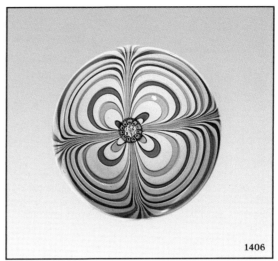

1406

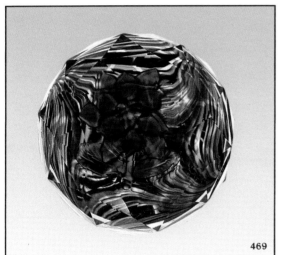

469

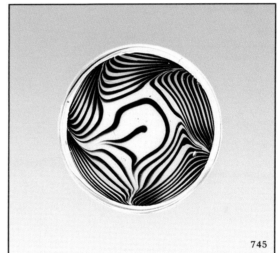

745

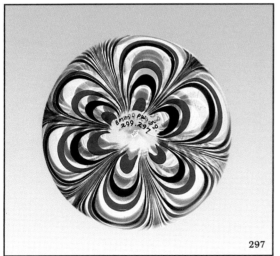

297

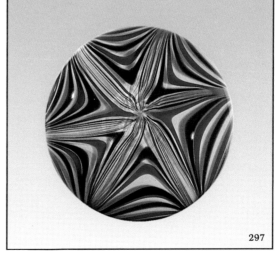

297

147
Clichy, 1845-55. Swirl motif: alternating opaque green and opaque white rods radiate from large dark red/green pastry mold cane. Polished concave colorless base; basal ring.
D: 2⁵⁄₁₆″ (5.9 cm.)
Bergstrom Bequest, 1958.
EHB acquisition: October, 1938.
Illus. 28, Bergstrom book, 1940; later editions.
No. 156, Pl. 13; Cloak Catalogue, 1969.
Ref.: *PCA Bulletin,* 1978; Fig. 21, p. 26.

196
Clichy, 1845-55. Swirl motif: alternating opaque pink and white flattened rods swirl from central green/white/pastel yellow honeycomb/white star center pastry mold cane. Polished concave colorless base.
D: 2¹⁄₁₆″ (5.3 cm.)
Bergstrom Bequest, 1958.
EHB acquisition: February, 1939.
No. 211, Pl. 13; Cloak Catalogue, 1969.

370
Clichy, 1845-55. Alternating turquoise-blue and opaque white rods swirl from central Clichy pink rose, green sepals. Polished concave colorless base; basal ring.
D: 2⅝″ (6.5 cm.)
Bergstrom Bequest, 1958.
EHB acquisition: March, 1941.
No. 389, Pl. 13; Cloak Catalogue, 1969.

546
Clichy, 1845-55. Swirl motif: alternating pale opaque amethyst and opaque white rods radiate from white/red/green pastry mold cane near crown to polished concave colorless base; basal ring.
D: 2⁹⁄₁₆″ (6.5 cm.)
Bergstrom Bequest, 1958.
EHB acquisition: Unrecorded.
No. 582, Pl. 13; Cloak Catalogue, 1969.

885
Clichy, 1845-55. Swirl type. Cobalt blue and white rods swirled alternately from central white/green/red pastry mold cane. Polished concave colorless base; basal ring.
D: 2⁵⁄₁₆″ (6.0 cm.)
Bequest of Mrs. L. E. Kaumheimer, 1973.

886
Clichy, 1845-55. Swirl type. Rose-pink and opaque white rods swirled alternately from large green/white pastry mold cane. Polished concave colorless base; basal ring. ("6838" etched in base; perhaps a dealer's mark.)
D: 2⁷⁄₁₆″ (6.2 cm.)
Bequest of Mrs. L. E. Kaumheimer, 1973.

1095
Clichy, 1845-55. Alternating opaque cobalt blue/opaque white/translucent turquoise flattened rods swirl from large center green/white pastry mold cane, red/white center. Polished concave colorless base; basal ring.
D: 3″ (7.6 cm.)
Museum Purchase, 1975.

297
Origin unknown, possibly English, 1850-70. Marbrie type. Colorless glass encases hollow-blown white opaline festooned with cobalt blue and dark red, loops in 6 sections simulating a 6-point star. Smooth concave pontil area.
D: 3⅜″ (8.6 cm.)
Bergstrom Bequest, 1958.
EHB acquisition: April, 1940.
No. 318, Pl. 34; Cloak Catalogue, 1969.

467
Saint Louis, 1845-55. Marbrie. High-domed opaque white ground; festooned red and green trailings form quatrefoil motif centered by blue/white cane cluster. Polished concave colorless base; basal ring.
D: 3¹⁄₁₆″ (7.8 cm.)
Bergstrom Bequest, 1958.
EHB acquisition: May, 1942.
No. 495, Pl. 20; Cloak Catalogue, 1969.
Ref.: McCawley, Patricia K.: *Antique Glass Paperweights from France,* 1968; No. 73.
No. 189, *The Corning Museum of Glass Exhibition Catalogue,* 1978.

469
Attributed to New England Glass Co., E. Cambridge, MA, 1867-88. (Motif also resembles the work of Nicholas Lutz at Boston & Sandwich Glass Co.) Marbrie type. Encased sphere festooned with red and white; at apex, a red flower with ten smooth petals, opaque red/green/goldstone center; pastel green stem, two leaves. Allover diamond faceting. Smooth flat colorless base.
D: 3⅜″ (8.6 cm.)
Bergstrom Bequest, 1958.
EHB acquisition: June, 1942.
No. 498, Pl. 43; Cloak Catalogue, 1969.
No. 250, New England Glass Company Exhibit, Toledo Museum of Art, Toledo, OH, 1963.

745
Origin unknown, attributed to Japan, 1960s. Shallow form; marbrie type. Thinly cased, opaque white core festooned with dark brown. Smooth flat colorless base.
D: 3¹⁄₁₆″ (7.8 cm.)
Gift of Mr. Robert A. Elder, Jr., 1969.

1406
Saint Louis, 1971. Marbrie type; alternate festoons on opaque white ground of chartreuse-green and turquoise-blue form 4 panels converging at signature cane (SL 1971) near dome. Polished flat colorless base.
D: 3″ (7.7 cm.)
Gift of Mrs. F. E. Seybold, 1980.

6, 334

289, 872

235, 1454, 525

440, 319

35

371

1632

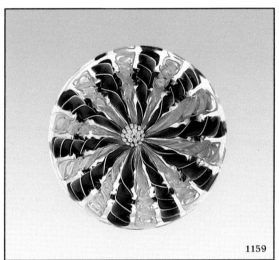

1159

146

387

466

6
Saint Louis, 1845-55. Crown weight; hollow; thickly encased. White-edged, red/green ribbon twists and white filigree spiral twists alternately radiate from central green/blue/white millefiori cane, converging at center base.
D: 3³/₁₆″ (8.1 cm.)
Bergstrom Bequest, 1958.
EHB acquisition: June, 1936.
No. 6, Pl. 20; Cloak Catalogue, 1969.
Ref.: *PCA Bulletin,* 1978; Fig. 6, p. 22.

235
Venetian, probably mid-19th century. Hollow, crown type. White filigree/goldstone and turquoise-blue/goldstone twists alternate over white opaline ground. Twists radiate from central bubble converging underside; pontil mark.
Ex collection: Marquis de Bailleul.
D: 2¹⁵/₁₆″ (7.4 cm.)
Bergstrom Bequest, 1958.
EHB acquisition: September, 1939.
Illus. 51, Bergstrom book, 1940; Illus. 49, later editions.
No. 251, Pl. 38; Cloak Catalogue, 1969.
Ref.: Hollister, Paul: *The Encyclopedia of Glass Paperweights,* 1969; p. 21.

289
New England Glass Co., E. Cambridge, MA, or Boston & Sandwich Glass Co., Sandwich, MA, ca. 1852. Hollow crown weight. White/red/green ribbon twists alternate with white filigree twists and pink/white ribbon spirals; at apex, a white/black star pastry mold cane with date "1825" (probably "1852" reversed when encased). Under date, 2 tiny rabbit silhouettes. Circular top facets; spiral flutes, circular and quatrefoil facets on sides. Polished concave colorless base.
D: 2⅜″ (6.1 cm.)
Bergstrom Bequest, 1958.
EHB acquisition: April, 1940.
Illus. 59, Bergstrom book, 1940; Illus. 57, later editions.
No. 310, Pl. 41; Cloak Catalogue.
Ref.: No. 252, *The Corning Museum of Glass Exhibition Catalogue,* 1978.

319
Bohemian, 1845-55. Crown weight. Central cluster of 8 millefiori canes from which radiate alternating dark cobalt blue and opaque white stave canes, not contiguous, converging at center of polished concave colorless base. 2 white silhouette canes resemble dancing devil type.
D: 2¹¹/₁₆″ (6.8 cm.)
Bergstrom Bequest, 1958.
EHB acquisition: June, 1940.
No. 340, Pl. 2; Cloak Catalogue, 1969.
Ref.: Hollister, Paul: *Encyclopedia of Glass Paperweights,* Fig. 10, p. 33.

334
Saint Louis, 1845-55. Crown weight; hollow. Alternately spaced white-edged red/green ribbon twists, white-edged blue/chartreuse ribbon twists and spiraled white filigree radiate from central cobalt blue/white millefiori floret, converging at center of polished concave colorless base; basal ring.
D: 3¼″ (8.3 cm.)
Bergstrom Bequest, 1958.
EHB acquisition: August, 1940.
Illus. 12, Bergstrom book, 1940; Illus. 13, later editions.
No. 354, Pl. 20; Cloak Catalogue, 1969.

440
Attributed to Bohemia, 1845-55. Crown motif. White filigree twists, alternately enclosing white, red, or cobalt blue twists, radiate from cluster of red/white millefiori canes centered by a red monkey silhouette. Polished concave colorless base. Note: encasing glass thicker than for usual crown weights; light in heft.
D: 2⁷/₁₆″ (6.2 cm.)
Bergstrom Bequest, 1958.
EHB acquisition: December, 1941.
No. 468, Pl. 20; Cloak Catalogue, 1969.
Ref.: No. 8, *The Corning Museum of Glass Exhibition Catalogue,* 1978.

525
Italian, probably Murano, ca. 1930. Crown type; white filigree rods and opaque pink/goldstone ribbon twists radiate alternately from apex, converging at flat colorless base.
D: 3⅛″ (7.9 cm.)
Bergstrom Bequest, 1958.
EHB acquisition: Unrecorded.
No. 559-A, Pl. 38; Cloak Catalogue, 1969.

872
New England Glass Co., East Cambridge, MA, 1852-1868. "Crown" type. Alternating red/white, blue/chartreuse, and white filigree ribbon twists swirled from compound amethyst cane/white star center close to surface. Hollow. Smooth colorless base; pontil mark; basal ring.
D: 2⅛″ (5.4 cm.)
Bequest of Mrs. L. E. Kaumheimer, 1973.

1454
Murano (Italian) 1960s-70s. Crown type. Alternating ribbon twists (yellow/white/goldstone/blue/pink/pale green) radiate from red/white center cane to polished flat colorless base; paper label: "F. Made in Italy. Murano Glass."
D: 3¹/₃₂″ (7.7 cm.)
Gift of Mrs. John Ogden and Henry Harnischfeger in memory of their parents, Mr. and Mrs. Walter Harnischfeger, 1981.

146
Hand Cooler.
Saint Louis, 1845-55. Hollow-blown colorless glass vertically ribbed with alternate rods of white-edged cobalt blue and red ribbon twists and spiraled white filigree.
L: 2⅞" (7.3 cm.); D: 2" (5.1 cm.)
Bergstrom Bequest, 1958.
EHB acquisition: October, 1938.
Illus. 22, Bergstrom book, 1940; later editions.
No. 155, Pl. 25; Cloak Catalogue, 1969.

371
Saint Louis, 1845-55. Rare crown motif: 2 red/blue/white ribbon twists, spiraled in opposite directions and alternated with spiraled white filigree, radiate from chartreuse/white center cane (forming a medallion) converging at point on base. Polished slightly concave colorless base; basal ring.
D: 2¾" (7.0 cm.)
Bergstrom Bequest, 1958.
EHB acquisition: March, 1941.
No. 390, Pl. 19; Cloak Catalogue, 1969.
Ref.: No. 184, *The Corning Museum of Glass Exhibition Catalogue,* 1978.
PCA Bulletin, 1978; Fig. 6, p. 22.

387
Paul Ysart, Wick, Scotland, 1930s. Crown type; high ovoid dome. Double-swirl white filigree rods, alternated with white filigree/red twist and white filigree/green twist rods, radiate from central bubble and form pinwheel design over translucent blue ground, converging at point near smooth base; pontil mark.
D: 3⁵⁄₁₆" (8.4 cm.)
Bergstrom Bequest, 1958.
EHB acquisition: May, 1941.
No. 408, Pl. 33; Cloak Catalogue, 1969.

466
Paul Ysart, Wick, Scotland, 1930-40. Crown weight. Spiraled pastel green filigree alternates with opaque red/white/blue ribbon twists and opaque red ribbon twists within coiled white filigree, all radiating from central bubble and converging at base; transparent blue-green ground. Colorless base, wide basal ring; pontil mark. Unsigned.
D: 3¼" (8.3 cm.)
Bergstrom Bequest, 1958.
EHB acquisition: May, 1942.
No. 494, Pl. 33; Cloak Catalogue, 1969.

1159
Saint Louis, 1845-55. Crown weight; hollow core. Red/white/blue ribbon twists alternated with white spiral filigree twists radiate from central lime-yellow/white/red center compound cane. Polished concave colorless base; trace of pontil mark; basal ring.
D: 3³⁄₁₆" (8.1 cm.)
Gift of Mrs. Florence Gosselin Marsh in memory of her husband, Raymond Clark Marsh, 1976.

1632
Perthshire Paperweights, Ltd., Crieff, Scotland, dated 1969. Crown motif. Red/white/cobalt blue ribbon twists alternate with spiraled white filigree; red/white/cobalt blue compound cane at apex. "P 1969" signature cane centers polished concave colorless base; basal ring. 350 edition.
D: 2¹⁵⁄₁₆" (7.5 cm.)
Gift of Mr. and Mrs. F. John Barlow, 1986.

823

5

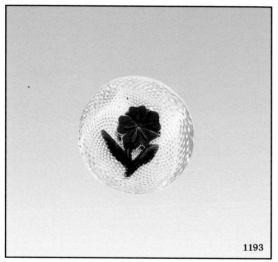

1193

1112

1113

339

205

1458

20

485

1308

51

5
Saint Louis, 1845-60. Rose-colored anemone; 5 smooth petals centered by 6 opaque yellow dots; black veining; 5 green sepals; 2 green leaves, stem; white latticinio cushion. Polished concave colorless base.
D: 2¾″ (7.0 cm.)
Bergstrom Bequest, 1958.
EHB acquisition: April, 1936.
No. 5, Pl. 19; Cloak Catalogue, 1969.

339
Chinese, 1925-40. Copy of rare mid-19th century Saint Louis weight. Yellowish glass, upright bouquet; 5 small varicolored opaque flowers, bubble centers; encircling green leaves drawn to white latticinio basket, red/white filigree-twist handle joined to basket on each side by millefiori cane. Flat smooth colorless base.
D: 2¹³⁄₁₆″ (7.2 cm.)
Bergstrom Bequest, 1958.
EHB acquisition: August, 1940.
No. 359, Pl. 62; Cloak Catalogue, 1969.

823
Saint Louis, 1845-55. Flat anemone flower: 5 smooth deep pink/white petals, black veining, yellow/black/green center; 5 narrow pointed green sepals, 2 narrow veined green leaves, stem. Polished colorless base cut with 32-point star.
D: 2¾″ (7.0 cm.)
Purchased from Fred A. Nagel Memorial Fund, 1971.

1112
Saint Louis, 1848-55. Magnum half-weight. White latticinio half-basket (ochre/white twist rim) filled with blue, white, ochre, and salmon-color flowers; green leaves. Polished concave colorless base; diamond-grid cut flat side.
D: 5½″ (13.9 cm.)
Gift of Mrs. Florence Gosselin Marsh in memory of her husband, Raymond Clark Marsh, 1976.
Ref.: No. 224, *The Corning Museum of Glass Exhibition Catalogue,* 1978.

1113
Saint Louis, 1845-55. Upright bouquet in white latticinio basket with coiled amber/white latticinio rim; coiled amber/blue/white handle fastened by millefiori cane on each side. Polished concave colorless base; basal ring.
D: 3⅛″ (7.9 cm.)
Gift of Mrs. Florence Gosselin Marsh in memory of her husband, Raymond Clark Marsh, 1976.
Ref.: McCawley, Patricia K.: *Antique Glass Paperweights from France,* 1968; 38 b/c.
No. 222, *The Corning Museum of Glass Exhibition Catalogue,* 1978.
PCA Bulletin, 1970; Fig. 1, p. 3.

1193
Saint Louis, 1848-55. Red pelargonium-type flower, 5 veined, white-edged petals; 2 green leaves, stem; double-swirl white latticinio cushion. Polished concave colorless base; basal ring.
D: 2⅛″ (5.4 cm.)
Gift of Mrs. Florence Gosselin Marsh in memory of her husband, Raymond Clark Marsh, 1976.

20
Boston & Sandwich Glass Co., Sandwich, MA, 1870-88; attributed to Nicholas Lutz. Deep pink double clematis-type flower (12 smooth pointed petals), 5 emerald-green leaves all accented by small bubbles, stem. Clichy-type rose, (green/white/red) center. Polished concave colorless base; basal ring.
D: 2⅞″ (7.3 cm.)
Bergstrom Bequest, 1958.
EHB acquisition: June, 1937.
No. 22, Pl. 41; Cloak Catalogue, 1969.

51
Boston & Sandwich Glass Co., 1869-88. Single opaque dark pink flower, 10 smooth petals, white geometric center cane; dewdrop bubbles on petals and 3 green leaves, stem; detached second green stem with red bud. Swirled white latticinio cushion. Smooth concave colorless base; wide basal ring.
W: 3¹⁄₁₆″ (7.8 cm.)
Bergstrom Bequest, 1958.
EHB acquisition: August, 1937.
Illus. 2, Bergstrom book, 1940; later editions.
No. 51, Pl. 41; Cloak Catalogue, 1969.

205
Saint Louis, 1848-55. Lampwork upright bouquet centered in swirled white latticinio basket rimmed with amber/white filigree spiral. Deep blue central flower surrounded by a white, a pink and 2 canes simulating flower heads; 14 green leaves. Polished concave base; basal ring.
D: 3″ (7.6 cm.)
Bergstrom Bequest, 1958.
EHB acquisition: February, 1939.
Illus. 11, Bergstrom book, 1940; later editions.
No. 220, Pl. 19; Cloak Catalogue, 1969.
Ref.: McCawley, Patricia K.: *Antique Glass Paperweights from France,* 1968; 38 b/c.
PCA Bulletin, 1984; Fig. 5, p. 39.

485
Boston & Sandwich Glass Co., 1855-88. 2 full-blown pink roses; pink bud, green sepals; 2 unusual green leaves (looped strands form leaf around stem); brown rod-like stem spiraled with yellow and green strands. Swirled white latticinio ground; smooth concave base.
D: 2⅞″ (7.3 cm.)
Bergstrom Bequest, 1958.
EHB acquisition: April, 1943.
No. 515, Pl. 41; Cloak Catalogue, 1969.
Ref.: Jokelson, Paul: *One Hundred of the Most Important Paperweights,* 1966; Pl. 81.

1308
Boston & Sandwich Glass Co., possibly Nicholas Lutz, ca. 1875. Cobalt blue flower (10 petals on 6 larger petals, over which are 6 goldstone petals); red-cased opaque white center; spaced dewdrop bubbles. 6 green leaves, stem. Polished colorless base; inverted circle surrounds pontil area; basal ring.
D: 3⁵⁄₃₂″ (8.1 cm.)
Gift of Robert S. Sage and Jeanne Sage Groves in memory of their parents, Charles H. and Lyda P. Sage, 1978.
Ref.: *PCA Bulletin,* 1954, 1987.

1458
Attributed to Boston & Sandwich, possibly Nicholas Lutz, 1869-88. Weedflower type: 2 red and 3 blue/white striped petals, all with gilt-aventurine spots; red/white/blue center cane set in white opaline; olive-green stem, 3 ribbed leaves. Smooth concave base.
D: 2¾″ (7.0 cm.)
Museum Purchase and gift of Mr. and Mrs. D. J. Wilken, 1981.
Ref.: No. 261, *The Corning Museum of Glass Exhibition Catalogue,* 1978.

242

386

97

1192

88

369

1161

317

284

434

1114

1290

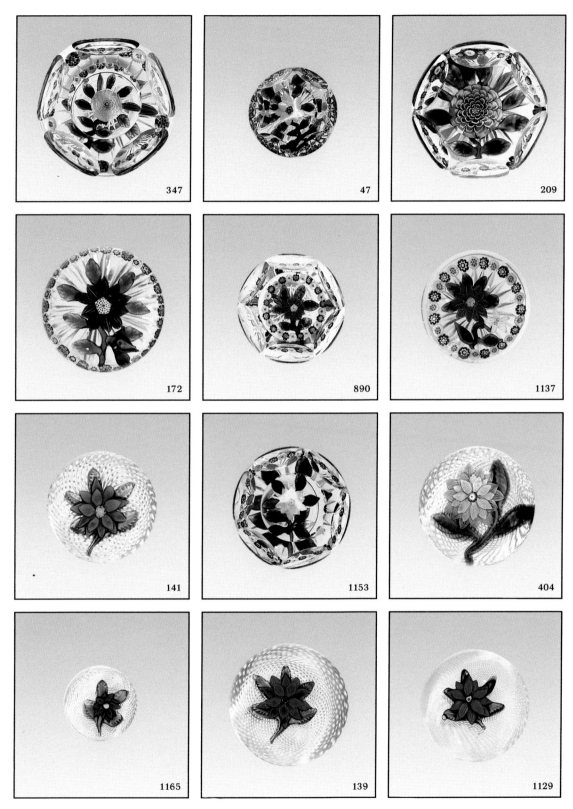

347

47

209

172

890

1137

141

1153

404

1165

139

1129

40

88
Saint Louis, 1848-55. Cane and lampwork. Chiffon-type pink camomile, yellow/white star cane center; 1 pink bud/green sepals; 4 green leaves, pointed stem; white latticinio cushion. Convex dome, 6 punties on curve. Polished concave colorless base; basal ring.
D: 3⅛″ (7.9 cm.)
Bergstrom Bequest, 1958.
EHB acquisition: November, 1937.
No. 93, Pl. 19; Cloak Catalogue, 1969.

97
Saint Louis, 1848-55. Chiffon-type, white camomile flower (green/white center cane), 1 white bud/green sepals; 4 green leaves, stem; swirled white latticinio on translucent red ground drawn to point forms tuft at base. Convex dome, 6 punties on curve. Polished concave colorless base; basal ring.
D: 2⁹⁄₁₆″ (6.6 cm.)
Bergstrom Bequest, 1958.
EHB acquisition: December, 1937.
Illus. 20, Bergstrom book, 1940; later editions.
No. 103, Pl. 19; Cloak Catalogue, 1969.

242
Baccarat, 1848-55. Lampwork pastel yellow buttercup-type flower, cup-shape petals (opaque white cased with transparent yellow); white stardust cane center. 8 pastel green leaves, sturdy stem; coral-red bud, green sepals. Polished concave colorless base, cut with 24-point star; basal ring.
D: 3″ (7.6 cm.)
Bergstrom Bequest, 1958.
EHB acquisition: September, 1939.
No. 258, Pl. 5; Cloak Catalogue, 1969.

284
Baccarat, 1845-55. Lampwork pastel yellow camomile flower, green/white arrow cane center; 6 green leaves, sturdy stem; dark red bud, green sepals. Peripheral circle of alternating white/blue star and serrated red/white canes. Polished concave colorless base deeply cut with 24-point star extending to curve.
D: 2½″ (6.3 cm.)
Bergstrom Bequest, 1958.
EHB acquisition: March, 1940.
No. 303, Pl. 5; Cloak Catalogue, 1969.

317
Saint Louis, 1845-55. Single pink camomile flower (no center cane), pink bud, green sepals, 3 green leaves, stem; white latticinio ground. Polished concave wide colorless base; basal ring.
D: 3⁵⁄₁₆″ (8.4 cm.)
Bergstrom Bequest, 1958.
EHB acquisition: June, 1940.
Illus. 53, Bergstrom book, 1940; Illus. 51, later editions.
No. 338, Pl. 41; Cloak Catalogue, 1969.

369
Saint Louis, 1848-55. White camomile flower (chiffon-type), pastel yellow cane stamen center; white bud/green sepals; 4 green leaves, stem. White, thinly cased with red, double-swirl latticinio ground; polished concave colorless base; basal ring.

D: 2½″ (6.3 cm.)
Bergstrom Bequest, 1958.
EHB acquisition: March, 1941.
No. 388, Pl. 20; Cloak Catalogue, 1969.

386
Baccarat, 1848-55. Cobalt blue/white buttercup flower with yellow/white star cane center; 8 green leaves, stem; blue bud, green sepals. Peripheral circle of serrated white/pink/green canes alternated with green/white/red canes. Polished concave colorless base cut with 16-point star; basal ring.
D: 3″ (7.6 cm.)
Bergstrom Bequest, 1958.
EHB acquisition: May, 1941.
No. 407, Pl. 5; Cloak Catalogue, 1969.

434
Saint Louis, 1848-55. White camomile (chiffon-type) flower, pastel yellow/red cane center; 4 green leaves, stem; white bud, green sepals. Opaque white latticinio/translucent red cushion. Polished concave colorless base; basal ring.
D: 3¹⁄₁₆″ (7.8 cm.)
Bergstrom Bequest, 1958.
EHB acquisition: October, 1941.
No. 462, Pl. 19; Cloak Catalogue, 1969.

1114
Saint Louis, 1848-55. White camomile flower, unusual chartreuse/white compound cane center; 1 white bud, green sepals; 2 green leaves, 4 stems. Polished concave colorless base; basal ring. (The camomile flower "cane" was made from bundled identical rods, reheated and pulled.)
D: 2¾″ (7.1 cm.)
Gift of Mrs. Florence Gosselin Marsh in memory of her husband, Raymond Clark Marsh, 1976.

1161
Baccarat, 1848-55. White camomile flower, yellow honeycomb cane center; 6 lettuce-green leaves, stem; peripheral circle of red/white/green arrow canes alternated with white/green star canes; polished slightly concave colorless base cut with 16-point star; basal ring.
D: 2¹⁄₁₆″ (5.2 cm.)
Gift of Mrs. Florence Gosselin Marsh in memory of her husband, Raymond Clark Marsh, 1976.

1192
Saint Louis, 1848-55. White camomile flower, yellow cane center, 1 white bud, green sepals; 4 green leaves, stem. Fine white double-swirl latticinio over translucent pink cushion. Polished concave colorless base; basal ring.
D: 2³⁄₃₂″ (5.2 cm.)
Gift of Mrs. Florence Gosselin Marsh in memory of her husband, Raymond Clark Marsh, 1976.

1290
Baccarat, 1848-55. Large single blue camomile flower (pom-pon). Multiple rows of cup-shaped petals centered by white stardust/yellow-white bull's-eye cane; curved green stem, 9 leaves; single vermilion-red bud. 24-point star-cut, polished concave colorless base.
D: 3⅛″ (7.9 cm.)
Museum Purchase, Alice B. Moore Memorial Fund, 1977.

47
Baccarat, 1848-55. White double clematis, 10 furrowed petals, compound center cane of green arrows/red star center; 6 green leaves, stems; white bud. Peripheral circle of alternating green and white cog canes. Top, 6 side punties. Polished colorless base; large deeply cut 24-point star extends to curve.
D: 2⁹⁄₁₆″ (6.5 cm.)
Bergstrom Bequest, 1958.
EHB acquisition: August, 1937.
No. 47, Pl. 6; Cloak Catalogue, 1969.

139
Saint Louis, 1845-55. Lampwork cobalt blue clematis; 15 striped, pointed petals, dark red center; 5 pale green leaves, stem. Double-swirl, white latticinio ground. Polished concave colorless base.
D: 2⅝″ (6.6 cm.)
Bergstrom Bequest, 1958.
EHB acquisition: October, 1938.
No. 148, Pl. 21; Cloak Catalogue, 1969.

141
Saint Louis, 1845-55. Lampwork red clematis, 15 faintly striped pointed petals, initial "B" on opaque yellow, *square* center. 5 pale green leaves, stem. Double-swirl white latticinio cushion. Polished concave colorless base; basal ring.
Ex collection: Oscar Wilde.
D: 2⅝″ (6.6 cm.)
Bergstrom Bequest, 1958.
EHB acquisition: October, 1938.
No. 150, Pl. 21; Cloak Catalogue, 1969.

172
Baccarat, 1848-55. Lampwork dark red clematis with 10 furrowed pointed petals, 5-sided yellow honeycomb cane center; red bud, green sepals, 7 green leaves, stem. Peripheral circle of predominantly red/white/blue canes. Polished concave colorless base cut with 24-point star; basal ring.
D: 2⅞″ (7.3 cm.)
Bergstrom Bequest, 1958.
EHB acquisition: December, 1938.
No. 184, Pl. 3; Cloak Catalogue, 1969.

209
Baccarat, 1845-55. Large camomile, salmon-pink shading to brown; yellow/white star cane center; 2 vermilion buds, green sepals; 7 green leaves, stem. Peripheral circle of alternating white/pink and green/white millefiori canes. Convex dome, 6 side punties. Polished concave colorless base cut with 24-point star; basal ring.
D: 3¼″ (8.3 cm.)
Bergstrom Bequest, 1958.
EHB acquisition: February, 1939.
No. 224, Pl. 2; Cloak Catalogue, 1969.
Ref.: No. 56, *The Corning Museum of Glass Exhibition Catalogue,* 1978.

347
Baccarat, 1845-55. Pale yellow camomile flower, green/white arrow cane center, surrounded by 7 green leaves, stem; 2 vermilion-red buds, green sepals. Peripheral circle of alternating white cog and red/green/white arrow canes. Top punty, 5 on curve. Polished concave colorless base cut with 24-point star.

D: 3⅛″ (7.9 cm.)
Bergstrom Bequest, 1958.
EHB acquisition: September, 1940.
No. 366, Pl. 7; Cloak Catalogue, 1969.

404
Saint Louis, 1848-55. Pink clematis (28 furrowed and striped pointed petals), blue/white cane center, 3 green leaves, stem; white latticinio ground. Polished concave colorless base.
D: 2¾″ (7.0 cm.)
Bergstrom Bequest, 1958.
EHB acquisition: August, 1941.
No. 424, Pl. 21; Cloak Catalogue, 1969.
Ref.: No. 197, *The Corning Museum of Glass Exhibition Catalogue,* 1978.

890
Baccarat, 1848-55. Small rust-red double clematis, pale yellow honeycomb cane center; red bud, green sepals; 6 green leaves, stem. Peripheral circle of alternating white stardust/red/white whorl-center and green/white/red star canes. Top, 6 side punties. 24-point star cut in polished colorless base; basal ring.
D: 2⁷⁄₁₆″ (6.3 cm.)
Bequest of Mrs. L. E. Kaumheimer, 1973.

1129
Saint Louis, 1848-55. Cobalt blue clematis flower, 15 striped pale blue petals, orange/yellow center; 5 green leaves, 3 stems; fine double-swirl white latticinio cushion; polished concave colorless base; basal ring.
D: 2²⁵⁄₃₂″ (7.0 cm.)
Gift of Mrs. Florence Gosselin Marsh in memory of her husband, Raymond Clark Marsh, 1976.

1137
Baccarat, 1848-55. Rust-red clematis (6 veined petals over 8), honeycomb cane center, set on 5 green leaves; 5-petal white flower, star/cane center; 2 green stems, 2 lower green leaves. Peripheral circle of alternating red/white and white/blue canes. Polished concave 24-point star cut colorless base; wide basal ring.
D: 2⁹⁄₁₆″ (6.5 cm.)
Gift of Mrs. Florence Gosselin Marsh in memory of her husband, Raymond Clark Marsh, 1976.

1153
Baccarat, 1845-55. Double white clematis with 10 furrowed petals, honeycomb cane center; white bud, green sepals; 8 green leaves, stem. Peripheral circle of alternating green/white/red florets and white star/red-white whorl canes. Top and 6 side punties; polished concave colorless base cut with 24-point star; basal ring.
D: 2⅞″ (7.3 cm.)
Gift of Mrs. Florence Gosselin Marsh in memory of her husband, Raymond Clark Marsh, 1976.

1165
Saint Louis, 1848-55. Unusual blue clematis (5 petals over 10), yellow matchhead center; 4 green leaves, 3 stems; fine double-swirl white latticinio cushion (double cushion when viewed from the side); polished concave colorless base; basal ring.
D: 2¹⁄₃₂″ (5.1 cm.)
Gift of Mrs. Florence Gosselin Marsh in memory of her husband, Raymond Clark Marsh, 1976.

382

45

346

874

873

1197

1191

1510

176

1125

897

487

41

426

252

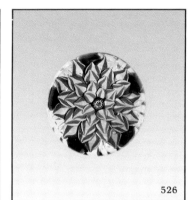

526

76

198

21

1145

366

1523

45
Saint Louis, 1848-55. Single clematis: deep pink-striped coral petals (5 over 10), opaque yellow center, set on spray of 4 green leaves, stem ending in point; white latticinio ground. Polished concave colorless base; basal ring.
D: 2⅛″ (5.4 cm.)
Bergstrom Bequest, 1958.
EHB acquisition: August, 1937.
No. 45, Pl. 24; Cloak Catalogue, 1969.

176
Baccarat, 1848-55. Lampwork translucent pastel turquoise-blue clematis, white star-cane center, 12 pointed furrowed petals; 2 turquoise-blue buds, green sepals; 5 green leaves, 3 stems, one crossing the other two. Polished almost flat colorless base cut with 16-point star; basal ring.
D: 2³⁄₁₆″ (5.5 cm.)
Bergstrom Bequest, 1958.
EHB acquisition: January, 1939.
No. 188, Pl. 6; Cloak Catalogue, 1969.

346
Baccarat, 1845-55. Lampwork salmon-pink clematis (10 grooved petals, white star/red whorl cane center); 6 pale green leaves, stem; red bud/green sepals. Peripheral circle of alternating white/green canes. White filigree ground extends to polished concave colorless base.
D: 2⅞″ (7.3 cm.)
Bergstrom Bequest, 1958.
EHB acquisition: September, 1940.
No. 365, Pl. 19; Cloak Catalogue, 1969.

382
Saint Louis, 1848-55. Cobalt blue clematis (15 striped pointed petals, ochre/white/blue star center cane), 4 pastel green leaves, short stem. Polished concave colorless base cut with 24-point star.
D: 3″ (7.6 cm.)
Bergstrom Bequest, 1958.
EHB acquisition: May, 1941.
No. 402, Pl. 19; Cloak Catalogue, 1969.

487
Saint Louis, 1848-55. White clematis flower, pointed grooved petals, amber/white/blue center cane; tips of 5 pastel green sepals visible. Flower centered on dark green aventurine cushion encircled by flattened white filigree twist torsade coiled with pink. Polished concave colorless base; basal ring. Note: Not the same weight shown in Illus. 10, Bergstrom book, which had 3 leaves, 3 stems, and different torsade; disposition unknown.
D: 2¾″ (7.0 cm.)
Bergstrom Bequest, 1958.
EHB acquisition: April, 1943.
No. 517, Pl. 23; Cloak Catalogue, 1969.
Ref.: McCawley, Patricia K.: *Antique Glass Paperweights from France,* 1968; p. 6.

873
Saint Louis, 1848-55. Pink-red clematis, white cog cane center; 5 green leaves, double stem. Polished concave colorless base cut with 16-point star; basal ring.
D: 2⅜″ (6.1 cm.)
Bequest of Mrs. L. E. Kaumheimer, 1973.

874
Baccarat, 1848-55. Double white clematis, 10 furrowed petals, green/white arrows/red star cane center; 5 veined lettuce-green leaves, stem. White stardust/green whorl canes alternate with red/white/green arrow canes at periphery. Polished concave colorless base cut with 24-point star.
D: 1²⁹⁄₃₂″ (4.8 cm.)
Bequest of Mrs. L. E. Kaumheimer, 1973.

897
Baccarat, 1848-55. Double white clematis with 12 furrowed petals; unusual red/white/blue arrow cane center surrounded by hexagonally placed white star canes with red centers. White bud, green sepals; 9 green leaves, stem. 24-point star cut in polished concave colorless base.
D: 2⅝″ (6.7 cm.)
Bequest of Mrs. L. E. Kaumheimer, 1973.

1125
Saint Louis, 1848-55. Pink clematis; 15 striped pink petals (5 over 5); 4 green leaves, 3 stems; green aventurine cushion. Polished concave colorless base; basal ring.
D: 3³⁄₃₂″ (7.8 cm.)
Gift of Mrs. Florence Gosselin Marsh in memory of her husband, Raymond Clark Marsh, 1976.
Ref.: Hollister, Paul: *The Encyclopedia of Glass Paperweights,* 1969; p. 105.

1191
Baccarat, 1848-55. Pale yellow clematis, 2 yellow buds, green sepals, 5 green leaves, entwined stems. Polished concave colorless base cut with 16-point star; basal ring.
D: 2³⁄₃₂″ (5.2 cm.)
Gift of Mrs. Florence Gosselin Marsh in memory of her husband, Raymond Clark Marsh, 1976.

1197
Baccarat, 1848-55. Miniature. White clematis with green/white arrow cane center; 5 green leaves, stem. Polished concave colorless base cut with 24-point star.
D: 1¹¹⁄₁₆″ (4.2 cm.)
Gift of Mrs. Florence Gosselin Marsh in memory of her husband, Raymond Clark Marsh, 1976.

1510
Baccarat, 1845-55. Miniature. Double lavender clematis (6 veined petals over 6), pale yellow honeycomb cane center, tiny star at apex; 5 green leaves, curved stem. Peripheral circle of predominantly red/white millefiori canes. Wide top punty, 7 oval punties on curve above 7 wider punties; polished 24-point star-cut colorless base. Note: the lavender clematis is less often seen.
D: 2″ (5.1 cm.)
Gift of Franklin Schuell in memory of Hazel McCormick Schuell, 1984.

21
Saint Louis, 1848-55. Striped pink dahlia, pink/white serrated cane center, on 5 spaced green leaves. Rough ground, concave colorless base cut with 24-point star.
D: 2¼″ (5.7 cm.)
Bergstrom Bequest, 1958.
EHB acquisition: Unrecorded.
No. 22A, Pl. 24; Cloak Catalogue, 1969.

76
Saint Louis, 1848-55. Large dahlia; 42 pink-striped, white opaline pointed petals on 6 spaced green leaves. Serrated yellow ochre/white/blue star center cane. Polished concave colorless base cut with 24-point star.
D: 2¹⁵⁄₁₆″ (7.4 cm.)
Bergstrom Bequest, 1958.
EHB acquisition: September, 1937.
No. 81, Pl. 19; Cloak Catalogue, 1969.

198
Saint Louis, 1848-55. Large purple lampwork dahlia; pointed, striped petals; serrated, ochre central cane, blue medallion center. Visible at periphery: tips of 5 green leaves. Frosted, concave colorless base cut with 24-point star.
D: 3¹⁄₁₆″ (7.8 cm.)
Bergstrom Bequest, 1958.
EHB acquisition: February, 1939.
Illus. 9, Bergstrom book, 1940; later editions.
No. 213, Pl. 24; Cloak Catalogue, 1969.

252
Saint Louis, 1848-55. Large amber-colored dahlia; dark brown veined petals in 6 star-shape overlapping layers on 5 emerald green leaves spaced to form 5-point star. Dark cobalt blue banded white floret, red star center, studs top 5 petals which also form 5-point star. Polished concave colorless base cut with 24-point star.
D: 2⅞″ (7.3 cm.)
Bergstrom Bequest, 1958.
EHB acquisition: August, 1939.
No. 269, Pl. 24; Cloak Catalogue, 1969.
Ref.: McCawley, Patricia K.: *Antique Glass Paperweights from France,* 1968; 4b, Pl. 18.

366
Saint Louis, 1848-55. Lampwork red/blue fuchsia flower, thin pink stem and stamens; large red bud, 2 smaller buds, 4 green leaves, sturdy orange stalk; double-swirl latticinio cushion. Polished concave colorless base; basal ring.
D: 2⅞″ (7.3 cm.)
Bergstrom Bequest, 1958.
EHB acquisition: December, 1940.
No. 385, Pl. 27; Cloak Catalogue, 1969.

426
Baccarat, 1848-55. Brick-red dahlia flower in profile. 20 veined petals, interspersed pinpoint bubbles; green sepals; 4 narrow pointed green leaves, stem. Polished concave colorless base cut with 32-point star. Uncommon.
D: 2¾″ (7.0 cm.)
Bergstrom Bequest, 1958.
EHB acquisition: September, 1941.
No. 450, Pl. 3; Cloak Catalogue, 1969.

526
Saint Louis, 1845-55. Large pink/white striped dahlia; 42 pointed petals layered in "star" arrangement; 6 spaced green leaves; ribbed ochre/white/blue center cane. Polished concave base cut with 24-point star.
D: 2⁹⁄₁₆″ (6.5 cm.)
Bergstrom Bequest, 1958.
EHB acquisition: Unrecorded.
No. 560, Pl. 24; Cloak Catalogue, 1969.
Ref.: No. 196, *The Corning Museum of Glass Exhibition Catalogue,* 1978.

1145
Saint Louis, 1848-55. Large purple dahlia, veined petals, serrated amber cane, blue cog center. 6 green leaves, stem. Large 24-point star cut in smooth concave colorless base. Excessively rare with stem.
D: 2⁹⁄₁₆″ (6.5 cm.)
Gift of Mrs. Florence Gosselin Marsh in memory of her husband, Raymond Clark Marsh, 1976.
Ref.: McCawley, Patricia K.: *Antique Glass Paperweights from France,* 1968; Pl. 7, 41 (b).

1523
Attributed to Saint Louis, 1848-55, possibly Clichy. 3-dimensional deep pink fuchsia flower, 2 deep pink buds, 11 green leaves, green stems, on opaque pale amber branch. Polished concave colorless base; basal ring. Note: Previously unrecorded example for either Saint Louis or Clichy. Saint Louis fuchsias appear on swirled white latticinio ground; fuchsias unrecorded among Clichy flower types.
D: 2²⁷⁄₃₂″ (7.3 cm.)
Museum Purchase, 1985.
Ref.: McCawley, Patricia K.: *Antique Glass Paperweights from France,* 1968; No. 44, Pl. 19, p. 15.

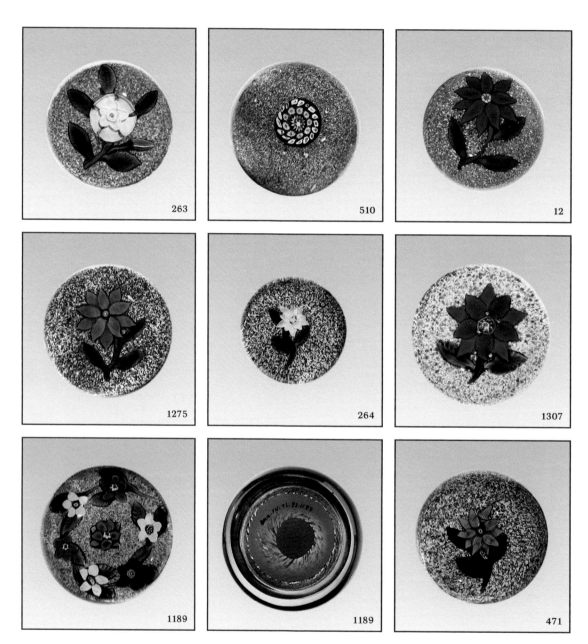

263

510

12

1275

264

1307

1189

1189

471

43

375

222

303

255

373

221

210

374

378

675

162

678

12
Boston & Sandwich Glass Co., Sandwich, MA, 1852-80. Cobalt blue clematis (10 pointed petals, white/red cane center), 3 green leaves, curved stem, red/white jasper ground. Smooth concave base; "jelly glass" ring.
D: 2⅝" (6.6 cm.)
Bergstrom Bequest, 1958.
EHB acquisition: May, 1936.
No. 12, Pl. 44; Cloak Catalogue, 1969.

263
Boston & Sandwich Glass Co., 1852-80. Lampwork buttercup type flower: 5 opaque white cupped petals, central white star with pink/white/yellow center; white bud, green sepals, 5 green leaves, stem; red/white jasper ground. Smooth concave colorless base; basal ring.
D: 2⅞" (7.3 cm.)
Bergstrom Bequest, 1958.
EHB acquisition: November, 1939.
No. 281, Pl. 44; Cloak Catalogue, 1969.

264
Saint Louis, 1845-55. Lampwork white clematis, 10 deeply furrowed pointed petals; yellow "matchhead" center; 3 green leaves, darker green pointed stem; green/white jasper cushion. Polished almost flat colorless base; trace of pontil mark.
D: 2⁷⁄₁₆" (6.2 cm.)
Bergstrom Bequest, 1958.
EHB acquisition: November, 1939.
No. 282, Pl. 20; Cloak Catalogue, 1969.

471
Saint Louis, 1848-60. Coral-pink clematis; 10 striped pointed petals, blue/white cane center; 3 dark green leaves, pointed stem; fine green/white jasper ground. Polished concave colorless base.
D: 3¹⁄₁₆" (7.8 cm.)
Bergstrom Bequest, 1958.
EHB acquisition: July, 1942.
No. 500, Pl. 24; Cloak Catalogue, 1969.

510
Saint Louis, 1845-55. Large compound concentric cane/floret center impressed in ruby/white jasper ground. Polished flat colorless base.
D: 2¹⁵⁄₁₆" (7.4 cm.)
Bergstrom Bequest, 1958.
EHB acquisition: Unrecorded.
No. 543, Pl. 23; Cloak Catalogue, 1969.

1189
Saint Louis, 1848-55. Cobalt blue, 2 red, and 3 white 5-petal flowers, various cane centers, surround single medium blue flower, white floret center; 15 green leaves, 4 stems; pink/white jasper ground. Polished colorless base, wide basal concavity; basal ring.
D: 3³⁄₁₆" (8.1 cm.)
Gift of Mrs. Florence Gosselin Marsh in memory of her husband, Raymond Clark Marsh, 1976.
Ref.: Hollister, Paul: *Encyclopedia of Glass Paperweights,* 1969; pp. 102-03.

1275
Boston & Sandwich Glass Co., 1869-88. Red clematis flower, 2 rows of overlapping petals, 5-over-5; central floret, 3 green leaves, stem; fine blue/white jasper ground; polished concave colorless base; basal ring.
D: 2¾" (7.0 cm.)
Museum Purchase, 1977.

1307
Boston & Sandwich Glass Co., 1852-80. Cobalt blue clematis (5 petals over 5), blue/white cog cane center; 2 green leaves, stem; accent bubbles; red/white/blue jasper ground. Smooth concave colorless base; trace of pontil mark.
D: 2¹⁵⁄₁₆" (7.5 cm.)
Gift of Robert S. Sage and Jeanne Sage Groves in memory of their parents, Charles H. and Lyda P. Sage, 1978.

162
Millville, NJ, 1905-12. 12-petal, white rose cased with transparent yellow-green "vaseline"; 3 opaque dark green leaves extend upward toward flower. Smooth flat colorless base.
D: 3⁷⁄₁₆″ (8.7 cm.)
Bergstrom Bequest, 1958.
EHB acquisition: November, 1938.
No. 171, Pl. 46; Cloak Catalogue, 1969.

210
Millville, NJ, 1905-12. Pink rose; 12 petals cased with transparent amber; 3 translucent green leaves. 3 side punties; smooth circular colorless foot; trace of pontil mark.
D: 3¼″ (8.3 cm.)
Bergstrom Bequest, 1958.
EHB acquisition: February, 1939.
No. 225, Pl. 46; Cloak Catalogue, 1969.

221
Millville, NJ, 1905-12. 12-petal red rose shading to pink; 3 chartreuse-green leaves extend to top of flower. Smooth colorless round foot with concavity.
D: 3¹¹⁄₁₆″ (9.4 cm.)
Bergstrom Bequest, 1958.
EHB acquisition: June, 1939.
Illus. 69, Bergstrom book, 1940; Illus. 67, later editions.
No. 236, Pl. 46; Cloak Catalogue, 1969.

222
Whitall, Tatum & Co., Millville, NJ, early 1900s. Opaque white water lily, yellow center, 16 tuberous pink stamens; green sepals. Smooth concave disk foot.
D: 3⅜″ (8.6 cm.)
Bergstrom Bequest, 1958.
EHB acquisition: June, 1939.
Pl. XIX, Bergstrom book, 1940; later editions.
No. 237, Pl. 46; Cloak Catalogue, 1969.

255
Millville, NJ, 1905-12. Red rose; 11 slightly translucent thin petals shade to pastel pink; 2 green stems (crossed at base of rose) support small green leaves extending toward top of flower. Smooth colorless circular foot; basal concavity.
D: 3⅝″ (9.2 cm.)
Bergstrom Bequest, 1958.
EHB acquisition: November, 1939.
No. 272, Pl. 46; Cloak Catalogue, 1969.

303
Millville, NJ, early 19th century. Greyish glass encases red rose shading to pink at tips of 12 petals; 1 stamen; 3 dark green leaves. Smooth flat circular foot; pontil mark.
D: 3⅝″ (9.2 cm.)
Bergstrom Bequest, 1958.
EHB acquisition: April, 1940.
No. 323, Pl. 46; Cloak Catalogue, 1969.

373
Millville, NJ, 1905-12; attributed to Ralph Barber. 15-petal yellow rose, yellow stamen, 3 pointed green leaves with pastel green edges. Smooth circular foot; pontil mark.
D: 3⅝″ (9.2 cm.)
Bergstrom Bequest, 1958.
EHB acquisition: March, 1941.
No. 393, Pl. 46; Cloak Catalogue, 1969.

374
Millville, NJ, 1905-12. 16-petal pink rose, 3 dark green leaves; motif placed close to crown. Smooth flat circular foot; pontil mark.
D: 3⅝″ (9.2 cm.)
Bergstrom Bequest, 1958.
EHB acquisition: March, 1941.
No. 394, Pl. 46; Cloak Catalogue, 1969.

375
Millville, NJ, 1905-12. Greyish glass encases dark red rose shading to pink; 16 petals, 3 green leaves. Smooth circular foot; pontil mark.
D: 3¾″ (9.6 cm.)
Bergstrom Bequest, 1958.
EHB acquisition: March, 1941.
No. 395, Pl. 46; Cloak Catalogue, 1969.

378
Millville, NJ, 1905-12. High-domed, colorless glass encases 13-petal red rose shading to pink, 3 green leaves, resting on base; smooth flat underside. Trace of pontil mark on crown.
D: 3½″ (8.9 cm.)
Bergstrom Bequest, 1958.
EHB acquisition: February, 1941.
No. 398, Pl. 46; Cloak Catalogue, 1969.

675
Charles Kaziun, Brockton, MA, early 1960s. Upright chrysanthemum (amethyst shading to white) on 4 green leaves, "K"/red hearts signature cane visible underside. Colorless collared pedestal base; underside polished flat with pontil concavity; basal ring.
D: 2¼″ (5.7 cm.)
No. 694, Pl. 54; Cloak Catalogue, 1969.
Gift of Mr. and Mrs. Ralph S. Johns, 1963.

678
Charles Kaziun, Brockton, MA, early 1960s. Upright crimp rose, pink shading to white; 4 veined green leaves. "K"/red hearts signature cane appears underside where leaves join. Colorless collared flat pedestal base, polished pontil area; basal ring.
D: 2¹⁄₁₆″ (5.3 cm.)
No. 697, Pl. 54; Cloak Catalogue, 1969.
Gift of Mr. and Mrs. Ralph S. Johns, 1963.

72

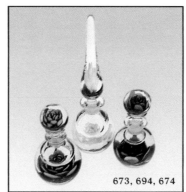

673, 694, 674

187

711

933

537

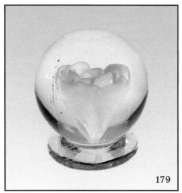

179

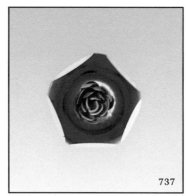

737

220

864

701, 702

703

1792

1609

1791

391

1144

1777

1588

GE-2

497

927

308

481

72
Attributed to Millville, NJ, early 20th century. Shaded pink rose: 11 thick petals drawn to point on concave translucent green ground. Flat smooth colorless base.
D: 3³⁄₁₆″ (8.1 cm.)
Bergstrom Bequest, 1958.
EHB acquisition: September, 1937.
No. 77, Pl. 48; Cloak Catalogue, 1969.

179
Whitall, Tatum & Co., Millville, NJ, 1905-12. Heavy colorless glass. Opaque white 19-petal rose drawn to point at base; no leaves. Circular foot, pontil mark.
D: 3⁹⁄₁₆″ (9.1 cm.)
Bergstrom Bequest, 1958.
EHB acquisition: January, 1939.
No. 192, Pl. 48, Cloak Catalogue, 1969.

187
Millville, NJ, attributed to Ralph Barber, 1905-12. Pink rose, 11 thick petals with pale pink edges; 3 dark green leaves. Thin circular foot frosted underside.
D: 3⅝″ (9.2 cm.)
Bergstrom Bequest, 1958.
EHB acquisition: January, 1939.
No. 200, Pl. 46; Cloak Catalogue, 1969.

220
Millville, NJ, 1905-12. 12-petal opaque white rose; no leaves. Circular foot bears pontil mark.
D: 3⅝″ (9.2 cm.)
Bergstrom Bequest, 1958.
EHB acquisition: June, 1939.
No. 235, Pl. 48; Cloak Catalogue, 1969.

537
Chinese, 1925-40. Copy of a Millville rose. Yellowish glass encases pink Millville-type rose, 14 petals shading to lighter pink at tips, 5 green leaves extending to base. Small, collared, circular flat foot; smooth underside.
D: 3⅛″ (7.9 cm.)
Bergstrom Bequest, 1958.
EHB acquisition: Unrecorded.
No. 573, Pl. 62; Cloak Catalogue, 1969.

673
Charles Kaziun, Brocton, MA, early 1960s. Spherical form; upright full-blown, shaded pink rose on 4 green leaves, "K" and hearts signature cane underside where leaves join. Polished flat colorless base; narrow neck, rounded rim. Stopper: miniature paperweight affixed to mereses and polished stopper end. Upright full-blown, shaded pink rose on 4 green leaves, "K" and hearts cane visible where leaves join underside.
Bottle H: 3¹¹⁄₁₆″ (9.4); D: 2″ (5.1 cm.)
Stopper L: 1⅞″ (4.7 cm.); D: 1½″ (2.9 cm.)
No. 692, Pl. 53; Cloak Catalogue, 1969.
Gift of Mr. and Mrs. Ralph S. Johns, 1963.

674
Charles Kaziun, Brockton, MA, early 1960s. Spherical scent bottle, enclosing in base a 3-dimensional (crimped) full-blown red rose, shading to pink, on 4 veined green aventurine leaves with "K"/red hearts signature cane underside where leaves join. Short neck ground for stopper; flat rim edge. Polished, flat colorless base. Ball-shaped, colorless glass stopper encloses 3-dimensional (crimped) red rose (shading to pink) on 4 veined green aventurine leaves. Collared stem; ground stopper end.
Bottle H: 3⅝″ (9.2 cm.); D: 1⅞″ (4.8 cm.)
Stopper L: 2″ (5.1 cm.); D: 1³⁄₃₂″ (2.8 cm.)
No. 693, Pl. 53; Cloak Catalogue, 1969.
Gift of Mr. and Mrs. Ralph S. Johns, 1963.

694
Charles Kaziun, Brockton, MA, early 1960s. Ovoid colorless glass encloses opaque white full-blown rose with 4 green leaves in base; "K" and red hearts signature cane underside where leaves join polished slightly concave base. Rimmed neck, ground for matching steeple-shaped stopper encasing upright opaque white rose, elongated petals, 4 green leaves; "K" signature cane under leaves.
Bottle H: 6½″ (16.2 cm.); D: 2¹⁄₁₆″ (5.3 cm.)
Stopper L: 4¹⁵⁄₃₂″ (11.4 cm.); D: ¹⁵⁄₁₆″ (2.4 cm.)
No. 713, Pl. 53; Cloak Catalogue, 1969.
Gift of Mr. and Mrs. Ralph S. Johns, 1963.

701
Francis Dyer Whittemore, Lansdale, PA, 1965. Miniature. Opaque white crimp rose on 4 green leaves, black "W" in yellow signature cane underside where leaves join. Sphere tilted on colorless collared pedestal, smooth foot, polished pontil concavity.
D: 2″ (5.1 cm.)
No. 721, Pl. 55; Cloak Catalogue, 1969.
Gift of Mr. and Mrs. Ralph S. Johns, 1965.

702
Francis Dyer Whittemore, Lansdale, PA, 1965. Upright full-blown crimp rose, red shading to pale pink, on 4 green leaves; black "W" in yellow signature cane underside where leaves join; colorless collared pedestal, smooth flat foot; trace of pontil mark.
D: 2⅛″ (5.4 cm.)
No. 722, Pl. 55; Cloak Catalogue, 1969.
Gift of Mr. and Mrs. Ralph S. Johns, 1965.

703
Francis Dyer Whittemore, Lansdale, PA, 1965. Yellow crimp rose surrounded by 3 green leaves; opaque grey with black "W" signature cane underside of rose. Colorless pedestal base, polished flat foot.
D: 2¹⁄₁₆″ (5.3 cm.)
No. 723, Pl. 55; Cloak Catalogue, 1969.
Gift of Mr. and Mrs. Ralph S. Johns, 1965.

711
John Degenhart (1884-1964), Cambridge, OH, ca. 1950. Greyish glass sphere encases marbled ruby-red/white crimp rose. Flat circular foot; smooth concave pontil area.
D: 2¹¹⁄₁₆″ (6.8 cm.)
No. 743, Pl. 52; Cloak Catalogue, 1969.
Gift of Mrs. John Degenhart in memory of her husband, John Degenhart, 1967.

737
Francis Dyer Whittemore, Lansdale, PA, 1968. Cobalt blue overlay. 3-dimensional pink crimp rose shades to pale pink at petal tips; 4 green leaves. Yellow signature cane with black "W" visible where leaves join. Top and base cut with flat punty; 5 smaller flat circular cuts on curve.
D: 2¹⁄₁₆″ (5.3 cm.)
Gift of Mr. and Mrs. Ralph S. Johns, 1968.

864
Robert Hamon, Scott Depot, WV, 1973. Miniature. Dark to pale amethyst crocus; 3 green leaves. Letter "H" in concavity of polished pedestal base. 34/250.
D: 1¹¹⁄₁₆″ (4.3 cm.)
Gift of Mr. W. F. Riley, 1973.

933
Joe St. Clair, Elwood, IN, 1960s. Crimp-type red rose, 15 petals; green leaves; pedestal base signed "Joe St. Clair."
D: 3″ (7.7 cm.)
Gift of Dr. M. J. Caldwell, 1974.

✳   ✳   ✳

GE-2
Rose Crimper.
Probably Whitall, Tatum & Company, Millville, NJ, early 20th century. Wrought brass; wooden handle. Used in making the Millville-type rose motifs.
D: 2⅛″ (5.4 cm.)
Bergstrom Bequest, 1958.
EHB acquisition: Unrecorded.
Illus. 72, Bergstrom book, 1940; Illus. 70, later editions.
No. 629, Pl. 47, Cloak Catalogue, 1969.

308
Ralph Barber, Whitall, Tatum & Co., Millville, NJ, 1905-12. Greyish glass encases 12-petal pink/pale pink crimp type rose; green stem, 2 branches: 5 green leaves and red bud on one, 4 leaves on the other. Sphere tilted on colorless baluster stem, disk foot; pontil mark. Rose faces side.
H: 6″ (15.2 cm.); D: 3½″ (8.9 cm.)
Bergstrom Bequest, 1958.
EHB acquisition: April, 1940.
Pl. XVIII, Bergstrom book, 1940; later editions.
No. 328, Pl. 45; Cloak Catalogue, 1969.
Ref.: No. 275, *The Corning Museum of Glass Exhibition Catalogue,* 1978.
Pepper, Adeline: *Glass Gaffers of New Jersey,* 1971; Pl. 16, pp. 252-260.

391
Millville, NJ, ca. 1905. Colorless glass sphere encases opaque white rose with 11 petals, some having black tips with red tint. No leaves. Foot formed from same gather that encases rose; pontil mark.
H: 4¼″ (10.8 cm.); D: 3″ (7.6 cm.)
Bergstrom Bequest, 1958.
EHB acquisition: May, 1941.
No. 411, Pl. 48; Cloak Catalogue, 1969.

481
Origin unknown, American, late 19th-early 20th century. Dark green glass encases rose with 11 pink/white striped petals; small central bubble. Circular foot; pontil mark.
D: 2¹⁵⁄₁₆″ (7.4 cm.)
Bergstrom Bequest, 1958.
EHB acquisition: November, 1942.
No. 511, Pl. 48; Cloak Catalogue, 1969.

497
Millville, NJ, ca. 1900. Opaque white crocus, 5 petals, yellow-tipped stamen; no leaves. Low, conical colorless glass foot; pontil mark.

D: 2⅞″ (7.3 cm.)
Bergstrom Bequest, 1958.
EHB acquisition: Unrecorded.
No. 527, Pl. 48; Cloak Catalogue, 1969.

927
Ronald Hansen, Mackinaw City, MI, 1960s. Full-blown, shaded pink rose on 4 veined green leaves; pink cane beneath; polished flat colorless base signed "Ronald Hansen." Made by Mr. Hansen for his daughter.
D: 2⅛″ (5.5 cm.)
Gift of Dr. M. J. Caldwell, 1974.

1144
Saint Louis, 1848-55. Pink camomile; central ochre/white/blue stamen cane; 1 brown bud, green sepals; 4 green leaves, stem; fine double-swirl latticinio cushion. Polished concave colorless base; basal ring.
D: 3″ (7.6 cm.)
Gift of Mrs. Florence Gosselin Marsh in memory of her husband, Raymond Clark Marsh, 1976.

1588
Francis D. Whittemore, Lansdale, PA, 1960s. Pink/mauve crimp rose on 4 green leaves; "W" cane underneath. Collared colorless pedestal base; polished pontil area in smooth flat foot.
H: 2²⁹⁄₃₂″ (7.4 cm.); D: 2¹⁄₁₆″ (5.3 cm.)
Bequest of J. Howard Gilroy, 1986.

1609
Probably O. J. "Skip" Woods, Millville, NJ, 1950s-70s. Footed Millville-type red crimp rose on 6 pale green leaves. Sphere signed "Woods" near broad, heavy concave colorless foot. Note: Woods became a glassblower at Kimble Glassblowing shop, Millville, in the early 1950s.
H: 3¹¹⁄₁₆″ (9.4 cm.); D: 3¼″ (8.3 cm.)
Bequest of J. Howard Gilroy, 1986.

1777
Chinese, 1950s-70s. Pink multipetaled water lily flower centers, 5 shaded green leaves drawn down to predominantly white spatter foot. 3 thick colorless collars on stem. Rough ground, flat base.
H: 5⅜″ (13.3 cm.); D: 3⅜″ (8.7 cm.)
Gift of Mrs. Harriet J. Jorgensen, 1987.

1791
Origin unknown, probably Millville, NJ, 20th century. Greyish glass. Crimped translucent white rose, 3 translucent dark green leaves. Collared, inverted foot, "4-lobe" shape pontil mark.
D: 3¹³⁄₃₂″ (8.7 cm.)
Gift of Mrs. Virginia Bensley Trowbridge, 1987.

1792
Pairpoint Glass Co., Inc., Sagamore, MA, 1972-73. Crimped, yellow rose drawn to base of colorless sphere, 4 mottled yellow-green leaves spaced between 4 green sepals; "p" in black cane beneath center of motif. Underside of pedestal base etched with grapes, leaves and tendrils; polished pontil concavity, signed "1973/49."
D: 3¹¹⁄₁₆″ (9.4 cm.)
Gift of Mrs. Virginia Bensley Trowbridge, 1987.

228

357

486

119

47

312

117

1432

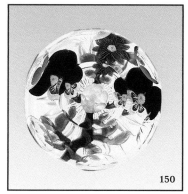

150

416

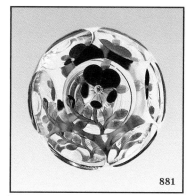

881

1127

367

385

1288

8

381

119

Attributed to New England Glass Co., East Cambridge, MA, 1853-88. Lampwork 5-petal, opaque white flower, blue cane center, on overlapping tiers of smooth pointed green leaves forming cross. White latticinio ground. All-over geometric faceting. Polished concave colorless base; wide basal ring.

D: 3¼" (8.3 cm.)

Bergstrom Bequest, 1958.

EHB acquisition: May, 1938.

Illus. 21, Bergstrom book, 1940; later editions.

No. 128, Pl. 16; Cloak Catalogue, 1969.

Ref.: No. 254, *The Corning Glass Museum Exhibition Catalogue,* 1978.

228

Attributed to Mt. Washington Glass Co., New Bedford, MA, 1870-90. Magnum. 3-dimensional motif: large frilled full-blown pink/yellow rose, goldstone center; 2 yellow buds/green sepals; 2 blue/yellow fruit pieces; 4 pastel green leaves near flower, smaller green leaves near buds; 2 varicolored butterflies near top of rose. Woman's hand (gold ring on wedding finger) holds sturdy green stem. Polished concave colorless base; basal ring.

D: 4¼" (10.8 cm.)

Bergstrom Bequest, 1958.

EHB acquisition: June, 1939.

Illus. 64, Bergstrom book, 1940; Illus. 62, later editions.

No. 244, Pl. 42; Cloak Catalogue, 1969.

Ref.: Jokelson, Paul: *One Hundred of the Most Important Paperweights,* 1966; Pl. 83.

357

Mount Washington Glass Works, New Bedford, MA, 1870-90. Magnum. 3-dimensional motif: amethyst/white full-blown rose, pink bud/green sepals, blue bud/green sepals; 4 red/4 yellow fruits; 4 pastel green leaves, darker green stem; multicolored butterfly above rose. Motif low in weight. Polished concave colorless base; basal ring.

D: 4⁵⁄₁₆" (10.9 cm.)

Bergstrom Bequest, 1958.

EHB acquisition: November, 1940.

No. 375, Pl. 42; Cloak Catalogue, 1969.

486

Mount Washington Glass Works, New Bedford, MA, 1870-90. Magnum. Large poinsettia, 12 veined bract-like red petals centered by numerous yellow, blue/orange upright "stamens"; 7 dark green leaves (made with same tool as for petals) surround flower; pointed green stem. High crown. Smooth flat colorless base; trace of pontil mark.

D: 3¹¹⁄₃₂" (8.5 cm.)

Bergstrom Bequest, 1958.

EHB acquisition: April, 1943.

No. 516, Pl. 42; Cloak Catalogue, 1969.

Ref.: Jokelson, Paul: *One Hundred of the Most Important Paperweights,* 1966; Pl. 85.

No. 266, *The Corning Museum of Glass Exhibition Catalogue,* 1978.

* * *

8

Baccarat, ca. 1855. Lampwork and millefiori motif. Pansy: 2 purple upper petals with "velvet" texture; 3 yellow lower petals (applied black veining), purple tips; central cane of white stars, red/white center; 1 bud, 2 green sepals; 7 green leaves, stem. Peripheral circle of red/white "cog" and blue/white floret canes. Hexagonally cut sides, pyramidal crown; polished colorless base cut with 24-point star; basal ring.

D: 2½" (6.3 cm.)

Bergstrom Bequest, 1958.

EHB acquisition: May, 1936.

No. 8, Pl. 3; Cloak Catalogue, 1969.

117

New England Glass Co., East Cambridge, MA, 1852-88. Lampwork: 3-dimensional floral and fruit spray; 4 flowers, green leaves, yellow bud, 2 red cherries, fruit pieces; white latticinio cushion; polished colorless concave base; basal ring.

D: 3¹³⁄₁₆" (9.7 cm.)

Bergstrom Bequest, 1958.

EHB acquisition: May, 1938.

Pl. XVI, Bergstrom book, 1940; later editions.

No. 126, Pl. 41; Cloak Catalogue, 1969.

150
Baccarat, 1845-55. Lampwork spray: 4 flowers, red bud, 2 green sepals: deeply cupped white buttercup-type/yellow star stamen center surrounded by two early Baccarat pansies with deep purple upper petals; cane-like lower petals with translucent blue/white veining/white serrated edges; yellow honeycomb cane centers. Red clematis, deeply furrowed petals, honeycomb cane center. 10 pale green leaves, darker green stem. Top punty, 6 smaller side punties. Polished concave colorless base cut with 24-point star.
D: 3¼″ (8.3 cm.)
Bergstrom Bequest, 1958.
EHB acquisition: October, 1938.
No. 159, Pl. 7; Cloak Catalogue, 1969.

312
New England Glass Co., 1852-68. Lampwork: purple, velvet-textured flower, opaque yellow center; scattered bubbles, 5 green leaves, pointed stems; swirled white latticinio ground. Concave quatrefoil faceting on dome, flutes between lobes; punties on curve. Polished concave colorless base.
D: 2½″ (6.3 cm.)
Bergstrom Bequest, 1958.
EHB acquisition: May, 1940.
No. 333, Pl. 42; Cloak Catalogue, 1969.

367
Baccarat, ca. 1855. Pansy (2 purple upper petals, 3 yellow lower petals lined with opaque white, purple tips and applied fine veining; central white star dust cane with red/white whorl center); purple bud, green sepals; 12 green leaves, stem. Polished concave colorless base cut with 24-point star; basal ring.
D: 2¹³⁄₁₆″ (7.2 cm.)
Bergstrom Bequest, 1958.
EHB acquisition: December, 1940.
No. 386, Pl. 3; Cloak Catalogue, 1969.

381
Attributed to Baccarat, 2nd half 19th century. Solid, colorless glass; large top punty, 6 smaller punties on curve. Polished concave base engraved and decorated with colored enamel: single purple/yellow pansy, green leaves and pink bud, within wreath of pink flowers alternating with green leaves. Basal ring.
D: 3⅛″ (7.9 cm.)
Bergstrom Bequest, 1958.
EHB acquisition: May, 1941.
No. 401, Pl. 9; Cloak Catalogue, 1969.

385
Clichy, 1848-55. "Johnny Jump-up" pansy: 2 purple upper petals, 3 lower yellow petals tipped with purple, center with purple veining. Thick dark green stem, 5 leaves; on end of second stem, purple bud with green sepals faces downward. Polished concave colorless base cut with 16-point star; basal ring.
D: 2½″ (6.3 cm.)
Bergstrom Bequest, 1958.
EHB acquisition: May, 1941.
No. 405, Pl. 13; Cloak Catalogue, 1969.

416
Baccarat, 1855-60. Pansy: 2 purple upper petals; 3 white-lined yellow lower petals, purple tips and veining; 7 green leaves, dark green stem; purple bud, green sepals. Center cane: yellow stars on red. Peripheral circle: white star/red whorl center canes alternate with blue/white honeycomb/blue-white star center canes. Polished concave colorless base cut with 24-point star; wide basal ring.
D: 3⅝″ (9.2 cm.)
Bergstrom Bequest, 1958.
EHB acquisition: September, 1941.
No. 438, Pl. 7; Cloak Catalogue, 1969.

881
Baccarat, 1848-55. Pansy: 2 deep purple upper and 3 black-veined yellow lower petals edged with purple and white, slightly cupped. Mauve and yellow bud, green sepals. White stardust/red/white whorl center cane. 10 green leaves, stems. Top, 6 side punties. Small 16-point star cut in polished concave colorless base.
D: 3³⁄₁₆″ (8.2 cm.)
Bequest of Mrs. L. E. Kaumheimer, 1973.

1127
Baccarat, 1848-55. Flat bouquet. Large purple/yellow pansy, white stardust/red whorl cane center; a rust-red clematis (6 over 6 petals), honeycomb cane center; 3 small cobalt blue flowers, each with white stardust/red whorl cane center, 5 furrowed petals. 2 green stalks, 4 stems, 13 leaves; 1 purple-yellow pansy bud, green sepals. Polished concave colorless base; basal ring.
D: 3³⁄₃₂″ (7.8 cm.)
Gift of Mrs. Florence Gosselin Marsh in memory of her husband, Raymond Clark Marsh, 1976.

1288
Clichy, 1848-55. Floral bouquet: Purple/yellow pansy (viola), 2 purple buds; 2 5-petal white flowers with yellow stamens, 2 white buds; multiple green leaves, stems, tied with pink ribbon. Multiple dewdrop bubbles. Polished concave colorless base; high dome.
D: 3⅜″ (8.6 cm.)
Gift of Florence Gosselin Marsh in memory of her husband, Raymond Clark Marsh, 1977.
Ref.: No. 151, *The Corning Museum of Glass Exhibition Catalogue,* 1978.

1432
Pete Lewis, Millville, NJ, 1981. Brown and veined-yellow pansy, white star-cane center; 1 brown/yellow filigree bud/green sepals, 4 green leaves, stem; thin white filigree cushion, small white "PL" cane. Top, 6 side punties; polished basal concavity and basal ring.
D: 2⁹⁄₁₆″ (6.6 cm.)
Gift of Mr. and Mrs. William L. Liebman, 1981.

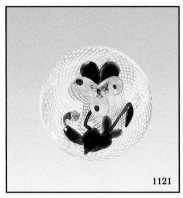

1121

870

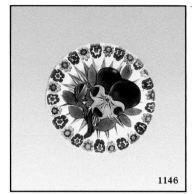

1146

1157

135

314

1132

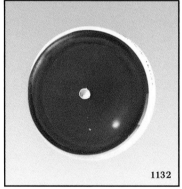

1132

236

1283

1143

1155

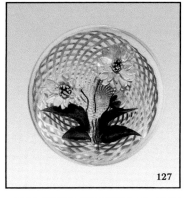

127

1170

1179

1131

1131

1178

523

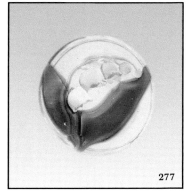

277

1173

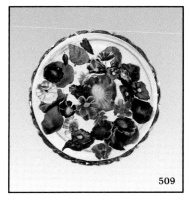

509

555

1142

135

Baccarat, ca. 1850. Flat bouquet, 4 flowers: pansy (2 purple upper, 3 yellow lower petals), blue/white primrose, yellow wheatflower (black dots), all with white star/red-white bull's eye center canes; full-blown red centered pink rose, red bud and blue bud, both with green sepals; 11 green leaves; 2 crossed stems. Polished concave colorless base; basal ring.
D: 3³⁄₁₆″ (8.1 cm.)
Bergstrom Bequest, 1958.
EHB acquisition: October, 1938.
Illus. 29, Bergstrom book, 1940; later editions.
No. 144, Pl. 3; Cloak Catalogue, 1969.
Ref.: McCawley, Patricia K., *Antique Glass Paperweights from France,* 1968; 28(b).

236

Probably Monot, père et fils, et Stumpf, Cristallerie de Pantin, Paris, France, ca. 1878. Full-blown, 3-dimensional translucent lemon-yellow rose, yellow bud/green sepals, 5 green leaves, stem; translucent cobalt blue ground; minute bubbles on motif and ground. High crown. Polished concave colorless base; basal ring. (This weight may have been made for 1878 Paris Exposition.)
D: 3″ (7.6 cm.)
Bergstrom Bequest, 1958.
EHB acquisition: September, 1939.
Pl. XVII, Bergstrom book, 1940; later editions.
No. 252, Pl. 27; Cloak Catalogue, 1969.
Ex collection: Marquis de Bailleul.
Ref.: No. 293, *The Corning Museum of Glass Exhibition Catalogue,* 1978.
PCA Bulletin, 1981, pp. 3-11.
McCawley, Patricia K.: *Antique Glass Paperweights from France,* 1968; 99(a).

314

Baccarat, 1845-50. Early example. Pansy; 2 purple upper petals with velvet texture, 3 lower petals of serrated opaque white canes with translucent blue centers veined with white; pale yellow/white honeycomb center cane. Red bud, 2 green sepals; 7 green leaves; stem. Polished concave colorless base cut with 24-point star.
D: 3¹⁄₁₆″ (7.8 cm.)
Bergstrom Bequest, 1958.
EHB acquisition: May, 1940.
Illus. 13, Bergstrom book, 1940; Illus. 14, later editions.
No. 335, Pl. 314; Cloak Catalogue, 1969.

870

Letter Weight.
Saint Louis, ca. 1848. Multi-faceted colorless glass knop encases rare, single pansy with amethyst and ochre petals, blue pastry mold cane with white flower center. 3 green leaves, stems drawn to point. 6-paneled colorless stem below knop, circular collar, heavy colorless, chamfered and beveled square base.
D: 3¹³⁄₁₆″ (9.6 cm.); Knop: 1⅝″ (4.1 cm.)
Gift of Dr. Jackson Blair in memory of Evangeline H. Bergstrom, 1973.

1121

Clichy, 1848-55. Lampwork. Pansy (2 purple top petals, 3 opaque pale yellow lower petals, each with purple spot; purple/white cane center, turquoise stamen), 3 green stems: one with purple bud, green sepals; one with pink

cane bud; 5 green leaves. Double swirl latticinio cushion, its apex drawn from below pansy to hole in polished concave colorless base; basal ring.
D: 2¾″ (7.1 cm.)
Gift of Mrs. Florence Gosselin Marsh in memory of her husband, Raymond Clark Marsh, 1976.

1132

French, possibly Pantin, ca. 1878. Opaque white full-blown rose with recessed marbled yellow/green/white center; 4 green leaf-like sepals; 1 white bud, 4 green sepals, and stem. Turquoise-green stalk, 5 broad green leaves. Motif has tiny bubble accents. Garnet red-cased white cushion; polished concave colorless base with center hole; basal ring. High dome.
D: 2⅞″ (7.3 cm.)
Gift of Mrs. Florence Gosselin Marsh in memory of her husband, Raymond Clark Marsh, 1976.

1143

French, possibly Pantin, ca. 1878. Water lily-type flower, cupped petals striped with blue, tall yellow center stamens; green stem drawn down to 5 translucent green leaves; colorless base; basal ring.
D: 2²⁵⁄₃₂″ (7.1 cm.)
Gift of Mrs. Florence Gosselin Marsh in memory of her husband, Raymond Clark Marsh, 1976.

1146

Baccarat, 1848-60. Typical Baccarat pansy: 2 deep purple, 3 yellow petals black-veined with purple spots; white star/red whorl center cane; bi-colored yellow/purple bud, green sepals. 8 green leaves, stem. Peripheral circle of alternating blue/white and white/red florets; polished concave colorless base cut with 24-point star; basal ring.
D: 2¹⁷⁄₃₂″ (6.4 cm.)
Gift of Mrs. Florence Gosselin Marsh in memory of her husband, Raymond Clark Marsh, 1976.

1155

French, possibly Pantin, ca. 1878. 5-petal white flower, black veining, yellow dots; yellow stamen center; 3 large veined dark green leaves; translucent green stem. Polished concave colorless base; basal ring.
D: 3¹⁄₁₆″ (7.7 cm.)
Gift of Mrs. Florence Gosselin Marsh in memory of her husband, Raymond Clark Marsh, 1976.

1157

Clichy, 1845-65. Dark purple viola-type flower; brown-veined yellow areas on lower petals; 1 dark purple bud, pale green sepals; 2 green stems, 7 green leaves, 2 pale green leaves; 3-dimensional arrangement. Polished concave colorless base; basal ring.
D: 3³⁄₁₆″ (8.1 cm.)
Gift of Mrs. Florence Gosselin Marsh in memory of her husband, Raymond Clark Marsh, 1976.

1283

French, possibly Pantin, ca. 1878. Single yellow aloe, green sepals, 4 small green leaves, 4 larger green leaves, centered on green glass and mica ground over white opaline. Polished concave colorless base.
D: 3⁹⁄₃₂″ (8.3 cm.)
Gift of Mrs. Florence Gosselin Marsh in memory of her husband, Raymond Clark Marsh, 1977.

127
Possibly Monot, père et fils, et Stumpf, Cristallerie de Pantin, Paris, France, 1870-1880. 3-dimensional motif low in weight on swirled white latticinio cushion: 2 opaque white flowers, pointed petals, green sepals; 4 raised green leaves, disjointed thin stems; 1 half-open white bud, green sepals (similar to flower in lizard weight No. 215). Opaque yellow stamens on green ground form flower centers. Polished concave colorless base; basal ring.
D: 3¼″ (8.3 cm.)
Bergstrom Bequest, 1958.
EHB acquisition: August, 1938.
Illus. 30, title page; Bergstrom book, 1940; later editions.
No. 136, Pl. 27; Cloak Catalogue, 1969.
Ref.: No. 288, *The Corning Museum of Glass Exhibition Catalogue,* 1978.

277
Origin unknown, probably French (possibly Pantin), late 19th century. Flat spray: Opaque white lily-of-the-valley blossoms, (3 in full bloom, 2 buds), thin stem, 2 large green leaves. Polished concave colorless base; basal ring.
D: 2¾″ (7.0 cm.)
Bergstrom Bequest, 1958.
EHB acquisition: January, 1940.
No. 296, Pl. 27; Cloak Catalogue, 1969.

509
Origin unknown, second half 19th century. High-domed, heavy glass encases varicolored deeply cupped, 3-dimensional flowers and opaque green leaves. Some flower centers are opaque yellow or white dots, others appear as filmy pastel yellow canes. Lower exterior half of weight deeply cut in diamond-shaped facets diminishing in size toward polished, almost flat base; faint basal ring. (Similar to No. 508.)
H: 3⅜″ (8.6 cm.); D: 3¾″ (9.6 cm.)
Bergstrom Bequest, 1958.
EHB acquisition: Unrecorded.
No. 542, Pl. 35; Cloak Catalogue, 1969.
Ref.: No. 276, *The Corning Museum of Glass Exhibition Catalogue,* 1978.

523
Origin unknown, French, possibly Pantin, ca. 1878. Full-blown, 3-dimensional pink/red rose, yellow stamen center, turquoise-green sepals; red bud with 1 green and 2 turquoise sepals; 3 turquoise-green leaves, 2 olive-green leaves; amethyst-encased white stem; white opaline ground. Polished concave colorless base; basal ring. Light in heft. (Similar to No. 216.)
D: 2¹¹⁄₁₆″ (6.8 cm.)
Bergstrom Bequest, 1958.
EHB acquisition: Unrecorded.
No. 558, Pl. 23; Cloak Catalogue, 1969.

555
Origin unknown, possibly Russian, ca. 1880. Formerly attributed to Mt. Washington Glass Works, New Bedford, MA, 1869-94. Bevel-edged, rectangular colorless glass encases 3-dimensional floral bouquet: 4 pink and 3 purple flowers (each with smooth, pointed petals and opaque ivory-white stamen centers), 2 pink buds with green sepals; numerous chartreuse-green leaves; 3 stems appear below pink/white striped "ribbon" drawn horizontally. Coarse, diamond-cut base.
Size: 5³⁄₁₆ x 3½ x 1¼″ (13.2 x 8.9 x 3.2 cm.)
Bergstrom Bequest, 1958.
EHB acquisition: Unrecorded.
No. 591, Pl. 42; Cloak Catalogue, 1969.
Ref.: *Antiques Magazine,* October, 1984; pp. 900-903.

1131
Attributed to Clichy, 1848-55. Lavender morning glory-type flower made from pastry mold cane; 2 green leaves, stem. Polished concave colorless base; basal ring.
D: 2²⁷⁄₃₂″ (7.2 cm.)
Gift of Mrs. Florence Gosselin Marsh in memory of her husband, Raymond Clark Marsh, 1976.

1142
French, possibly Pantin, ca. 1878. Delicate yellow flower, a brown holly-like leaf on each of its 5 rimmed petals, all drawn down to green stem underneath. 5 large, veined 3-dimensional leaves; tiny bubble accents. Polished concave colorless base; basal ring.
D: 2³¹⁄₃₂″ (7.5 cm.)
Gift of Mrs. Florence Gosselin Marsh in memory of her husband, Raymond Clark Marsh, 1976.

1170
French, possibly Pantin, ca. 1878. Yellow dahlia-type flower, green veining, dark yellow center with brown dots; dark green stem, 2 veined green leaves. Wide, grid-cut, colorless base.
D: 3³⁄₁₆″ (8.1 cm.)
Gift of Mrs. Florence Gosselin Marsh in memory of her husband, Raymond Clark Marsh, 1976.

1173
Origin unknown, possibly French or Bohemian, late 19th-early 20th century. 4 pink/white roses; 2 pink buds, green sepals; 24 green leaves, stems. Polished wide colorless base with concavity.
D: 3⁹⁄₃₂″ (8.3 cm.)
Gift of Mrs. Florence Gosselin Marsh in memory of her husband, Raymond Clark Marsh, 1976.

1178
French, probably Pantin, ca. 1878. Orange and yellow dahlia (or chrysanthemum) with brown center. Opaque yellow petals cased with transparent red. Light green stem, 2 dark green veined leaves; star-cut colorless base.
D: 3⁵⁄₃₂″ (8.0 cm.)
Gift of Mrs. Florence Gosselin Marsh in memory of her husband, Raymond Clark Marsh, 1976.

1179
French, possibly Pantin, ca. 1878. Shaded pink rose, yellow center; 1 pink bud, pale turquoise sepals; 2 pale turquoise-green leaves, 3 pale olive-green leaves; 5 turquoise sepals and stem; flat opaque white ground. Smooth colorless base, polished pontil area; wide basal ring.
D: 3⁷⁄₃₂″ (8.2 cm.)
Gift of Mrs. Florence Gosselin Marsh in memory of her husband, Raymond Clark Marsh, 1976.

508

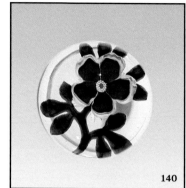

140

67

892

318

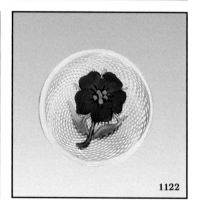

1122

231

257

218

128

784

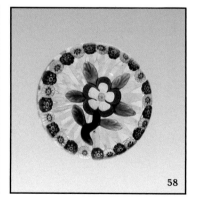

58

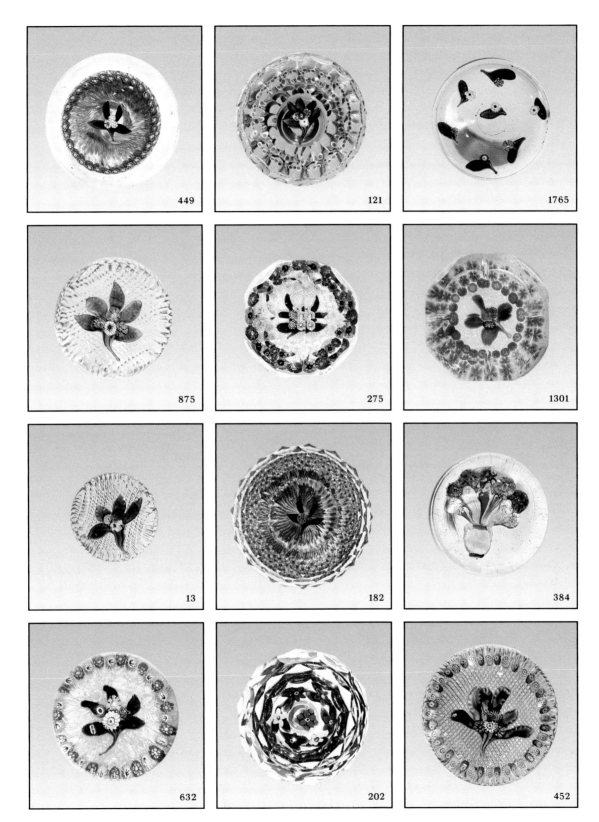

449

121

1765

875

275

1301

13

182

384

632

202

452

52

58
Baccarat, 1848-55. Blue primrose: 5 opaque white petals bordered with cobalt blue, yellow honeycomb center cane; sturdy dark green stem, 6 green leaves. Peripheral circle of white/green and red/white whorl and star canes. Polished concave colorless base cut with small 24-point star.
D: 2½" (6.3 cm.)
Bergstrom Bequest, 1958.
EHB acquisition: August, 1937.
No. 60, Pl. 6; Cloak Catalogue, 1969.

67
Baccarat, 1848-55. Primrose: 6 white recessed petals, red edges, pointed tips, white stardust center cane with red/white whorl; 11 green leaves, stem. Polished concavity of colorless base deeply cut with 16-point star; basal ring.
D: 2¾" (7.0 cm.)
Bergstrom Bequest, 1958.
EHB acquisition: September, 1937.
No. 72, Pl. 6; Cloak Catalogue, 1969.

128
Probably Saint Louis, 1848-55. Spray of 2 cobalt blue flowers in full bloom (green/yellow stamen centers), 3 partly open buds, green sepals, 5 pastel green leaves; 3 stems, one crossing the other two. White double-swirl latticinio ground; polished concave colorless base; trace of pontil mark; basal ring.
D: 2¹³⁄₁₆" (7.2 cm.)
Bergstrom Bequest, 1958.
EHB acquisition: August, 1938.
No. 137, Pl. 24; Cloak Catalogue, 1969.
Ref.: No. 206, *The Corning Museum of Glass Exhibition Catalogue,* 1978.

140
Baccarat, 1848-55. Lampwork cupped cobalt blue primrose, white edge, white stardust/red whorl cane center; 11 dark green leaves, stem. Polished concave colorless base cut with small 24-point star.
D: 2¹³⁄₁₆" (7.2 cm.)
Bergstrom Bequest, 1958.
EHB acquisition: October, 1938.
No. 149, Pl. 6; Cloak Catalogue, 1969.

218
Baccarat, 1848-55. Lampwork red flower with 5 rounded petals, white stardust/red-white whorl center cane; red bud with green sepals; 6 green leaves, stem. Polished concave colorless base cut with small 24-point star; basal ring.
D: 2½" (6.3 cm.)
Bergstrom Bequest, 1958.
EHB acquisition: May, 1939.
No. 233, Pl. 3; Cloak Catalogue, 1969.

231
Baccarat, 1848-55. Lampwork primrose flower; 5 vermilion-red petals, cupped white edges; white stardust/red-white whorl center cane; 11 green leaves, stem. High crown. Polished concave colorless base cut with small 16-point star.
D: 3¼" (8.3 cm.)
Bergstrom Bequest, 1958.
EHB acquisition: July, 1939.
No. 247, Pl. 7; Cloak Catalogue, 1969.

257
Saint Louis, ca. 1848-55. Single flower head: raised, narrow, pointed opaque white striped with pink petals; cobalt blue/yellow star center cane; dewdrop bubbles on petals, 2 green leaves, stem; translucent amethyst ground. Convex dome, sides cut in horizontal ovals with corner flutes effecting squared form; polished flat colorless base.
D: 2⁵⁄₁₆" (5.8 cm.)
Bergstrom Bequest, 1958.
EHB acquisition: November, 1939.
No. 274, Pl. 23; Cloak Catalogue, 1969.

318
Baccarat, ca. 1850. Flat bouquet low in weight: 1 white clematis (yellow/red honeycomb center); 1 red/white primrose (white stars/pale blue/white whorl center); 8 green leaves, double crossed stems; 5 small gentian blue flowers each centered by pale blue/white whorl and star canes, 8 small green leaves, 5 stems. Large top punty, flat periphery; 6 side punties; polished colorless base cut with 24-point star.
D: 3⅜" (8.6 cm.)
Bergstrom Bequest, 1958.
EHB acquisition: June, 1940.
No. 339, Pl. 5; Cloak Catalogue, 1969.

508
Origin unknown, second half of 19th century. High-domed, heavy glass; exterior lower half cut in diminishing diamond-shaped facets toward polished concave base; basal ring. Near base: 3 pansies (3 yellow-cased opaque white lower petals, 2 purple upper petals); 9 opaque green leaves, purple bud/opaque green sepals, stem.
H: 3⁷⁄₁₆" (8.7 cm.); D: 3⅞" (9.9 cm.)
Bergstrom Bequest, 1958.
EHB acquisition: Unrecorded.
No. 541, Pl. 35; Cloak Catalogue, 1969.

784
Cristalleries de Val St. Lambert, Liège, Belgium, mid-19th century. 8 opaque white petals festooned in loops of red/blue/green, blue/white/red serrated cane center form single flower; 5 emerald green leaves, 3 leaves on stem. Peripheral red/green/blue/white ribbon twist torsade. Shallow dome, 12 thumbprint cuts on curve. Polished convex colorless base; wide basal ring.
D: 3" (7.6 cm.)
Museum Purchase, 1970.

892
Baccarat, 1848-55. Deep blue primrose: 6 white-edged petals overlaid with 6 smaller puce enamel petals with white stardust/red/white whorl center. 13 green leaves, stems. Polished concave colorless base.
D: 2¾" (6.9 cm.)
Bequest of Mrs. L. E. Kaumheimer, 1973.

1122
Attributed to Saint Louis, 1848-55. Cobalt blue primrose (lined with white), 5 shaded petals, black marking, green center with 6 sulphur-yellow and black dots; 5 fine green sepals, 2 pointed green leaves, stem. Fine double swirl white latticinio cushion. Polished concave colorless base; basal ring.
D: 2¹¹⁄₁₆" (6.7 cm.)
Gift of Mrs. Florence Gosselin Marsh in memory of her husband, Raymond Clark Marsh, 1976.

13
Saint Louis, 1845-55. Flat floral spray: 4 cane florets on 4 pale green leaves; stems drawn to point. Strawberry diamond-cut, concave colorless base.
D: 2³⁄₁₆" (5.5 cm.)
Bergstrom Bequest, 1958.
EHB acquisition: May, 1936.
No. 15, Pl. 23; Cloak Catalogue, 1969.

121
Saint Louis, 1848-55. Flat floral bouquet: 3 millefiori canes (predominantly pale blue/deep blue/salmon-pink), white flower with tiny white petals centered by red-lined star; 5 emerald green leaves, 3 stems; circle of alternating white/blue/red canes and serrated chartreuse canes with square center rod. Top punty; allover side honeycomb faceting extends almost to basal ring of amber-flashed, concave base.
D: 3" (7.6 cm.)
Bergstrom Bequest, 1958.
EHB acquisition: June, 1938.
No. 130, Pl. 20; Cloak Catalogue, 1969.

182
Possibly New England Glass Co., E. Cambridge, MA, 1852-80. Small flat spray: 3 florets centered on 4 pointed green leaves float above millefiori basket formed by pink/white/blue/yellow canes drawn downward from the rim. Allover honeycomb faceting, except for small top punty. Smooth concave colorless base, rough pontil mark; basal ring.
D: 3½" (8.0 cm.)
Bergstrom Bequest, 1958.
EHB acquisition: January, 1939.
No. 195, Pl. 42; Cloak Catalogue, 1969.
Ref.: No. 250, *The Corning Museum of Glass Exhibition Catalogue,* 1978.

202
Saint Louis, 1848-55. Flat motif, low in weight; 6 cane-centered, lampwork flowers (2 cobalt blue, 2 white, 1 ochre, 1 rust-red, green leaves, stems) form wreath around central blue flower on 5 green leaves. Deep top punty indicates possible use as wafer tray; honeycomb faceting on curve; polished concave colorless base.
D: 2⅞" (7.3 cm.)
Bergstrom Bequest, 1958.
EHB acquisition: February, 1939.
No. 217, Pl. 28; Cloak Catalogue, 1969.

275
New England Glass Co., 1852-1880. Flat spray motif: 3 white canes form stylized flower set on 4 green leaves, stem. 2 circles of ochre/dark blue and pastel canes surround flower, white latticinio cushion. Concave quatrefoil faceting with flute cuts between lobes on dome, punties of 2 sizes on curve. Polished concave colorless base; basal ring.
D: 2⅝" (6.6 cm.)
Bergstrom Bequest, 1958.
EHB acquisition: November, 1939.
Illus. 79, Bergstrom book, 1940; Illus. 77, later editions.
No. 294, Pl. 42; Cloak Catalogue, 1969.

384
Origin unknown. Formerly attributed to Saint Louis. Varicolored floret bouquet, the 11 millefiori canes drawn down into an opaque white flowerpot with 2 handles.

Red/white filigree twist, to right, at periphery of weight, visible only from side. Polished flat colorless base.
D: 2¹³⁄₁₆" (7.2 cm.)
Bergstrom Bequest, 1958.
EHB acquisition: May, 1941.
No. 404, Pl. 27; Cloak Catalogue, 1969.

449
New England Glass Co., ca. 1855. Small flat spray: 3 white florets centered among 4 pointed dark green leaves above cone-shaped millefiori basket, its rim formed by concentric circles of blue/white and pink/white/blue canes. Successive circles of yellow/pink and white/pink/green canes are drawn downward and swirled to ¼" opening above polished concave colorless base; basal ring.
D: 3¹⁄₁₆" (7.8 cm.)
Bergstrom Bequest, 1958.
EHB acquisition: January, 1942.
No. 478, Pl. 42; Cloak Catalogue, 1969.

452
Saint Louis, 1845-55. Flat spray: 5 stylized millefiori cane "flower heads" set on 6 curled, serrated green leaves, pointed stems. Peripheral circle of alternating pink/white and green/white canes. Strawberry-cut, amber-flashed flat base.
D: 3¹⁄₁₆" (7.8 cm.)
Bergstrom Bequest, 1958.
EHB acquisition: February, 1942.
No. 481, Pl. 24; Cloak Catalogue, 1969.

632
Saint Louis, 1845-55. Stylized flat floral spray: 4 millefiori canes (white, salmon, chartreuse) on 5 green leaves with curved stem; upset muslin cushion low in weight; peripheral circle of alternating chartreuse/white/black anchor silhouette canes and blue/white/red anchor canes. Polished concave colorless base; basal ring.
D: 2⅞" (7.3 cm.)
No. 648, Pl. 25; Cloak Catalogue, 1969.
Gift of Mrs. Gordon Mahlke in memory of her mother, Mrs. William A. Hall, 1959.

875
Saint Louis, 1848-55. Nosegay of 4 millefiori canes: yellow, blue (7 "anchor" canes), white, and pink with anchor cane center; 5 veined green leaves, 2 curved stems. Strawberry diamond-cut, concave colorless base.
D: 2¹⁸⁄₃₂" (6.6 cm.)
Bequest of Mrs. L. E. Kaumheimer, 1973.

1301
Chinese, 1930s. Flat posy motif. Yellowish glass. Pink/blue/white star center canes; white/lilac/green center canes concentrically arranged at periphery; latticinio cushion. Quatrefoil faceting on dome. Polished concave colorless base; basal ring.
D: 3" (7.7 cm.)
Gift of Robert S. Sage and Jeanne Sage Groves in memory of their parents, Charles H. and Lyda P. Sage, 1978.

1765
Saint Louis, 1845-55. 7 scattered "sprigs:" green leaves, stems, each with millefiori cane "flower:" 3 white/red florets; 1 each, cobalt blue/white/red, ochre/white/cobalt blue, pink/white, rust/white/cobalt blue. Polished concave colorless base; trace of pontil; wide basal ring.
D: 2¹⁵⁄₁₆" (7.5 cm.)
Museum Purchase, 1987.

835

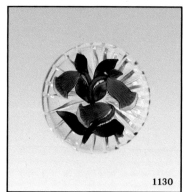

1130

1119

243

169

260

1128

230

171

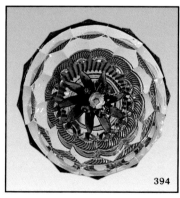

394

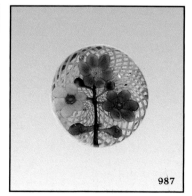

987

403

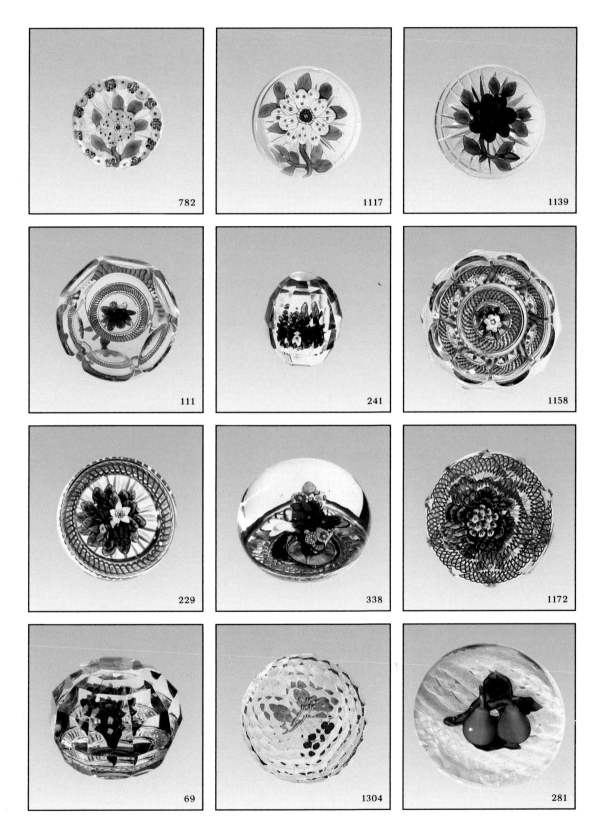

782

1117

1139

111

241

1158

229

338

1172

69

1304

281

54

169
Saint Louis, 1848-55. Lampwork open crimson/blue fuchsia flower, long red stamens; pink stems; 1 long, 2 small crimson buds; 4 green leaves; on amber branch. White latticinio cushion. Polished concave colorless base; basal ring.
D: 3 1/16" (7.8 cm.)
Bergstrom Bequest, 1958.
EHB acquisition: December, 1938.
Illus. 52, Bergstrom book, 1940; Illus. 50, later editions.
No. 181, Pl. 19; Cloak Catalogue, 1969.

171
Clichy, 1848-55. Lampwork flat bouquet: red/white striped, 6-petal flower, dark blue dots encircle cane center; dark blue clematis, furrowed petals, white star cane center; opaque white flower, dark blue spot on each of 6 petals, pink/green floret center. Amethyst-blue stems; 18 green leaves. Polished concave colorless base.
D: 2 1/2" (6.3 cm.)
Bergstrom Bequest, 1958.
EHB acquisition: December, 1938.
No. 183, Pl. 2; Cloak Catalogue, 1969.

230
Clichy, 1845-55. Flat bouquet: deep blue and mauve clematis flowers, furrowed petals and cane centers, each with bud, flank large pink Clichy rose; bud with green sepals, 2 groups of 3 green leaves; pointed stems crossed by pink "ribbon." Polished concave colorless base; basal ring.
D: 3 3/16" (8.1 cm.)
Bergstrom Bequest, 1958.
EHB acquisition: July, 1939.
Illus. 27, Bergstrom book, 1940; later editions.
No. 246, Pl. 18; Cloak Catalogue, 1969.

243
Baccarat, 1848-55. Lampwork flat spray: 6 deep pink clematis buds (green sepals) in symmetrical tiers on vertical green stems, 2 large and 5 smaller green leaves. Polished concave colorless base cut with small 16-point star.
D: 3 1/16" (7.8 cm.)
Bergstrom Bequest, 1958.
EHB acquisition: September, 1939.
No. 259, Pl. 7; Cloak Catalogue, 1969.

260
Baccarat, 1848-55. Lampwork: 3 white bell flowers, 1 bud, all with furrowed petals, green sepals; 4 green stems, 7 green leaves. Polished concave colorless base; basal ring.
D: 3" (7.6 cm.)
Bergstrom Bequest, 1958.
EHB acquisition: November, 1939.
No. 278, Pl. 2; Cloak Catalogue, 1969.

394
Saint Louis, 1848-55. Magnum. Upright bouquet: central white flower, 2 dark blue and 2 salmon-pink flowers, 4 millefiori canes surrounded by 10 pastel green leaves. White/red filigree torsade. Honeycomb facets enlarge toward wide polished concave colorless base; basal ring. Convex dome.
D: 4 1/16" (10.3 cm.)
Bergstrom Bequest, 1958.
EHB acquisition: May, 1941.
No. 414, Pl. 20; Cloak Catalogue, 1969.

403
Boston & Sandwich Glass Co., Sandwich, MA, ca. 1870; or New England Glass Co., E. Cambridge, MA, 1852-80. Upright bouquet in white latticinio basket: central dark blue flower/cane center; blue/white/translucent pink flowers; 3 canes; all surrounded by 6 spaced, veined dark green leaves. Polished concave colorless base; wide basal ring.
D: 2 9/16" (6.5 cm.)
Bergstrom Bequest, 1958.
EHB acquisition: August, 1941.
No. 423, Pl. 41; Cloak Catalogue, 1969.

835
Baccarat, 1845-55. "Crown Imperial": 3 salmon-colored bell flowers; 8 green leaves, stems. Polished concave colorless base; narrow basal ring.
D: 2 7/8" (7.3 cm.)
Museum Purchase, The Evelyn Campbell Cloak Memorial Fund, 1972.
Ref.: No. 58, *The Corning Museum of Glass Exhibition Catalogue,* 1978.

987
Red Chinese, 1970 or earlier (possibly 1930s). Greyish glass encases flat bouquet of 3 6-petal flowers: yellow (red-yellow center), orange (yellow-red center), and blue (red-yellow center); 1 yellow-red bud; 3 green leaves, stem. Loosely formed white latticinio cushion. Rough-polished pontil area, colorless base.
D: 2 5/16" (6.4 cm.)
Gift of Dr. M. J. Caldwell, 1974.

1119
Baccarat, 1848-55. Flat spray of partly open white clematis flowers, 1 bud, all with green sepals; 4 green leaves, entwined stems (separated near ends). Polished concave colorless base; basal ring. (Also called "tulip buds" and found with 4 or 6 flowers.)
D: 3" (7.4 cm.)
Gift of Mrs. Florence Gosselin Marsh in memory of her husband, Raymond Clark Marsh, 1976.

1128
Clichy, 1848-55. Flat bouquet: 1 stylized purple cane flower, compound yellow/moss cane center, green sepals; 1 pink cane flower, compound pink/moss cane center, green sepals; 1 garnet-red cane flower, green sepals; 1 green bud; 2 pink stems, a green stem, 8 leaves each highlighted by 2 rows of tiny bubbles. Polished concave colorless base; basal ring. Note: flower centers have unusual combinations of moss canes, stars, whorls and medallions.
D: 2 31/32" (7.5 cm.)
Gift of Mrs. Florence Gosselin Marsh in memory of her husband, Raymond Clark Marsh, 1976.
Ref.: No. 141, *The Corning Museum of Glass Exhibition Catalogue,* 1978.

1130
Baccarat, 1848-55. 3 salmon-colored gentians lined with white; 1 bud; 6 green leaves, curved stems; polished concave star-cut base. Rare with bud.
D: 2 1/2" (6.4 cm.)
Gift of Mrs. Florence Gosselin Marsh in memory of her husband, Raymond Clark Marsh, 1976.

69
Saint Louis, 1848-55. Small upright lampwork bouquet: salmon-pink center flower, a white, and a blue flower (all with opaque yellow centers); 2 florets; green leaves ending in point; white filigree torsade near base. Allover geometric faceting becomes larger toward polished concave colorless base; basal ring.
D: 2¹⁵⁄₁₆″ (7.4 cm.)
Bergstrom Bequest, 1958.
EHB acquisition: September, 1937.
No. 74, Pl. 20; Cloak Catalogue, 1969.

111
Saint Louis, 1848-55. Lampwork and cane motif. Upright bouquet: red/white/blue flowers, 2 canes; 4 pale green leaves drawn to point at colorless base; at periphery, finely coiled red/white torsade, without core. Top punty, 6 punties on curve. Polished concave base; basal ring.
D: 3″ (7.6 cm.)
Bergstrom Bequest, 1958.
EHB acquisition: May, 1938.
No. 119, Pl. 20; Cloak Catalogue, 1969.

229
Baccarat, 1848-55. Lampwork upright bouquet: small, varicolored flowers surrounded by green leaves, stems drawn down to point at base center. White star/red whorl canes center amethyst/white blossoms; red/blue flowers have rod-like vertical petals. White filigree torsade coiled with cobalt blue placed low in polished concave colorless base cut with 24-point star; basal ring.
D: 2⅞″ (7.3 cm.)
Bergstrom Bequest, 1958.
EHB acquisition: July, 1939.
No. 245, Pl. 7; Cloak Catalogue, 1969.

241
Hand Cooler.
Saint Louis, 1848-55. Ovoid cut in 10-sided rectangular facets encases joined upright bouquets (one facing upward, the other downward) of red/white/blue single flowers among green leaves. Polished flat top and base.
H: 2⁵⁄₁₆″ (5.9 cm); D: 1¹⁵⁄₁₆″ (4.9 cm.)
Bergstrom Bequest, 1958.
EHB acquisition: September, 1939.
Illus. 22, Bergstrom book, 1940; later editions.
No. 257, Pl. 25; Cloak Catalogue, 1969.

281
Origin unknown, French, possibly Pantin, ca. 1878. 2 dark amber/yellow pears (translucent pastel green star-with-bubble blossom ends), rose-colored stems (amber cased with red); 3 emerald green leaves, stems; deep amethyst encased white branch. Varied patterns of white filigree twists (laid parallel) form ground above polished concave colorless base; basal ring.
D: 3⁹⁄₁₆″ (9.1 cm.)
Bergstrom Bequest, 1958.
EHB acquisition: February, 1940.
Pl. XI, Bergstrom book, 1940; later editions.
No. 300, Pl. 18; Cloak Catalogue, 1969.
Ref.: No. 154, *The Corning Museum of Glass Exhibition Catalogue,* 1978.

338
Saint Louis, 1845-55. Upright bouquet: cobalt blue center flower and white flower, a red cane bud, 4 florets, green leaves. Basal torsade: twisted flat white filigree within salmon-pink coil. High crown. Polished concave colorless base cut with small 24-point star; basal ring.
D: 3¼″ (8.3 cm.)
Bergstrom Bequest, 1958.
EHB acquisition: August, 1940.
No. 358, Pl. 28; Cloak Catalogue, 1969.

782
Baccarat, ca. 1850. Miniature. Yellow wheatflower, 10 black-spotted round petals; green stalk, 6 leaves; peripheral circle of alternating white star and red/white/green arrow canes. Polished concave colorless base cut with 16-point star; basal ring.
D: 2″ (5.0 cm.)
Museum Purchase, 1970.

1117
Baccarat, ca. 1850. White wheatflower, 12 petals with blue dots; compound stardust/blue-white center cane; 1 white bud, green sepals; 11 green leaves, 2 stems. Polished concave colorless base cut with 24-point star.
D: 2⁹⁄₁₆″ (6.5 cm.)
Gift of Mrs. Florence Gosselin Marsh in memory of her husband, Raymond Clark Marsh, 1976.

1139
Baccarat, ca. 1850. Full-blown garnet-red rose, 1 red bud, green sepals; 2 green stems, 9 leaves. Polished concave 24-point star-cut colorless base; basal ring.
D: 2²⁷⁄₃₂″ (7.2 cm.)
Gift of Mrs. Florence Gosselin Marsh in memory of her husband, Raymond Clark Marsh, 1976.

1158
Saint Louis, 1845-55. Small upright floral bouquet surrounded by small red and white coiled filigree torsade between "mercury" rings low in base. Top punty; multiple circular facets on curve. Polished concave colorless base cut with 24-point star; basal ring.
D: 3⁵⁄₃₂″ (8.0 cm.)
Gift of Mrs. Florence Gosselin Marsh in memory of her husband, Raymond Clark Marsh, 1976.

1172
Baccarat, 1848-55. Upright floral bouquet set in multiple lettuce-green leaves; 2 salmon cane-centered flowers, 2 each white, blue and red buds; large central red/white/blue arrow cane. Fine white filigree coiled with blue torsade low in weight. Allover faceting. Polished concave colorless base cut with 24-point star; basal ring.
D: 3⁵⁄₃₂″ (8.0 cm.)
Gift of Mrs. Florence Gosselin Marsh in memory of her husband, Raymond Clark Marsh, 1976.

1304
Saint Louis, 1848-55. 2 red cherries, fine pale green stems, 3 veined green leaves accented by tiny bubbles; amber branch. Motif low in weight, allover geometric faceting. Polished concave strawberry diamond-cut base.
D: 3⁹⁄₁₆″ (9.1 cm.)
Gift of Robert S. Sage and Jeanne Sage Groves in memory of their parents, Charles H. and Lyda P. Sage, 1978.

1804

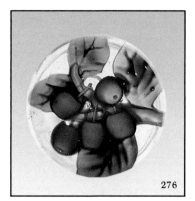

276

62

217

157

1169

99

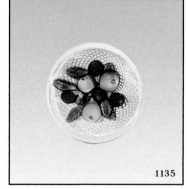

1135

889

780

1152

1761, 1690

425

161

1430

130

216

138

1140

87

733

1194

402

1630

56

62
Saint Louis, 1848-55. Cluster of 8 cherries or currants, 8 parallel amber stems bound with opaque white "cord" twist. 5 green leaves near stem ends. Polished concave colorless base cut with 24-point star; basal ring.
D: 2¹⁵⁄₁₆″ (7.4 cm.)
Bergstrom Bequest, 1958.
EHB acquisition: September, 1937.
No. 66, Pl. 19; Cloak Catalogue, 1969.

99
Boston and Sandwich Glass Co., Sandwich, MA, or New England Glass Co., East Cambridge, MA, 1852-80. 2 pears, apple, cherry, plum, and radish; 7 pointed, varied green leaves, stems; accent bubbles on or near fruit. Smooth colorless base, polished concave pontil area; basal ring.
D: 3³⁄₁₆″ (8.1 cm.)
Bergstrom Bequest, 1958.
EHB acquisition: December, 1937.
Illus. 55, Bergstrom book, 1940; Illus. 53, later editions.
No. 105, Pl. 41; Cloak Catalogue, 1969.

157
Origin unknown, French, possibly Pantin, ca. 1878. 2 clusters of red currants; translucent green stems; rose-amber stalk; 3 green leaves. Motif low in weight. Polished concave colorless base; basal ring.
D: 3⅛″ (8.0 cm.)
Bergstrom Bequest, 1958.
EHB acquisition: October, 1938.
No. 166, Pl. 28; Cloak Catalogue, 1969.

217
Saint Louis, 1848-55. 2 yellow pears, a peach, and 4 cherries, yellow stems, 10 leaves, in double-spiral white latticinio basket. Polished concave colorless base; basal ring.
D: 2¹¹⁄₁₆″ (6.8 cm.)
Bergstrom Bequest, 1958.
EHB acquisition: May, 1939.
No. 232, Pl. 19; Cloak Catalogue, 1969.

276
Origin unknown, French, possibly Pantin, ca. 1878. Cluster of 5 cherries; translucent red-cased/amber stems, "Y" shape branch; 4 green, veined leaves; accent bubbles at blossom end of each cherry. Polished concave colorless base; basal ring.
D: 3⅛″ (8.0 cm.)
Bergstrom Bequest, 1958.
EHB acquisition: January, 1940.
Illus. 19, Bergstrom book, 1940; later editions.
No. 295, Pl. 2, Cloak Catalogue, 1969.
Ref.: No. 300, *The Corning Museum of Glass Exhibition Catalogue,* 1978.

780
Baccarat, 1848-55. 2 apricot fruits, yellow shading to orange, centered on stalk with 6 green leaves. Polished concave colorless base; basal ring.
Ex collection: Miss Olga Drexel Dahlgren.
D:2¾″ (7.0 cm.)
Museum Purchase, 1970.
Ref.: *PCA Bulletin,* 1966-67; Illustrated cover.
No. 71, *The Corning Museum of Glass Exhibition Catalogue,* 1978.

889
Baccarat, 1848-55. 2 coral-pink strawberries, 1 green strawberry; green stems, 7 green leaves. 16-point star cut in polished concave colorless base.
D: 2⅞″ (7.2 cm.)
Bequest of Mrs. L. E. Kaumheimer, 1973.

1135
Saint Louis, 1848-55. 2 red/yellow pears, 1 green/yellow pear (all with green blossom ends), 4 cherries (3 with green stems), 7 leaves; stems pulled near base of deeply cupped, double-spiral white latticinio basket. Trace of pontil mark in polished concave colorless base; basal ring.
D: 2¼″ (5.7 cm.)
Gift of Mrs. Florence Gosselin Marsh in memory of her husband, Raymond Clark Marsh, 1976.

1152
French, possibly Saint Louis, 1855-78. 3 pears: 1 large in olive/green/ochre cased with transparent red; one of smaller pears is yellow/orange cased with transparent red; the other is yellow/orange cased with amber. Opaque rust blossom end and stems. 4 green veined leaves; 2 chartreuse leaves; bubble accents. Single latticinio cushion in polished colorless base; basal ring.
D: 2¹¹⁄₁₆″ (6.9 cm.)
Gift of Mrs. Florence Gosselin Marsh in memory of her husband, Raymond Clark Marsh, 1976.
Ref.: Imbert, R.; Amic, Y.: *Les Presse-Papiers Francais de Cristal,* 1948; Fig. 44, p. 48.

1169
Saint Louis, 1845-55. Yellow-green pear, orange pear and peach, 3 red cherries each with yellow stems; 9 green leaves; white latticinio cushion in polished concave colorless base, basal ring. Top and 6 side punties.
D: 3³⁄₁₆″ (8.1 cm.)
Gift of Mrs. Florence Gosselin Marsh in memory of her husband, Raymond Clark Marsh, 1976.
Ref.: No. 228, *The Corning Museum of Glass Exhibition Catalogue,* 1978.

1690
Perthshire Paperweights, Ltd., Crieff, Scotland, dated 1980. Pear, orange, lemon, 3 cherries, 5 green stems; olive-green leaves; double swirl white latticinio cushion. Polished colorless basal concavity; "P 1980" cane; basal ring.
D: 2¹⁵⁄₃₂″ (6.3 cm.)
Gift of Mr. and Mrs. F. John Barlow, 1986.

1761
Perthshire Paperweights, Ltd., Crieff, Scotland, ca. 1980; unsigned. Cluster of pear; orange; lemon; 3 cherries; 3 stems; 12 leaves; double swirl white latticinio cushion. Wide top punty; circle of oval cuts in 2 sizes near crown, 8 side ovals. Polished colorless basal concavity; basal ring. One of a kind.
D: 2⁷⁄₁₆″ (6.2 cm.)
Gift of Mr. and Mrs. F. John Barlow, 1986.

1804
Saint Louis, dated 1971. Sprigs of cherries set in "wheel" pattern; white double swirl latticinio cushion. Pink/white "SL 1971" cane. Wide top punty, 6 side punties. Polished concave colorless base.
D: 3⁵⁄₃₂″ (8.1 cm.)
Gift of Mrs. Virginia Bensley Trowbridge, 1987.

87
Saint Louis, 1848-55. Spoke arrangement of 7 lampwork vegetables (probably turnips, radishes and carrot): 2 opaque white, 3 amethyst, 1 each red and amber, with green "leaf" tops at periphery. Green "core" drawn to base of white double swirl latticinio basket. Polished almost flat colorless base.
D: 3¹⁄₁₆″ (7.8 cm.)
Bergstrom Bequest, 1958.
EHB acquisition: November, 1937.
Illus. 18, Bergstrom book, 1940.
No. 92, Pl. 23; Cloak Catalogue, 1969.
Ref.: McCawley, Patricia K.: *Antique Glass Paperweights from France,* 1968; No. 67.

130
New England Glass Co., East Cambridge, MA, ca. 1860. Lampwork cluster of 5 yellow/red pears (each with bubble at blossom end) and 4 red berries; 8 dark green leaves; stems drawn to base of coarse, white latticinio basket. Polished concave colorless base; basal ring.
D: 2⁷⁄₁₆″ (6.2 cm.)
Bergstrom Bequest, 1958.
EHB acquisition: September, 1938.
Illus. 3, Bergstrom book, 1940; later editions.
No. 139, Pl. 43; Cloak Catalogue, 1969.

138
Saint Louis, 1845-55. Lampwork cluster of 2 rose-amber pears, 1 yellow-green pear, 4 red cherries, thin yellow stems, 8 opaque green leaves; swirled white latticinio basket. Top punty, 6 oval side punties. Polished slightly concave colorless base; basal ring.
D: 2¹⁵⁄₁₆″ (7.4 cm.)
Bergstrom Bequest, 1958.
EHB acquisition: October, 1938.
No. 147, Pl. 21; Cloak Catalogue, 1969.

161
Attributed to Mt. Washington Glass Works, New Bedford, MA, 1870-90. Magnum. 5 ripe strawberries, 4 opaque white/pink-center blossoms on pale green leaves, tiny bubbles enhancing motif. Polished concave colorless base; basal ring.
D: 4³⁄₁₆″ (10.6 cm.)
Bergstrom Bequest, 1958.
EHB acquisition: November, 1938.
Illus. 54, Bergstrom book, 1940; Illus. 52, later editions.
No. 170, Pl. 41; Cloak Catalogue, 1969.
Ref.: Jokelson, Paul: *One Hundred of the Most Important Paperweights,* 1966; Pl. 95.

216
Origin unknown, French, possibly Pantin, ca. 1878. Large lampwork amber-rose pear (green-star blossom end with bubble), curved opaque pastel olive-green stem; 1 rose-red cherry, 1 deep red berry (both with translucent pastel green stems); turquoise-blue stalk and 2 leaves, 3 emerald-green leaves; opaque white ground. High-domed. Polished concave colorless base; basal ring.
D: 2¾″ (7.0 cm.)
Bergstrom Bequest, 1958.
EHB acquisition: May, 1939.
No. 231, Pl. 23; Cloak Catalogue, 1969.

402
Saint Louis, 1848-55. White flower with yellow stamens, 2 strawberries (1 cerise, 1 pastel pink) each with green sepals; 4 green leaves, stem; double-swirl white latticinio ground. Polished flat colorless base, trace of pontil mark; basal ring.
D: 2¹³⁄₁₆″ (7.2 cm.)
Bergstrom Bequest, 1958.
EHB acquisition: August, 1941.
No. 422, Pl. 41; Cloak Catalogue, 1969.

425
Saint Louis, 1848-55. Cluster of small bluish-purple grapes, thin pastel green stem, 2 green leaves attached to pastel orange branch (placed low in weight). Polished slightly concave colorless base with fine strawberry cutting; basal ring. Large top punty, 8 smaller punties on curve, 8 larger punties below.
D: 3¹⁄₁₆″ (7.8 cm.)
Bergstrom Bequest, 1958.
EHB acquisition: September, 1941.
No. 449, Pl. 21; Cloak Catalogue, 1969.
Ref.: McCawley, Patricia K.: *Antique Glass Paperweights from France,* 1968; No. 59, Pl. 23.
Kaplan, Leo: *From a Private Collection,* Fig. 4, pp. 28-30.

733
Saint Louis, 1950s. 5 stylized vegetables (2 red, 1 white, 1 green, 1 yellow), 6 green leaves; coarse white latticinio cushion. Polished concave colorless base; basal ring.
D: 3⅛″ (7.9 cm.)
Gift of Mr. Franklin Schuell, 1968.

1140
Saint Louis, 1848-55. 6 white, red, and purple root vegetables with green leaves alternate in radial cluster; double-swirl white latticinio basket. Polished concave colorless base; wide basal ring.
D: 2¾″ (7.0 cm.)
Gift of Mrs. Florence Gosselin Marsh in memory of her husband, Raymond Clark Marsh, 1976.

1194
Saint Louis, 1848-55. Miniature. Pale orange peach, translucent pale green cane in blossom end; 3 emerald green leaves, accent bubbles; pale green stem. Motif low in weight. Polished almost flat colorless base; basal ring.
D: 2″ (5.1 cm.)
Gift of Mrs. Florence Gosselin Marsh in memory of her husband, Raymond Clark Marsh, 1976.

1430
Saint Louis, 1845-55. 3 dark amethyst Damson plums on curved amber branch encircled by fine white stems; 5 green leaves. Polished concave colorless base cut with 24-point star basal ring.
D: 2¹⁷⁄₃₂″ (6.5 cm.)
Museum Purchase, 1981.

1630
Origin unknown, probably French, ca. 1878, possibly Cristallerie de Pantin. Single transparent red-cased amber pear, red and amber stem and branch; 3 shaded green ridged leaves covered with multiple tiny bubbles. Polished concave colorless base; basal ring.
D: 1³¹⁄₃₂″ (5.5 cm.)
Gift of Mrs. Virginia Bensley Trowbridge, 1986.

463

1063, 1064

92

442

1341

113

529

948

1317

427

175

631, 630, 628, 626, 627

859

515

1124

1164

256

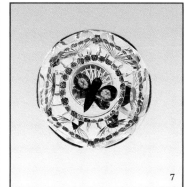

7

118

280

383

167

1156

195

92
New England Glass Co., East Cambridge, MA, ca. 1860.
Translucent amber blown glass apple, stem pressed into
applied concave colorless disk base. Pontil mark in
blossom end.
Apple D: 2⅚₆″ (5.8 cm.); D: approx. 2½″ (6.3 cm.) base.
Bergstrom Bequest, 1958.
EHB acquisition: November, 1937.
Illus. 61, 1940 Bergstrom book; Illus. 59, later editions.
No. 97, Pl. 43; Cloak Catalogue, 1969.

113
New England Glass Co., ca. 1860. Hollow blown pear,
brown shading to yellow; black blossom end; stem joins
applied colorless glass disk base.
Pear D: 2″ (5.1 cm.); D: 3³⁄₁₆″ (8.1 cm.) base.
Bergstrom Bequest, 1958.
EHB acquisition: May, 1938.
Illus. 62, 1940 Bergstrom book; Illus. 60, later editions.
No. 121, Pl. 43; Cloak Catalogue, 1969.

175
Doorknob.
Saint Louis, 1848-55. Fuchsia, blue center, pink stamens,
pink stem looped over amethyst stalk; 4 leaves, 2 red
buds; swirled white latticinio ground; colorless base
and shank.
D: 2¹³⁄₁₆″ (7.2 cm.)
Bergstrom Bequest, 1958.
EHB acquisition: June, 1939.
No. 187, Pl. 25; Cloak Catalogue, 1969.

427
Origin unknown, possibly Venetian, late 19th-early 20th
century. Colorless glass apple, applied colorless veined
leaf at top, encases translucent ruby-red sphere with
spaced bubbles and goldstone flecks; pontil mark.
D: 3¼″ (8.3 cm.)
Bergstrom Bequest, 1958.
EHB acquisition: October, 1941.
No. 454, Pl. 38; Cloak Catalogue, 1969.

442
New England Glass Co., ca. 1860-80. Blown pear, amber
shading to green-yellow; colorless glass disk base. Black
blossom end and stem.
Pear D: 2⅜″ (6.1 cm.); D: 2¹⁵⁄₁₆″ (7.4 cm.) base.
Bergstrom Bequest, 1958.
EHB acquisition: December, 1941.
No. 471, Pl. 43; Cloak Catalogue, 1969.

463
Saint Louis, 1848-55. Hollow-blown quince, opaque white
cased with yellow shading to deep amber; blue cane blos-
som end; white opaline stem. Square colorless glass base;
underside polished flat, basal concavity.
Quince D: 2¹³⁄₁₆″ (7.2 cm.); D: 3⅝″ x 3⅝″ (9.2 x 9.2 cm.)
base.
Bergstrom Bequest, 1958.
EHB acquisition: April, 1942.
No. 491, Pl. 43; Cloak Catalogue, 1969.

529
Attributed to Hobbs, Brockunier & Co., Wheeling, WV,
ca. 1886. Amber-encased, free-blown pear of opaque
white glass shading to rose toward top; amber stem. Small
hole in flattened underside.
D: 2⅝″ (6.6 cm.)
Bergstrom Bequest, 1958.
EHB acquisition: Unrecorded.
No. 563, Pl. 43; Cloak Catalogue, 1969.

626, 627, 628, 630, 631
Glass Flowers.
Venetian, 1860s.
626 Red dahlia-type flower; 2 applied leaves.
627 Pansy; 3 yellow lower petals, 2 purple upper petals.
Applied leaf.
628 Tulip; 6 jagged-edged white petals striped with red.
Applied leaf.
630 Daisy type; 12 amber-cased opaque white petals.
Applied leaf.
631 Blue/white dahlia-type glass flower. 2 applied leaves.
Bergstrom Bequest, 1958.
EHB acquisition: Unrecorded.
No. 766, Pl. 63; Cloak Catalogue, 1969.

948
Rainbow Glass, Huntington, WV, 1968-72. Translucent
amber-red apple, green stem; concave base.
D: 2⅝″ (6.7 cm.)
Gift of Dr. M. J. Caldwell, 1974.

1063, 1064
Door Knobs (pair).
Saint Louis, 1848-55. Chartreuse-yellow pear, 3 red
cherries, 4 green leaves, swirled white latticinio ground.
Brass mount.
D: 2″ (5.1 cm.)
Gift of Alfred M. King in memory of his wife, Barbara S.
King, 1974.
Ref.: Jokelson, Paul: *Antique French Paperweights*, 1955;
No. 317.

1317
Origin unknown (possibly American). Encased mica-
flecked black glass pear, black stem; blossom end mark;
flat side area.
H: 3⁹⁄₁₆″ (9.1 cm.); D: 2³⁄₁₆″ (5.5 cm.)
Gift of Robert S. Sage and Jeanne Sage Groves in memory of their parents, Charles H. and Lyda P. Sage, 1978.

1341
Murano, probably 20th century. Hollow blown pear,
yellow streaked with translucent green and pastel red;
green "flower" end; stem with applied veined leaf.
H: 3¹⁹⁄₃₂″ (9.2 cm.); D: 2¹⁹⁄₃₂″ (6.6 cm.)
Gift of Paul Hollister, 1978.

7
Baccarat, 1845-55. Butterfly: translucent amethyst fili-gree body; black head, 2 blue eyes; transparent blue antennae; wings of flattened varicolored canes lined with opaque white. Peripheral circle of red/white/green arrow canes alternate with white/blue star canes. Top and 6 side punties. 24-point star cut underside of polished, almost flat colorless base; basal ring.
D: 2⅞" (7.3 cm.) Bergstrom Bequest, 1958.
EHB acquisition: May, 1936.
No. 7, Pl. 6; Cloak Catalogue, 1969.

118
Baccarat, ca. 1850. Butterfly: translucent amethyst fili-gree body, black head, 2 blue eyes, 2 black antennae; matching upper and lower wings of flattened red/blue/green rods, some whorl centers, lined with opaque white. Above white clematis-type flower (12 furrowed pointed petals); 8 leaves, stem; white bud/sepals. Polished con-cave colorless base cut with 24-point star.
D: 3¹⁄₁₆" (7.8 cm.) Bergstrom Bequest, 1958.
EHB acquisition: May, 1938.
Pl. V, Bergstrom book, 1940 and later editions.
No. 127, Pl. 4; Cloak Catalogue, 1969.

167
Saint Louis, ca. 1848. Hollow-blown green/white jasper sphere crowned by molded, coiled, gilded, mottled green/white lizard. Smooth concave base; trace of pontil mark.
D: 3³⁄₁₆" (8.1 cm.)
Bergstrom Bequest, 1958.
EHB acquisition: November, 1938.
No. 177, Pl. 21; Cloak Catalogue, 1969.

195
Saint Louis, ca. 1848. Molded lizard on hollow-blown sphere of white opaline overlaid with pink. Floral faceting on curve. Concave polished base; center hole.
D: 3⁷⁄₁₆" (8.7 cm.) Bergstrom Bequest, 1958.
EHB acquisition: February, 1939.
Illus. 7, Bergstrom book, 1940.
No. 209, Pl. 21; Cloak Catalogue, 1969.
Ref.: No. 234, *The Corning Museum of Glass Exhibition Catalogue,* 1978.

256
Baccarat, 1848-55. Butterfly: amethyst filigree body, black head, 2 blue eyes, black antennae; upper wings red/yellow/brown canes, lower wings blue/green/red, canes flattened and lined with opaque white; scrambled white filigree ground; peripheral circle of alternating white stardust/green-white whorl and red/white/green arrow canes. Polished concave colorless base.
D: 2¼" (5.7 cm.) Bergstrom Bequest, 1958.
EHB acquisition: Undated.
No. 273, Pl. 6; Cloak Catalogue, 1969.

280
Baccarat, ca. 1850. Butterfly: amethyst filigree body, black head and antennae; 2 turquoise eyes; upper wings with red/blue/white arrow cane centers; lower wings with red/green/blue bull's eye centers—the canes flat-tened and lined with opaque white. Peripheral circle of alternating white/red/yellow center florets and white/blue/green arrow canes. Polished concave colorless base cut with 24-point star; basal ring.
D: 3⅛" (7.9 cm.) Bergstrom Bequest, 1958.
EHB acquisition: February, 1940.

Pl. XIII, Bergstrom book, 1940 and later editions.
No. 299, Pl. 4; Cloak Catalogue, 1969.

383
Baccarat, 1848-55. Butterfly: translucent amethyst en-cased filigree body, black head, 2 antennae, 2 turquoise eyes, upper wings of varicolored canes with white/red centers, lower wings blue/green/red whorl center canes (lined with opaque white) above white flower (6 furrowed petals beneath 6 rust petals), 7 leaves, stem. Polished flat colorless base cut with 16-point star.
D: 2¼" (5.7 cm.) Bergstrom Bequest, 1958.
EHB acquisition: May, 1941.
No. 403, Pl. 6; Cloak Catalogue, 1969.

515
Baccarat, 1845-55. Butterfly: amethyst filigree body, black head, 2 blue eyes, 2 black antennae, upper wings of mar-bled varicolored canes, lower wings of blue/green/red canes (lined with opaque white), above white clematis-type flower (12 furrowed pointed petals); 8 leaves and stem; white bud, sepals. 12 miter cuts alternate with 12 petal cuts underside of polished concave colorless base.
D: 3³⁄₁₆" (8.1 cm.) Bergstrom Bequest, 1958.
EHB acquisition: Unrecorded.
No. 549, Pl. 4; Cloak Catalogue, 1969.

859
Clichy, 1845-55. Extremely rare. Clichy butterfly: 3-dimen-sional, shaded amber/yellow body, 2 black/blue eyes, 2 black antennae, 6 black legs; upper wings: pink-lined white tubular canes, yellow centers; lower wings: pink/green Clichy rose canes. Polished concave colorless base.
D: 2⅝" (6.7 cm.)
Museum Purchase, 1973.
Ref.: No. 153, *The Corning Museum of Glass Exhibition Catalogue,* 1978.

1124
Baccarat, 1848-55. Butterfly: amethyst filigree body, black head, 2 turquoise eyes, 2 blue antennae; blue/white/green/salmon-red millefiori cane wings. Butterfly above 1 white clematis (6 over 6 furrowed petals); and 1 6-petal white clematis; 8 leaves, stems. Polished con-cave colorless base cut with 24-point star; wide basal ring.
D: 2¹³⁄₁₆" (7.2 cm.)
Gift of Mrs. Florence Gosselin Marsh in memory of her husband, Raymond Clark Marsh, 1976.

1156
Origin unknown. Greyish glass encases pink/white cane-winged butterfly (translucent cobalt blue body, legs and antennae; 2 orange eyes) above yellow, double-petaled flower. 6 leaves, stem. Irregular white filigree coil at periphery surrounds twisted white filigree rods laid parallel to form cushion above smooth flat colorless base.
D: 3⅛" (8.0 cm.)
Gift of Mrs. Florence Gosselin Marsh in memory of her husband, Raymond Clark Marsh, 1976.

1164
Origin unknown. Butterfly with pink/blue cane wings lined with white, green body, orange eyes, blue antennae and two back legs; white clematis with 10 leaves. Polished concave colorless base.
D: 2¹¹⁄₃₂" (6.0 cm.)
Gift of Mrs. Florence Gosselin Marsh in memory of her husband, Raymond Clark Marsh, 1976.

215

244

94

396

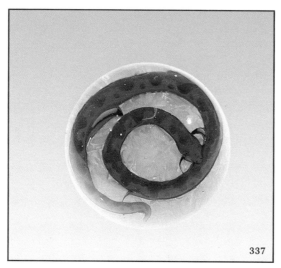

337

108

302

1282

1177

1784

1784

1314

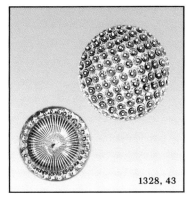

1328, 43

232

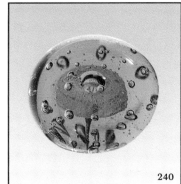

240

239

29

1313

94
Baccarat, 1848-55. Coiled opaque green snake, brown marking (linked ovals interspersed with dots) along its spine; scrambled white filigree ground; polished concave colorless base; basal ring.
D: 3¹/₁₆″ (7.8 cm.)
Bergstrom Bequest, 1958.
EHB acquisition: November, 1937.
No. 99, Pl. 21; Cloak Catalogue, 1969.
Ref.: No. 77, *The Corning Museum of Glass Exhibition Catalogue,* 1978.

108
Saint Louis, 1848-55. Slender coiled pale green snake, darker green spots and line from head to tail; red eyes and nostrils; white muslin ground extends to concave polished colorless base. Wide top punty, geometric faceting on curve.
D: 3″ (7.6 cm.)
Bergstrom Bequest, 1958.
EHB acquisition: February, 1938.
No. 115, Pl. 23; Cloak Catalogue, 1969.

215
Attributed to French, Pantin, ca. 1878. Magnum. High-dome. Coiled faceted green overlay/pastel yellow lizard; striped yellow/black bumblebee, bubbly colorless wings; upright cupped white flower, yellow stamens; 10 dark green leaves; multiple dewdrop bubbles. Green "grass" and "sandy" ground on white opaline. Polished concave colorless base; basal ring. (White flower resembles characteristics of No. 127.)
D: 4⅛″ (10.5 cm.)
Bergstrom Bequest, 1958.
EHB acquisition: May, 1939.
Illus. 6, Bergstrom book, 1940; later editions.
No. 230, Pl. 21; Cloak Catalogue, 1969.
Ref.: No. 280, *The Corning Museum of Glass Exhibition Catalogue,* 1978.
PCA Bulletin, 1981; pp. 2-11.

244
French, attributed to Monot, Père et Fils, et Stumpf, Pantin, ca. 1878. High-dome. Red-eyed black Mesazoic creature of dinosaur type, applied yellow spots; 3 plants: a white "morning glory" type flower with 4 upright black stamens, turned-down pointed and shaded green leaves; 1 cup-shaped red-petal flower (no sepals), yellow stamens, 9 upright and several mature shaded green leaves; 1 white-edged tiny tulip-like pink flower, yellow stamens, 4 upright and several turned-down shaded green leaves. Ground: sand-like particles on translucent emerald green glass and white opaline. Polished concave colorless base; basal ring.
D: 4⅛″ (10.5 cm.)
Bergstrom Bequest, 1958.
EHB acquisition: September, 1939.
No. 261, Pl. 7; Cloak Catalogue, 1969.

337
Baccarat, ca. 1850. Lampwork opaque red snake (green markings along spine: linked ovals interspersed with dots) coiled on scrambled white filigree ground. Polished concave colorless base; basal ring.
D: 3¹/₁₆″ (7.8 cm.)
Bergstrom Bequest, 1958.
EHB acquisition: August, 1940.
Pl. VI, Bergstrom book, 1940; later editions.
No. 357, Pl. 21; Cloak Catalogue, 1969.

396
Attributed to Saint Louis, 1848-55. Opaque emerald green snake, red eyes and nostrils, coiled on red/white jasper ground. Wide, shallow top punty. Beveled-edge, linked diamond faceting from punty edge to basal periphery. Polished concave colorless base.
D: 2¹⁵/₁₆″ (7.4 cm.)
Bergstrom Bequest, 1958.
EHB acquisition: May, 1941.
No. 416, Pl. 21; Cloak Catalogue, 1969.

29
Attributed to Castleford, Yorkshire, mid-late 19th century. Ovoid-shaped green bottle glass encases translucent upright floral motif: 2-layered 5-petal flowers (bubble center), stems drawn to base of "flower pot." Smooth flat base; basal ring.
H: 3⅞" (9.9 cm.); D: 3" (7.6 cm.)
Bergstrom Bequest, 1958.
EHB acquisition: June, 1937.
Illus. 46, Bergstrom book, 1940; Illus. 44, later editions.
No. 30, Pl. 33; Cloak Catalogue, 1969.

43
Origin unknown, possibly French, 19th century. Encased mold-blown hollow colorless glass; allover closely spaced circular indentations become radial strands ending at basal center. Trapped air creates silvery appearance. Smooth concave colorless base.
D: 3⅝" (9.2 cm.)
Bergstrom Bequest, 1958.
EHB acquisition: June, 1937.
No. 43, Pl. 49; Cloak Catalogue, 1969.

232
Origin unknown, possibly English, Stourbridge area; late 19th century. Mold-blown colorless glass with intaglio portrayal of royal British seal (lion, unicorn and House of Windsor motto: "Dieu et Mon Droit") encases hollow blown cobalt blue sphere; peripheral ribbed pattern, inside curve, drawn to basal center; trace of pontil mark.
D: 3⅛" (8.0 cm.)
Bergstrom Bequest, 1958.
EHB acquisition: July, 1939.
No. 248, Pl. 34; Cloak Catalogue, 1969.
Ref.: Hollister, Paul: *The Encyclopedia of Glass Paperweights,* 1969; Fig. 185, pp. 182-183.

239
Castleford, or Wakefield, Yorkshire, 2nd half 19th century. Ovoid translucent green bottle glass encases silver foil floral motif: near crown, a 12-petal flower, narrow stem extends downward to translucent "vase" with 4 small silver foil flowers above its scalloped rim. Flat base, pontil mark; basal ring.
H: 4⅛" (10.5 cm.); D: 2¼" (5.7 cm.)
Bergstrom Bequest, 1958.
EHB acquisition: September, 1939.
No. 255, Pl. 33; Cloak Catalogue, 1969.
Ref.: Hollister, Paul: *The Encyclopedia of Glass Paperweights,* 1969; pp. 177-180.

240
Castleford, Yorkshire, 2nd half 19th century. Heavy, spherical transparent dark green bottle glass encases large, elongated center bubble below translucent umbrella-shaped motif covered with bubbles; spaced bubbles scattered in crown and sides of base. Circular ridge of final glass gather appears on pontil-marked flat base.
D: 4¼" (10.8 cm.)
Bergstrom Bequest, 1958.
EHB acquisition: September, 1939.
No. 256, Pl. 33; Cloak Catalogue, 1969.

302
Saint Louis, last half 19th century. Coiled cobalt blue snake, decorated with gilt, applied to frosted white opaline sphere; gilt tongue on sphere. Smooth flat base.
D: 3⅛" (7.9 cm.)
Bergstrom Bequest, 1958.
EHB acquisition: April, 1940.
Illus. 8, Bergstrom book, 1940; later editions.
No. 322, Pl. 21; Cloak Catalogue, 1969.

1177
Baccarat, 1845-55. Coiled snake with light green spots on pale green body; 2 red eyes and nostrils; green, tan, and mica ground. Polished concave colorless base; basal ring.
D: 3¼" (8.2 cm.)
Gift of Mrs. Florence Gosselin Marsh in memory of her husband, Raymond Clark Marsh, 1976.
Ref.: McCawley, Patricia K.: *Antique Glass Paperweights from France,* 1968; No. 90.

1282
Baccarat, 1848-55. Coiled rust-red and brown-spotted green snake (2 black/white eyes); green glass/mica ground. Polished concave colorless base; basal ring. Slight trace of pontil mark.
D: 2¹³⁄₁₆" (7.4 cm.)
Gift of Mrs. Florence Gosselin Marsh in memory of her husband, Raymond Clark Marsh, 1977.

1313
English, probably Castleford, late 19th century. Tall, ovoid green bottle glass; multiple elongated bubbles; basal concavity; pontil mark.
H: 6¼" (15.9 cm.); D: 2⁷⁄₃₂" (7.3 cm.)
Gift of Robert S. Sage and Jeanne Sage Groves in memory of their parents, Charles H. and Lyda P. Sage, 1978.

1314
English, possibly Castleford, late 19th century. High-domed dark green bottle glass sphere; translucent "flower-pot" motif. Concave base; pontil mark.
D: 3⁵⁄₃₂" (8.1 cm.)
Gift of Robert S. Sage and Jeanne Sage Groves in memory of their parents, Charles H. and Lyda P. Sage, 1978.

1328
Origin unknown, possibly English, late 19th century. Mold-blown "quilted" hollow cushion. Polished flat colorless base; basal ring.
D: 2²⁵⁄₃₂" (7.1 cm.)
Gift of Paul Hollister, 1978.

1784
J. Kilner & Sons, Wakefield, Yorkshire, England, 1865-76. Green bottle glass encases 3 foil-like "flowers," bubble centers; stems drawn into flower pot. Trail of blue near dome. Rough pontil mark visible in base through attached glass wafer impressed in relief: "J. Kilner Maker Wakefield."
D: 3⁷⁄₃₂" (8.2 cm.)
Given in memory of Cedric Arthur Kilner by his sons: Donald D. Kilner and Kenneth A. Kilner, great, great grandsons of the factory founder, John Kilner, 1987.

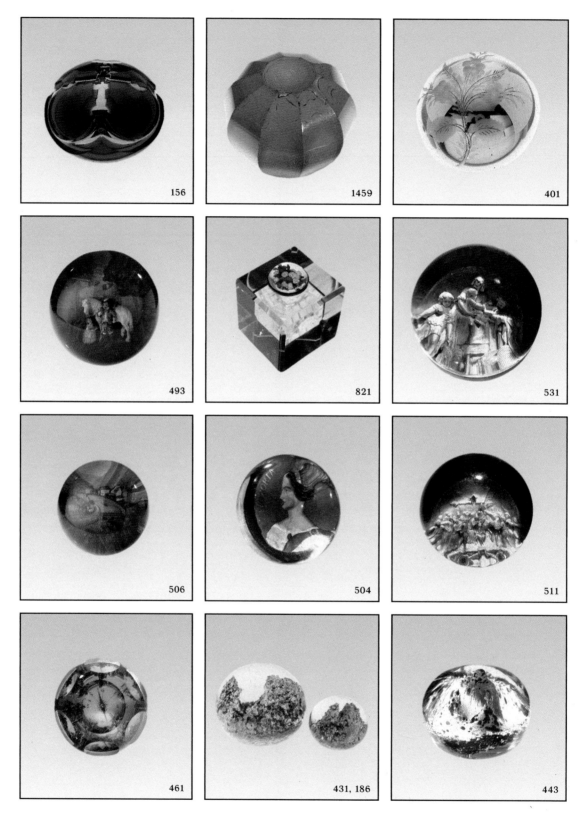

156

1459

401

493

821

531

506

504

511

461

431, 186

443

535

473

200

499

501

62

156
James Powell & Sons, London, England, 1850-60. Hollow-blown, ruby-cased colorless glass, lined with silver; cut with central quatrefoil, semi-circles between 4 lobes. Underside of base encloses metal disk imprinted with "Patent Hale Thomson's London."
D: 2¹³⁄₁₆″ (7.2 cm.)
Bergstrom Bequest, 1958.
EHB acquisition: October, 1938.
No. 165, Pl. 34; Cloak Catalogue, 1969.
Ref.: Wakefield, Hugh: *Nineteenth Century British Glass,* 1961, p. 34; 1982, p. 74.

186
Baccarat, ca. 1900. Miniature. Green glass and sand-like silica drawn up into 2 peaks. Polished slightly concave colorless base; basal ring.
D: 1¹³⁄₁₆″ (4.7 cm.)
Bergstrom Bequest, 1958.
EHB acquisition: December, 1938.
No. 199, Pl. 2; Cloak Catalogue, 1969.

401
New England Glass Co., E. Cambridge, MA, ca. 1855. Blown mercury ("silvered") glass engraved with floral spray on dome. Smooth slightly concave base reveals ½-inch hole beneath encasing glass; polished pontil area.
D: 3³⁄₁₆″ (8.1 cm.)
Bergstrom Bequest, 1958.
EHB acquisition: August, 1941.
No. 421, Pl. 44; Cloak Catalogue, 1969.

431
Attributed to Baccarat, 1900-1916. "Sand Dunes" (also referred to as "Rock") motif: sand-like glass mottled with translucent green drawn up in 3 peaks. Polished slightly concave colorless base; basal ring.
D: 2¹⁵⁄₁₆″ (7.4 cm.)
Bergstrom Bequest, 1958.
EHB acquisition: October, 1941.
No. 458, Pl. 7; Cloak Catalogue, 1969.

443
Origin unknown, possibly Pantin, ca. 1878. "Seascape" motif. Emerald green, white opaline, sand-like ground drawn up into 3 peaks. Sand moves when weight is tipped. Polished basal concavity; wide basal ring.
D: 3³⁄₁₆″ (8.1 cm.)
Bergstrom Bequest, 1958.
EHB acquisition: December, 1941.
No. 472, Pl. 4; Cloak Catalogue, 1969.

461
Origin unknown, possibly English, 19th century. Solid colorless glass dome, top punty, 6 horizontal oval facets on curve, set over functioning compass encircled by wreath of metallic green leaves and 2 bunches of tiny pink glass grapes. Circular marble base.
D: 3⅛″ (7.9 cm.)
Bergstrom Bequest, 1958.
EHB acquisition: March, 1942.
No. 489, Pl. 58; Cloak Catalogue, 1969.

493
Origin unknown, ca. mid-19th century. Pinchbeck type. Thick convex lens-like glass crown; pewter base. Genre scene; gold alloy in relief; hand-painted man and child, each holding goblet; white horse at watering trough; background of trees, house and mountain.
D: 3¼″ (8.3 cm.)
Bergstrom Bequest, 1958.
EHB acquisition: Unrecorded.
No. 523, Pl. 57; Cloak Catalogue, 1969.
Ref.: *American Collector,* November, 1945; pp. 6-8.

504
Origin unknown, mid-19th century. Pinchbeck type; pewter base. Thick, lens-like convex colorless glass crown covers hand-painted relief portrait (slightly to dexter) of Queen Victoria wearing royal crown; sculpted in French tripoli; scarlet ceramic ground; "Victoria" in Pinchbeck gold letters left of portrait.
D: 3¼″ (8.3 cm.)
Bergstrom Bequest, 1958.
EHB acquisition: Unrecorded.
Illus. 82, Bergstrom book, 1948.
No. 536, Pl. 57; Cloak Catalogue, 1969.

506
Origin unknown, mid-19th century. Pinchbeck type; pewter base. Thick, lens-type colorless glass dome covers gold alloy; painted scene, in relief, portrays river, boat, bridge and distant mountains.
D: 2¾″ (7.0 cm.)
Bergstrom Bequest, 1958.
EHB acquisition: Unrecorded.
No. 538, Pl. 57; Cloak Catalogue, 1969.

511
Origin unknown, mid-19th century. Pinchbeck weight; velvet-covered pewter base. Thick convex lens-type colorless glass dome. Gold alloy portrays in relief a group of peasants and dog before cottages and trees; symbolic farmer's tools and ox-head below.
D: 2¾″ (7.0 cm.)
Bergstrom Bequest, 1958.
EHB acquisition: Unrecorded.
Illus. 83, Bergstrom book, 1948.
No. 545, Pl. 57; Cloak Catalogue, 1969.

531
Origin unknown, mid-19th century. Pinchbeck type; collared circular marble base. Gold alloy, in relief, portrays: mother, 3 children, 2 hens, and basket. Thick, convex lens-type dome.
D: 2¹⁵⁄₁₆″ (7.4 cm.)
Bergstrom Bequest, 1958.
EHB acquisition: Unrecorded.
No. 567, Pl. 57; Cloak Catalogue, 1969.

821
Boston & Sandwich Glass Co., Sandwich, MA, 1860-88. Beveled colorless cube. Top center: encased miniature "composition" bouquet of red/pink/white, and yellow roses, green leaves, stems "tied" with white ribbon. Metal mount; embedded ceramic shank.
D: 1¾″ (4.5 cm.) each side.
Gift of George Ingham, 1970.
Ref.: Lee, Ruth Webb: *Sandwich Glass Handbook,* 1947; Pl. 24.

1459
Attributed to Friedrich Egermann Workshop, Haida, near Blottendorf, Bohemia, ca. 1830. Globular green stained with yellow-ochre and dark blue; red glass core; circular top facet, 10 vertical side panels; polished concave base; basal ring.
D: 3⅛″ (7.9 cm.)
Museum Purchase, 1982.

* * *

200
Attributed to Baccarat, 1845-55. Encased pink/white overlay disk portrays cameo-carved trotting horse; peripheral circle of blue/white/green arrow canes alternated with white star/green center canes. Top, 6 side punties; polished flat colorless base. Note: These disks, or plaques, were formerly thought to be enameled.
D: 3¼″ (8.3 cm.)
Bergstrom Bequest, 1958.
EHB acquisition: February, 1939.
Illus. 24, Bergstrom book, 1940.
No. 215, Pl. 4; Cloak Catalogue, 1969.

473
Baccarat, 1845-55. Cameo-carved, blue laid over opaque white circular glass plaque portrays shaded cobalt blue horse galloping over turf. Dark blue, narrow-banded plaque edge encircled by alternating white and dark red millefiori canes. Top, 6 side punties. Polished flat colorless base; basal ring.
D: 3⅜″ (8.5 cm.)
Bergstrom Bequest, 1958.
EHB acquisition: September, 1942.
No. 503, Pl. 2; Cloak Catalogue, 1969.
Ref.: Jokelson, Paul: *One Hundred of the Most Important Paperweights,* 1966; Pl. 19.
McCawley, Patricia K.: *Antique Glass Paperweights from France,* 1968; No. 88.
No. 37, *The Corning Museum of Glass Exhibition Catalogue,* 1978.

499
Origin unknown, possibly late 19th century. Hollow crown (top punty, 6 smaller punties on upper curve) encloses blown opaque white swan, pink eyes, beak, and festooned wings. Applied colorless glass base lined with mica-flecked translucent green glass. (For similar construction, see No. 501.)
D: 3⅛″ (7.9 cm.)
Bergstrom Bequest, 1958.
EHB acquisition: November, 1943.
No. 531, Pl. 58; Cloak Catalogue, 1969.
Ref.: Jokelson, Paul: *One Hundred of the Most Important Paperweights,* 1966; Pl. 2.
Hollister, Paul: *Encyclopedia of Glass Paperweights,* 1969; pp. 196-197.

501
Origin unknown, possibly late 19th century. Hollow crown (top and 6 side punties) encloses milk glass latticework basket containing blue/white roses surrounded by red roses. Applied colorless base flashed with translucent green on top; diamond-cut edge.
D: 3⁵⁄₁₆″ (8.4 cm.)
Bergstrom Bequest, 1958.
EHB acquisition: November, 1943.
No. 533, Pl. 58; Cloak Catalogue, 1969.
Ref.: Hollister, Paul: *Encyclopedia of Glass Paperweights,* 1969; pp. 196-197.

535
Origin unknown, possibly Baccarat, late 19th century. "Ducks in a Pond." Thick, hollow colorless glass dome; top punty, 5 on curve. 3 opaque pale yellow ducks, striped with brown/red/green; brown bills; colorless "pond" base encircled by green/white jasper. Dome appears to be fused to flanged flat base cut with 32-point star.
D: 3⅛″ (7.9 cm.)
Bergstrom Bequest, 1958.
EHB acquisition: Unrecorded.
Illus. 16, Bergstrom book, 1940; Illus. 12, later editions.
No. 571, Pl. 8; Cloak Catalogue, 1969.
Ref.: McCawley, Patricia K.: *Antique Glass Paperweights from France,* 1968; No. 96.

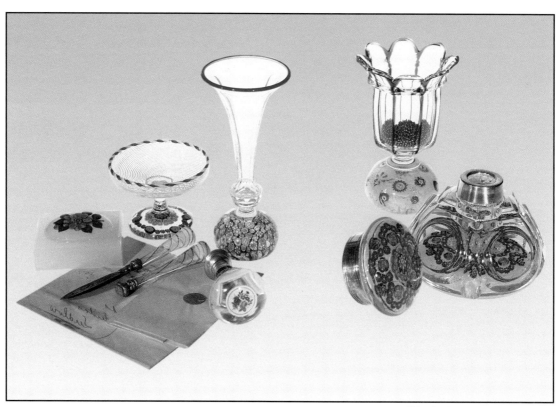

183, 191, 576, 577, 575, 214, 348

1106, 1107

1106, 1107

214, 192

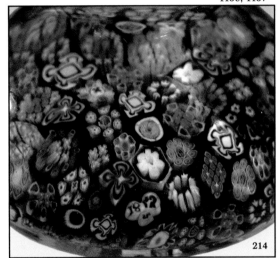

214

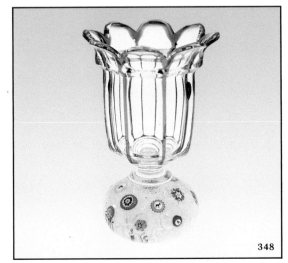

348

348

Ink Bottle, stoppered.
Clichy, 1845-55.
Lent from the collection of Mrs. Arthur Rubloff.

183
Clichy, 1848-55. Rectangular verre opaline, top centered by oval colorless glass medallion encasing flat lampwork motif: single pink flower, round pincered petals, a tiny rose with green sepals in center; pink bud, green stem, 7 green leaves. Petals and leaves show "waffle" pattern of tiny bubbles.
Size: 2⅝ x 2⅜" (6.6 x 6.1 cm.)
Bergstrom Bequest, 1958.
EHB acquisition: January, 1939.
No. 196, Pl. 15; Cloak Catalogue, 1969.

191
Wafer Tray.
Clichy, 1845-55. Swirled white filigree bowl, red/white ribbon twist rim, colorless stem; flat circular foot encases 3 concentric circles of millefiori canes (6 pink/green Clichy roses); large central green cane, yellow stamen center.
Bowl D: 3¼" (8.3 cm.); Foot: 2¹⁄₁₆" (5.2 cm.)
Bergstrom Bequest, 1958.
EHB acquisition: February, 1939.
P. 41, Bergstrom book, 1940; p. 42, later editions.
No. 204, Pl. 17; Cloak Catalogue, 1969.

214
Vase.
Saint Louis, dated 1845. Trumpet-shaped, vase cut with 10 vertical flutes above diamond-cut small spherical knop; cobalt blue/opaque white rim edge. Applied paperweight base encases predominantly pink and blue close millefiori canes, 1 cane with "SL 1845" in reverse. Polished slightly concave colorless base. An early example of Saint Louis millefiori decoration.
H: 5¾" (14.7 cm.); D: 2¹⁄₁₆" (5.3 cm.) base.
Bergstrom Bequest, 1958.
EHB acquisition: May, 1939.
P. 41, Bergstrom book, 1940; p. 42, later editions.
No. 229, Pl. 25; Cloak Catalogue, 1969.

348
Vase.
Baccarat, dated 1848. Green-flashed colorless glass bowl cut to 8 green-edged panels with flared scalloped rim. Circular, step-cut colorless bowl base, short collared stem. Paperweight base: spaced millefiori canes; arrow canes, goat, dog, rooster, pair of lovebirds, and pelican silhouettes; date "B 1848." Scrambled white filigree ground; polished flat colorless base.
H: 5⅛" (13.1 cm.); D: 2½" (6.3 cm.)
Bergstrom Bequest, 1958.
EHB acquisition: October, 1940.
No. 367, Pl. 8; Cloak Catalogue, 1969.

575
Glass Seal.
Baccarat, early to mid-19th century. Strawberry-cut knob end encloses sulphide disk painted with floral spray and leaves. 6-sided stem, circular groove cuts below faceted knop. In seal end is a portrait of French author, Vicomte François René de Châteaubriand (1768-1848), incised in onyx mounted in brass.
L: 2¾" (7.0 cm.)
Bergstrom Bequest, 1958.
EHB acquisition: Unrecorded.
No. 615, Pl. 23; Cloak Catalogue, 1969.
Ref.: Jokelson, Paul: Sulphides: The Art of Cameo Incrustation, 1968; Fig. XXV.

576
Letter Opener.
Origin unknown, probably French, 19th century. Handle encloses spiraled fine white and red filigree. Gilt decoration on steel blade; brass mount.
L: 5⅛" (13.1 cm.)
Bergstrom Bequest, 1958.
EHB acquisition: Unrecorded.
No. 616, Pl. 38; Cloak Catalogue, 1969.

577
Sealing Tool.
Origin unknown, probably French, 19th century. Handle encloses spiraled fine white and red filigree. Brass mounting on seal end is similar to that on 576.
L: 3⁵⁄₁₆" (8.4 cm.)
Bergstrom Bequest, 1958.
EHB acquisition: Unrecorded.
No. 616, Pl. 38; Cloak Catalogue, 1969.

192

Hand Cooler.

Saint Louis, 1845-55. Ovoid encases close millefiori canes collected in one gather; unusual example.

L: 2⅞″ (7.3 cm.); D: 2³⁄₁₆″ (5.5 cm.)

Bergstrom Bequest, 1958.

EHB acquisition: February, 1939.

Illus. 22, Bergstrom book, 1940; later editions.

No. 205, Pl. 27; Cloak Catalogue, 1969.

Ref.: No. 163, *The Corning Museum of Glass Exhibition Catalogue,* 1978.

214

Vase.

Saint Louis, dated 1845. Trumpet-shaped vase cut with 10 vertical flutes above diamond-cut small spherical knop; cobalt blue/opaque white rim edge. Applied paperweight base encases predominantly pink and blue close millefiori canes, 1 cane with "SL 1845" in reverse. Polished concave colorless base. An early example of Saint Louis millefiori decoration.

H: 5¾″ (14.7 cm.); D: 2¹⁄₁₆″ (5.3 cm.) base.

Bergstrom Bequest, 1958.

EHB acquisition: May, 1939.

P. 41, Bergstrom book, 1940; p. 42, later editions.

No. 229, Pl. 25; Cloak Catalogue, 1969.

348

Vase.

Baccarat, dated 1848. Green-flashed colorless glass bowl cut to 8 green-edged panels with flared scalloped rim. Circular, step-cut colorless bowl base, short collared stem. Paperweight base: spaced millefiori canes; arrow. Canes; goat, dog, rooster, pair of lovebirds, and pelican silhouettes; date "B 1848." Scrambled white filigree ground; polished flat colorless base.

H: 5⅛″ (13.1 cm.); D: 2½″ (6.3 cm.)

Bergstrom Bequest, 1958.

EHB acquisition: October, 1940.

No. 367, Pl. 8; Cloak Catalogue, 1969.

1106, 1107

Vase (pair).

Clichy, 1845-50. Probably made to order as mantel ornaments. Blown, scrambled millefiori, spherical body, tall flared neck (shape similar to that of certain Chinese porcelain vases). Typical Clichy canes include many roses of different sizes and one fully signed "CLICHY" cane. Gold ormolu scrolled leaf footed base. (Other recorded examples slightly different in shape.)

H: 11½″ (29.3 cm.); Overall: 13½″

Museum Purchase, 1975.

Ref.: *PCA Bulletin,* 1977, p. 32.

274, 212, 144, 490, 569, 207

380

490

316

1823

110

1302

360, 361

307

25

144
Saint Louis, dated 1848. Millefiori mushroom motif: 6 concentric circles of white/blue/green canes. Circle of white stardust canes, green/white whorl centers. Outer circle, drawn down to point at base, forms tuft; "SL 1848" in black cane at periphery. Torsade of twisted flat opaque white rods coiled with salmon-pink. Polished colorless base etched with No. 26 and cut with small 16-point star; basal ring.
D: 3 1/16" (7.8 cm.)
Bergstrom Bequest, 1958.
EHB acquisition: October, 1938.
No. 153, Pl. 27; Cloak Catalogue, 1969.
Ref.: McCawley, Patricia K.: *Antique Glass Paperweights from France,* 1968; 79(a).
PCA Bulletin, 1969; Fig. 5, p. 15.

207
Bowl, covered.
Attributed to Saint Louis, 1848-55. Honeycomb-faceted glass bowl decorated with overall gilt vermiculation; gilt-banded rim and base. Obverse: (in relief) oval translucent white medallion painted in pastel colors with 2 birds on branches. Polished colorless base cut with 32-point star. Matching cover with spherical glass finial encasing upright bouquet: 3 flowers (red, white and blue), 2 florets; green leaves.
H: 5 5/8" (14.3 cm.); D: 4 1/2" (11.5 cm.)
Bergstrom Bequest, 1958.
EHB acquisition: February, 1939.
Illus. 10, p. 41, Bergstrom book, 1940; p. 42, later editions.
No. 222, Pl. 25; Cloak Catalogue, 1969.

212
Vase.
Saint Louis, 1845-55. Vase with concentric millefiori paperweight base. Flared conical bowl encases 2" band of double-swirl white filigree, rim and base bordered by a salmon-pink/white ribbon twist. Waisted and faceted 6-sided colorless stem. In base: 7 concentric circles of millefiori canes (predominantly blue, green, and white) surround large serrated red central cane. Peripheral circle of salmon-pink/white canes drawn to center of polished slightly concave colorless base; basal ring.
H: 6 5/8" (16.9 cm.); D: 4 1/4" (5.1 cm.) bowl.
Bergstrom Bequest, 1958.
EHB acquisition: May, 1939.
P. 41, Bergstrom book, 1940; p. 42, later editions.
No. 227, Pl. 25; Cloak Catalogue, 1969.

274
Vase.
Saint Louis, 1840-50. Tapered, bulbous colorless form; encases fine white filigree alternating with opaque white flattened rods spiraled from base to flared scalloped rim edge flanged base encircled by encased coral-pink and white filigree ribbon twist.
H: 11 1/2" (29.2 cm.)
Bergstrom Bequest, 1958.
EHB acquisition: Unrecorded.
No. 293, Pl. 22; Cloak Catalogue, 1969.

490
Scent Bottle, stoppered.
Saint Louis, 1845-50. Ovoid spiraled white filigree glass body, flared rim edged in cobalt blue; colorless glass collar joins bottle to macedoine paperweight base encasing a variety of compound canes, ribbon and white filigree twists. Polished concave colorless base; basal ring. Blown, ball-shaped, spiraled white filigree stopper.
H: 5 1/2" (13.9 cm.); D: 2" (5.1 cm.) base.
Stopper D: 1" (2.6 cm.); L: 1 3/4" (4.5 cm.)
Bergstrom Bequest, 1958.
EHB acquisition: April, 1943.
No. 520, Pl. 26; Cloak Catalogue, 1969.

569
Shot Glass.
Saint Louis, 1845-50. Horizontally ribbed colorless glass encases alternating canes: cobalt blue lined with opaque white and white filigree spiraled from rounded base to rim. Double collar. Paperweight base encases central blue/white millefiori cane surrounded by 5 spaced salmon/white canes and peripheral circle of yellow/white canes alternating with dark blue/white/red canes. Polished concave colorless base; basal ring.
H: 3 7/16" (8.7 cm.); D: 1 3/4" (7.0 cm.) base.
Bergstrom Bequest, 1958.
EHB acquisition: Unrecorded.
No. 611, Pl. 26; Cloak Catalogue, 1969.

25
Mantel Ornament.
Origin unknown, possibly Whitall, Tatum & Co., Millville, NJ, late 19th-early 20th century. Tall, slightly tapered form. Mottled varicolored spatter glass and goldstone drawn upward from base form "devil's fire" peaks within an inch of top. Applied colorless standard, knopped stem, flat circular foot.
H: 10%₁₆" (26.8 cm.)
Bergstrom Bequest, 1958.
EHB acquisition: April, 1937.
No. 26, Pl. 59; Cloak Catalogue, 1969.
Ref.: Pepper, Adeline: *The Glass Gaffers of New Jersey,* 1971; p. 260.

110
Vase.
Saint Louis, 1845-55. Bell shape, colorless glass bowl, cobalt blue/white flat filigree twist applied to rim; upper half engraved with flowers and leaves; 11-sided lower half cut with circular grooves. Scrambled millefiori canes, ribbon and filigree rods in paperweight base; polished concave underside; basal ring.
H: 5¾" (14.6 cm.); D: 2¾" (7.0 cm.) base.
Bergstrom Bequest, 1958.
EHB acquisition: April, 1938.
P. 41, Bergstrom book, 1940; p. 42, later editions.
No. 118, Pl. 25; Cloak Catalogue, 1969.

307
Mantel Ornament or Paperweight.
Origin unknown, 19th century. Ovoid. Multiple colored glass nodules from base to top of crown. Collared footed base, pontil mark.
H: 4¼" (10.8 cm.); D: 2⅝" (6.6 cm.)
Bergstrom Bequest, 1958.
EHB acquisition: May, 1940.
No. 327, Pl. 61; Cloak Catalogue, 1969.

316
Vase.
Bohemian, dated 1848, possibly Josephinenhutte, Schreiberhau, Silesia. Small, cylindrical, opaque white overlay, circular facets; colorless glass collar; paperweight base. Spaced multicolor millefiori canes include date "J 1848," 2 "Clichy-type" pink roses (one within circle of white/red star canes), and a colored moth silhouette; upset red/white, blue/white, and white filigree ground. Polished slightly concave colorless base; wide basal ring. Note: original flared rim of this vase appears to have been cut down.
H: 4" (10.2 cm.); D: 2½" (6.3 cm.) base.
Bergstrom Bequest, 1958.
EHB acquisition: May, 1940.
No. 337, Pl. 38; Cloak Catalogue, 1969.
Ref.: Hollister, Paul: *Encyclopedia of Glass Paperweights,* 1969/1970; Fig. 8, p. 30.
Spiegl, Walter: *Paperweights*, 1987; p. 119.

360, 361
Mantel Ornament (pair).
Attributed to Clichy, mid-19th century. Tall, tapered; vertical string of multicolored glass nodules from base to top. Collared, circular footed colorless base; trace of pontil mark in concavity.
H: 14½" (36.8 cm.)
Bergstrom Bequest, 1958.
EHB acquisition: December, 1940.
No. 378, Pl. 9; Cloak Catalogue, 1969.

380
Baccarat, 1848-55. Triple tier form. Top tier: white wheat-flower, blue dots, cobalt blue/white star center cane; red and blue buds; green leaves. Middle tier: 3 concentric circles of varicolored canes surround serrated red/white cane. Bottom tier: spaced millefiori canes include arrow and star; dog, goat, deer, pelican, cockerel, and devil silhouettes; scrambled white filigree ground. 5 small punties on curve; polished concave colorless base.
H: 3¹⁄₁₆" (7.8 cm.); D: 2½" (6.3 cm.) base.
Bergstrom Bequest, 1958.
EHB acquisition: May, 1941.
No. 400, Pl. 8; Cloak Catalogue, 1969.

490
See Pl. 65.

1302
Wafer Tray.
Saint Louis, 1845-55. Blue-edged ruffled colorless glass bowl. Scrambled millefiori paperweight base. Polished flat colorless underside; basal ring.
H: 3" (7.6 cm.); D: 3⅜" (8.6 cm.) rim; D: 2⅝" (6.6 cm.) base.
Gift of Robert S. Sage and Jeanne Sage Groves in memory of their parents, Charles H. and Lyda P. Sage, 1978.

1823
Vase.
Saint Louis, dated 1973. Thistle shape, colorless glass bowl encases white filigree swirled from base to flared rim; applied pink/white filigree twist edge. Colorless double mereses between bowl and applied paperweight base: concentric millefiori canes include "SL 1973." Polished colorless basal concavity; basal ring.
H: 5⅛" (13.1 cm.); D: 3⁷⁄₃₂" (8.3 cm.) rim; D: 2¹⁵⁄₃₂" (6.3 cm.) base.
Gift of Mrs. Virginia Bensley Trowbridge, 1987.

393, 1158, 394, 530, 567, 287

489

581, 582

254

412

305

1402

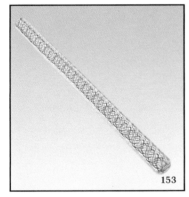

153

330

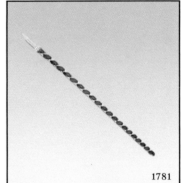

1781

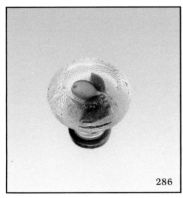

286

354, 355

266, 265

287
Scent Bottle, stoppered.
Saint Louis, 1840-50. Colorless glass bottle encloses opaque white filigree swirled from base to top of tall tapered neck, becoming finer toward top. Applied opaque white/red/blue ribbon twist encircles shoulder and rim. Finely swirled white latticinio drawn from shank top to tip of steeple stopper finial; opaque white/red/blue ribbon twist applied to rim edge.
H: 7½" (13.3 cm.)
Stopper D: 1¹⁵⁄₃₂" (3.8 cm.); L: 3½" (8.9 cm.)
Bergstrom Bequest, 1958.
EHB acquisition: March, 1940.
P. 41, Bergstrom book, 1940; p. 42, later editions.
No. 307, Pl. 26; Cloak Catalogue, 1969.

393
Vase.
Saint Louis, 1845-55. Allover honeycomb facets enlarge toward flared rim; applied white filigree/red coil edge. 5-sided waisted stem joins conical bowl to paperweight base. Small upright floral bouquet: central white flower, 2 dark blue and 2 red flowers, 4 florets, surrounded by 10 pastel green leaves. Fine white filigree/red torsade without core (matching rim); air rings. Polished concave colorless base.
H: 13" (32.9 cm.); D: 4⅛" (10.5 cm.) base.
Bergstrom Bequest, 1958.
EHB acquisition: May, 1941.
No. 413, Pl. 22; Cloak Catalogue, 1969.

394
Saint Louis, 1848-55. Magnum. Upright bouquet: central white flower, 2 dark blue and 2 salmon-pink flowers, 4 millefiori canes surrounded by 10 pastel green leaves. White/red filigree torsade. Honeycomb facets enlarge toward wide polished concave colorless base; basal ring. Convex dome.
D: 4¹⁄₁₆" (10.3 cm.)
Bergstrom Bequest, 1958.
EHB acquisition: May, 1941.
No. 414, Pl. 20; Cloak Catalogue, 1969.

530
Wafer Tray.
Saint Louis, 1845-55. Flared, colorless glass bowl; rim edged with spiraled pink/white filigree. Colorless collar; macedoine paperweight base contains millefiori canes, ribbon and filigree twists. Polished concave colorless base; basal ring.
H: 3" (7.6 cm.)
Bergstrom Bequest, 1958.
EHB acquisition: Unrecorded.
P. 41, Bergstrom book, 1940; p. 42, later editions.
No. 566, Pl. 26; Cloak Catalogue, 1969.

567
Vase.
Saint Louis, 1840-50. Cylindrical, horizontally-ribbed colorless glass, narrow neck, flared rim, encases red-over-opaque white canes alternating with fine white filigree spiraled from base to rim. Polished concave colorless base; basal ring.
H: 4⅝" (10.9 cm.); D: 2⅛" (5.4 cm.)
Bergstrom Bequest, 1958.
EHB acquisition: Unrecorded.
No. 609, Pl. 26; Cloak Catalogue, 1969.

1158
Saint Louis, 1845-55. Small upright floral bouquet surrounded by small red and white coiled filigree torsade between "mercury" rings low in base. Top punty; multiple circular facets on curve. Polished, concave, colorless base cut with 24-point star; basal ring.
D: 3⁵⁄₃₂" (8.0 cm.)
Gift of Mrs. Florence Gosselin Marsh in memory of her husband, Raymond Clark Marsh, 1976.

153
Straightedge.
Possibly Saint Louis, 19th century. Colorless glass rod, cut to 8 sides, encases white filigree coiled around red and blue spiral twists. Polished flat ends.
L: 10″ (25.5 cm.); D: ½″ (1.2 cm.)
Bergstrom Bequest, 1958.
EHB acquisition: October, 1938.
No. 162, Pl. 35; Cloak Catalogue, 1969.

254
Shot Glass.
Saint Louis, 1845-55. Horizontally rib-cut, bell-shape, colorless glass bowl encases spiraled white filigree and pastel pink rods joined by colorless glass collar to crown-type paperweight base: fine white filigree rods alternated with red/green/white and yellow-green aventurine/white ribbon twists, all radiating from large central floret. Polished colorless underside of base.
H: 3½″ (8.9 cm.); D: 1¾″ (4.4 cm.)
Bergstrom Bequest, 1958.
EHB acquisition: October, 1939.
P. 41, Bergstrom book, 1940; p. 42, later editions.
No. 271, Pl. 26; Cloak Catalogue, 1969.

265, 266
Doorknob (pair).
Attributed to Dorflinger Glass Works, White Mills, PA, 1852-1910. Spaced millefiori canes (pink, cobalt, blue, green, ochre); fine quality serrated canes with 5-point stars predominate. Brass mount.
D: 1¹³⁄₁₆″ (4.6 cm.)
Bergstrom Bequest, 1958.
EHB acquisition: November, 1939.
No. 283, Pl. 43; Cloak Catalogue, 1969.

286
Doorknob.
Attributed to Saint Louis, 1848-55. Single pear, yellow shading to green, bubble blossom end, yellow stem; 2 green leaves; double-swirl white latticinio ground. Wide cut flat dome. Colorless shank; brass mount.
D: 2″ (5.1 cm.)
Bergstrom Bequest, 1958.
EHB acquisition: March, 1940.
No. 306, Pl. 25; Cloak Catalogue, 1969.

305
Inkwell.
Attributed to Bristol, England, 1850-60. Cylindrical colorless glass; wineglass shape, translucent cobalt blue interior. Basal ring; pontil mark.
H: 4⁵⁄₁₆″ (10.9 cm.); D: 2⁵⁄₁₆″ (5.8 cm.)
Bergstrom Bequest, 1958.
EHB acquisition: May, 1940.
No. 325, Pl. 36; Cloak Catalogue, 1969.

330
Witch Ball and Stand.
English, early 19th century. Hollow, blown transparent cobalt blue ball (hole in base); matching mold-blown bowl-shaped ribbed stand; flared rim; circular foot.
Stand H: 2⅜″ (6.1 cm.); D: 4½″ (11.4 cm.); D: 3⁵⁄₁₆″ (8.5 cm.) rim.
Bergstrom Bequest, 1958.
EHB acquisition: May, 1940.
P. 41, Bergstrom book, 1940; p. 42, later editions.
No. 351, Pl. 36; Cloak Catalogue, 1969.

354, 355
Doorknob (pair).
American, 1852-75. Possibly New England Glass Co., or Boston & Sandwich Glass Co. Hollow blown colorless glass lined with gilt; opaque white overlay; star, circular, and oval facets. Brass fitting; steel shank.
D: 2″ (5.1 cm.)
Bergstrom Bequest, 1958.
EHB acquisition: November, 1940.
No. 373, Pl. 58; Cloak Catalogue, 1969.

412
Letter Seal.
Origin unknown, probably American, 19th-20th century. Diamond-faceted colorless glass seal; handle encloses cobalt blue and white spirals; monogram "EB" engraved in seal end.
L: 3¼″ (8.3 cm.)
Bergstrom Bequest, 1958.
EHB acquisition: August, 1941.
No. 432, Pl. 49; Cloak Catalogue, 1969.

489
Vase.
Saint Louis, 1845-55. Transparent ruby glass, waisted form, encased white filigree twist rim. Double collar of colorless glass joins vase to paperweight base; large salmon/white/blue serrated center cane surrounded by 5 red/white/green spaced canes; peripheral circle of alternating blue/white and chartreuse/white canes; scrambled white filigree ground. Polished slightly concave colorless base; basal ring.
H: 5″ (12.6 cm.)
Bergstrom Bequest, 1958.
EHB acquisition: April, 1943.
No. 519, Pl. 26; Cloak Catalogue, 1969.

581, 582
Lamp (pair).
Origin unknown, possibly Boston & Sandwich Glass Co., Sandwich, MA, 1825-70. Ruby/white overlay cylindrical glass fonts cut with vertical miters to 4 panels decorated with circular and square faceting (fluid-burning). Brass mounting for double wicks and attached snuffers. Brass baluster mount on square marble base.
H: 11″ (27.9 cm.)
Bergstrom Bequest, 1958.
EHB acquisition: Unrecorded.
No. 621, Pl. 58; Cloak Catalogue, 1969.

1402
Vase.
Bohemian, ca. 1847. Classic form, flared neck; colorless glass overlaid with opaque white; circular and oval facets on neck and shoulder; body with arched panels and diamonds; faceted colorless paperweight base encases spaced millefiori canes on white filigree ground.
H: 8¾″ (22.3 cm.)
Museum Purchase, 1979.

1781
Glass Nib.
Charles Kaziun, Sr., Brockton, MA, 1987. Encased green/cerise, pink/white ribbon twist cane.
L: 7¹³⁄₃₂″ (19.9 cm.)
Gift of Charles Kaziun, Sr., 1987.

813

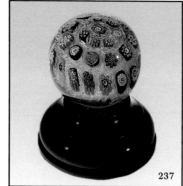

237

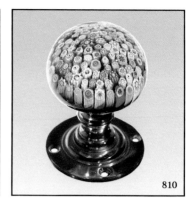

810

1207

295, 296

15

245

1311

868

388, 389

1303, 1, 1427

249, 250

69

1367, 227

300, 301

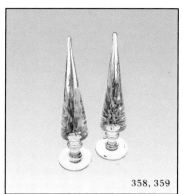
358, 359

1202

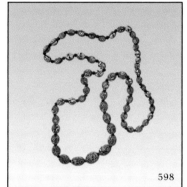
598

362, 16

79

352

328

568, 405, 569

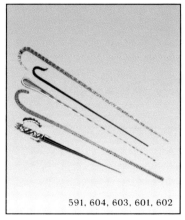
591, 604, 603, 601, 602

34

1
Ink Bottle, stoppered.
Whitefriars (James Powell & Sons, Ltd., London). Colorless glass bottle. 5 concentric circles of purple/white/pink canes, 1 cane dated "1848"; pontil mark. Colorless glass stopper, probably not original, encases 4 concentric circles of lavender/white canes.
H: 6″ (15.3 cm.); D: 4⅝″ (11.7 cm.)
Stopper D: 2¹⁷⁄₃₂″ (6.5 cm.); L: 3⅛″ (8.0 cm.)
Bergstrom Bequest, 1958.
EHB acquisition: March, 1935.
No. 5, p. 41, Illus. 49, Bergstrom book, 1940; p. 42, Illus. 47, later editions.
No. 1, Pl. 35; Cloak Catalogue, 1969.
Ref.: *PCA Bulletin,* 1987; "The Myth of Whitefriars."
The attributions for 1 and 22 have been researched by John Smith, London, and were found to be false. These bear fake dates and were produced during the 1930s by John Walsh-Walsh, Ltd., Birmingham, England.

15
Mantel Ornament.
Origin unknown. 2 layers of multicolored spatter, elongated central bubble surrounded by 4 bubbles. Colorless standard with baluster stem and flat, circular foot.
H: 5⅝″ (14.3 cm.); D: 3½″ (8.3 cm.) sphere.
Bergstrom Bequest, 1958.
EHB acquisition: May, 1936.
No. 17, Pl. 60; Cloak Catalogue, 1969.

237
Newel Post.
Clichy, 1845-55. Colorless glass sphere; spaced millefiori canes set in white filigree cushion. White filigree rods appear between canes in chequer pattern.
Ex collection: Oscar Wilde.
D: 3⁹⁄₁₆″ (9.1 cm.) Bergstrom Bequest, 1958.
EHB acquisition: September, 1939.
No. 12, p. 41, Bergstrom book, 1940; p. 42, later editions.
No. 253, Pl. 18; Cloak Catalogue, 1969.

245
Pairpoint Corp., New Bedford, MA, 1910-20s. Spherical, footed weight; red and white rods form ovoid motif. Engraved floral/leaf decoration top of crown. Flat circular foot with floral/leaf designs, and fine cross-cutting.
D: 2¾″ (7.0 cm.); D: 3¼″ (8.3 cm.) foot.
Bergstrom Bequest, 1958.
EHB acquisition: September, 1939.
Illus. 65, Bergstrom book, 1940; Illus. 53, later editions.
No. 262, Pl. 42; Cloak Catalogue, 1969.

249, 250
Mantel Ornaments (pair).
Attributed to Stourbridge, England, 19th century. Greenish glass encases central bubble/varicolored spatter on yellow lily-type bubble flower; 3 flowers spaced near periphery, all drawn to base. Inverted colorless glass collar; double mereses above and below waisted chartreuse stem. Circular, concave, colorless foot; smooth base.
H: 5⅞″ (15.0 cm.); D: 3¼″ (8.3 cm.)
Sphere D: 4⅛″ (10.5 cm.) Bergstrom Bequest, 1958.
EHB acquisition: September, 1939.
No. 3, p. 41, Bergstrom book, 1940; p. 42, later editions.
Nos. 266-267, Pl. 33; Cloak Catalogue, 1969.

295, 296
Doorknobs, not identical.

Clichy, 1845-55. Patterned millefiori canes, white filigree ground. Central Clichy rose surrounded by florets. Brass fitting marked: "E.C.J.NE/Breveté S.G.D.G."
D: 2⅛″ (5.4 cm.) Bergstrom Bequest, 1958.
EHB acquisition: April, 1940.
Illus. 56, Bergstrom book, 1940; Illus. 54, later editions.
No. 316, Pl. 17; Cloak Catalogue, 1969.

388, 389
Mantel Ornament (pair).
Origin unknown. Tapered upper portion, encases varicolored spatter glass over opaque white and goldstone drawn up into "devil's fire" peaks. Applied stemmed colorless glass standard with thick flat circular foot.
H: 6½″ (16.5 cm.) Bergstrom Bequest, 1958.
EHB acquisition: May, 1941.
No. 409, Pl. 59; Cloak Catalogue, 1969.

810
Doorknob.
Perthshire Paperweights, Ltd., Crieff, Scotland, 1969-70. Millefiori canes on cobalt blue ground. Brass mount.
D: 2⁵⁄₁₆″ (5.8 cm.)
Gift of Mrs. C. A. Peterson, 1970.

813
Doorknob.
Perthshire Paperweights, Ltd., 1969-70. Patterned millefiori. Cobalt blue ground. Brass mount.
D: 2¼″ (5.6 cm.)
Gift of John McFedries, 1970.

868
Murano, ca. 1972. White filigree twist "crown" motif. Colorless collar, plain stem, and wide foot.
H: 6¹⁄₁₆″ (15.3 cm.); D: 3⅝″ (9.3 cm.)
Gift of The Woman's Tuesday Club, Neenah, WI, and Paul Kelvin, 1973.

1207
Mantel Ornament.
Origin unknown. Double tier of multicolor spatter; baluster stem, circular flat foot, dome punty.
H: 5³⁄₁₆″ (13.2 cm.); D: 2½″ (6.3 cm.) sphere.
Gift of Mrs. Florence Gosselin Marsh in memory of her husband, Raymond Clark Marsh, 1976.

1303
Ink Bottle, stoppered.
Chinese, 1930s. Yellowish glass, bulbous form; footed; Concentric millefiori canes. Matching stopper.
H: 5″ (12.8 cm.); D: 3″ (7.6 cm.)
Stopper D: 1¾″ (4.5 cm.)
Gift of Robert S. Sage and Jeanne Sage Groves in memory of their parents, Charles H. and Lyda P. Sage, 1978.

1311
Newel Post.
Clichy, 1845-55. Sphere encases spaced concentric millefiori canes. 7 Clichy roses encircle central pastry mold cane. Brass mount.
H: 6⅜″ (16.0 cm.); D: 3¹³⁄₁₆″ (9.7 cm.)
Gift of Robert S. Sage and Jeanne Sage Groves in memory of their parents, Charles H. and Lyda P. Sage, 1978.

1427
Chinese, 1930s. Yellow glass encases concentric millefiori canes; smooth, concave base marked "China."
D: 2⁷⁄₁₆″ (6.2 cm.)
Gift of Carl W. Fischer, 1981.

16
Millville, NJ, attributed to Marcus Kuntz, 1900-10. "Devil's fire" motif. Smooth base, pontil mark.
D: 3⁹⁄₁₆" (9.1 cm.)   Bergstrom Bequest, 1958.
EHB acquisition: May, 1936.
No. 18, Pl. 47; Cloak Catalogue, 1969.

34
Ink Bottle, stoppered.
Millville, NJ, attributed to Emil Stanger, ca. 1900. Colorless glass body encases white lily, coarse spatter glass. Collared, circular foot; pontil mark. Matching stopper.
H: 10¼" (26.0 cm.)   Bergstrom Bequest, 1958.
EHB acquisition: June, 1937.
Illus. 75, Bergstrom book, 1940; Illus. 73, later editions.
No. 34, Pl. 47; Cloak Catalogue, 1969.

79
Millville, NJ, probably work of Emil Stanger or Marcus Kuntz; ca. 1900. White "crimp" lily fused with spatter glass. Smooth circular foot; trace of pontil mark.
D: 3½" (8.9 cm.)   Bergstrom Bequest, 1958.
EHB acquisition: October, 1937.
Illus. 73, Bergstrom book, 1940; Illus. 71, later editions.
No. 84, Pl. 47; Cloak Catalogue, 1969.

227
Necklace.
Possibly Egyptian, 1st-3rd century, B.C. "Eye" beads alternate with pink quartz and gold beads.
L: 15½" (39.5 cm.)   Bergstrom Bequest, 1958.
EHB acquisition: June, 1939.
Illus. 1, Bergstrom book, 1940; Illus. 1, later editions.
No. 243, Pl. 62; Cloak Catalogue, 1969.

300, 301
Doorknobs.
Probably New England Glass Co.; possibly Boston & Sandwich Glass Co.; ca. 1855-60. Silvered glass base, overlaid with colorless glass flashed with green (301-cobalt blue). Intricate decorative faceting. Brass fitting.
D: 2¹³⁄₁₆" (7.2 cm.); 301 D: 2¹¹⁄₁₆" (6.8 cm.)
Bergstrom Bequest, 1958.
EHB acquisition: April, 1940.
Illus. 58, Bergstrom book, 1940; Illus. 56, later editions.
No. 321, Pl. 44; Cloak Catalogue, 1969.

328
Millville, NJ; probably Emil Stanger or Marcus Kuntz, ca. 1900. White "crimp" lily, spatter glass decoration. Collared, colorless stem; circular flat foot, pontil mark.
H: 4⅝" (11.7 cm.); D: 3⅛" (8.0 cm.)
Bergstrom Bequest, 1958.
EHB acquisition: July, 1940.
No. 349, Pl. 47; Cloak Catalogue, 1969.

352
Ink Bottle, stoppered.
Millville, NJ; attributed to Marcus Kuntz. "Devils fire" motif. Stopper: panel-cut.
H: 5½" (13.9 cm.)   Bergstrom Bequest, 1958.
EHB acquisition: October, 1940.
No. 371, Pl. 48; Cloak Catalogue, 1969.

358, 359
Mantel Ornament (pair).
Origin unknown, possibly Whitall Tatum & Co., Millville, NJ, early 20th century. Steeple shape. Pastel-colored glass drawn upward into peaks and spikes. Applied color-less circular foot; bladed, knopped stem.
H: 11" (27. 9 cm.)   Bergstrom Bequest, 1958.
EHB acquisition: December, 1940.
No. 376, Pl. 36; Cloak Catalogue, 1969.

362
Ink Bottle, stoppered.
Millville, NJ, 1900-10. "Devil's fire" motif. Pontil mark. Matching spire stopper.
H: 7" (17.8 cm.)   Bergstrom Bequest, 1958.
EHB acquisition: November, 1940.
No. 380, Pl. 47; Cloak Catalogue, 1969.

405
Saint Louis, 1845-55. Concentric millefiori mushroom motif. Twisted white rods within blue coil form torsade. Polished concave colorless base cut with 24-point star.
D: 3¹⁄₁₆" (7.8 cm.)   Bergstrom Bequest, 1958.
EHB acquisition: August, 1941.
No. 425, Pl. 27; Cloak Catalogue, 1969.

568
Scent Bottle, stoppered.
Saint Louis, 1840-50. Cylindrical colorless glass, encases cobalt blue canes, alternated with white filigree. Hollow-blown, stopper: spiraled blue and white filigree canes.
H: 4½" (11.4 cm.)   Bergstrom Bequest, 1958.
EHB acquisition: Unrecorded.
No. 610, Pl. 37; Cloak Catalogue, 1969.

569
Shot Cup, footed.
Saint Louis, 1845-50. Horizontally ribbed glass encases canes: cobalt blue lined with opaque white and white filigree. Base: central millefiori cane surrounded by 5 salmon/white canes and peripheral circle of canes.
H: 3⁷⁄₁₆" (8.7 cm.); D: 1¾" (7.0 cm.) base.
Bergstrom Bequest, 1958.
EHB acquisition: Unrecorded.
No. 611, Pl. 26; Cloak Catalogue, 1969.

598
Necklace.
Italian, 1930s. 62 millefiori glass beads.
L: 40" (101.6 cm.)   Bergstrom Bequest, 1958.
EHB acquisition: Unrecorded.
No. 640, Pl. 38; Cloak Catalogue, 1969.

601, 602, 603, 604 (591 Sword)
Walking Canes.
English, possibly Stourbridge area.
Bergstrom Bequest, 1958.
EHB acquisition: Unrecorded.
No. 644, Pl. 37; Cloak Catalogue, 1969.
No. 633, Pl. 60; Cloak Catalogue, 1969 (Sword).

1202
Scent Bottle, stoppered.
Attributed to Saint Louis, 1845-50. Octagonal, horizontally ribbed colorless glass encases alternating yellow and white rods. Stopper, hexagonal form.
H: 3⅜" (8.5 cm.)
Gift of Mrs. Florence Gosselin Marsh in memory of her husband, Raymond Clark Marsh, 1976.

1367
Millefiori Fragments.
Roman, 2nd-4th century A.D.
Gift of Mr. and Mrs. Dwight P. Lanmon, 1979.

498

1824

299

612, 583, 584

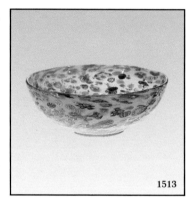

1513

321, 320

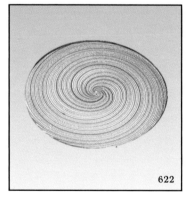

622

621

624

625

609

617

519

223

514

1521

616, 343, 345, 344

605, 607

1511

28

304

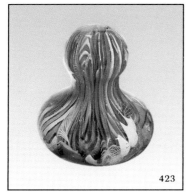

423

1310

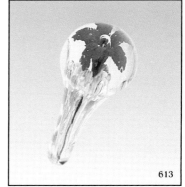

613

299
Doorstop.
Tiffany Studios, Long Island, NY, ca. 1900. Aquamarine glass encloses "undersea" motif: millefiori cane "rocks" and sea urchins. Unsigned concave base; basal ring.
D: 5⁵⁄₁₆″ (13.4 cm.); Wt: 6 lbs.   Bergstrom Bequest, 1958.
EHB acquisition: April, 1940.
Illus. 68, Bergstrom book, 1940; Illus. 66, later editions.
No. 320, Pl. 44; Cloak Catalogue, 1969.

320, 321
Footed Tumblers.
Attributed to Saint Louis, 1840-50. Double overlay: white/red (321 cobalt blue/white). Spaced trefoil and quatrefoil cuttings encircle bowl, 3 miter cuts surround base; 6-sided colorless stem extends to foot, encased overlay cut with 12 petal and 12 miter facets underside.
H: 4⅜″ (11.1 cm.); D: 2⅞″ (7.3 cm.) foot.
Bergstrom Bequest, 1958.
EHB acquisition: June, 1940.
No. 341, 342, Pl. 16; Cloak Catalogue, 1969.

498
Doorstop.
Tiffany Studios, 1900. Transparent green glass encases "undersea" motif: flattened blue/white filigree rod, with translucent blue-green tentacles; concavity signed "L. C. Tiffany Favrile/3914 P."
D: 4¹⁵⁄₁₆″ (12.5 cm.)   Bergstrom Bequest, 1958.
EHB acquisition: November, 1943.
No. 529, Pl. 44; Cloak Catalogue, 1969.

583
Plate.
Saint Louis, 1840-50. Top side of colorless glass overlaid with opaque white and green. Gilt-edged rim cut with vines, berries, and leaves; base medallion cut in 12 alternating petals and miters.
D: 6¼″ (15.9 cm.)   Bergstrom Bequest, 1958.
EHB acquisition: Unrecorded.
No. 623, Pl. 15; Cloak Catalogue, 1969.

584
Scent Bottle, stoppered.
Origin unknown, 1840-50. Blue/white double overlay; gilt decoration. Leaf and floral facets encircle bowl; 4 cuts on shoulder; 4 oval cuts on neck. Number "31" scratched in basal concavity. Stopper cut to 8 sides.
H: 5½″ (13.9 cm.); D: 1¹³⁄₁₆″ (4.7 cm.) bottle.
Stopper L: 2⁹⁄₃₂″ (5.9 cm.); D: ¾″ (2.0 cm.)
Bergstrom Bequest, 1958.
EHB acquisition: Unrecorded.
No. 624, Pl. 15; Cloak Catalogue, 1969.

609
Wineglass.
Origin unknown, 1850-80. Rosaline craquelle, bowl, gilt rim band; between gilt collars, a 6-sided colorless stem encases ruby/white filigree spiraled around ribbon twist. Craquelle foot flashed with rosaline on underside.
H: 6⅛″ (15.6 cm.); D: 3³⁄₁₆″ (8.1 cm.) bowl.
Bergstrom Bequest, 1958.
EHB acquisition: Unrecorded.
No. 649, Pl. 37; Cloak Catalogue, 1969.

612
Glass Box, covered.
Bohemian, 19th century.

Box: ruby glass overlaid with opaque white, gilt decoration. 8 gilt-edged facets on sides.
Cover: ruby glass overlaid with opaque white, gilt decoration. Top cut with 8-petal medallion, 8 gilt petals in center. Figure-eight, gilt-edged cuts encircle curve and sides.
D: 3¹⁵⁄₁₆″ (10.1 cm.)   Bergstrom Bequest, 1958.
EHB acquisition: Unrecorded.
No. 727, Pl. 9; Cloak Catalogue, 1969.

617
Cup and Saucer.
Origin unknown, possibly Nicholas Lutz, Sandwich, MA, ca. 1870. Flattened spiraled yellow filigree alternately striped with double pink/white filigree twists. Applied foot; colorless stem and handle. Matching saucer.
Cup D: 2⅞″ (7.3 cm.); Saucer D: 4¾″ (12.1 cm.)
Bergstrom Bequest, 1958.
EHB acquisition: Unrecorded.
No. 732, Pl. 38; Cloak Catalogue, 1969.

621
Bowl.
Origin unknown, 1920-30. Flattened spiral twists of white/blue. Encased white spiral at rim.
D: 9″ (22.9 cm.)   Bergstrom Bequest, 1958.
EHB acquisition: Unrecorded.
No. 761, Pl. 63; Cloak Catalogue, 1969.

622
Plate.
Origin unknown, 1920-30. Cased swirled rods: white/yellow/pink/goldstone. Applied red rim.
D: 6¹⁵⁄₁₆″ (17.7 cm.)   Bergstrom Bequest, 1958.
EHB acquisition: Unrecorded.
No. 762, Pl. 63; Cloak Catalogue, 1969.

624
Bowl.
Origin unknown, probably Italian, 1920-30. Spiraled white filigree rods, red centers. White filigree rim.
D: 8″ (20.4 cm.)   Bergstrom Bequest, 1958.
EHB acquisition: Unrecorded.
No. 764, Pl. 63; Cloak Catalogue, 1969.

625
Finger Bowl and Underplate.
Origin unknown. Free-blown, colorless glass with goldstone threading; ruffled rim. Matching underplate.
Bowl D: 4¹³⁄₁₆″ (10.6 cm.)   Plate D: 6½″ (16.5 cm.)
Bergstrom Bequest, 1958.
EHB acquisition: Unrecorded.
No. 765, Pl. 63; Cloak Catalogue, 1969.

1513
Bowl.
Attributed to Ysart brothers, Perth, Scotland, 1930-40. Hand-blown, white opaline glass, embedded with canes cased with colorless glass. Shallow, colorless foot.
H: 3⅞″ (9.9 cm.); D: 10⁷⁄₁₆″ (26.6 cm.)
Museum Purchase, 1984.

1824
Bowl.
Monart Glass, Perth, Scotland, 1930-40. Blown. Base etched "Monart/Scotland/BS insignia."
D: 4¹⁷⁄₃₂″ (11.6 cm.)
Gift of Mrs. Virginia Bensley Trowbridge, 1987.

28
Probably English, Isle of Wight, late 19th or early 20th century. Colorless glass filled with colored sand.
H: 9¼″ (23.5 cm.); D: 3⁷⁄₁₆″ (8.7 cm.) base.
Bergstrom Bequest, 1958.
EHB acquisition: June, 1937.
No. 29, Pl. 61; Cloak Catalogue, 1969.

223
Goblet.
English, attributed to Bristol, 18th-19th century. Round funnel form; engraved bowl. Stem encases red/white/blue ribbon spiral. Low circular foot; pontil mark.
H: 10⅛″ (25.8 cm.); Bowl D: 4⅝″ (11.8 cm.)
Bergstrom Bequest, 1958.
EHB acquisition: June, 1939.
Illus. 11, p. 41, Bergstrom book, 1940; p. 42, later editions.
No. 238, Pl. 35; Cloak Catalogue, 1969.

304
Witch Ball.
English, early 19th century. Hollow, blown. Mottled red/blue/green over white. Ball is lined with plaster of Paris; hole in center of base. (Hung by the superstitious near cottage doorways to ward off evil spirits.)
D: 5¼″ (13.3 cm.)   Bergstrom Bequest, 1958.
EHB acquisition: April, 1940.
No. 17, p. 41, Bergstrom book, 1940; p. 42, later editions.
No. 324, Pl. 36; Cloak Catalogue, 1969.

343
Gemel Flask.
Origin unknown, possibly English, late 19th century. Opaque white glass festooned with red. Applied blue lip.
H: 10″ (25.4 cm.)   Bergstrom Bequest, 1958.
EHB acquisition: August, 1940.
No. 363, Pl. 37; Cloak Catalogue, 1969.

344
Flask.
Attributed to England, mid-19th century. Opaque white glass festooned with red.
H: 7½″ (19.0 cm.)   Bergstrom Bequest, 1958.
EHB acquisition: August, 1940.
No. 364, Pl. 36; Cloak Catalogue, 1969.

345
Flask.
Origin unknown, probably English, 19th century. Amethyst glass festooned with white.
H: 6⅝″ (16.8 cm.)   Bergstrom Bequest, 1958.
EHB acquisition: Unrecorded.
No. 364A, Pl. 36; Cloak Catalogue, 1969.

423
Letter Weight.
Origin unknown, 19th century. Scrambled strands of white filigree and colored twist rods drawn from base to knob top of weight.
D: 3¼″ (8.3 cm.)   Bergstrom Bequest, 1958.
EHB acquisition: September, 1941.
No. 446, Pl. 34; Cloak Catalogue, 1969.

514
Flask.
Attributed to Nicholas Lutz, Boston & Sandwich Glass Co., 1875; or Saint Louis, 1852. Yellow/blue and red/green ribbon twists, alternating with twisted white filigree, drawn up to flared neck. Polished flat colorless base.

H: 3¹⁵⁄₁₆″ (10.1 cm.); W: 3″ (7.6 cm.)
Bergstrom Bequest, 1958.
EHB acquisition: Unrecorded.
No. 548, Pl. 44; Cloak Catalogue, 1969.

519
Flask.
Origin unknown, possibly Venetian. Blue rods and stripes of goldstone spiraled from base to neck.
H: 6½″ (16.5 cm.); W: 3¹⁄₁₆″ (7.8 cm.)
Bergstrom Bequest, 1958.
EHB acquisition: Unrecorded.
No. 553, Pl. 38; Cloak Catalogue, 1969.

605
Glass Rod.
Origin unknown, 19th century. Red/white/blue threads spiraled around opaque white core.
L: 6″ (15.3 cm.)   Bergstrom Bequest, 1958.
EHB acquisition: Unrecorded.
No. 645-a, Pl. 37; Cloak Catalogue, 1969.

607
Glass Pen.
Origin unknown, 19th century. Opaque white glass rod with red stripes.
L: 6″ (15.3 cm.)   Bergstrom Bequest, 1958.
EHB acquisition: Unrecorded.
No. 645-c, Pl. 37; Cloak Catalogue, 1969.

613
Darner.
Joe St. Clair, St. Clair Glass Works, Elwood, IN, early 1950s. 5-petal red lily-type flower made of glass chips.
L: 5¼″ (13.3 cm.)   Bergstrom Bequest, 1958.
EHB acquisition: Unrecorded.
No. 728, Pl. 49; Cloak Catalogue, 1969.

616
Flask.
English, attributed to Bristol area, mid-19th century. Cased opaque white glass festooned with blue.
H: 8¾″ (22.2 cm.)   Bergstrom Bequest, 1958.
EHB acquisition: Unrecorded.
No. 730, Pl. 37; Cloak Catalogue, 1969.

1310
Mallet.
American, late 19th century. Twisted, colorless handle. Mallet end encloses blue/pink/green lily with bubble.
Mallet D: 2⁵⁄₁₆″ (5.9 cm.); L: 11″ (28.0 cm.)
Gift of Robert S. Sage and Jeanne Sage Groves in memory of their parents, Charles H. and Lyda P. Sage, 1978.

1511
Gene Baxley, Corydon, IN, 1981. "The Intoxicated Gourd," pink selenium glass, free-form shape. Base signed "Gene Baxley 1981 Corydon Indiana." Edition of 10.
H: 5¼″ (13.4 cm.); D: 3½″ (9.0 cm.)
Gift of Gene Baxley, 1984.

1521
Obelisk.
Possibly Boston & Sandwich Glass Co., 1880-1900. Colorless glass, with "vase" cutting and hand-painted decoration. Separate beveled rectangular glass base.
H: 5″ (12.3 cm.)
Base: 4¼ x 2½ x ¾″ (10.9 x 6.4 x 2.0 cm.)
Gift of James C. Myers, 1985.

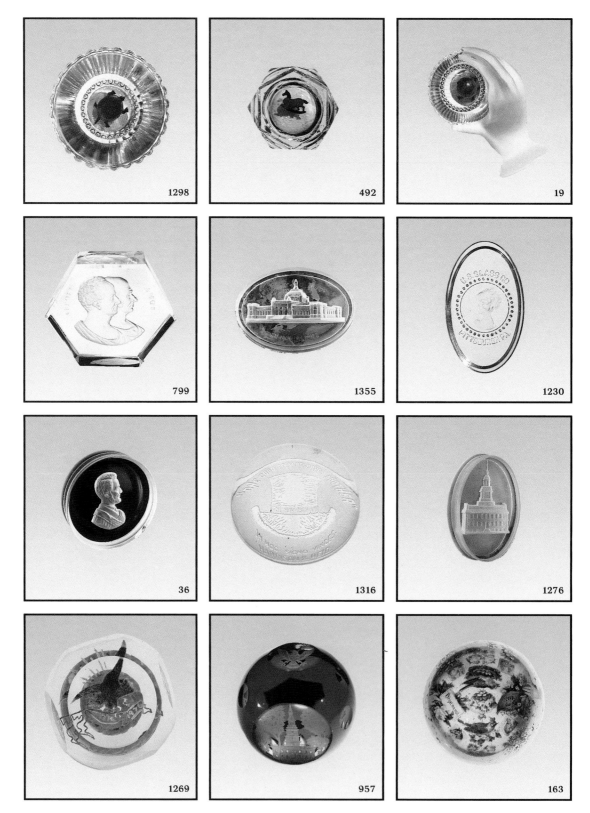

1298

492

19

799

1355

1230

36

1316

1276

1269

957

163

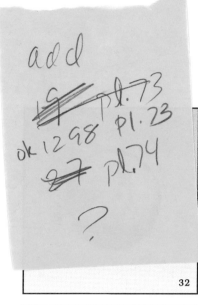

32

224, 152

27

86

33

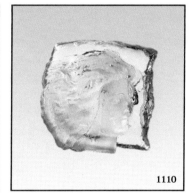

1110

512

2

521

562

444

42

19

Possibly Gillinder & Sons, Philadelphia, PA, 1876. U.S. Centennial souvenir. Frosted hand holds hollow, circular pressed glass weight containing brown turtle with moving black head, legs, and tail; green paper ground. Fluted exterior sides; inside crown, circle of pressed beading. (A patent for this type of turtle weight without the hand was issued to H. E. Geron, Springfield, OH, in 1948. However, Gillinder may also have made these weights without the hand.)
H: 4¼" (10.8 cm.); D: 2½" (6.3 cm.)
Bergstrom Bequest, 1958.
EHB acquisition: June, 1937.
No. 21, Pl. 61; Cloak Catalogue, 1969.

36

Gillinder & Sons, 1876. Pressed round flat form, frosted edge grooved with two rings. In base: frosted intaglio profile bust, to sinister, of Abraham Lincoln.
D: 3¼" (8.3 cm.)
Bergstrom Bequest, 1958.
EHB acquisition: April, 1937.
No. 36, Pl. 43; Cloak Catalogue, 1969.

163

Boston & Sandwich Glass Co., Sandwich, MA, ca. 1880. Sentimental Victorian enamel transfers (mottoes, birds, bouquets, animals) closely spaced on colorless blown sphere encased with transparent green bottle-type glass. Hollow interior filled with white plaster. Small open base sealed with ceramic clay.
D: 2⅞" (7.3 cm.)
Bergstrom Bequest, 1958.
EHB acquisition: November, 1938.
Illus. 60, Bergstrom book, 1940; Illus. 58, later editions.
No. 172, Pl. 44; Cloak Catalogue, 1969.

492

Origin unknown, possibly Gillinder & Sons, ca. 1876. Miniature. Hollow core encloses small black horse (moveable head and tail), with red blanket, resting on white paper disk inserted underside of weight. Top cut flat, diamond faceting on curve. (Construction similar to No. 19.)
D: 1⅞" (4.8 cm.)
Bergstrom Bequest, 1958.
EHB acquisition: April, 1943.
No. 522, Pl. 61; Cloak Catalogue, 1969.

799

New England Glass Co., E. Cambridge, MA, 1848-52. Flat hexagonal cut and beveled. Frosted double portrait profiles to dexter, of Abbott and Amos Lawrence; pressed intaglio in base. "Abbott and Amos Lawrence" engraved in half circle above portrait.
D: 3⁹⁄₁₆" (9.1 cm.)
Gift of Friends of Bergstrom, 1970.

957

Royale Germania Crystal, West Germany, 1971. Translucent amethyst-red overlay cut with circular facets on curve. Polished flat dome engraved with American Eagle. Larger flat surface on side engraved with trees and Independence Hall. Polished flat base engraved "1971 Royale 160," surrounded by miter cuts. No. 160/600 edition commemorating the designation, about 1816, of Philadelphia's Independence Hall.

H: 3¹¹⁄₁₆" (11.5 cm.); D: 4" (10.2 cm.)
Gift of Dr. M. J. Caldwell, 1974.

1230

U. S. Glass Company, Pittsburgh, PA, 1892. Chicago World's Fair souvenir, duo commemorative: introduction of the incandescent lamp and recognition of women's rights. Pressed oval colorless glass; flashed dark pink edge above frosted intaglio female profile portrait, surrounded by spaced gold dots simulating light bulbs, and "U. S. Glass Co. Pittsburgh PA." impressed in base.
L: 2¾" (7.0 cm.); W: 4½" (11.2 cm.)
Gift of Mr. and Mrs. Silas Spengler, 1976.

1269

Fred Wilkerson, Moundsville, WV, 1976. Die motif: grey/white eagle, orange talons hold Bicentennial banner "1776/1976"; outline of West Virginia at left; blue/white/red spatter cushion. Top and 4 side punties; polished flat colorless base. "W" signature forms part of State outline.
D: 3¹³⁄₃₂" (8.7 cm.)
Gift of Fred Wilkerson, 1977.

1276

Gillinder & Sons, ca. 1876. Oval, gavel-molded edge, intaglio in base impressed "Independence Hall." Polished top, frosted edge and base.
L: 4⅞" (12.5 cm.)
Museum Purchase, 1977.

1298

Gillinder & Sons, ca. 1876. U. S. Centennial souvenir. Pressed dome; hollow core encloses dark brown turtle with moving head, tail, and legs. Beige paper and green simulated leather base.
D: 3¹⁄₁₆" (7.9 cm.)
Gift of Robert S. Sage and Jeanne Sage Groves in memory of their parents, Charles H. and Lyda P. Sage, 1978.

1316

American, ca. 1888. Souvenir. Shallow dome; frosted flat base acid-etched intaglio with image of beaver hat inscribed "The Harrison Hat"; above it, "One Good Term Deserves Another"; below it, "In Hoc Signo Vinces"/ "Harrison & Reid."
D: 3¹⁄₃₂" (7.7 cm.)
Gift of Robert S. Sage and Jeanne Sage Groves in memory of their parents, Charles H. and Lyda P. Sage, 1978.

1355

Gillinder & Sons, ca. 1876. Frosted, collared, oval polished top reveals image of Memorial Hall, pressed intaglio in base; "1776/1876" above, "Memorial Hall" below. A souvenir of the U. S. Centennial Exposition, Fairmount Park, Philadelphia, 1876.
D: 3⅜" (8.6 cm.); L: 4⅞" (12.4 cm.)
Gift of Mr. and Mrs. Stan Gores, 1979.

*   *   *

2

Origin unknown, American, 1890-1910. Sepia reproduction on paper of the painting "The Cherub Choir" fastened to concave underside of colorless glass disk.
H: 1" (2.5 cm.); D: 3" (7.6 cm.)
Bergstrom Bequest, 1958.
EHB acquisition: Unrecorded.
No. 1A, Pl. 60; Cloak Catalogue, 1969.

27
Marble.
Attributed to German or American manufacture, 1850-1910. Sulphide figure of a lamb.
D: 2″ (5.1 cm.)
Bergstrom Bequest, 1958.
EHB acquisition: June, 1937.
No. 28, Pl. 59; Cloak Catalogue, 1969.
Ref.: Baumann, Paul: *Collecting Antique Marbles,* 1970.

32
Marble.
Attributed to German or American manufacture, 1840-1926. Sulphide figure of young girl kneeling with mallet in hand.
D: 2¹³⁄₁₆″ (7.2 cm.)
Bergstrom Bequest, 1958.
EHB acquisition: June, 1937.
No. 33, Pl. 59; Cloak Catalogue, 1969.

33
Marble.
Attributed to German or American manufacture, 1840-1926. Yellowish glass encases sulphide figure of child in sitting position blowing horn.
D: 1¹³⁄₁₆″ (4.7 cm.)
Bergstrom Bequest, 1958.
EHB acquisition: Unrecorded.
No. 33, Pl. 59; Cloak Catalogue, 1969.

42
Wilfred Smith & Co., New York, NY, 1900. Pressed rectangular colorless glass souvenir. Beaded edge frames underside opening for photograph of First Presbyterian Church, Neenah, WI, at time of dedication, 1900-1901; oval inset shows Rev. John E. Chapin, D.D. Printed on paper base: "Manufactured by Wilfred Smith & Co., 150 Nassau St., New York."
Size: 2¹¹⁄₁₆ x 4⅛ x ⅞″ (6.8 x 10.5 x 2.2 cm.)
Bergstrom Bequest, 1958.
EHB acquisition: June, 1937.
No. 42, Pl. 50; Cloak Catalogue, 1969.

86
Maker unknown: "L.L."; Paris, France, 1889. Snow weight. Thin colorless glass sphere encloses replica of Eiffel Tower. Dried ceramic flakes surround Tower base, liquid having evaporated. Sphere mounted on square ceramic base; "L.L. Paris Made In France" impressed underside.
D: 2⁹⁄₁₆″ (6.5 cm.)
Base: 1¾ x 1¾ x ⅞″ (4.5 x 4.5 x 2.2 cm.)
Bergstrom Bequest, 1958.
EHB acquisition: November, 1937.
No. 91, Pl. 37; Cloak Catalogue, 1969.

152
French, 1870-90. Snow weight. Thin, colorless glass sphere encloses facade of castle and girl flying a balloon.
Square: 1⅞″ (4.7 cm.)
Bergstrom Bequest, 1958.
EHB acquisition: October, 1938.

224
Origin unknown, French, late 19th century. Snow weight. Thin colorless glass sphere encloses replica of the Marie Antoinette Chalet, Petit Trianon in Versailles; in foreground, woman holds red parasol. Sphere is attached to rectangular marble base.

Sphere D: 3¾″ (9.5 cm.); Base: 2⅞ x 4¼″ (7.2 x 10.8 cm.)
Bergstrom Bequest, 1958.
EHB acquisition: June, 1939.
Illus. 23, Bergstrom book, 1940; later editions.

444
Origin unknown, American, possibly New York State, ca. 1893. Souvenir. Reproduction on paper of "World's Columbian Exposition 1893 Machinery Hall" fastened to underside of flat colorless glass rectangle; rounded corners.
Size: 4⅛ x 2⅝ x ⅞″ (10.5 x 6.6 x 2.2 cm.)
Bergstrom Bequest, 1958.
EHB acquisition: December, 1941.
No. 473, Pl. 60; Cloak Catalogue, 1969.

512
Attributed to Austria, last half 19th century. Flat, bevel-edged, rectangular colorless glass covers sulphide plaque portraying 2 horses, lion, foliage, hillside, rocks. Entrapped air gives silvery appearance outlining the scene. "Patented G.S. & Co." impressed lower front edge of sulphide. Paper label: "J. & L. Lobmeyr, Wien" on side. Paper covers underside.
Size: 5⅝ x 3⅜ x ¾″ (14.3 x 8.6 x 1.9 cm.)
Bergstrom Bequest, 1958.
EHB acquisition: Unrecorded.
No. 546, Pl. 57; Cloak Catalogue, 1969.

521
New England Glass Co., E. Cambridge, MA, 1876-88. Pressed, glass replica of Plymouth Rock, showing crack in rock and date "1620." Base rim, "A rock in the wilderness welcomed our sires/from bondage far over the dark rolling sea/on that holy altar they kindled the fires/Jehovah which glow in our bosom for thee." On rim edge: "Mary Chilton was the first to land upon the rock Dec. 21, 1620. In attempting to raise up the rock in 1776 (for sight-seers), it was split asunder. This is a facsimile of the upper part. Pilgrim Rock trademark Providence Ink Stand Co. 1876."
L: 4⅛″ (10.5 cm.)
Bergstrom Bequest, 1958.
EHB acquisition: Unrecorded.
Illus. 82, Bergstrom book, 1940; Illus. 80, later editions.

562
Origin unknown, American, probably late 19th century. Heavy, pressed colorless glass rectangle; convex top (footed at corners) covers "mother-of-pearl" plaque on which is painted a gilt medallion, the center inscribed "Notes." Gilt leaf and scroll design on salmon-pink and black ground surrounds medallion. Underside of plaque coated with wax to hold it in place.
Size: 4 x 2¾ x 1⅜″ (10.2 x 7.0 x 4.0 cm.)
Bergstrom Bequest, 1958.
EHB acquisition: Unrecorded.
No. 601, Pl. 60; Cloak Catalogue, 1969.

1110
Libbey Glass Co., Toledo, OH, 1893. Molded, 3-dimensional frosted colorless glass relief profile of female head with flowing hair; irregular squared base; large basal concavity embossed with "World's Fair 1893" and "Libbey Glass Co. Toledo, Ohio."
D: 2³¹⁄₃₂ x 2²⁹⁄₃₂″ (7.6 x 7.4 cm.)
Gift of Mrs. Charles Decker, 1976.
Ref.: Fauster, Carl: *Libbey Glass Since 1818,* 1979; Fig. 3, p. 228.

1295

1599

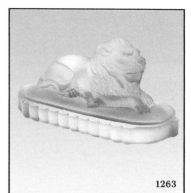

1263

1315

1315

946

1253

1433

1705

39, 41, 1547, 40

838

1356, 1329, 1266, 1085

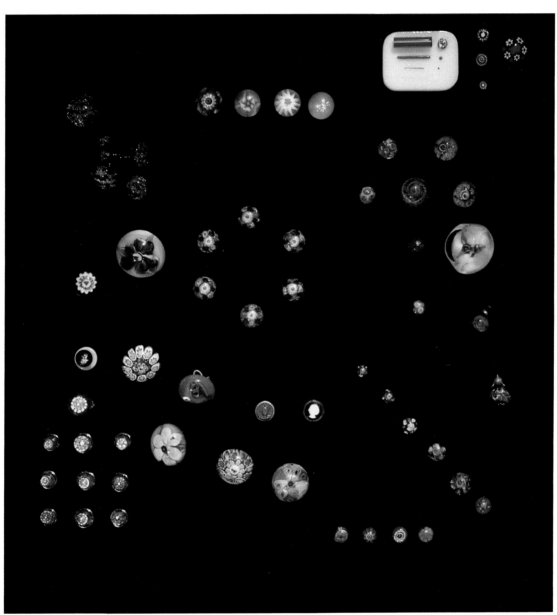

101, 398, 571, 579, 580, 595, 596, 597, 1233, 1296, 1319, 1472, 1473, 1474, 1476, 1618

39
American, possibly Boston & Sandwich Glass Co., Sandwich, MA, 1852-88. Transparent amber-flashed glass icosahedron.
D: 2⁷⁄₁₆″ (6.2 cm.)
Bergstrom Bequest, 1958.
EHB acquisition: June, 1937.
No. 39, Pl. 60; Cloak Catalogue, 1969.

40
American, possibly Boston & Sandwich Glass Co., 1860-88. Bevel-edged colorless glass cube.
1¾″ (4.5 cm.) each side.
Bergstrom Bequest, 1958.
EHB acquisition: 1936.
No. 40, Pl. 61; Cloak Catalogue, 1969.

41
American, possibly Boston & Sandwich Glass Co., 1860-88. Transparent blue glass cube; polished slightly beveled edges.
1⅝″ (4.1 cm.) each side.
Bergstrom Bequest, 1958.
EHB acquisition: 1936.
No. 41, Pl. 61; Cloak Catalogue, 1969.

838
Max Erlacher, Corning, NY, 1971. "Bird in the Nest." Shallow, colorless Steuben designed; copperwheel-engraved intaglio by Erlacher. Polished flat base signed "MRE '71" and "No. 10." Edition of 100.
D: 3¹¹⁄₁₆″ (9.4 cm.)
Museum Purchase, 1972.

946
Fenton Art Glass, Williamstown, WV, 1969. Circular plaque, the underside impressed "Apollo II 1969" in frosted center. At periphery: "One Small Step for a Man, One Giant Leap for Mankind."
D: 3⅞″ (10.0 cm.)
Gift of Dr. M. J. Caldwell, 1974.

1085
Origin unknown, probably Bohemian, 2nd half 19th century. Souvenir. Shallow colorless glass dome; red concave base engraved intaglio with street scene inscribed "Kaiserstrasse in Kranzenzbad."
D: 2⁹⁄₁₆″ (6.6 cm.)
Gift of David Kingsbaker, 1974.

1253
Whitefriars (English), Wealdstone, 1976. American flag is surrounded by close-packed white star canes including blue/white Bicentennial cane (1776-1976 and Whitefriars monk silhouette); peripheral circle of blue/white star canes; smooth "jelly glass" inverted colorless base. Large top punty, 5 side punties.
D: 3¹⁄₁₆″ (7.8 cm.)
Museum Purchase, 1976.

1263
Gillinder & Sons, Philadelphia, PA, ca. 1876. Frosted, molded lion on oval base; ribbed sides; hollow base impressed "Gillinder & Sons Philadelphia Pa."
H: 2¾″ (6.9 cm.); W: 2²⁵⁄₃₂″ (7.1 cm.)
L: 5¹¹⁄₁₆″ (14.4 cm.)
Museum Purchase, 1976.

1266
Origin unknown, probably Bohemian, 2nd half 19th

century. "Spa" souvenir. Solid colorless glass, blue-flashed concave base; inscribed "Trinkhalle in Baden."
D: 2¹³⁄₃₂″ (6.1 cm.)
Museum Purchase, 1977.

1295
Ronald E. Hansen, Mackinaw City, MI, 1967. Lampwork "Spanish galleon" on pedestal.
H: 8¹⁵⁄₁₆″ (22.7 cm.); W: 7¼″ (18.5 cm.)
Gift of Ronald E. Hansen, 1977.

1315
Origin unknown, possibly English (Stourbridge area), late 19th century. Shallow, hollow glass dome impressed intaglio with dahlia design, affixed to blue-over-brass base. Underside imprinted: "Cristaux-Nouveautes de J. & Cie Fabricants Btes (s.g.d.g.) paris 5mf Serie No. Paris."
D: 3″ (8.9 cm.)
Gift of Robert S. Sage and Jeanne Sage Groves in memory of their parents, Charles H. and Lyda P. Sage, 1978.

1329
Origin unknown, possibly French, 19th century. "Spa" souvenir. Shallow colorless dome, shallow foot; base flashed with red and engraved with scene of railway bridge over the Rhine River at Kehl. Inscribed: "Le Pont de Kehl."
D: 3⅛″ (7.9 cm.)
Gift of Paul Hollister, 1978.

1356
Attributed to Bohemia, 19th century. "Spa" souvenir. Red-flashed base engraved with stag, to sinister in forest scene. Periphery of dome protrudes slightly from circular, straight-sided base.
D: 2²³⁄₃₂″ (6.9 cm.)
Gift of Mrs. F. E. Seybold, 1979.

1433
Colin Terris, Caithness Glass, Ltd., Wick, Scotland, 1981. Swirled pink/white and green/white star canes, compound central legend cane; mottled translucent dark blue base polished flat, signed "60/750" "Caithness Scotland" "Celebration." Souvenir of The Prince of Wales/Lady Diana Spencer wedding, July 29, 1981.
D: 2⅞″ (7.3 cm.)
Gift of Mr. and Mrs. William L. Liebman, 1981.

1547
Origin unknown, possibly Boston & Sandwich Glass Co., Sandwich, MA, 19th century. Transparent turquoise-blue icosahedron. D: 2¹⁵⁄₁₆″ (7.5 cm.)
J. Howard Gilroy Bequest, 1986.

1599
Ed St. Clair, Elwood, IN, 1960s. Ovoid colorless glass, spaced bubbles, encases ceramic replica of "Liberty Bell" placed above red/white/blue crimp cushion. "Ed St. Clair" impressed in pontil area of smooth flat base.
D: 3¹³⁄₃₂″ (8.7 cm.)
Bequest of J. Howard Gilroy, 1986.

1705
Perthshire Paperweights, Ltd., Crieff, Scotland, dated 1981. High colorless dome encases "Royal Wedding Crown" motif (date "24.7.81" and border of wedding bells). Polished colorless basal concavity encloses "P 1981" cane; basal ring.
D: 2⅝″ (6.7 cm.)
Gift of Mr. and Mrs. F. John Barlow, 1986.

101
Attributed to Boston & Sandwich Glass Co., Sandwich, MA, 1880.
Bergstrom Bequest, 1958.
EHB acquisition: Unrecorded.
No. 620, Pl. 50; Cloak Catalogue, 1969.

398
Origin unknown, possibly Millville, NJ area, ca. 1910.
Bergstrom Bequest, 1958.
EHB acquisition: Unrecorded.
No. 418, Pl. 45; Cloak Catalogue, 1969.

571
Glass Bead.
Origin unknown, possibly Chinese, 1930s.
Bergstrom Bequest, 1958.
EHB acquisition: Unrecorded.
No. 612A, Pl. 50; Cloak Catalogue, 1969.

579
Attributed to Thure Erickson, Brockton, MA, 1945.
Bergstrom Bequest, 1958.
EHB acquisition: Unrecorded.

580
Cuff Links.
Attributed to Frank X. Weinman, Boston, MA, ca. 1940.
Bergstrom Bequest, 1958.
EHB acquisition: Unrecorded.
No. 619, Pl. 50; Cloak Catalogue, 1969.

595
Attributed to Winfield Rutter, Millville, NH, ca. 1940.
Bergstrom Bequest, 1958.
EHB acquisition: Unrecorded.
No. 638, Pl. 50; Cloak Catalogue, 1969.

596
Charles Kaziun, 1940-45.
Bergstrom Bequest, 1958.
EHB acquisition: Unrecorded.
No. 637, Pl. 53; Cloak Catalogue, 1969.

597
Attributed to Clichy, 1845-55.
Bergstrom Bequest, 1958.
EHB acquisition: Unrecorded.
No. 639, Pl. 50; Cloak Catalogue, 1969.

1233
John Gooderham, Sault Ste. Marie, Ontario, 1976.
Gift of John Gooderham, 1976.

1296
Ronald Hansen, Mackinaw City, MI, 1977.
Gift of Ronald Hansen, 1977.

1319
Glass Bead.
Origin unknown, possibly French, 19th century.
Gift of Robert S. Sage and Jeanne Sage Groves in memory of their parents, Charles H. and Lyda P. Sage, 1978.

1472, 1473
Origin unknown, possibly English, ca. 1840-90.
Acquisition unknown, ca. 1969-70.

1474
Millefiori Glass Canes.
Origin unknown, probably Italian, ca. 1970.
Acquisition unknown.

1476
Origin unknown.
Acquisition unknown.

1618
Origin unknown, 1960s-70s.
Bequest of J. Howard Gilroy, 1986.

573, 574, 1555, 572

65

1556, 1066

50

48, 49

433

390

116

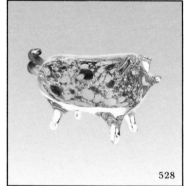

528

629

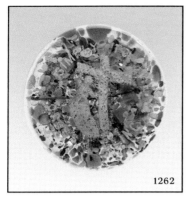

1262

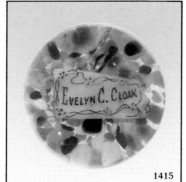

1415

253

981

1605

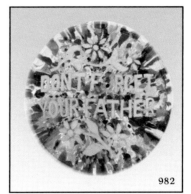

982

77

351

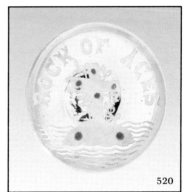

520

731

760

550

48
Origin unknown, possibly Spain, late 19th-early 20th century. Free-form glass hen; pontil mark underside.
L: 4½" (11.4 cm.)
Bergstrom Bequest, 1958.
EHB acquisition: August, 1937.
No. 48, Pl. 60; Cloak Catalogue, 1969.

49
Origin unknown, possibly Spain, late 19th-early 20th century. Free-form glass hen; pontil mark underside.
L: 3¼" (8.3 cm.)
Bergstrom Bequest, 1958.
EHB acquisition: August, 1937.
No. 49, Pl. 60; Cloak Catalogue, 1969.

50
Origin unknown, possibly Bristol area, 1850-60. Free-form translucent sapphire-blue glass swan; pontil mark on its back.
H: 3¾" (9.6 cm.); W: 3¼" (8.3 cm.)
Bergstrom Bequest, 1958.
EHB acquisition: August, 1937.
No. 50, Pl. 45; Cloak Catalogue, 1969.

65
Attributed to Venice, ca. 1930. Sparkling colorless glass encases near surface "Roman" spiral. Central spiral of coarse opaque white filigree. Flat smooth base.
D: 2¹⁵⁄₁₆" (5.8 cm.)
Bergstrom Bequest, 1958.
EHB acquisition: September, 1937.
No. 70, Pl. 59; Cloak Catalogue, 1969.

116
Attributed to Bristol area, 1850-60. Translucent sapphire-blue, free-form glass hen applied to crown of blown glass sphere mottled with spatter glass; smooth flattened base; pontil mark.
D: 3¾" (9.6 cm.)
Bergstrom Bequest, 1958.
EHB acquisition: May, 1938.
Illus. 44, Bergstrom book, 1940; Illus. 42, later editions.
No. 124, Pl. 33; Cloak Catalogue, 1969.

390
American; 19th century. Free-form, translucent brown glass turtle.
L: 5¾" (14.6 cm.)
Bergstrom Bequest, 1958.
EHB acquisition: May, 1941.
No. 410, Pl. 60; Cloak Catalogue, 1969.

433
Zanesville Glass Works, Zanesville, OH; ca. 1850. Translucent brown, free-form glass turkey; cylindrical stem; smooth flat circular foot.
D: 2¹³⁄₁₆" (7.2 cm.) foot.
Bergstrom Bequest, 1958.
EHB acquisition: October, 1941.
No. 461, Pl. 45; Cloak Catalogue, 1969.

528
Origin unknown, probably Stourbridge area, England, 19th century. Free-form glass pig.
L: 4" (10.2 cm.)

Bergstrom Bequest, 1958.
EHB acquisition: Unrecorded.
No. 562, Pl. 60; Cloak Catalogue, 1969.

572
Marble.
Attributed to German or American manufacture, 1850-1926. Bubbly, colorless glass encases white-striped red/green/blue rods spiraled from apex to base; white filigree "net" center core.
D: 2" (5.1 cm.); Circumf.: 6¼" (15.9 cm.)
Bergstrom Bequest, 1958.
EHB acquisition: Unrecorded.
No. 613, Pl. 59; Cloak Catalogue, 1969.

573
Marble.
Attributed to German or American manufacture, 1846-1926. Spiraled white strands near surface; twisted central opaque yellow core edged with translucent red; double strands of translucent dark green between each twist from apex to base.
D: 2" (5.1 cm.)
Bergstrom Bequest, 1958.
EHB acquisition: Unrecorded.

574
Marble.
Attributed to German or American manufacture, 1850-1926. "Onionskin" type. Sections of red and blue spatter slightly swirled over opaque white.
D: 2¹⁄₁₆" (5.3 cm.); Circumf.: 6½" (16.5 cm.)
Bergstrom Bequest, 1958.
EHB acquisition: Unrecorded.
No. 614, Pl. 59; Cloak Catalogue, 1969.

629
Origin unknown, probably American, 19th-early 20th century. Morning glory-type flower. Blown stem, shaped flower form.
D: 4³⁄₃₂" (10.4 cm.); L: 5⁷⁄₃₂" (13.3 cm.)
Bergstrom Bequest, 1958.
EHB acquisition: Unrecorded.
No. 766d, Pl. 63; Cloak Catalogue, 1969.

1066
Marbles.
A-G, I-Q, S and T: Probably German, Thuringen area, 1846-60. H and R: Origin unknown, German or American, 1850-1920.
Gift of Mrs. Kathleen Hatcher, 1974.
Ref.: Baumann, Paul: Collecting Antique Marbles, 1970.

1555
Marble.
Germany; 1850-1920. Large, "onionskin" type. Mottled red/yellow/green swirled near top. One small flat end.
D: 2⁵⁄₃₂" (5.5 cm.)
Bequest of J. Howard Gilroy, 1986.

1556
Marble.
Germany; 1850-1920. Swirled mottled red/green/yellow/mica. Pontil mark one end.
D: 1¼" (3.2 cm.)
Bequest of J. Howard Gilroy, 1986.

77
Attributed to Millville, NJ, ca. 1900. Yellowish glass encases flat opaque white motto "Home Sweet Home to Mother"; crimped pink/yellow/white spatter glass ground over translucent pink spatter glass "basket" down to smooth colorless base; pontil mark.
D: 3⅜" (8.6 cm.)
Bergstrom Bequest, 1958.
EHB acquisition: October, 1937.
No. 82, Pl. 48; Cloak Catalogue, 1969.

253
Attributed to Michael Kane, Millville, NJ, ca. 1900. Die-made, horizontal motif: finely ground colored glass portrays hunter in blue coat aiming at wild fowl, brown/white dog pointing; fallen log in foreground. Allover geometric faceting expands near smooth flat base. Note: the "hunter and dog" theme may have been inspired by Baccarat ceramic incrustation, 1845-55; see No. 201.
D: 3¾" (9.6 cm.)
Bergstrom Bequest, 1958.
EHB acquisition: October, 1939.
Illus. 77, Bergstrom book, 1940; Illus. 75 later editions.
No. 270, Pl. 46; Cloak Catalogue, 1969.
Ref.: *American Collector*, November, 1938; p. 14.
Pepper, Adeline: *The Glass Gaffers of New Jersey*, 1971; p. 260.

351
Millville, NJ, attributed to Michael Kane, 1880-1910. Die-made, thin flat motif of finely ground opaque white glass vertically placed in weight. "Home Sweet Home" in half-circle above log cabin, double path to door, fence, and tree. Top punty, 1 punty on each side frames motif. Smooth concave circular foot.
D: 3½" (8.9 cm.)
Bergstrom Bequest, 1958.
EHB acquisition: October, 1940.
No. 370, Pl. 47; Cloak Catalogue, 1969.
Ref.: *American Collector*, April, 1938, p. 9.

520
Attributed to Millville, NJ, 1880-1905. "Die" motif: opaque white powdered glass portrays cross on a mound (decorated with 6 red dots), foliage and ground, "Rock of Ages" above cross. Smooth flat base; pontil mark.
D: 3¼" (8.3 cm.)
Bergstrom Bequest, 1958.
EHB acquisition: Unrecorded.
No. 554, Pl. 48; Cloak Catalogue, 1969.

550
Edward Rithner, Wellsburg, WV, 1940-50. "Bergstrom" in white powdered glass near crown. Layer of dark red spatter over opaque white through which 4 elongated bubbles extend to colorless base; pontil mark.
D: 3⁷⁄₁₆" (8.7 cm.)
Bergstrom Bequest, 1958.
EHB acquisition: Unrecorded.
No. 586, Pl. 49; Cloak Catalogue, 1969.
Ref.: *PCA Bulletin*, 1966-67.

731
John Gentile, Gentile Glass Co., Star City, WV, 1966. American flag with 13 stars on opaque white cushion. Words "Old" and "Glory" in cobalt blue appear above and below flag. Wide top punty; 8 punties in 2 sizes on curve. "JG" insignia in blue encased underside of base. (This type weight, first made before 1920 by John's father, Peter Gentile, was revived by John after 1950.)
D: 3⅜" (8.6 cm.)
Gift of Mrs. Jean S. Melvin, 1968.
Ref.: *The Gatherer*, Wheaton Village, Millville, NJ; August, 1981.

760
John Gentile, WV, 1964. "Die" weight. "From A Friend" within a wreath (powdered white glass) above blue/red/yellow spatter glass cushion. Smooth colorless base and pontil area.
D: 3⁷⁄₁₆" (8.5 cm.)
Gift of Mrs. Jean S. Melvin, 1969.

981
Origin unknown, American, possibly William Degenhart, Cambridge, OH, 1960s. White "die" motto, "Don't Forget Your Mother" above crimped multicolor spatter. Polished flat colorless base.
D: 3⅜" (8.6 cm.)
Gift of Dr. M. J. Caldwell, 1974.

982
Origin unknown, American, possibly William Degenhart, 1960s. White "die" motto, "Don't Forget Your Father" above crimped multicolor spatter. Polished flat colorless base.
D: 3⅜" (8.6 cm.)
Gift of Dr. M. J. Caldwell, 1974.

1262
Millville, NJ, ca. 1900. "Die" weight. Low in weight; motto: "Simply To Thy Cross I Cling" above crimped multicolor spatter; smooth colorless base; pontil mark.
D: 3⅜" (8.6 cm.)
Gift of Mrs. Walter Kuester, 1976.

1415
Possibly Degenhart (Crystal Art Glass), Cambridge, OH, 1960s. Bubbly colorless glass encloses floral-decorated white plaque inscribed in blue: "Evelyn C. Cloak," multicolor chip/white spatter ground; polished flat colorless base.
D: 3³⁄₁₆" (8.1 cm.)
Gift of Evelyn Campbell Cloak, 1967.

1605
American, probably John Degenhart, early 1930s. Rectangular white glass plaque painted with "Summer Scene" (house, fence, road in rural setting), signed "Picha 3 Pat. J.S..." Layer of multicolor spatter above layer of white spatter. Polished flat colorless base.
D: 3⅝" (9.2 cm.)
Bequest of J. Howard Gilroy, 1986.
Ref.: Melvin, Jean S.: *American Glass Paperweights and Their Makers*, 1970; p. 46.

104

762

356

464

GE-1

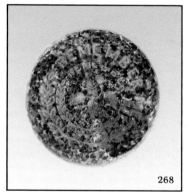

268

505

715

1061

934

553

761

336, 335

699

1564, 1099, 1100

929

78

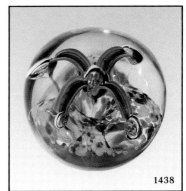

1438

697

819

272

610

14

774

GE-1
Origin unknown, Millville, NJ, or possibly Pittsburgh, PA, 1880-1910. Circular steel plate, 1 side incised "Remember Me" (in reverse) in wreath motif (used in making paperweight No. 268); the other side incised "Friendship" (in reverse), 2 hearts with arrow, and branch of leaves.
D: 2½" (6.3 cm.)
Bergstrom Bequest, 1958.
EHB acquisition: Unrecorded.
Illus. 71, Bergstrom book, 1940; Illus. 69, later editions.
No. 285-A, Pl. 47; Cloak Catalogue, 1969.

104
Origin unknown, possibly Pittsburgh, late 19th-early 20th century. Magnum. Encased opaque greyish-white glass plaque etched in black with bust portrait of American Indian (probably Iroquois) with long hair, earrings, head feathers, and necklace of boar's teeth. Green/red/blue spatter glass surrounds plaque. Smooth colorless base, pontil mark.
D: 3¹¹⁄₁₆" (9.4 cm.)
Bergstrom Bequest, 1958.
EHB acquisition: January, 1938.
No. 111, Pl. 61; Cloak Catalogue, 1969.

268
Artist unknown, Millville, NJ, 1880-1910. Dome-shape; powdered white glass die motif: "Remember Me" motto, wreath of leaves encircles central spray of rosebud, stem, 4 leaves; motif floats above multicolor spatter ground. Top punty. Smooth flat colorless base; polished central concavity. See Die: GE-1.
D: 3⁵⁄₁₆" (8.4 cm.)
Bergstrom Bequest, 1958.
EHB acquisition: November, 1939.
Illus. 70, Bergstrom book, 1940; Illus. 68, later editions.
No. 285, Pl. 47; Cloak Catalogue, 1969.

356
Gear Shift Knob.
Charles or John Degenhart, Crystal Art Glass Co., Cambridge, OH, 1930s. Opaque white glass plaque, outlined in blue, bears name of "R. Barber" in black letters. 4 small lily-type flowers (2 yellow/2 pink, each with bubble center) decorate plaque corners; varicolored spatter ground. Flat top, geometric facets on curve. Steel mount. ("R. Barber" is a coincidence; knob was not made by Ralph Barber in Millville, NJ. Many of these gear shift knobs were made to order by the Degenharts; confirmed by Mrs. Elizabeth Degenhart, Crystal Art Glass Co., April, 1974.)
D: 2" (5.1 cm.)
Bergstrom Bequest, 1958.
EHB acquisition: November, 1940.
No. 374, Pl. 50; Cloak Catalogue, 1969.

464
Millville, NJ, attributed to Michael Kane, 1880-1910. Vertically placed, die-made thin opaque white flat portrayal of ship, red flag, blue sea; 3 side punties. Smooth circular foot; pontil mark.
D: 3¾" (9.6 cm.)
Bergstrom Bequest, 1958.
EHB acquisition: April, 1942.
No. 492, Pl. 47; Cloak Catalogue, 1969.

505
Attributed to Millville, NJ, 1880-1905. Dome shape: die-made opaque white flat sailboat with flag, birds in flight, lighthouse, and waves; translucent dark amber ground approximately ½" thick. Frosted central concavity in flat base. (Similar to No. 520.)
D: 3⁵⁄₁₆" (8.4 cm.)
Bergstrom Bequest, 1958.
EHB acquisition: Unrecorded.
No. 537, Pl. 48; Cloak Catalogue, 1969.

553
Peter Gentile, G-F Glass Co., Morgantown, W. VA., ca. 1947. Heavy, spherical form. Large opaque white flying bird, orange head and yellow bill, near crown over spaced bubbles. (This type weight patented by John G. Funfrock, 1948.)
D: 3⁷⁄₁₆" (8.7 cm.)
Bergstrom Bequest, 1958.
EHB acquisition: Unrecorded.
No. 589, Pl. 52; Cloak Catalogue, 1969.

715
Joseph Zimmerman and Gene Baxley, Zimmerman Art Glass Co., Corydon, IN, 1967. Enameled floral spray motif designed by Mrs. Lucie Webb: blue/pink/yellow flowers, green leaves; translucent cobalt blue cushion. Smooth, flattened colorless base impressed with letter "Z" in pontil area.
D: 3¼" (8.3 cm.)
Gift of Joseph Zimmerman, 1967.
No. 747, Pl. 56; Cloak Catalogue, 1969.

761
Edward Rithner, Wellsburg, WV, ca. 1950. Stylized powdered glass flower: 5 turquoise/pink/white petals, bubble center drawn down into red-on-white spatter crimp cushion with 4 spaced smaller bubbles. Smooth colorless base, rough-ground pontil area.
D: 3¹⁄₁₆" (7.7 cm.)
Gift of Mrs. Jean S. Melvin, 1969.

762
Crystal Art Glass Co., Cambridge, OH, 1968. Opaque white glass plaque inscribed "Home Sweet Home" within floral border; 2 layers of varicolored spatter. Smooth colorless base.
D: 3⅜" (8.7 cm.)
Gift of Mrs. Jean S. Melvin, 1969.

934
Bob St. Clair, Elwood, IN, 1970s. Multicolor crimp motif, 8 teardrop bubbles. Shallow dome; "Bob St. Clair" impressed in pontil area of colorless base.
D: 3¾" (9.5 cm.)
Gift of Dr. M. J. Caldwell, 1974.

1061
Carl Kraft, Toledo, OH, 1973. Commemorative paperweight sponsored by The Glass Collectors Club of Toledo to recognize the founding by Edward Drummon Libbey of the glass industry in Toledo in 1888. On layer of opaque white: "85th Anniversary Glass Industry in Toledo, Ohio 1888-1973 Toledo, Ohio, The Glass Capital of the World" and 2-story log fort, all in cobalt blue. Cobalt blue/white marbleized ground. Smooth base inscribed "494" and impressed "Kraft Toledo, Ohio." 494/500.
D: 3⅛" (7.9 cm.)
Gift of Mrs. John S. Pilner, 1974.

14
Benjamin A. Leach, Fowlerton, IN, 1896-98. Tiny bubbles and yellow spatter glass cushion punctuated by central bubble; 4 bubbles near periphery; translucent brown ground; flat, frosted base.
D: 3⅜″ (8.6 cm.) Bergstrom Bequest, 1958.
EHB acquisition: March, 1935.
Illus. 83, Bergstrom book, 1940; Illus. 81, later editions.
No. 16, Pl. 49; Cloak Catalogue, 1969.

78
Danish, 1880-1920. A layer of varicolored spatter glass through which 5 elongated bubbles extend down to smaller layer of spatter above smooth flat base; pontil mark.
D: 3¹¹⁄₁₆″ (9.4 cm.) Bergstrom Bequest, 1958.
EHB acquisition: October, 1937.
No. 83, Pl. 40; Cloak Catalogue, 1969.

272
Swedish. Early 20th century. 2 layers of coarse spatter, predominantly orange, centered by bubble and 4 peripheral elongated bubbles drawn to smooth flat base.
D: 3⁷⁄₁₆″ (8.7 cm.) Bergstrom Bequest, 1958.
EHB acquisition: Unrecorded.
No. 291, Pl. 40; Cloak Catalogue, 1969.

335, 336
Mantel Ornament with Stand (pair).
Ravenna Glass Works, Ravenna, OH, late 19th century. Globular. Expanded crimped "lily": opaque white and multicolor spatter punctuated by central bubble and 4 elongated bubbles, all drawn to base. Polished flat pontil area. Sphere rests on separate green glass stand encasing multicolor glass strands. Applied colorless glass threads encircle exterior. Conical foot; trace of pontil mark.
Ball D: 3⅜″ (8.6 cm.); Stand H: 4⅞″ (12.5 cm.)
Bergstrom Bequest, 1958.
EHB acquisition: August, 1940.
No. 356, Pl. 49; Cloak Catalogue, 1969.

610
American, possibly Fostoria Glass, Fostoria, OH, 1880-1900. 4-petal lily (red/pink/white), elongated central bubble. Petals curve downward to base, each with elongated bubbles near tip. Flat frosted base; pontil mark.
D: 3¹¹⁄₁₆″ (9.4 cm.) Bergstrom Bequest, 1958.
EHB acquisition: Unrecorded.
No. 718, Pl. 44; Cloak Catalogue, 1969.

697
St. Clair Glass Works, Elwood, IN, early 1960s. 8 sections of opaque white marbled with caramel glass (made at Indiana Tumbler & Goblet Co., Greentown, IN, ca. 1900); elongated bubble center, bubble between each section. Smooth base, pontil mark.
D: 3⁷⁄₁₆″ (8.7 cm.)
No. 716, Pl. 55; Cloak Catalogue, 1969.
Gift of Neenah-Menasha Early American Glass Club, 1964.

699
Doorstop.
John St. Clair, Elwood, IN, ca. 1930. Aquamarine glass encloses aqua/white spatter glass crimp design in 2 layers simulating lily-type pattern, punctuated by 6 elongated bubbles and central bubble. Aqua/white spatter ground.

Colorless base, pontil mark.
D: 8¹⁄₁₆″ (20.4 cm.); Wt.: 11½ lbs.
No. 719, Pl. 49; Cloak Catalogue, 1969.
Gift of Joseph St. Clair, 1964.

774
Edward J. Mazerski, Union Glass Co., Somerville, MA, 1969. Morning glory-type flower made from fragments of Mount Washington Burmese glass. 3 "flowers," each with central bubble, drawn down to spatter glass cushion with 3 alternating bubbles. Polished pontil area.
D: 3⁷⁄₁₆″ (8.8 cm.)
Gift of Mrs. Evelyn Campbell Cloak, 1970.

819
John Gentile, Star City, WV, 1960s. 3 "flowers" of white/pink/blue spatter glass, each centered by bubble drawn into 2 matching layers of spatter with 3 additional bubbles near periphery. Smooth flat colorless base.
H: 4¼″ (10.7 cm.); D: 4⁷⁄₁₆″ (11.2 cm.)
Gift of John Clary, 1970.

929
Joe Zimmerman, Corydon, IN, 1972. 6 spaced teardrop bubbles drawn to pink/green spatter "lilies." Smooth base.
D: 3″ (7.6 cm.)
Gift of Dr. M. J. Caldwell, 1974.

1099
Colin Terris and Peter Holmes, Caithness Glass, Ltd., Wick, Scotland, 1970. Planet series, "SATURN." Cobalt blue spatter "ring" encircles transparent bubble "sphere" above blue particles and bubbles crimped amethyst ground forming 9 peaks; 9 spaced peripheral bubbles. Polished flat base inscribed "SATURN Colin Terris. Peter Holmes. 1970. No. 19/500."
D: 3¹⁄₃₂″ (7.7 cm.)
Gift of Colin Terris & Peter Holmes, 1975.

1100
Caithness Glass, Ltd., 1970. Planet series, "VENUS." Multiple bubbles cover central amethyst twisted core; 8 "petals" at periphery; blue/white particle ground. Trail of transparent bubbles in "space." Polished flat base inscribed "VENUS Colin Terris Peter Holmes 1970 No. 19/500."
D: 3″ (7.6 cm.)
Gift of Colin Terris & Peter Holmes, 1975.

1438
Origin unknown, possibly Alex Stelzer, Libbey Glass Co., Toledo, OH, 1940s. 4 striped "petals," a bubble at each tip and center; spatter cushion; colorless base, pontil mark; basal ring.
D: 3⅜″ (8.6 cm.)
Gift of Mrs. John Ogden and Henry Harnischfeger in memory of their parents, Mr. and Mrs. Walter Harnischfeger, 1981.

1564
Caithness Glass, Ltd., 1971. Planet series: "URANUS." 3 spaced red canes surrounded by 6 bubbles. Amethyst "hilly" ground covered with bubbles and powdered blue glass. Polished flat base signed "URANUS Colin Terris Peter Holmes 1971. No. 180/500. Caithness."
D: 3³⁄₃₂″ (7.8 cm.)
Bequest of J. Howard Gilroy, 1986.

422

1270

1047

712

1794

548

814

164

120

438

844

656

35

1010

773

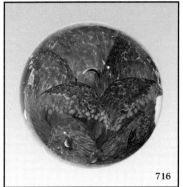
716

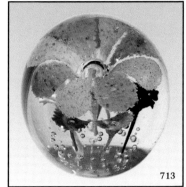
713

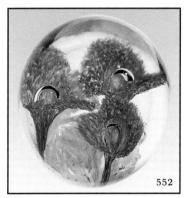
552

747

61

976

395

540

754

120
Corning, NY, ca. 1935. Large flower, bubble center, 4 translucent deep blue petals bordered with pink/opaque white. Opaque blue/white stem extends to flat colorless base.
D: 3½″ (8.9 cm.)
Bergstrom Bequest, 1958.
EHB acquisition: June, 1938.
No. 129, Pl. 51; Cloak Catalogue, 1969.

164
Ernst Von Dohln, Dorflinger Glass Works, White Mills, PA, early 1900s. Heavy, sparkling glass encases green lily motif; 4 large upright green petals lined with opaque white. Elongated central bubble, smaller bubble between petals. Polished flat colorless base.
D: 3⁷⁄₁₆″ (8.7 cm.)
Bergstrom Bequest, 1958.
EHB acquisition: November, 1938.
No. 173, Pl. 51; Cloak Catalogue, 1969.

422
Origin unknown, possibly Dorflinger Glass Works, White Mills, PA, 1890-1910. Heavy sparkling colorless glass encases upright 4-petal motif, each with single large millefiori cane at tip. Opaque white petals overlaid with red/cobalt blue/green (elongated bubble center) rest on multicolored ground. Superior quality, serrated canes enclose 5-point stars in various designs.
D: 3¼″ (8.3 cm.)
Bergstrom Bequest, 1958.
EHB acquisition: September, 1941.
No. 445, Pl. 44; Cloak Catalogue, 1969.
Ref.: *PCA Bulletin,* 1987.

438
Attributed to Ravenna Glass Co., Ravenna, OH, late 19th century. Opaque white lily; 5 narrow petals; central bubble and lily stem extend to base. 5 trumpet-like flowers (yellow/green/pastel blue/dark blue/white; bubble centers) appear at basal periphery. Frosted flat base; pontil mark. (Design patented by Henry Miller, Pittsburgh, PA, 1890.)
D: 3½″ (8.9 cm.)
Bergstrom Bequest, 1958.
EHB acquisition: October, 1941.
No. 466, Pl. 45; Cloak Catalogue, 1969.

548
G-F Glass Co., Morgantown, WV, 1947. Gentile-Funfrock became Gentile Glass Co., Star City, WV, in 1948. Ovoid; 3 opaque white spatter calla lilies (bubble centers), green stems extend to base between sections of transparent blue glass cushion with spaced bubbles. Smooth base; paper label: "Funfrock, April 14, 1947."
D: 3⁵⁄₁₆″ (8.4 cm.)
Bergstrom Bequest, 1958.
EHB acquisition: Unrecorded.
No. 584, Pl. 52; Cloak Catalogue, 1969.

656
Origin unknown, midwest American, late 19th-early 20th century. Near dome, a central red lily, 5 narrow petals, bubble center. Red stem extends to varicolored spatter/opaque white crimp ground.
D: 2¹³⁄₁₆″ (7.2 cm.)
No. 675, Pl. 45; Cloak Catalogue, 1969.
Museum Purchase, 1963.

712
Gertrude Gentile, Gentile Glass Co., Star City, WV, 1967. Ovoid; 3 opaque white, blue-centered lily-type flowers; elongated bubble centers; spaced smaller bubbles near smooth, colorless base; concave pontil area. Paper label: "Handcrafted by Gertrude Gentile, Star City, W. VA."
D: 3³⁄₁₆″ (8.1 cm.)
No. 744, Pl. 56; Cloak Catalogue, 1969.
Gift of Mrs. Jean S. Melvin, 1967.

814
Blair R. Hardenburg, Corning, NY, 1965. Near crown; large lily, 5 opaque white petals, wide cobalt blue stripes; bubble center. Frosted bowl-shaped cushion. Smooth flat base signed "B H"/"65."
D: 3¹⁄₁₆″ (7.9 cm.)
Gift of Blair R. Hardenburg, 1970.

844
Carl Erickson, Bremen, OH, 1943-61. 3 translucent emerald green calla lilies, bubble centers, drawn down into pastel yellow/orange spatter cushion. Smooth colorless base.
D: 3⁷⁄₁₆″ (8.7 cm.)
Gift of Prof. and Mrs. F. H. Knower, 1972.

1047
Czechoslovakian, early 1970s. Greyish glass encases 3 bubbles, partially covered with blue/green/orange above miniscule bubble-covered dark green ground. Polished flat colorless base.
D: 3⅝″ (9.3 cm.)
Gift of Dr. M. J. Caldwell, 1974.

1270
Holmegaard Glassworks, Naestved, Denmark, 1977. Ovoid; central bubble surrounded by 4 peripheral bubbles, all drawn to spatter "lilies" of blue/white/yellow; multicolor cushion; polished flat colorless base. Paper label: "Holmegaard."
D: 2²¹⁄₃₂″ (6.8 cm.)
Gift of Møgen Schluter, 1977.

1794
Pairpoint Glass Co., Inc., Sagamore, MA, 1972. Shallow form. Crimped tortoiseshell motif, bubbles within crimps near periphery. "No. 28" scratched in base, the center die-stamped "1872/1972/Van Son."
D: 3¹¹⁄₃₂″ (9.8 cm.)
Gift of Mrs. Virginia Bensley Trowbridge, 1987.

35
Origin unknown, late 19th-early 20th century. 2 tiers of spatter glass lined with opaque white: top layer predominantly red; lower green. Central bubble near dome, 4 spaced bubbles extend downward through layers. Concave center in flattened colorless base.
D: 3¼″ (8.3 cm.)
Bergstrom Bequest, 1958.
EHB acquisition: June, 1937.
No. 35, Pl. 63; Cloak Catalogue, 1969.

61
Origin unknown, possibly Boston & Sandwich Glass Co., Sandwich, MA, 1870-88. High-crowned, colorless glass encases "diamond-quilted" mottled pink/white cushion; spaced bubbles in each indenture; large central bubble. Cushion thinly cased with transparent amber. Flat smooth colorless base. Possibly New England Glass Company; also seen in green and blue.
D: 2¹⁵⁄₁₆″ (7.4 cm.)
Bergstrom Bequest, 1958.
EHB acquisition: September, 1937.
No. 65, Pl. 50; Cloak Catalogue, 1969.

395
American, probably Dorflinger Glass Works, White Mills, PA, early 1900s. Heavy, colorless glass encases red, white, and blue upright lily flower with 4 double-layer petals, the colored glass being laid over opaque white: red on top side of upper layer and blue on underside of lower layer. Large central elongated bubble, smaller bubbles between petals. Polished flat colorless base.
D: 3⅛″ (7.9 cm.)
Bergstrom Bequest, 1958.
EHB acquisition: May, 1941.
No. 415, Pl. 51; Cloak Catalogue, 1969.

540
Steuben Glass, Corning, NY, Paul A. Holton, 1941. Large lily-type flower, 5-point pink blue-bordered petals; central bubble. Stem extends to mottled green/opaque white base. Inscribed "Steuben 1941" on flat underside.
D: 3³⁄₁₆″ (8.1 cm.)
Bergstrom Bequest, 1958.
EHB acquisition: Unrecorded.
No. 576, Pl. 51; Cloak Catalogue, 1969.

552
G-F Glass Co., Morgantown, WV, (Gentile-Funfrock), 1946. 3 deep pink and white spatter lilies, bubble centers; stems extend to bottom edge of thick ground of opaque white with spaced bubbles. Flat colorless base bears paper label: "Funfrock, April 11, 1946." Note: Similar to No. 548.
D: 3⁷⁄₁₆″ (8.7 cm.)
Bergstrom Bequest, 1958.
EHB acquisition: Unrecorded.
No. 588, Pl. 52; Cloak Catalogue, 1969.

713
Frank Hamilton, Gentile Glass Co., Star City, WV, 1967. Ovoid; near crown, a large flower with 8 fine spatter glass petals of alternating green/yellow. Bubble center extends toward base. Below flower: 5 smaller "lily" forms (blue/white/black/yellow/green); spaced bubbles near polished flat base, slight pontil concavity.
D: 3⅝″ (9.2 cm.)
No. 745, Pl. 56; Cloak Catalogue, 1969.
Gift of Mrs. Jean S. Melvin, 1967.

716
Joseph Zimmerman and Gene Baxley; Zimmerman Art Glass Co., Corydon, IN, 1967. Near crown, pink spatter over opaque white, lily-type crimp flower, central bubble. Basal periphery: 5 upright pink/white petals, bubble centers. Letter "Z" impressed in pontil area of flattened, colorless base.
D: 3⅜″ (8.6 cm.)
No. 748, Pl. 56; Cloak Catalogue, 1969.
Gift of Joseph Zimmerman, 1967.

747
Frank Hamilton, Gentile Glass Co., Star City, WV, 1967. Large "flower" near crown: 4 blue alternate with 4 white spatter glass petals; "frosty" central bubble. Layer of red/white/blue spatter with 6 tendrils surrounds stem, all drawn down to polished pontil area; smooth flat colorless base.
D: 3⁹⁄₁₆″ (9.0 cm.)
Gift of Mrs. Jean S. Melvin, 1969.
Ref.: Melvin, Jean S.: *American Glass Paperweights and Their Makers,* 1967, 1970; pp. 221-222.

754
Bookend.
John Degenhart, Cambridge, OH, ca. 1950. Blue/white spatter "flower"; central bubble and 4 smaller bubbles near periphery tilted on scallop-edged, semicircular flat colorless base.
D: 3⁵⁄₁₆″ (8.4 cm.)
Gift of Mrs. Jean S. Melvin, 1969.
Ref.: Melvin, Jean S.: *American Glass Paperweights and Their Makers,* 1967, 1970; pp. 44-55.

773
Edward J. Mazerski, Union Glass Co., Somerville, MA, 1969. 5-petal "flower" (umbrella form), central bubble; made from red/white/blue/aqua glass fragments excavated at site of Boston & Sandwich Glass Co., Sandwich, MA. Smooth base.
D: 3½″ (9.0 cm.)
Gift of Mrs. Evelyn Campbell Cloak, 1970.

976
F. M. Konstglas, Sweden, ca. 1970. Magnum. Bubble-centered multicolor spatter "flowers" stems drawn toward base, 1 near dome, 3 spaced near periphery. Pontil area polished flat.
D: 4³⁄₁₆″ (10.8 cm.)
Gift of Dr. M. J. Caldwell, 1974.

1010
F. Murano, Italy, 1960s. Ovoid; multicolor millefiori canes swirled in pyramidal form; 6 spaced peripheral teardrop bubbles. Polished flat base.
H: 4¼″ (10.5 cm.); D: 3″ (7.7 cm.)
Gift of Dr. M. J. Caldwell, 1974.

997, 999, 931

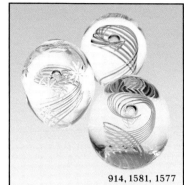

914, 1581, 1577

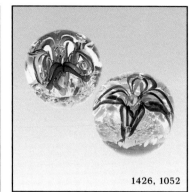

1426, 1052

979, 964

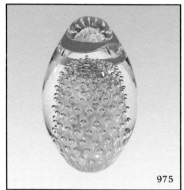

975

751, 764, 1029

845

947, 1600, 790

1292

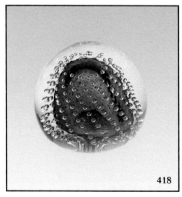

418

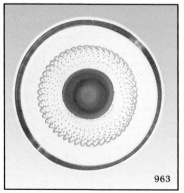

963

1021, 1020, 1049

910, 912

1563

549, 271

1038

1522

1424

122

38

720

84

753

758

418
Origin unknown, possibly Pairpoint Corp., New Bedford, MA, 1910-1920. Swirled bubbles surround hollow-blown red core.
D: 3¹³⁄₁₆″ (8.1 cm.) Bergstrom Bequest, 1958.
EHB acquisition: September, 1941.
No. 440, Pl. 42; Cloak Catalogue, 1969.

751
Hand Cooler.
John Gentile, Gentile Glass Co., Star City, WV, 1966. Spatter glass and bubbles swirled toward crown.
D: 2¼″ (5.7 cm.)
Gift of Mrs. Jean S. Melvin, 1969.

764
John Gentile, 1968. Ovoid; turquoise and white rods spiraled from base to crown, spiraled spaced bubbles.
D: 3¼″ (8.4 cm.)
Gift of Mrs. Jean S. Melvin, 1969.

790
Pilgrim Glass Corp., Ceredo, WV, 1969. Large central bubble. Exterior striped with orange-colored glass. Circle of thumbprint cuts near base cut with 16-point star; signed "Fred Ogren 1970."
D: 3¹⁄₁₆″ (7.8 cm.)
Gift of Fred Ogren, 1970.

845
Carl Erickson, Bremen, OH, 1943-1961. Black cushion covered with multiple bubbles. Basal ring signed "Erickson."
D: 2¹³⁄₁₆″ (7.1 cm.)
Gift of Prof. and Mrs. F. H. Knower, 1972.

914
Blair Hardenburg, Corning, NY, 1960s. Pink and white ribbons spiral central teardrop. Oval cuts encircle base signed "B.H. 71."
D: 3³⁄₁₆″ (7.8 cm.)
Gift of Blair Hardenburg, 1973.

931
Joe Zimmerman, Corydon, IN, 1972. Yellow/orange/green spatter glass, 6 bubbles, drawn to rough-ground base.
D: 2⁵⁄₁₆″ (5.8 cm.)
Gift of Dr. M. J. Caldwell, 1974.

947
Pilgrim Glass, Ceredo, WV, early 1970s. Ovoid; large bubble within orange spiral. Polished flat base.
D: 2³⁄₁₆″ (5.8 cm.)
Gift of Dr. M. J. Caldwell, 1974.

963
Whitefriars Glass, Ltd., Wealdstone, England, ca. 1970. Shallow cylindrical; spaced bubbles enclose orange "mushroom." Polished flat top and base.
D: 3⁷⁄₁₆″ (8.9 cm.)
Gift of Dr. M. J. Caldwell, 1974.

964
Kosta Glassworks, Kosta, Sweden, ca. 1970. Cobalt blue spiral. Signed "Kosta 90962." 10 spires signed "Kosta 96099 Landstrand."
D: 3¹⁄₁₆″ (7.8 cm.)
Gift of Dr. M. J. Caldwell, 1974.

975
F. M. Konstglas, Ronneby, Sweden, ca. 1970. Ovoid; bubbles surround core creating a "pineapple."
H: 4⅞″ (12.4 cm.); D: 3¹⁄₁₆″ (7.9 cm.)
Gift of Dr. M. J. Caldwell, 1974.

979
Gulla-Kruf, Sweden, ca. 1970. Elongated central bubble surrounded by 5 spherical bubbles. Polished flat base.
D: 3⅛″ (8.1 cm.)
Gift of Dr. M. J. Caldwell, 1974.

997, 999
Origin unknown, India, ca. 1970. 3 multicolor and "goldstone" spatter "flowers." Double crimp motif.
D: 2⁹⁄₁₆″ (6.6 cm.) each.
Gift of Dr. M. J. Caldwell, 1974.

1020, 1021
Murano, Italy, 1960-1970. Apple and pear; applied leaf. Polished flat base.
H: 5″ (12.8 cm.) pear; D: 3½″ (9.0 cm.) apple
Gift of Dr. M. J. Caldwell, 1974.

1029
Murano, 1960-70. Ovoid. Green/white filigree spiral. Polished flat base.
H: 3¹⁄₁₆″ (7.8 cm.); D: 2½″ (6.4 cm.)
Gift of Dr. M. J. Caldwell, 1974.

1049
Czechoslovakia, early 1970s. Pear. Polished flat base.
H: 4¾″ (12.0 cm.)
Gift of Dr. M. J. Caldwell, 1974.

1052
Portugal, ca. 1970. 4-petal flower outlined in red and green. Polished flat colorless base.
D: 2½″ (6.3 cm.)
Gift of Dr. M. J. Caldwell, 1974.

1292
John Murphy, Cameron, WV, 1972. Lily-bubble design on green cushion; polished base signed "J Murphy."
D: 3½″ (8.9 cm.)
Gift of Mrs. Wanda Stevens in memory of her husband, Harold Stevens, 1977.

1426
Origin unknown, 20th century. 4-petal flower, drawn down to spatter cushion.
D: 2²¹⁄₃₂″ (6.7 cm.)
Gift of Carl W. Fischer, 1981.

1577
Steuben Glass, Corning, NY, 1960-1970. Ovoid; 8 white rods spiraled from base to point of central teardrop. Polished flat base signed "Steuben."
D: 3³⁄₃₂″ (7.9 cm.)
Bequest of J. Howard Gilroy, 1986.

1581
Blair Hardenburg, 1970. Ovoid; green/white spiral from base to central bubble. Polished base signed "BH '70."
H: 3³⁄₁₆″ (8.2 cm.); D: 3⅛″ (8.0 cm.)
Bequest of J. Howard Gilroy, 1986.

1600
Pilgrim Glass, 1960s. Ovoid frosted glass. Bubbles surround interior amber form, encasing large teardrop.
H: 2⅞″ (7.3 cm.); D: 2⁵⁄₃₂″ (5.5 cm.)
Bequest of J. Howard Gilroy, 1986.

38
Czechoslovakia, 1918-38. Ovoid form; allover faceting pointed at top. Five 5-petal opaque white flowers variously streaked with cobalt blue/orange/yellow; bubble centers; stems drawn down to translucent green spatter "mound." Polished flat base.
D: 2¹³⁄₁₆″ (7.2 cm.)
Bergstrom Bequest, 1958.
EHB acquisition: June, 1937.
No. 38, Pl. 40; Cloak Catalogue, 1969.

84
Czechoslovakia, 1918-38. Single orange nasturtium-type flower (6 petals/bubble center) above varicolored spatter ground. Rows of graduated pink loops surround motif. Smooth flat colorless base.
D: 2⅞″ (7.3 cm.)
Bergstrom Bequest, 1958.
EHB acquisition: November, 1937.
No. 89, Pl. 40; Cloak Catalogue, 1969.

122
Czechoslovakia, 1918-38. 3 flowers: opaque red, yellow-green, and purple, each with 8 petals and bubble center; colorless stems and 5 thin peripheral bubbles project from varicolored spatter pot. Haphazard faceting reaches point at top; 5- and 6-sided facets at curve. Polished flat colorless base.
D: 3″ (7.6 cm.)
Bergstrom Bequest, 1958.
EHB acquisition: June, 1938.
No. 131, Pl. 40; Cloak Catalogue, 1969.

271
Ernst von Dohln, Dorflinger Glass Works, White Mills, PA, early 1900s. Colorless "flint" glass encases cobalt blue lily lined with opaque white. 4 large upright petals, elongated bubble center (small bubble between petals) extend to colorless base; pontil mark.
D: 3⁷⁄₁₆″ (8.7 cm.)
Bergstrom Bequest, 1958.
EHB acquisition: November, 1939.
No. 290, Pl. 51; Cloak Catalogue, 1969.

549
Paul Holton, Corning, NY, 1941. Large blue and pink lily-type flower, silver flecks, bubble center, 5 opaque white-bordered petals. Stem extends to mottled green ground lined with opaque white. Smooth flat colorless base inscribed "Steuben, Nov. 1941." Note: Nos. 540 and 549 signed "Steuben" are not official products of the Steuben factory. Colored glass has not been produced there since 1933. They are more correctly "offhand paperweights" made by Steuben workers during off-hours.
D: 3¹¹⁄₁₆″ (9.4 cm.)
Bergstrom Bequest, 1958.
EHB acquisition: Unrecorded.
No. 585, Pl. 51; Cloak Catalogue, 1969.

720
Strathearn Glass, Ltd., Crieff, Scotland, 1967. Ovoid. Red lily flower and stem, 5 smooth pointed petals, bubble center; 3 narrow green leaves, all rising from deep cushion with black center surrounded by multicolored spatter which includes 1 ochre-colored cane bearing "S" signature. Flat smooth colorless base.
H: 3½″ (8.9 cm.); D: 2¼″ (5.7 cm.)
No. 752, Pl. 39; Cloak Catalogue, 1969.
Gift of Arthur Gorham, 1967.

753
John Kreutz, Silverbrook Art Glass Co., Flanders, NY, 1960s. Ovoid. Near surface: 4 stylized frond-like sprays (blue/red/yellow/white) stem from fine spatter glass and ovoid mica cushion. Polished flat base.
D: 3″ (7.6 cm.)
Gift of Mrs. Jean S. Melvin, 1969.

758
John Kreutz, 1960s. 3 translucent blue flowers/yellow centers near crown; coarsely frosted "mushroom" cushion. Red festooning forms peripheral border. Smooth flat base.
D: 3⁷⁄₁₆″ (8.8 cm.)
Gift of Mrs. Jean S. Melvin, 1969.

910
Pairpoint Glass Co., Sagamore, MA, 1971. Translucent turquoise swan on colorless sphere encasing multiple spaced bubbles. Colorless pedestal foot.
H: 6⁷⁄₁₆″ (16.3 cm.); D: 2⅝″ (6.7 cm.)
Gift of Mr. and Mrs. Joseph Beckenbach in memory of Evelyn Campbell Cloak, 1973.

912
Pairpoint Glass Co., 1971. Translucent amethyst glass snake, in 3 coils around colorless glass sphere encasing multiple spaced bubbles; baluster stem; circular footed base. Pontil mark.
H: 4¹¹⁄₁₆″ (11.9 cm.); D: 2⅞″ (7.3 cm.)
Gift of Mr. and Mrs. Joseph Beckenbach in memory of Evelyn Campbell Cloak, 1973.

1038
Italian, 1960-70. Quadrant-pressed colorless sphere encases in each section a bubble-centered flower (blue/pink/green/orange), stems drawn to polished flat base. Paper label: "Decora Imports, Inc., New York Made in Italy."
D: 3¼″ (8.0 cm.)
Gift of Dr. M. J. Caldwell, 1974.

1424
India, 1950s-60s. Shallow dome; 2 "flowers," 1 yellow/green/red, 1 blue/white/orange stem from sides of red/blue/green spatter "bower." Rough-ground, flat base; trace of pontil.
D: 2¹⁷⁄₃₂″ (6.5 cm.)
Gift of Carl W. Fischer, 1981.

1522
Harvey K. Littleton, Verona, WI, 1972. (1 of 5 paperweights made with factory canes while visiting Val St. Lambert Glassworks, Liège, Belgium.) Ovoid. Alternately spaced, spiraled red/white and amethyst/white ribbon twist rods, bubble inclusions, form vertical crown-like motif. Tall, flat oval cut on 2 opposite sides of exterior. "H. K. Littleton 1972 VSL" signed on mitered periphery of wide, polished flat base.
H: 3⅜″ (8.6 cm.); D: 2²⁵⁄₃₂″ (7.1 cm.)
Gift of Harvey K. Littleton, 1985.

1563
Caithness Glass, Scotland, 1971. Powdered blue glass on amethyst cushion; large spaced peripheral bubbles. On surface: 2 etched cormorants. Polished flat base signed "No. 71/500 Caithness Scotland."
D: 3¼″ (8.3 cm.)
Bequest of J. Howard Gilroy, 1986.

269

1826

495

1076, 1475

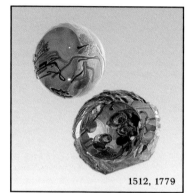

1512, 1779

709

759

690

940

1214

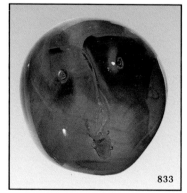

833

1509

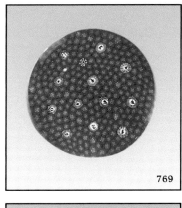

769

1065

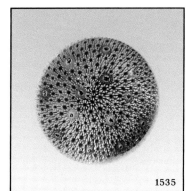

1535

677

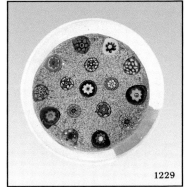

1229

671

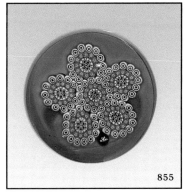

855

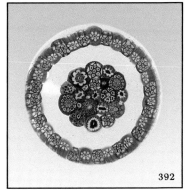

392

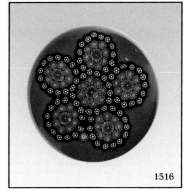

1516

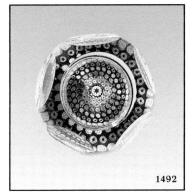

1492

1505

1561

86

269
Czechoslovakia, 1918-38. 5 morning glories, varicolored stripes on opaque white petals; narrow stems project from opaque white/green/blue spatter glass cushion, multiple tiny bubbles. Flat top punty, 4 on curve, each encircled by small radial miter cuts "framing" a flower. Vertical leaf and stem facets appear between side punties. Polished flat colorless base.
D: 3 5/16" (8.4 cm.)
Bergstrom Bequest, 1958.
EHB acquisition: November, 1939.
Illus. 42, Bergstrom book, 1940; Illus. 40, later editions.
No. 287, Pl. 36; Cloak Catalogue, 1969.

495
Czechoslovakia, 1918-38. Dome shape 5 opaque varicolored flowers, round petals, bubble centers; central flower near crown; 4 spaced flowers near periphery. Stems extend to double-layered varicolored spatter ground. Contiguous concave cuttings encircle flat top; 4 oval side punties. Flat colorless base.
D: 3 9/16" (9.1 cm.)
Bergstrom Bequest, 1958.
EHB acquisition: Unrecorded.
No. 525, Pl. 40; Cloak Catalogue, 1969.

690
Harvey K. Littleton, Verona, WI, early 1960s. Transparent dark blue, non-lead glass blown in mushroom shape encasing vertical deep amber canes, large bubble in core, small bubble near dome. Polished flat base; unsigned.
H: 4 1/2" (11.4 cm.); D: 3 3/16" (8.1 cm.)
Museum Purchase, 1963.
No. 709, Pl. 55; Cloak Catalogue, 1969.

709
Dominick Labino, Grand Rapids, OH, 1967. Free-form, hot glass technique. Transparent green glass sphere encloses abstract trapped air motif. Polished flat base inscribed "Labino 1967."
D: 3 5/8" (9.2 cm.)
Gift of Friends of Bergstrom, 1967.
No. 760, Pl. 55; Cloak Catalogue, 1969.

759
Charles B. Windsor, Jr., Blenko Glass Co., Milton, WV, 1969. Milky yellow spiral from bubble near crown to polished flat base.
D: 3" (7.6 cm.)
Gift of Mrs. Jean S. Melvin, 1969.

833
Andre Billeci, Campbell, NY, 1971. Free-form, hot glass technique. Struck silver glass with "ghost eyes" inclusions in deep amber shading to honey color. High dome; polished flat base signed "Andre Billeci."
D: 3 11/16" (9.3 cm.)
Gift of Friends of Bergstrom, 1971.

940
Jennings Bonnell, Big Pine Key, FL, 1970. 3 shaded orange flowers centered by tiny bubbles drawn down to pale green/white mottled cushion; 3 spaced teardrop bubbles. Polished flat colorless base signed "J B 3.10.70." Top and side faceting. Certificate.
D: 1 13/16" (4.6 cm.)
Gift of Dr. M. J. Caldwell, 1974.

1076
Robert Barber, Pomeroy, OH, 1973. Free-form pink selenium soda-lime formula glass; interior air sculpture motif; exterior indentures. Rough-ground flat base signed "Robert Barber '73" near periphery.
D: 3 3/8" (8.5 cm.)
Museum Purchase, 1974.

1214
Dr. Robert C. Fritz, San Jose, Ca, 1976. Free-form amber selenium lead glass; inverted central cone-shaped inclusion surrounded by 3 triple "finger" forms. Signed "Fritz."
D: 4 1/2" (11.4 cm.)
Gift of Dr. Robert C. Fritz, San Jose, CA, 1976.

1475
Sculpture.
Bill Slade, Neptune Beach, FL, 1981. Tall oval form; paperweight technique; multi-layered "silver" veil motif, vertical central rod of amber/rust-red/brown. "Slade 81" signed near frosted flat base.
H: 7 11/16" (19.1 cm.); W: 2 7/8" (7.3 cm.); D: 1 9/16" (4.0 cm.) base.
Gift of Mrs. H. M. Canfield, 1982.

1509
Vase.
Dr. Robert C. Fritz, San Jose, CA, 1982. Wide base tapering to a small, crown-like finial; elongated oil carbon-smoked inclusion; vertical central and side openings with tear-shaped horizontal bubbles. Signed "Fritz" near perimeter of polished flat base. Entitled "Homage to Henry Moore"; Petro Series, 1982.
H: 6 3/8" (16.0 cm.); W: 3 11/16" (9.4 cm.)
Gift of Mrs. Robert C. Fritz, 1983.

1512
John C. Macpherson, Andover, MN, 1984. Spherical form; yellowish glass with iridized surface: amber, green, and blue. Linear motif of multicolored glass fibers embedded in surface. Pheriphery of frosted flat base signed "John Macpherson '84."
D: 3 1/32" (7.7 cm.)
Gift of John C. Macpherson, 1984.

1779
Douglas J. Becker, Bethel, MN, dated 1987. Trailed, iridized surface. Angle-cut flat side; 2 smaller cuts on opposite sides reflect encased iridized, multi-color decorated partial sphere enclosing 3 bubbles of various sizes each reflecting a mosaic-like image. Polished flat base signed "Douglas J. Becker 1987."
D: 3 1/16" (7.8 cm.)
Gift of Douglas J. Becker, 1987.

1826
Michael Boylen, West Burke, VT, 1973. Free-form dichroic trapped air motif: amber, blue, white. Signed "Michael Boylen 1730" at periphery of frosted flat base.
D: 3" (7.7 cm.)
Gift of Mrs. Virginia Bensley Trowbridge, 1987.

392
Paul Ysart, Wick, Scotland, ca. 1940. Greyish glass; patterned millefiori motif: central cluster of varicolored canes includes green/white/red "PY" signature; peripheral circle of alternating blue/white and ochre canes. Polished flat colorless base.
D: 3″ (7.6 cm.)
Bergstrom Bequest, 1958.
EHB acquisition: May, 1941.
No. 412, Pl. 40; Cloak Catalogue, 1969.

671
Charles Kaziun, Brockton, MA, 1950-60. Spaced millefiori: 6 green/red pastry mold canes, opaque white centers, surround green center cane with red hearts encircling blue-on-white "K" signature cane; opaque pale pink (moonglow) ground. Colorless, short-stemmed polished flat circular foot; pontil concavity.
D: 2 1/16″ (5.3 cm.)
No. 690, Pl. 54; Cloak Catalogue, 1969.
Gift of Mr. and Mrs. Ralph S. Johns, 1963.

677
Charles Kaziun, early 1960s. 19 spaced pastry mold millefiori canes, predominantly white, on translucent cobalt blue ground. "K" with red hearts signature cane visible in center of smooth, concave base.
D: 2⅜″ (6.1 cm.)
No. 696, Pl. 53; Cloak Catalogue, 1969.
Gift of Mr. and Mrs. Ralph S. Johns, 1963.

769
Baccarat, dated 1969. 12 spaced Zodiac silhouette canes and date "1969." Small dark cobalt blue/pink/white carpet ground. High crown; polished flat colorless base, etched Baccarat insignia.
D: 3 5/16″ (8.4 cm.)
Gift of Baccarat, Inc., 1970.

855
Saint Louis, 1972. Patterned millefiori in "doily" motif: 6 adjoining circles of serrated pink/white, white star, and white/dark red canes surround small white/yellow canes. Serrated white/dark red canes (star centers) surround each circle. Blue/white "SL 1972" signature cane; motif high in weight. Transparent blue base. Polished concave base; basal ring.
D: 3 1/16″ (7.8 cm.)
Gift of Cristalleries de St. Louis, 1973.

1065
Saint Louis, 1973. Supermagnum Piedouche. 607 multicolored millefiori glass canes in concentric motif, including "SL 1973" and "9" canes. Twisted white torsade rims double latticinio "hourglass" pedestal and periphery of base. 9/10.
H: 9½″ (24.1 cm.); D: 9 13/16″ (25.062 cm.)
Gift of Paul Jokelson, 1974.
Ref.: *PCA Bulletin,* 1973; pp. 15-20.

1229
Ysart brothers, John Moncrieff, Ltd., Perth, Scotland, 1930-40. Spaced millefiori canes on fine blue/white jasper cushion. Colorless base; pontil mark.
D: 3 11/32″ (8.5 cm.)
Gift of Mrs. F. E. Seybold, 1976.
Ref.: *The Glass Club Bulletin,* No. 118, December, 1976; pp. 3-9.
Spinning Wheel, Vol. 24, No. 7-8, July, 1968; p. 22.

1492
Whitefriars (English), 1981-83; 6 concentric circles of varicolored millefiori canes surround central serrated red/white/blue star center cane. Bright yellow/white outer circle; blue/white "monk" Whitefriars symbol in circle 3. Top, 5 side punties. Deep indentation in colorless base reveals concave millefiori disk insert.
D: 3″ (7.6 cm.)
Gift of Mr. and Mrs. William L. Liebman, 1983.

1505
Wafer Tray.
Saint Louis, 1983. Translucent emerald-green bowl, opaque white ribbon twist/filigree rim; colorless stem/mereses; paperweight base: concentric varicolored millefiori motif, "SL 1983" cane; peripheral circle of green/white/red star canes drawn to polished pontil area of colorless base; basal ring. 30/100.
H: 3 15/16″ (10.0 cm.); D: 4 15/32″ (11.4 cm.) bowl.
Gift of Mr. and Mrs. William L. Liebman, 1983.

1516
Saint Louis, 1984. Patterned millefiori canes, predominantly yellow, red, white and 3 shades of blue in circular "doily" motif. "SL 1984" signature cane. Orange ground lined with white. Polished concave colorless base; basal ring. 1/150.
D: 2 15/16″ (7.5 cm.)
Gift of Mr. and Mrs. William L. Liebman, 1984.

1535
Baccarat, dated 1973. Spaced Zodiac silhouettes in varicolored canes on white/red floret carpet ground. Polished flat colorless base etched with Baccarat insignia, "No. 5" and date "1973."
D: 2 15/16″ (7.5 cm.)
Bequest of J. Howard Gilroy, 1986.

1561
Whitefriars Glass, Ltd., Wealdstone, England, 1970. Smooth concave basal disk encases central "Mayflower" silhouette cane surrounded by 5 concentric millefiori cane circles: blue/white, white star/"1620-1970," and white monk signature; pink/white; pale turquoise/white; cobalt blue/white canes. Wide top punty, 5 side punties.
D: 3 5/32″ (8.1 cm.)
Bequest of J. Howard Gilroy, 1986.

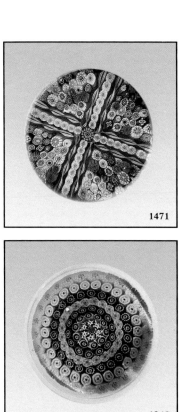

1471

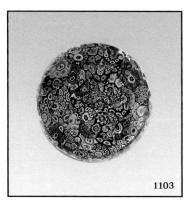

1103

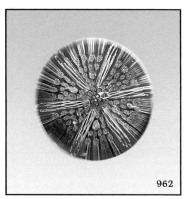

962

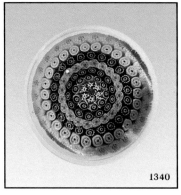

1340

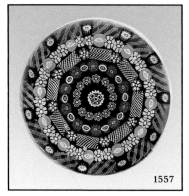

1557

801

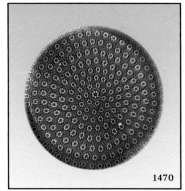

1470

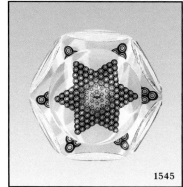

1545

1223

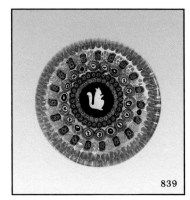

839

1218

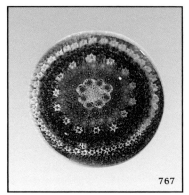

767

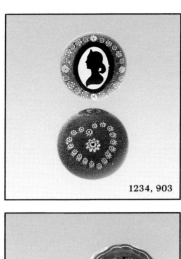

1234, 903

670

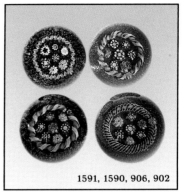

1591, 1590, 906, 902

1704, 1711

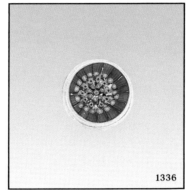

1336

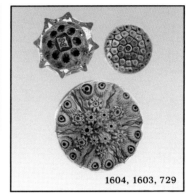

1604, 1603, 729

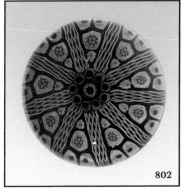

802

1825

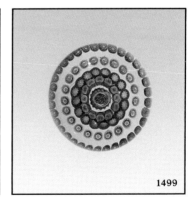

1499

952

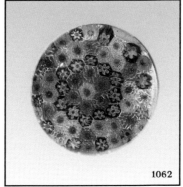

1062

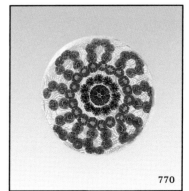

770

767
Baccarat, dated 1969. 9 concentric circles of green/deep pink/mustard-yellow/blue/white star/pink and blue canes; central cluster of turquoise/ white quatrefoil canes. "1969" cane near periphery. Polished flat colorless base; etched Baccarat insignia.
D: 3¼" (8.2 cm.)
Gift of Cristalleries de Baccarat, 1970.

801
Strathearn Glass, Ltd., Crieff, Scotland, 1970. Patterned millefiori: yellow/blue/white/brown canes arranged between white filigree rods radiate in spoke motif from central cluster of yellow/red/white canes. Opaque cobalt blue ground.
D: 2½" (6.3 cm.)
Gift of Mrs. C. A. Peterson, 1970.

839
Baccarat, dated 1972. Concentric millefiori. 5 circles of canes: blue/white; yellow/white, (one dated "B 1972") alternate with red/white; pale green with small black silhouettes representing all Gridel figures used in antique Baccarat weights; red/white; and lilac/white. Large central black cane with white squirrel silhouette. Polished colorless base etched with Baccarat signature and "16.5.1972," the date of the 1972 Bergstrom Paperweight Tour visit to Baccarat glass works.
D: 3⅛" (7.9 cm.)
Gift of Cristalleries de Baccarat, 1972.

962
Whitefriars Glass, Ltd., Wealdstone, England, dated 1971. Panel millefiori: mauve/pink/green/blue canes separated by 5 white filigree "spokes"; central cluster of small canes. 1971/monk signature cane in 1 panel. Translucent cobalt blue ground. Smooth "jelly glass" concave base.
D: 3¹⁄₁₆" (7.9 cm.)
Gift of Dr. M. J. Caldwell, 1974.

1103
Perthshire Paperweights, Ltd., Crieff, Scotland, 1975. Scrambled millefiori canes; "P 1975" signature cane. Smooth concave colorless base. 19/350.
D: 2¹¹⁄₁₆" (6.9 cm.)
Gift of Mrs. Susan Szekeres, 1975.

1218
Paul Ysart, Wick, Scotland, 1976. Heart-patterned millefiori motif: cobalt blue/pink/white florets meet large black/white PY signature cane. At periphery, tubular white filigree rods drawn to smooth colorless base form basket effect. Polished pontil area.
D: 2¾" (7.0 cm.)
Gift of Paul Jokelson, 1976.

1223
Saint Louis, 1975. Patterned millefiori canes, in close-packed rows, drawn down near center of base. "SL 1975" signature cane near periphery. Polished concave colorless base.
D: 2²¹⁄₃₂" (7.6 cm.)
Gift of Paul Jokelson, 1976.

1340
Attributed to Saint Louis, 1952-53. High-dome; concentric millefiori canes form convex cushion low in weight; polished flat base marked "=M."

D: 2³¹⁄₃₂" (7.6 cm.)
Gift of Paul Hollister, 1978.

1470
Saint Louis, 1981. Blue/white/red millefiori cane carpet ground. Polished concave colorless base reveals pink "SL 1981" signature cane. 2/200.
D: 3¹⁄₁₆" (7.8 cm.)
Gift of Mr. and Mrs. William L. Liebman, 1982.

1471
Saint Louis, 1981. "Cross" motif. Close millefiori canes divided by white/green stardust canes and pink/white ribbon twists form 4 panels, one including pink/white "SL 1981" signature cane; opaque mauve cushion. Polished concave colorless base; basal ring.
D: 2⅞" (7.4 cm.)
Gift of Mr. and Mrs. William L. Liebman, 1982.

1545
Saint Louis, dated 1971. Dark red/white star-patterned millefiori canes, "SL 1971" center cane; opaque white ground. Wide top punty, 6 side punties. Polished concave colorless base etched "No. 993"; basal ring.
D: 3³⁄₁₆" (8.1 cm.)
Bequest of J. Howard Gilroy, 1986.

1557
Paul Ysart, Caithness Glass, Wick, Scotland, 1950s-70s. Magnum. 5 circles of concentric millefiori canes and white/yellow filigree; 4th circle punctuated by opaque pink canes alternated with white/green star canes. White filigree rods alternate with blue/white star canes. Peripheral circle; yellow filigree and green/white pastry mold canes. "PY" signature cane. Dark green ground. Wide, polished flat base.
D: 3¾" (9.6 cm.)
Bequest of J. Howard Gilroy, 1986.

*   *   *

670
Door Knob.
Paul Ysart, Scotland, mid-20th century. Patterned millefiori canes set in opaque blue ground. Central cluster of canes. Peripheral circle of canes alternate with serrated canes and radially laid white filigree rod segments. Brass mount.
D: 3" (7.6 cm.)
No. 689, Pl. 40; Cloak Catalogue, 1969.
Gift of Mr. and Mrs. Ralph S. Johns, 1963.

729
Vasart Glass, Crieff, Scotland, 1960s. Patterned millefiori set on opaque aqua ground. Pastel pastry mold and serrated canes intersperse filigree twists laid radially from central cluster of varicolored rods. Smooth flat colorless base.
D: 2¾" (7.0 cm.)
No. 734, Pl. 39; Cloak Catalogue, 1969.
Gift of Paul Jokelson, 1967.

770
Baccarat, dated 1969. Patterned millefiori; central cluster of pink rods within 2 circles of canes and 8 loops of canes. Date "1969" in blue rods. Thin white filigree ground. Polished flat colorless base, etched Baccarat insignia.
D: 2¹⁵⁄₁₆" (7.4 cm.)
Gift of Baccarat, Inc., 1970.

802
Strathearn Glass, Ltd., Crieff, Scotland, 1970. Patterned millefiori, spoke motif. Opaque cobalt blue ground; smooth colorless base; pontil mark.
D: 3⅛″ (7.9 cm.)
Gift of Mrs. C. A. Peterson, 1970.

902
Charles Kaziun, Brockton, MA, 1973. 7 spaced canes: (Clichy-type rose, whale, rabbit, turtle, 4-leaf clover, and heart) encircled by filigree torsade including blue/white "K" signature cane; goldstone on pink opaline ground lined with alabaster, revealing gold "K." Polished concave colorless base.
D: 2⅛″ (5.4 cm.)
Gift of Charles Kaziun, 1973.

903
Charles Kaziun, 1973. Apricot and white heart canes in heart pattern. Turquoise and goldstone ground lined with alabaster. Gold "K" in polished colorless base.
D: 2³⁄₃₂″ (5.3 cm.)
Gift of Charles Kaziun in memory of Evangeline H. Bergstrom, 1973.

906
Charles Kaziun, 1973. 7 spaced canes (Clichy-type rose, goose, 4-leaf clover, heart, duck, rabbit, and duck-centered arrow cane). Pink/white compound torsade includes blue/white "K" signature cane; goldstone on turquoise ground lined with alabaster, gold "K"; polished concave colorless base.
D: 2⁵⁄₃₂″ (5.4 cm.)
Gift of Charles Kaziun, 1973.

952
Baccarat, 1970-71. Scrambled canes. Polished flat colorless base; etched Baccarat insignia.
D: 2⅞″ (7.4 cm.)
Gift of Dr. M. J. Caldwell, 1974.

1062
Chinese, 1930s. Scrambled millefiori canes and filigree rods. Shallow dome.
D: 3⅛″ (8.0 cm.)
Gift of Gordon L. Hess in memory of his wife, Leone Elward Hess, 1974.

1234
Charles Kaziun, 1976. Large white cane features black silhouette, to dexter, of Princess Eugénie; peripheral circle of canes include "K" signature; goldstone on pink ground lined with alabaster; gold "K" underneath. Polished flat colorless base.
D: 2³⁄₁₆″ (5.6 cm.)
Gift of Charles Kaziun, 1976.

1336
Josephinenhütte, Czechoslovakia, ca. 1930. Miniature. Imitation of Whitefriars concentric millefiori; "jelly glass" base.
D: 1¹³⁄₁₆″ (4.6 cm.)
Gift of Paul Hollister, 1978.

1499
Baccarat, 1982. Open concentric millefiori motif. Outer circle includes "B 1982" cane. Polished flat colorless base; etched Baccarat insignia.
D: 2¹⁹⁄₃₂″ (6.6 cm.)
Gift of Mr. and Mrs. William L. Liebman, 1983.

1590
Charles Kaziun, 1960s. Patterned millefiori: 6 canes (rabbit, fish, shamrock, turtle, duck, heart) surround "Clichy"-type rose; blue ribbon twist torsade coiled with white filigree, "K" signature cane between ends. Goldstone ground on amethyst lined with alabaster, gold "K" in center. Polished concave colorless base; wide basal ring.
D: 2¹⁄₁₆″ (5.3 cm.)
Bequest of J. Howard Gilroy, 1986.

1591
Charles Kaziun, 1960s. White filigree twist torsade with "K" cane surround 6 canes (shamrock, millefiori, turtle, compound shamrock, heart, duck) and central fish/arrow cane. Goldstone ground on amethyst lined with alabaster centered by gold "K." Polished concave colorless base; basal ring.
D: 2³⁄₃₂″ (5.4 cm.)
Bequest of J. Howard Gilroy, 1986.

1603
Strathearn Glass, Crieff, Scotland, 1960s. Miniature. Shallow form. Concentric millefiori. Side pressed in 8 "flutes" converging at center of rough-ground base.
D: 2¹⁄₁₆″ (5.3 cm.)
Bequest of J. Howard Gilroy, 1986.

1604
Origin unknown (English), 1970s. Miniature. Concentric millefiori canes in pastel colors. Mottled yellow ground. Smooth basal concavity bears gold label: "Hand Made in Great Britain for LPW."
D: 1⁹⁄₁₆″ (4.0 cm.)
Bequest of J. Howard Gilroy, 1986.

1704
Perthshire Paperweights, Ltd., dated 1981. Amber/white double overlay; wide flat dome; cut, scalloped edges. 6 large oval side punties. Multicolored millefiori convex cushion. Polished colorless basal concavity; "P 1981" cane; basal ring. 7/250.
D: 2⁹⁄₁₆″ (7.1 cm.)
Gift of Mr. and Mrs. F. John Barlow, 1987.

1711
Perthshire Paperweights, Ltd., 1982. Patterned millefiori. Amber/white canes form 8-point star. "P" cane center. 2 circles of green canes; circle of blue/white canes. Wide top punty, sides diamond-cut to level of motif. Medallion-cut colorless base. 129/300.
D: 2¼″ (5.7 cm.)
Gift of Mr. and Mrs. F. John Barlow, 1986.

1825
Whitefriars Glass, Ltd., Wealdstone, England, dated 1972. Polished rectangular colorless glass "block" encases vertically arranged white staves, cobalt blue/white, green/white, amber/white, black/white, white/green, and red/white/blue star canes; signature cane "1972/white monk symbol."
H: 1⁹⁄₃₂ x 2¹⁄₁₆ x 2½″ (3.3 x 5.3 x 6.4)
Gift of Mrs. Virginia Bensley Trowbridge, 1987.

680, 682, 1593, 681, 679

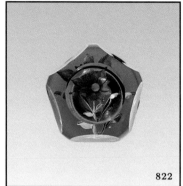

822

684, 907, 685

507

1526

672

1247

741

1249

905, 655

1244

904, 901, 676

1494

1584

1248

700

1246

1816

1489

1585

1529

1245

1627

1815

507
Charles Kaziun, Brockton, MA, early 1940s. Miniature.
Rose surrounded by 4 leaves, goldstone/1 blue cane;
cobalt blue ground. Polished concave base.
D: 1¾″ (4.5 cm.)   Bergstrom Bequest, 1958.
EHB acquisition: Unrecorded.
No. 539, Pl. 53; Cloak Catalogue, 1969.

655
Charles Kaziun, early 1960s. Rose with 3 pastry mold
canes; turquoise ground, gold "K" underside; top punty,
4 side punties. Tilted on polished pedestal base.
D: 1¼″ (3.2 cm.)
No. 674, Pl. 54; Cloak Catalogue, 1969.
Museum Purchase, 1963.

672
Charles Kaziun, early 1960s. Double overlay; rose. Pol-
ished colorless base cut with 16-point star. Top, 5 side
punties.
D: 2¼″ (5.7 cm.)
No. 691, Pl. 53; Cloak Catalogue, 1969.
Gift of Mr. and Mrs. Ralph S. Johns, 1963.

676
Charles Kaziun, early 1960s. Central millefiori cane
flower. At periphery, 6 spaced canes. Opaque white
ground; gold "K." Tilted on polished pedestal base.
D: 1⁷⁄₁₆″ (6.2 cm.)
No. 695, Pl. 54; Cloak Catalogue, 1969.
Gift of Mr. and Mrs. Ralph S. Johns, 1963.

679
Charles Kaziun, early 1960s. Sub-miniature. Lily; gold-
flecked cobalt blue ground lined with white; gold "K."
Top and 6 side punties; tilted on polished pedestal base.
H: 1¼″ (3.2 cm.); D: 1″ (2.6 cm.)
No. 698, Pl. 53; Cloak Catalogue, 1969.
Gift of Mr. and Mrs. Ralph S. Johns, 1963.

680
Charles Kaziun, early 1960s. Sub-miniature. Lily; gold-
flecked turquoise ground lined with white. Gold "K." Top
and 6 side punties. Tilted on polished pedestal base.
H: 1¼″ (3.2 cm.); D: ¹⁵⁄₁₆″ (2.4 cm.)
No. 699, Pl. 53; Cloak Catalogue, 1969.
Gift of Mr. and Mrs. Ralph S. Johns, 1963.

681
Scent Bottle, stoppered.
Charles Kaziun, early 1960s. Lily; gold-flecked pink
ground, gold "K"; 6 side punties; polished concave color-
less base; ground neck, flat rim. Matching stopper.
Bottle H: 1³¹⁄₃₂″ (5.2 cm.); D: 1⅜″ (4.0 cm.)
Stopper H: 1⁹⁄₁₆″ (4.0 cm.); D: ¹³⁄₁₆″ (2.3 cm.)
No. 700, Pl. 54; Cloak Catalogue, 1969.
Gift of Mr. and Mrs. Ralph S. Johns, 1963.

682
Scent Bottle, stoppered.
Charles Kaziun, early 1960s. Lily; gold-flecked blue
ground lined with alabaster; 6 punties. Gold "K." Sub-
miniature weight stopper; top, 6 side punties.
H: 3″ (7.6 cm.); D: 1⅜″ (4.0 cm.) bottle.
Stopper L: 1²³⁄₁₆″ (4.4 cm.); D: ²⁹⁄₃₂″ (2.3 cm.)
No. 701, Pl. 54; Cloak Catalogue, 1969.
Gift of Mr. and Mrs. Ralph S. Johns, 1963.

684
Charles Kaziun, early 1950s. Miniature. Rose; gold bee;
3 pastry mold canes; white filigree over cobalt blue
ground, gold "K." Tilted on polished pedestal base.
D: 1⁷⁄₁₆″ (3.7 cm.)
No. 703, Pl. 53; Cloak Catalogue, 1969.
Gift of Mr. and Mrs. Ralph S. Johns, 1963.

685
Charles Kaziun, 1950-60. Pastel millefiori canes arranged
on white filigree over amethyst ground. Tilted on polished
pedestal base.
D: 1⅛″ (2.8 cm.)
No. 704, Pl. 54; Cloak Catalogue, 1969.
Gift of Mr. and Mrs. Ralph S. Johns, 1963.

741
Charles Kaziun, 1969. Convolvulus on trellis over blue
ground lined with opaque white. Initials "ECC" (Evelyn
Campbell Cloak) in gold; gold "69"; 2 gold bees; gold
"K." (Presented upon publication of Mrs. Cloak's book.)
D: 2¼″ (5.8 cm.)
Gift of Friends of Bergstrom, August, 1969.

822
Paul Stankard, Mantua, NJ, 1970. Orange flower; 7
leaves, stem; white bud. Top punty, 5 side punties. Blue
footed base, polished flat. "PS" cane underside of flower.
D: 2¹⁄₁₆″ (5.2 cm.)
Gift of Arthur Gorham, 1970.

901
Charles Kaziun, 1973. Pansy; gold bee; alabaster ground;
gold "K"; polished concave colorless base; basal ring.
D: 2³⁄₃₂″ (5.3 cm.)
Gift of Charles Kaziun, 1973.

904
Charles Kaziun, 1973. Poinsettia; gold bee; alabaster
ground; gold "K"; polished concave colorless base.
D: 2³⁄₁₆″ (5.6 cm.)
Gift of Charles Kaziun, 1973.

905
Charles Kaziun, 1973. Pastry mold canes in heart arrange-
ment; alabaster ground; gold "K"; polished concave color-
less base.
D: 2¹⁄₁₆″ (5.2 cm.)
Gift of Charles Kaziun in memory of Evangeline H.
Bergstrom, 1973.

907
Charles Kaziun, 1973. Lily; white latticinio cushion,
amethyst ground; gold "K." Tilted on footed, baluster stem.
D: 1¹³⁄₃₂″ (3.8 cm.)
Gift of Charles Kaziun in memory of Evangeline H.
Bergstrom, 1973.

1244
Paul Stankard, 1976. Orange/yellow/white flowers, 3
white/3 orange buds; 2 blackberries; green stems, leaves.
At periphery: red/white cane, blue "S." Polished concave
colorless base; basal ring.
D: 2³¹⁄₃₂″ (7.6 cm.)
Gift of Mr. and Mrs. Walter LaPatrick, 1976.

1247
Paul Stankard, 1975. Meadowwreath flower; 2 yellow bud spikes; Green/white ground, "PS" underside. Polished concave colorless base signed "A100075" and "Especially for Pat." Top and 5 side punties; basal ring.
D: 2¾" (7.0 cm.)
Gift of Mr. and Mrs. Walter LaPatrick, 1976.

1249
Paul Stankard, 1977. Flax flower, 2 buds; 8 leaves, stems. At periphery, yellow cane with "S"; "25277." Polished concave colorless base; basal ring.
D: 2³¹/₃₂" (7.6 cm.)
Gift of Mr. and Mrs. Walter LaPatrick, 1976.

1526
Paul Stankard, 1985. "Catteleya Epiphytic" orchid; branch with lichen. Red ground lined with white. Blue "S" cane underside of polished concave colorless base, signed "A356 1985."
D: 3¹/₁₆" (7.8 cm.)
Gift of Mrs. William A. Draheim, 1985.

1593
Charles Kaziun, early 1960s. Miniature. Lily; gold-flecked turquoise ground, gold "K." Colorless foot; wide basal ring.
H: 1¹⁵/₁₆" (5.0 cm.); D: 1⁵/₁₆" (3.4 cm.)
Bequest of J. Howard Gilroy, 1986.

*   *   *

700
Charles Kaziun, Brockton, MA, 1964-65. White and blue striped convolvulus flower, blue bud with green sepals, 3 green leaves, stems; transparent amethyst ground. Smooth, concave base reveals gold "K" beneath flower.
D: 2" (5.1 cm.)
No. 720, Pl. 54; Cloak Catalogue, 1969.
Gift of Mr. and Mrs. Ralph S. Johns, 1965.

1245
Paul Stankard, Mantua, NJ, 1976. "Triple Wild Rose" motif; multiple pale yellow stamens; green leaves, stems. blue ground; red-bordered white signature cane with blue "S" underside. Polished concave colorless base; basal ring.
D: 2⅞" (7.3 cm.)
Gift of Mr. and Mrs. Walter LaPatrick, 1976.

1246
Paul Stankard, 1976. "Trilaflora" bouquet of 3 orange, 5 blue, 2 yellow, 2 pale yellow, 3 white bellflowers, 5 blue lupine, 5 orange buds; green leaves, stems. At periphery below motif, blue "S" in red-bordered white cane. Polished flat colorless base.
D: 2⁹/₃₂" (7.4 cm.)
Gift of Mr. and Mrs. Walter LaPatrick, 1976.
Ref.: *PCA Bulletin*, 1973, 1977, 1978.

1248
Paul Stankard, 1976. Orange daylily, long, black-tipped pale yellow stamens, 3 orange buds; 6 long green leaves, stems. Below motif, at periphery, a red-bordered, white cane with blue "S" used only during U.S. Bicentennial year. Polished concave colorless base; basal ring.
D: 2¹⁵/₁₆" (7.4 cm.)
Gift of Mr. and Mrs. Walter LaPatrick, 1976.

1489
Paul Stankard, 1983. "Glass Botanical." Tapered, beveled flat top, sides and base; 5 upright 3-dimensional, rust-red, Arizona desert flowers, each with 5 petals, yellow stamens, olive-green leaves and stems; layer of "soil" with tap-root system beneath. "Stankard #46 1983" signed near base.
H: 4¹/₃₂" (10.3 cm.); Base: 2³/₃₂ x 2⁹/₃₂" (5.4 x 5.9 cm.)
Gift of Mr. and Mrs. William L. Liebman, 1983.

1494
Paul Stankard, 1980. White Arethusa orchid, rust/orange spots, pink pod. Green stamens, stem, 3 leaves; gray/white root system. Polished concave pontil area in colorless base. Black "S" in small white cane at periphery inscribed "A232 1980 Experimental."
D: 3" (7.7 cm.)
Gift of Mr. and Mrs. William L. Liebman, 1983.

1529
Paul Stankard, 1982. Colorless glass "block" form encases 3-dimensional rose motif: 1 white rose, 1 pink, 3 buds with green sepals; multiple green leaves, stems. Spotted brown and sand ground, tangled root system below. Periphery of base signed "To Pat, Love, Paul '82."
H: 4¹¹/₃₂" (11.1 cm.)
Gift of Mrs. Walter LaPatrick in memory of her husband, Walter LaPatrick, 1986.

1584
Paul Stankard, 1974. Single red plantain, one of "Herbal" series; variegated green leaves, brown roots; opaque white ground. Polished concave colorless base signed "A558 1974 (C)" and "PS" black on white cane; basal ring.
D: 2¹⁷/₃₂" (6.7 cm.)
Bequest of J. Howard Gilroy, 1986.
Ref.: Stankard, Paul: *The First Decade,* 1979; No. 19B, p. 21.

1585
Paul Stankard, 1974. "Forget-me-not" floral spray: 5 flowers, 3 stems of buds, 3 leaves; amethyst roots; opaque white ground. Polished colorless base signed "1974 A 500"; in center: "PS" black on white cane. Basal ring.
D: 2¹¹/₃₂" (6.0 cm.)
Bequest of J. Howard Gilroy, 1986.

1627
Ray Banford, Hammonton, NJ, 1986. 2 pink roses, 2 pink buds with sepals; 9 green leaves, 6 stems; translucent cobalt blue, polished concave base. Black "B" in white signature cane at base of stems. Basal ring.
D: 2³¹/₃₂" (7.5 cm.)
Gift of Ray and Robert Banford in memory of Arthur Rubloff and Maurice Lindon, 1986.

1815
Paul Stankard, dated 1975. "Meadowwreath" with root system; translucent yellow ground. "PS" black/white signature cane in polished concave colorless base signed "28/50/1975/A 892"; basal ring.
D: 2¹¹/₁₆" (6.0 cm.)
Gift of Mrs. Virginia Bensley Trowbridge, 1987.

1816
Paul Stankard, ca. 1977. Pastel yellow Paphiopedilum orchid, green/brown sepals; 4 green leaves, stem; translucent cobalt blue base; polished pontil concavity; basal ring. "S" (black/yellow) signature cane inside periphery above "30977/50/75" signed on surface.
D: 2²⁹/₃₂" (7.4 cm.)
Gift of Mrs. Virginia Bensley Trowbridge, 1987.

1493

1517, 1231

1628

915

1507

738

1813

1597

1464

1495

1497, 1595, 1232

1079

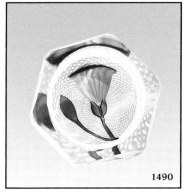

1490

689

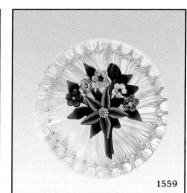

1559

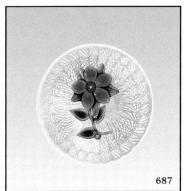

687

1795

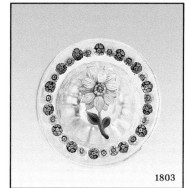

1803

739

1785

1586

1814

1467

797

738
Ronald E. Hansen, Mackinaw City, MI, 1969. Floral bouquet: 2 "heart" flowers, a blue-white morning glory, mauve and blue flowers, blue "cane" flower; green leaves; opaque turquoise cushion extends to polished flat base signed "Ronald E. Hansen." Top, 6 side punties.
D: 2³⁄₁₆" (5.5 cm.)
Museum Purchase, 1969.

915
Carolyn M. Smith, Millville, NJ, 1973. White dogwood flower: 4 petals, yellow stamen center; 1 white bud; 2 crossed/brown stems, 6 leaves; mottled cranberry-red ground. White "CS" signature cane. Polished flat colorless base signed "Carolyn Marie Smith." Top, 5 side punties.
D: 2¼" (5.7 cm.)
Gift of Miss Karen M. Smith, 1973.

1079
Hugh E. Smith, Millville, NJ, 1974. 2 white calla lilies, 3 green leaves, 7 stems, "HS" signature cane; cranberry-red fine jasper ground. Large top punty, 5 side punties (cut by Mrs. Carolyn Smith). Polished flat base signed "Hugh Edmund Smith 12/9/1974."
D: 2¹⁄₁₆" (5.2 cm.)
Gift of Mrs. Hugh E. Smith in memory of Heather Lynn Smith, 1975.

1231
Ray Banford, Hammonton, NJ, 1976. "Three Roses." 11 green leaves, stem, amethyst ground, "B" signature cane. Polished flat colorless base.
D: 2⁷⁄₁₆" (6.2 cm.)
Gift of Mr. and Mrs. Ray Banford in memory of Adolph Macho, 1976.

1232
Robert Banford, Hammonton, NJ, 1976. "Three Flowers in Vase": pink, rust, and cobalt blue with yellow cane center; 3 stems, 18 leaves; festooned in amethyst/white vase on pebbled blue ground with blue and white "B" signature cane. Polished flat colorless base.
D: 2¹⁵⁄₃₂" (6.3 cm.)
Gift of Robert Banford in memory of Mr. Arthur Gorham, 1976.

1464
Debbie Tarsitano, Elmont, NY, 1981. 3 poppies, yellow stamens, and lily-of-the-valley; 20 leaves, 3 vertical stems. Top punty, 6 smaller side punties. 16-point star-cut, polished concave colorless base; basal ring. "DT" white/black signature cane under lower leaf.
D: 2¹¹⁄₁₆" (6.8 cm.)
Gift of William L. Liebman, 1982.

1493
Ray Banford, 1982-83. Yellow/white double overlay: top punty encircled by 7 small punties; 7 larger side punties. Full-blown pink/white rose on 5 green petals; 1 pink/white bud, 3 sepals; 2 green stems, each with leaf, twisted. White/black "B" signature cane. Polished concave colorless pontil area in base.
D: 2⅞" (7.3 cm.)
Gift of Mr. and Mrs. William L. Liebman, 1983.

1495
John Deacons, Jay Glass, Crieff, Scotland, ca. 1983. Translucent rose-red overlay. 2 blue flowers (white star cane centers), each with 6 cupped petals; 1 half-open blue flower, 1 blue bud; 4 green stems, 5 leaves, 7 sepals; upset white filigree cushion. Wide top punty, 6 oval side punties. Polished concave colorless base; basal ring. Green/white "A" cane; white cane with symbols.
D: 2²¹⁄₃₂" (6.9 cm.)
Gift of Mr. and Mrs. William L. Liebman, 1983.

1497
Debbie Tarsitano, Elmont, NY, ca. 1981. 3 striped pink, 5-petal flowers, each on 5 green leaves; curved brown stem, 6 leaves; green vase with 3 blue panels. Top punty, 6 punties on curve. Polished concave colorless base cut with 16-point star; "DT" signature cane.
D: 2¾" (7.0 cm.)
Gift of Mr. and Mrs. William L. Liebman, 1983.

1507
Ray Banford, 1980-82. Opaque pale blue/white crested bird on branch of grey-brown shrub; 4 other branches; 9 striped amethyst/white buds; 14 striped green leaves. White "B" signature cane; polished concave opaque white base; basal ring. Wide top punty; 6 smaller side punties.
D: 2²⁷⁄₃₂" (7.2 cm.)
Gift of Mr. and Mrs. William L. Liebman, 1983.

1517
Ray Banford, 1983-84. Ovoid. Top punty, column-cut sides; central pink rose low in weight surrounded by 4 smaller pink roses; black "B" white cane; amethyst ground, opaque white base, inverted scallop edge, polished concavity; basal ring.
D: 2¹⁄₁₆" (5.2 cm.)
Gift of Mr. and Mrs. William L. Liebman, 1984.

1595
Robert Banford, 1976-77. High-domed colorless glass encases, near top, a bee with white filigree wings; low in weight: a 6-petal coral flower (yellow stamen center), 1 partially opened pink flower and a bud; 15 green leaves, 2 stems; "B" (red/white/blue) signature cane; blue polished flat base.
D: 2¹⁹⁄₃₂" (6.6 cm.)
Bequest of J. Howard Gilroy, 1986.

1597
Ray Banford, 1975-79. Miniature. 3-dimensional motif: 2 pink roses set among 8 striped chartreuse leaves and stem on tilted gilt/aventurine ground. Blue cane with white "B." Polished flat colorless base.
D: 1¹¹⁄₁₆" (4.3 cm.)
Bequest of J. Howard Gilroy, 1986.

1628
Robert Banford, 1986. Gingham-cut red/white double overlay; wide top punty encircled by red/white ring. 5 forget-me-not flowers, yellow/black cane stamens; green sepals. 2 blue buds, sepals; 8 leaves. Red "B" in white/blue signature cane. Polished concave colorless base; basal ring.
D: 2²¹⁄₃₂" (7.5 cm.)
Gift of Ray and Robert Banford in memory of Arthur Rubloff and Maurice Lindon, 1986.
Ref.: *PCA Bulletin,* 1977, 1985-86.

1813
Ray Banford, ca. 1980. Pink rose, 1 bud; green striped sepals, 7 leaves, 2 stems. Red "B" in white signature cane. Wide top punty, 5 side punties. Polished concave white base.
D: 2¹⁵⁄₃₂″ (6.3 cm.)
Gift of Mrs. Virginia Bensley Trowbridge, 1987.

*   *   *

687
Paul Ysart, Caithness Glass, Wick, Scotland, 1963. Lampwork and filigree cane motif: floating, 5-petal pink flower with orange pastry mold center cane; 5 green leaves under flower, 3 leaves on stem; "PY" signature cane between stem and lower leaf. Peripheral circle of tubular white filigree rods pulled to base form basket. Smooth flat base; trace of pontil mark.
D: 2¹⁵⁄₁₆″ (7.4 cm.)
No. 706, Pl. 40; Cloak Catalogue, 1969.
Gift of Mr. and Mrs. Ralph S. Johns, 1963.

689
Paul Ysart, 1963. Pink flower with 5 grooved, pointed petals and orange pastry mold center cane; 5 green leaves surround flower, 3 green leaves on stem near "PY" signature cane. Circle of red and pink canes at periphery; translucent olive-green ground. "Caithness 1963" scratched on flat base.
D: 3″ (7.6 cm.)
No. 708, Pl. 40; Cloak Catalogue, 1969.
Gift of Mr. and Mrs. Ralph S. Johns, 1963.

739
Francis Dyer Whittemore, Lansdale, PA, 1969. White clematis-type flower (10 pale blue-striped pointed petals), 1 striped white bud; blue/white cane center with tiny black "W"; 2 dark green stems, 4 leaves. Smooth concave colorless base.
D: 2⅜″ (6.0 cm.)
Museum Purchase, 1969.

797
Joe Barker, Newark, DE, 1970. Lampwork motif: shaded blue flower: 10 brown-striped, pointed petals on 5 striped, pointed green leaves; striped green stem and 3 leaves. Translucent cobalt blue-flashed flat base inscribed at periphery: "Joe Barker."
D: 2¼″ (5.7 cm.)
Gift of Friends of Bergstrom, 1970.

1467
Saint Louis, 1982. White lily-of-the-valley, 6 green leaves; opaque vermilion-red ground; top punty and 6 side punties. Smooth, slightly concave base reveals "SL 1982" yellow signature cane. 86/200.
D: 3¼″ (7.9 cm.)
Gift of William L. Liebman, 1982.

1490
Saint Louis, 1983. Ribbed white convolvulus lined and edged with red; 2 green sepals, 2 stems, leaf; double swirl white latticinio cushion, "SL 1983" salmon/white cane underneath. Wide top punty, 6 on side. Smooth concave colorless base. 7/200.
D: 2³¹⁄₃₂″ (7.6 cm.)
Gift of Mr. and Mrs. William L. Liebman, 1983.

1559
Paul Ysart, 1960s-70s. Bouquet: large, cobalt-striped, turquoise-blue 5-petal center flower below 5 small 5-petal flowers; pale amethyst, pale blue-white, yellow/red center, dark amethyst tulip, white/red center, and striped pink with red "PY" cane center; 12 veined green leaves, 3 stems. White filigree rod basket. Caithness label on smooth base; pontil mark.
D: 2³¹⁄₃₂″ (7.6 cm.)
Bequest of J. Howard Gilroy, 1986.
Ref.: *PCA Bulletin,* 1970; pp. 41-43.

1586
Francis D. Whittemore, Lansdale, PA, 1970s. Red rose and bud with sepals; 7 pale green leaves, 5 stems. "W" in yellow cane under rose. Polished concave colorless base; basal ring.
D: 2¹⁷⁄₃₂″ (6.7 cm.)
Bequest of J. Howard Gilroy, 1986.
Ref.: Melvin, Jean S.: *American Glass Paperweights and Their Makers,* 1970; pp. 202-207.

1785
Saint Louis, dated 1984. "Nympheas de Monet" (Monet's Water Lilies). Special edition for the Claude Monet Museum at Giverny. 1 white water lily, yellow/red/white cane center; 2 white buds, green sepals, 7 green lily pads (1 beneath flower); opaque turquoise-blue ground. Wide top punty, 6 side punties. "SL 1984" signature cane in smooth concave base.
D: 3³⁄₁₆″ (8.2 cm.)
Gift of Mrs. H. M. Canfield, 1987.

1795
Inkwell, stoppered.
Paul Ysart, 1950s. Large, heavy; yellowish glass. Low in base: shaded pink lampwork flower (5 petals over 5), compound pink/chartreuse/white cane center; green stem, 4 leaves; "PY" cane. Peripheral circle of red/white/colorless/amber canes; translucent mottled cobalt blue base polished flat. Short rimmed neck ground for mushroom shape stopper: central red/white/green cane. Peripheral circle of red/white/colorless/amber canes match those in inkwell.
H: 3⅜″ (8.6 cm.); D: 4¹⁄₃₂″ (10.3 cm.)
Stopper L: 2¹³⁄₃₂″ (6.1 cm.); D: 2″ (5.2 cm.)
Gift of Mrs. Virginia Bensley Trowbridge, 1987.

1803
Saint Louis, dated 1954. White-veined, pastel pink double clematis (6 petals over 6); compound white star/pink whorl cane center; striped green stem, 2 leaves. Peripheral circle of alternating green/white/red and white star/green/red canes; "SL 1954" white star/red signature cane. Wide, polished concave colorless base.
D: 3¹⁄₁₆″ (7.8 cm.)
Gift of Mrs. Virginia Bensley Trowbridge, 1987.

1814
Debbie Tarsitano, Valley Stream, NY, ca. 1982. Floral bouquet: large shaded purple dahlia set on 7 green leaves; yellow wheatflower, blue wheatflower (each set on 5 green leaves); 5 stems of white lily-of-the-valley flowers; 4 green stems tied with pink "ribbon." "DT" signature cane. Polished concave colorless base; basal ring.
D: 2¾″ (7.0 cm.)
Gift of Mrs. Virginia Bensley Trowbridge, 1987.
Ref.: *PCA Bulletin,* 1978, 1979, 1980, 1981, 1983.

793

854

1543

1221

827

1780

1487

1219

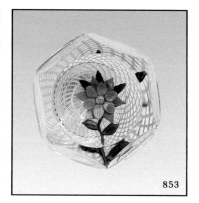

853

1357

1358

772, 1254, 1255, 1594

93

1469

1756, 1478

1745

1612

1498

1800

1801

1220

1483

1797

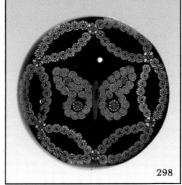

298

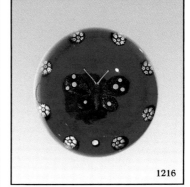

1216

772
Francis Dyer Whittemore, Lansdale, PA, 1969. Shaded lavender flower, 2 buds (1 partially open), green sepals and stems extending below 2 large green leaves. Translucent cobalt blue, polished flat base. Yellow cane with black "W" visible underside motif.
D: 2⁷⁄₁₆" (6.1 cm.)
Gift of Francis Dyer Whittemore, 1970.

793
Cristalleries de Saint Louis, France, 1970. Large blue dahlia, "SL 1970" chartreuse center cane. Top, 6 side punties. Polished concave colorless base; basal ring. 449/800.
D: 3¼" (8.2 cm.)
Gift of Cristalleries de Saint Louis, 1970.

827
Baccarat, 1971. Stylized millefiori cane flowers: 7 pale yellow pointed petals, purple/white cluster-cane center; pale opaque green stem, 4 leaves. Near periphery: small white stardust cane with "1971" in black numerals. Translucent cerulean blue cushion. Polished flat colorless base etched with Baccarat signature, series number "93" and year "1971."
D: 3" (7.6 cm.)
Gift of Baccarat, Inc., 1971.

853
Saint Louis, 1972. Pastel turquoise clematis: 6 pointed petals "SL 1972" white center cane encircled by tiny chartreuse-yellow canes. 5 green leaves, stem. Tiny bubbles on petals and leaves. Double-swirl white latticinio ground. Wide top punty, 6 smaller side punties. Polished concave colorless base.
D: 3³⁄₁₆" (8.1 cm.)
Bergstrom Bequest, 1958.
EHB acquisition: 1973.

854
Saint Louis, 1971. Flat cluster of 3 5-petal flowers (blue/red/chartreuse-yellow), each with center cane, "SL 1971" in yellow flower center; 14 green leaves; 2 stems; set into thin opaque white cushion. Wide top punty, 6 side punties. Polished concave colorless base; basal ring.
D: 3¼" (8.2 cm.)
Bergstrom Bequest, 1958.
EHB acquisition: 1973.

1219
Saint Louis, 1976. 2 long-stemmed pale yellow "Clichy-like" cane roses, pink centers: 1 white bud, green sepals; 10 green leaves, 3 green stems, pink thorns; opaque cornflower-blue ground. Smooth concave colorless base reveals "SL 1976" signature cane.
D: 3³⁄₁₆" (8.1 cm.)
Gift of Paul Jokelson, 1976.

1221
Saint Louis, 1973. Pastry mold cane flower, 5 white/chartreuse petals lined with pink, centered by chartreuse/white "SL 1973" signature cane. 1 white bud, green sepals and stems, 3 leaves; orange ground lined with opaque white. Polished concave base. 2/250.
D: 3⁵⁄₃₂" (8.0 cm.)
Gift of Paul Jokelson, 1976.

1254
Francis D. Whittemore, Lansdale, PA, 1976. 3 purple violets, green sepals, 2 green leaves at base of 3 green stems; opaque white cushion, yellow/deep blue/white "W" signature cane underside. Top punty, 7 oval side punties. Polished concave colorless base.
D: 1½" (4.5 cm.)
Gift of Francis D. Whittemore, 1976.

1255
Francis D. Whittemore, 1976. Encased in high-dome, pink cyclamen, 1 pink bud with sepal; 4 tan stems; 2 with green leaf, "W" signature cane underside; emerald ground. Top punty, 5 side punties; polished concave base.
D: 2⁵⁄₁₆" (5.9 cm.)
Gift of Francis D. Whittemore, 1976.

1357
Saint Louis, dated 1979. 2 cobalt blue cornflowers, 1 bud with 4 green sepals; 6 green leaves, stems. Top, 6 side punties; polished star-cut base centered by mauve/green "SL" signature cane. At periphery, etched: "Bergstrom Art Center 1979/1/200." Commissioned by Friends of Bergstrom to commemorate the Museum's Silver Anniversary.
D: 3" (7.6 cm.)
Gift of Friends of Bergstrom, 1979.

1358
Lampwork Parts.
Saint Louis, France, 1979. Lampwork components for "Blue Cornflowers" paperweight.
Gift of Cristalleries de Saint Louis, Bitsche, France, 1979.

1487
Saint Louis, 1982. Near dome, a 5-petal blue striped white flower with "SL 1982" signature cane center; 6 green leaves, stem; double swirl white latticinio spherical ground drawn near center of polished concave colorless base; basal ring. 25/200.
D: 2³¹⁄₃₂" (7.6 cm.)
Gift of William L. Liebman, 1982.

1543
Saint Louis, dated 1970. Chartreuse flower, "SL 1970" signature cane center; chartreuse bud, green sepals; 9 green leaves, 2 stems; translucent cobalt blue ground. Top, 6 side punties. Polished flat colorless base numbered "293."
D: 2⁹⁄₃₂" (8.4 cm.)
Bequest of J. Howard Gilroy, 1986.

1594
Origin unknown, possibly Ronald E. Hansen, Mackinaw City, MI, 1960s. Translucent amethyst multipetaled flower, yellow stamen center, set on 4 narrow pointed green leaves, spray of white lily-of-the-valley buds between each. Transparent cobalt blue ground. Rough-polished flat base.
D: 1¹¹⁄₃₂" (3.4 cm.)
Bequest of J. Howard Gilroy, 1986.

1780
Ken Rosenfeld, North Hollywood, CA, 1987. 3 pastel yellow flowers (5 petals), green sepals, orange stamens; 1 yellow bud, green sepals. 1 shaded blue flower, white stamens, green sepals; 1 blue bud, green sepals. 6 shaded green stems, 9 leaves. "R" cane. Signed "Ken Rosenfeld '87." Translucent amethyst ground, polished basal concavity.
D: 3⅜" (7.9 cm.)
Gift of Ken Rosenfeld, 1987.

298
Paul Ysart, Perth, Scotland, 1935-40. Patterned mille-
fiori butterfly; orange lampwork body and antennae;
ochre millefiori cane wings. Chain garland (3 pink and
3 green links) encircles butterfly on opaque cobalt blue
ground. Smooth concave base.
D: 3¾″ (9.6 cm.)
Bergstrom Bequest, 1958.
EHB acquisition: April, 1940.
Illus. 43, Bergstrom book, 1940; Illus. 41, later editions.
No. 319, Pl. 33; Cloak Catalogue, 1969.

1216
Paul Ysart, Wick, Scotland, 1976. Goldstone butterfly: 4
yellow spots on wings, rust body, chartreuse antennae;
peripheral circle of spaced green and white star canes
and "PY" signature cane; translucent dark cobalt blue
ground; polished flat colorless base.
D: 2¾″ (7.1 cm.)
Gift of Paul Jokelson, 1976.

1220
Saint Louis, 1974. "Honeycomb" cane-type dahlia, white-
edged red petals centered by "SL 1974" signature cane.
Polished concave colorless base. 23/400.
D: 2⅞″ (7.3 cm.)
Gift of Paul Jokelson, 1976.

1469
Saint Louis, 1982. 4 ripe strawberries, yellow seeds;
aqua sepals, stems; green leaves; flat double spiral white
latticinio cushion. Wide top punty, 5 side punties. Smooth
concave colorless base reveals yellow "SL 1982" signature cane. 8/200.
D: 3″ (7.7 cm.)
Gift of William L. Liebman, 1982.

1478
Perthshire Paperweights, Ltd., Crieff, Scotland, 1981.
"Acorn and Oak Leaf." 2 amber/green acorns, 6 green oak
leaves, buds, stem; fine white latticinio cushion. Small
oval side cuts above 8 larger linked ovals; wide top punty;
polished concave colorless base; "P 1981" cane; basal
ring. 94/300.
D: 2⁵⁄₁₆″ (5.9 cm.)
Gift of William L. Liebman, 1982.

1483
Jay Glass, Crieff, Scotland, 1980. Blue/white primrose-
type flower, cane center; 6 green leaves, stem. Polished
concave colorless base, "J 1980" and "A" canes.
D: 2¹³⁄₃₂″ (6.1 cm.)
Gift of William L. Liebman, 1982.

1498
Delmo Tarsitano, Elmont, NY, ca. 1982. 3 red strawberries, green sepals; 3 green stems, 8 leaves. 3 white
strawberry blossoms, yellow stamens. Polished concave
colorless base; "DT" signature under leaf. Wide basal
ring.
D: 3¹⁄₁₆″ (7.8 cm.)
Gift of Mr. and Mrs. William L. Liebman, 1983.

1612
John Gentile, Star City, WV, 1964-70. Ripe strawberry
(spaced bubble "seeds"), green sepals, between 2 white
blossoms (yellow stamen centers); 3 pale green stems,
3 green leaves; white signature cane ("JG" in blue). Wide
polished flat base.
D: 3⅛″ (8.0 cm.)
Bequest of J. Howard Gilroy, 1986.

1745
Perthshire Paperweights, Ltd., 1986. 2 ripe strawberries,
green sepals; 5-petal white flower, yellow cane center; 3
white buds, green sepals; 5 green stems; 5 strawberry
leaves; pink "P" cane. Wide top punty, 4 oval side punties,
a small oval and circular punty between each. Crosscut-
diamond, polished basal concavity; basal ring. 82/300.
D: 2⁹⁄₁₆″ (6.5 cm.)
Gift of Mr. and Mrs. F. John Barlow, 1986.

1756
Perthshire Paperweights, Ltd., dated 1983. Faceted
encased elaborately faceted amber/white double overlay
encases 3 amber/dark green acorns, pale green stems and
branch, 6 scallop-edge leaves. Wide top punty, edge scalloped by 2 adjoining rows of oval punties; 4 horizontal
oval punties, 2 sizes of vertical ovals between each. Polished colorless basal concavity; "P 1983" cane; basal ring.
One of a kind.
D: 3⁵⁄₁₆″ (8.4 cm.)
Gift of Mr. and Mrs. F. John Barlow, 1986.

1797
Paul Ysart, Wick, Scotland, 1950s-70s. Lampwork
butterfly: orange-tipped yellow antennae and head, red
aventurine body. 3 green spots and red aventurine spot on
pink upper wings; red aventurine spot on amber lower
wings. Peripheral circle of green/white/pink canes alternated with pink/white/chartreuse canes. Green/white/
red "PY" cane. Mottled blue ground. Polished flat colorless base.
D: 2⅞″ (7.3 cm.)
Gift of Mrs. Virginia Bensley Trowbridge, 1987.

1800
Baccarat, dated 1974. 3 ripe strawberries (black "seeds,"
green sepals). White 5-petal flower, pink center; green
stems, 3 leaves, "B 1974" cane. Transparent blue base,
wide basal ring, pontil area etched with Baccarat insignia
and "193/240."
D: 2¹⁵⁄₁₆″ (7.5 cm.)
Gift of Mrs. Virginia Bensley Trowbridge, 1987.

1801
Baccarat, dated 1977. Butterfly (2 yellow antennae, black
body, 2 white eyes; amber/white/blue millefiori cane
forms upper and lower wings) above white flower with
5 cupped petals, pink/white cane center. 1 white bud,
orange stripe, sepals; 2 chartreuse stems, 2 leaves. Pastel
blue/white star "B 1977" signature cane. Transparent
blue base, polished basal ring and pontil area etched with
Baccarat insignia and "67/250/1977."
D: 3¼″ (8.3 cm.)
Gift of Mrs. Virginia Bensley Trowbridge, 1987.

1449

545

725

1611

1154

1078

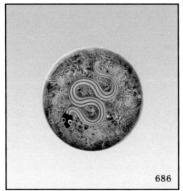

686

688

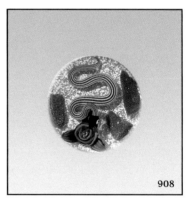

908

726

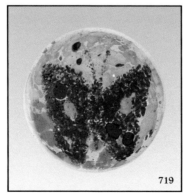

719

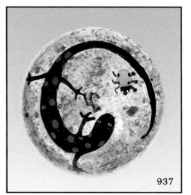

937

285

1589

1235

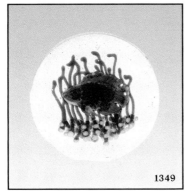

1349

1460

1463

397

1805

1411

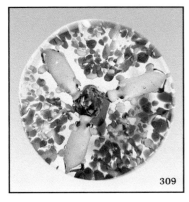

309

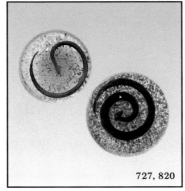

727, 820

516

545
Peter Gentile, G-F Glass Co., Morgantown, WV, ca. 1947.
G-F Glass Co. (Gentile-Funfrock) became the Gentile
Glass Co., Star City, WV, in 1948, the year John G.
Funfrock patented this type weight. Opaque white and
yellow butterfly with blue cane body; opaque red/white
flower with stem; high in crown, spaced bubbles below.
Polished concave colorless base.
D: 3⁵/₁₆″ (8.4 cm.)
Bergstrom Bequest, 1958.
EHB acquisition: Unrecorded.
No. 581, Pl. 52; Cloak Catalogue, 1969.

686
Charles Kaziun, Brockton, MA, early 1960s. Red-striped,
opaque yellow snake (double "S" form), black head,
green/white eyes; scrambled fine white filigree over translucent amethyst ground; "K" with red hearts signature
cane visible underside. Polished concave colorless base.
D: 2⅜″ (6.1 cm.)
No. 705, Pl. 53; Cloak Catalogue, 1969.
Gift of Mr. and Mrs. Ralph S. Johns, 1963.

688
Paul Ysart, Wick, Scotland, 1963. Dragonfly with yellow-
spotted goldstone body, 2 red eyes, 4 mottled green cane
wings. Peripheral circle of serrated green and white millefiori canes. "PY" signature cane; translucent olive-green
ground. "Caithness 1963" scratched on flat base.
D: 3″ (7.6 cm.)
No. 707, Pl. 40; Cloak Catalogue, 1969.
Gift of Mr. and Mrs. Ralph S. Johns, 1963.

719
Adolph Macho, Sr., Vineland, NJ, 1960s. Near crown:
orange spatter butterfly with blue/yellow spots. Opaque
white spatter ground. Partly frosted, flat colorless base
signed "A. Macho."
D: 3⅛″ (7.9 cm.)
No. 751, Pl. 56; Cloak Catalogue, 1969.
Gift of Mrs. Jean Ricksecker, 1967.

725
A. F. Carpenter, Pasadena, CA, 1966. Single red poinsettia, 16 smooth pointed petals, pale red dotted opaque
yellow disk center; 5 green leaves, stem. Dewdrop bubbles on petals and leaves. Periphery of frosted flat base
inscribed "Harold J. Hacker 1966." Note: Although signed
by Hacker, this weight was made by A. F. Carpenter.
D: 2⁵/₁₆″ (5.8 cm.)
No. 757, Pl. 55; Cloak Catalogue, 1969.
Gift of Harold J. Hacker, 1967.

726
A. F. Carpenter, 1965. Black glass lizard (green spots)
stands on thin translucent layer of finely spattered yellow
glass and gold mica. "Harold J. Hacker 1965" inscribed
near periphery of polished colorless base. (See No. 725.)
D: 2³/₁₆″ (5.5 cm.)
No. 758, Pl. 55; Cloak Catalogue, 1969.
Gift of Harold J. Hacker, 1967.
Ref.: Melvin, Jean S.: *American Glass Paperweights and
Their Makers,* 1967; p. 169.

908
Charles Kaziun, 1973. Red/yellow striped serpent coiled
near gold butterfly resting on red Sandwich-type rose on
3 striped green leaves; bronze aventurine "boulders" on
turquoise/white jasper ground. Tiny gold "K" in polished
concave base.
D: 2⅛″ (5.4 cm.)
Gift of Charles Kaziun in memory of Evangeline H.
Bergstrom, 1973.

937
John Gentile, Star City, WV, ca. 1972. Orange-spotted
black salamander; green/black bug; translucent yellow/
green ground. Polished flat base etched in crosscut pat-
tern. Unsigned.
D: 3½″ (8.9 cm.)
Gift of Dr. M. J. Caldwell, 1974.
Ref.: Melvin, Jean S.: *American Glass Paperweights and
Their Makers,* 1970; pp. 60-77.

1078
Paul Ysart, ca. 1970. Coiled iridescent garnet-red snake,
cerise and chartreuse spots, raised head, 2 chartreuse/
black eyes; white chips resembling glistening stones
imbedded in green ground with "PY" signature cane.
High-dome; polished flat colorless glass base.
D: 3″ (7.7 cm.)
Gift of Paul Ysart, 1974.

1154
Baccarat, 1845-55. Salmon-pink camomile, 2 rust-
colored buds, green sepals; 6 green leaves, stem; peripheral circle of white/salmon and blue/red arrow canes.
Top and 5 side punties. Polished concave colorless base
cut with 24-point star.
D: 2⁹/₁₆″ (6.5 cm.)
Gift of Mrs. Florence Gosselin Marsh in memory of her
husband, Raymond Clark Marsh, 1976.

1449
Murano, 1960s-70s. Yellowish glass. White daisy flower,
22 petals with yellow marking; multiple opaque yellow
rods form large stamen center. Polished flat base. Paper
label: "Murano Glass. Made in Italy."
D: 3⁵/₃₂″ (8.0 cm.)
Gift of Mrs. John Odgen and Henry Harnischfeger in memory of their parents, Mr. and Mrs. Walter Harnischfeger,
1981.

1611
John Gentile, 1964-70. Coiled dark brown salamander
with goldstone-striped spine; "JG" cane, 4 small pieces
of goldstone, 3 green/brown stylized branches on yellow-
orange powdered glass ground. Polished flat colorless base.
D: 2²⁷/₃₂″ (7.3 cm.)
Bequest of J. Howard Gilroy, 1986.

285
Origin unknown. Opaque white mushroom with dark red top bordered in white, stems from translucent cloudy green ground, numerous tiny bubbles. Colorless flattened base, trace of pontil mark.
D: 2⁹⁄₁₆″ (6.5 cm.)
Bergstrom Bequest, 1958.
EHB acquisition: March, 1940.
No. 305, Pl. 61; Cloak Catalogue, 1969.

309
Philip Bunamo, Union Glass Co., Somerville, MA, ca. 1910. Magnum. 3 opaque white pigs face central green basket; sparse multicolored chip ground. Smooth flat colorless base.
D: 3⅞″ (9.9 cm.)
Bergstrom Bequest, 1958.
EHB acquisition: May, 1940.
Illus. 67, Bergstrom book, 1940; Illus. 65, later editions.
No. 329, Pl. 44; Cloak Catalogue, 1969.

397
Paul Ysart, Wick, Scotland, 1930s. Green/brown striped snake, large red eyes, coiled on thin translucent bubbly green ground on fine white spatter. Smooth concave base; pontil mark.
D: 2⅞″ (7.3 cm.)
Bergstrom Bequest, 1958.
EHB acquisition: May, 1941.
No. 417, Pl. 2; Cloak Catalogue, 1969.

516
Union Glass Co., Somerville, MA; probably Philip Bunamo, ca. 1908-10. Magnum. High crown. 2 opaque white doves (translucent pink wings, blue rimmed red eyes, red beaks) look into central green nest with 2 opaque white eggs. Nest is surrounded by 2 cobalt blue flowers with white centers; 2 pink flowers with pale blue centers, pale green leaves, stems. Small bubbles on birds and flowers. Smooth, flat colorless base.
D: 3⅞″ (9.9 cm.)
Bergstrom Bequest, 1958.
EHB acquisition: Unrecorded.
No. 453, Pl. 44; Cloak Catalogue, 1969.

727
A. F. Carpenter, Pasadena, CA, 1965. Amethyst snake, raised orange head, coiled on thin translucent green spatter ground flecked with goldstone. Periphery of small smooth base inscribed "Harold J. Hacker, 1965."
D: 2¼″ (5.7 cm.)
No. 759, Pl. 55; Cloak Catalogue, 1969.
Gift of Harold J. Hacker, 1967.

820
A. F. Carpenter, 1970. Lampwork motif. Coiled tan and black snake with head upright; orange/green/yellow/brown ground in thin layer above polished flat colorless base.
D: 2½″ (6.3 cm.)
Gift of A. F. Carpenter, 1970.

1235
Harold J. Hacker, Buena Park, CA, 1976. 3 angleworms, spiraled with pastel orange, cobalt blue heads, on pointed green leaf, center hole; 6-petal flat dark blue flower, covered with bubbles; translucent blue spatter ground. Polished flat colorless base signed twice at periphery: "Harold J. Hacker."
D: 2²⁵⁄₃₂″ (7.1 cm.)
Gift of Harold J. Hacker, 1976.
Ref.: Melvin, Jean S.: *American Glass Paperweights and Their Makers,* 1970; p. 171.

1349
Janet Kelman, Royal Oak, MI, dated 1977. Orange/brown/black goldfish, green-stemmed marine flowers, white/orange buds. Polished concave colorless base signed at perimeter: "Janet Kelman '77 P-001."
D: 2³¹⁄₃₂″ (7.5 cm.)
Gift of Habatat Galleries, 1978.

1411
Saint Louis, 1980. Gilded molded coiled lizard on scroll-gilded and floral-faceted hollow paperweight; deep pink/white double overlay on colorless glass reflects multi-interior images. 16-point star-cut, concave base bears "SL 1980 55/300" etched in gold. No. 55/150 distributed in the U.S.
D: 3⁵⁄₁₆″ (8.4 cm.)
Gift of William L. Liebman, 1980.

1460
Baccarat, 1979. Coiled green/yellow serpent, 2 white/black eyes; brown/ivory/yellow/green "rock" ground, white/black "B 1979" cane. Polished concave base etched with Baccarat insignia, "84/300" and "1979"; basal ring.
D: 3⅛″ (8.0 cm.)
Gift of William L. Liebman, 1982.

1463
Baccarat, 1975. Yellow seahorse streaked with brown, its striped tail coiled around yellow-veined green seaweed; 4 leaves; multi-bubble, layered translucent green and blue ground; polished concave base etched with Baccarat insignia, "80/260," and "1975."
D: 3¹⁄₁₆″ (7.8 cm.)
Gift of William L. Liebman, 1982.

1589
Roland Ayotte, Nashua, NH, 1970s. Early weight. Red cardinal on brown branch. Top and 5 side punties. Polished concave colorless base; basal ring.
D: 2⁵⁄₃₂″ (5.5 cm.)
Bequest of J. Howard Gilroy, 1986.
Ref.: *PCA Bulletin,* 1982, 1979.

1805
Baccarat, dated 1977. Yellow ochre snail, brown striped shell, 2 pastel green antennae. 2 5-petal amethyst/white flowers (1 with pointed petals), white/red cane centers; 1 white 5-petal flower, red/white cane center; each flower set on 5 brown-striped green leaves. Translucent dark green ground, multiple tiny bubbles, 5 white "rocks"; "B 1977" signature cane. Polished concave base etched with Baccarat insignia and "37/300"; basal ring.
D: 3¹⁄₁₆″ (7.8 cm.)
Gift of Mrs. Virginia Bensley Trowbridge, 1987.

1720, 1721, 1718

1736, 1723, 1673

1634, 1653, 1689

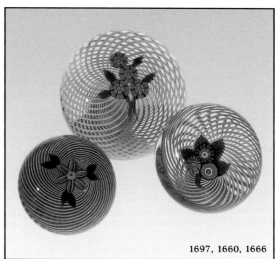

1697, 1660, 1666

1730, 1636

1759, 1671, 1647

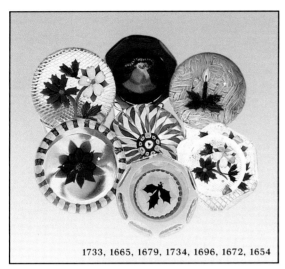

1733, 1665, 1679, 1734, 1696, 1672, 1654

1638, 1725, 1643

1726, 1746, 1692

1737, 1655, 1674

1688, 1687, 1675

1716, 1707, 1686

1634
Perthshire Paperweights, Ltd., Crieff, Scotland, dated 1970. Amethyst overlay; wide top punty; 5 circular side punties. Compound center cane; 5 spaced millefiori canes. Wide polished concave colorless base cut with 16-point star; signed "P 1970 AM JA"; basal ring. 32/150.
D: 2¹³⁄₁₆″ (7.2 cm.)
Gift of Mr. and Mrs. F. John Barlow, 1986.

1636
Perthshire Paperweights, Ltd., dated 1971. Crown motif. Amethyst ground. Polished concave colorless base encloses "JA" canes within circle of green/white canes; basal ring. 15/150.
D: 2²⁵⁄₃₂″ (7.1 cm.)
Gift of Mr. and Mrs. F. John Barlow, 1986.

1647
Perthshire Paperweights, Ltd., dated 1973. 6 silhouette canes (swan, deer, sailboat, Scottie dog, squirrel) and "P 1973" cane on carpet ground. Top and 5 side punties. Amethyst base; polished basal concavity; basal ring. 76/350.
D: 2¹⁹⁄₃₂″ (6.6 cm.)
Gift of Mr. and Mrs. F. John Barlow, 1986.

1653
Perthshire Paperweights, Ltd., dated 1974. Amethyst/white double overlay. Wide top punty, 8 oval side punties above 8 circular punties. Convex millefiori cushion includes "P 1974" cane. Amethyst ground lined with white. Polished colorless basal concavity. 300 edition.
D: 2¹³⁄₁₆″ (7.2 cm.)
Gift of Mr. and Mrs. F. John Barlow, 1986.

1660
Perthshire Paperweights, Ltd., dated 1976. "Forget-me-not" motif: latticinio cushion. Polished colorless base, "P 1976" cane in pontil area; basal ring. 397 edition.
D: 3⅛″ (8.0 cm.)
Gift of Mr. and Mrs. F. John Barlow, 1986.

1666
Perthshire Paperweights, Ltd., 1977. Nosegay set on 4 green leaves; centered on latticinio cushion. High flat dome. Polished colorless base, "P" cane; basal ring. 149/400.
D: 2¹³⁄₃₂″ (6.2 cm.)
Gift of Mr. and Mrs. F. John Barlow, 1986.

1671
Perthshire Paperweights, Ltd., dated 1977. Spaced millefiori on carpet ground. Tulip silhouette cane encircled by 6 green canes, 6 blue canes; 6 large silhouettes: robin, flower, heather, cane flower, woodpecker, roses. Wide polished colorless base; "P 1977" cane. 110/400.
D: 3³⁄₁₆″ (8.1 cm.)
Gift of Mr. and Mrs. F. John Barlow, 1986.

1673
Perthshire Paperweights, Ltd., dated 1978. 8 green/pink/white oval canes, form medallion encircled by row of canes. Translucent green ground; polished pontil area; "P 1978" cane. Wide top punty. 258/300.
D: 3³⁄₃₂″ (7.9 cm.)
Gift of Mr. and Mrs. F. John Barlow, 1986.

1689
Perthshire Paperweights, Ltd., 1980. Red flash overlay. Wide top punty, 2 rows side facets: 6 circular punties above row of 6 oval punties; blue flower, "P" cane center, encircled by garland of buds, 2 leaves; green cushion. Polished colorless basal concavity; basal ring. 133/300.
D: 2²³⁄₃₂″ (7.0 cm.)
Gift of Mr. and Mrs. F. John Barlow, 1986.

1697
Perthshire Paperweights, Ltd., dated 1981. 6-petal pink flower; 3 pairs of leaves. Fine white swirl on translucent amber cushion. Polished colorless basal concavity; "P 1981" cane; basal ring. 168/350.
D: 2³⁄₃₂″ (5.4 cm.)
Gift of Mr. and Mrs. F. John Barlow, 1986.

1718
Perthshire Paperweights, Ltd., dated 1983. 5 millefiori canes, stems, 10 leaves, form circle; ring of cog canes; upset white filigree ground. Wide top punty; 8 circular side punties above 2 rows of 8 oval punties. Polished colorless basal concavity; "P 1983" cane; basal ring. 50/300.
D: 2²⁷⁄₃₂″ (7.3 cm.)
Gift of Mr. and Mrs. F. John Barlow, 1986.

1720
Perthshire Paperweights, Ltd., 1983. Miniature bouquet; two 6-petal flowers; 12 leaves, 6 stems. 2 peripheral rings of millefiori canes with 1 "P" cane. 138/300.
D: 2²⁹⁄₃₂″ (7.1 cm.)
Gift of Mr. and Mrs. F. John Barlow, 1986.

1721
Perthshire Paperweights, Ltd., dated 1983. Pink water lily, blue/white butterfly; 2 pink buds; 3 leaves; mottled multicolor cushion. Wide top punty; 2 rows of 5 circular side punties. Wide polished colorless basal concavity; "P 1983" cane; basal ring. 86/300.
D: 2²⁷⁄₃₂″ (7.3 cm.)
Gift of Mr. and Mrs. F. John Barlow, 1986.

1723
Perthshire Paperweights, Ltd., dated 1983. Lampwork 15-petal yellow flower. 2 leaves, stem. Patterned millefiori peripheral canes. Translucent amethyst ground. Polished basal concavity; "P 1983" cane; basal ring. 300 edition.
D: 2¹⁵⁄₃₂″ (6.3 cm.)
Gift of Mr. and Mrs. F. John Barlow, 1986.

1730
Perthshire Paperweights, Ltd., dated 1984. 3-dimensional, 8-over-8 ochre petals, on 8 leaves at apex of swirled filigree twists drawn to center of polished colorless basal concavity; "P 1984" cane; basal ring. 147/300.
D: 2²⁹⁄₃₂″ (7.4 cm.)
Gift of Mr. and Mrs. F. John Barlow, 1986.

1736
Perthshire Paperweights, Ltd., 1985. 3 5-petal primroses on 5 leaves. Between each flower a millefiori cane. Peripheral circle of compound canes; "P" cane. Wide top punty, 5 side punties; radial-cut colorless basal concavity. 127/250.
D: 3⅛″ (7.8 cm.)
Gift of Mr. and Mrs. F. John Barlow, 1986.

1759
Perthshire Paperweights, Ltd., dated 1983. Multicolor close millefiori mushroom. Wide top punty; 2 rows of oval side punties. Polished colorless basal concavity; "P 1983" cane; basal ring. One of a kind.
D: 3″ (7.6 cm.)
Gift of Mr. and Mrs. F. John Barlow, 1986.

1638
Perthshire Paperweights, Ltd., Crieff, Scotland, dated 1971. "Christmas Holly"; upset white filigree ground. "P 1971" cane. 250/250.
D: 2¹⁹⁄₃₂" (6.7 cm.)
Gift of Mr. and Mrs. F. John Barlow, 1986.

1643
Perthshire Paperweights, Ltd., 1972. Mistletoe. Vermilion ground. 300 edition.
D: 2¹⁷⁄₃₂" (6.4 cm.)
Gift of Mr. and Mrs. F. John Barlow, 1986.

1654
Perthshire Paperweights, Ltd., dated 1974. English Christmas robin. "P 1974" cane; basal ring. 73/325.
D: 2³¹⁄₃₂" (7.6 cm.)
Gift of Mr. and Mrs. F. John Barlow, 1986.

1655
Perthshire Paperweights, Ltd., dated 1975. "Tudor Rose"; 8 spaced millefiori canes. Mottled blue ground. "P 1975" cane. 123/400.
D: 3³⁄₁₆" (8.1 cm.)
Gift of Mr. and Mrs. F. John Barlow, 1986.

1665
Perthshire Paperweights, Ltd., 1976. Poinsettia; circle of green/white and white star canes. "P" cane. 57/350.
D: 3" (7.7 cm.)
Gift of Mr. and Mrs. F. John Barlow, 1986.

1672
Perthshire Paperweights, Ltd., dated 1977. Christmas bells. Translucent ruby ground; "P 1977" cane. 4/325.
D: 3" (7.7 cm.)
Gift of Mr. and Mrs. F. John Barlow, 1986.

1674
Perthshire Paperweights, Ltd., dated 1978. Sprig of heather; circle of green/white and amethyst/white canes; blue ground. "P 1978" cane. 245/300.
D: 2¹⁷⁄₃₂" (6.5 cm.)
Gift of Mr. and Mrs. F. John Barlow, 1986.

1675
Perthshire Paperweights, Ltd., 1978. 3 bluebells; "P" cane. Top punty. 2 rows of 8 side punties.
D: 2⁵⁄₃₂" (5.8 cm.)
Gift of Mr. and Mrs. F. John Barlow, 1986.

1679
Perthshire Paperweights, Ltd., dated 1978. White overlay. Holly encircled by green/white/amethyst canes; white cushion; "P 1978" cane. 51/352.
D: 2½" (6.3 cm.)
Gift of Mr. and Mrs. F. John Barlow, 1986.

1686
Perthshire Paperweights, Ltd., dated 1979. Angel silhouette cane; spaced circles of stars set in cobalt blue ground; "P 1979" cane; basal ring. 295/325.
D: 3" (7.7 cm.)
Gift of Mr. and Mrs. F. John Barlow, 1986.

1687
Perthshire Paperweights, Ltd., 1980. Pink rose; pink bud. Pink/white "P" cane. Wide top punty; 2 rows of oval side punties, smaller near radial-cut base. 149/300.
D: 2¹⁹⁄₃₂" (6.6 cm.)
Gift of Mr. and Mrs. F. John Barlow, 1986.

1688
Perthshire Paperweights, Ltd., 1980. Green flash overlay; pink rose; pink bud, 4 leaves. "P" cane. 120/200.
D: 2¹¹⁄₃₂" (6.0 cm.)
Gift of Mr. and Mrs. F. John Barlow, 1986.

1692
Perthshire Paperweights, Ltd., dated 1980. "Sunflower" encircled by nosegays. Cobalt blue cushion lined with white; "P 1980" cane; basal ring. 329/450.
D: 2¼" (5.5 cm.)
Gift of Mr. and Mrs. F. John Barlow, 1986.

1696
Perthshire Paperweights, Ltd., dated 1980. "Christmas Candle." Scrambled white filigree rod cushion, translucent blue ground. "P 1980" cane; basal ring. 283/300.
D: 2²⁵⁄₃₂" (7.1 cm.)
Gift of Mr. and Mrs. F. John Barlow, 1986.

1707
Perthshire Paperweights, Ltd., dated 1981. Christmas silhouettes (church, Santa Claus, Christmas tree, snowman, sleigh) surround central white doily. Translucent green ground; "P 1981" cane; basal ring. 300 edition.
D: 2⅞" (7.3 cm.)
Gift of Mr. and Mrs. F. John Barlow, 1986.

1716
Perthshire Paperweights, Ltd., dated 1982. Shepherd, black ground. "P 1982" cane; basal ring. 44/350.
D: 2¹⁵⁄₁₆" (7.5 cm.)
Gift of Mr. and Mrs. F. John Barlow, 1986.

1725
Perthshire Paperweights, Ltd., dated 1983. Christmas "Holly Wreath." Upset white filigree ground. "P 1983" cane; basal ring. 350 edition.
D: 2²⁹⁄₃₂" (7.4 cm.)
Gift of Mr. and Mrs. F. John Barlow, 1986.

1726
Perthshire Paperweights, Ltd., dated 1984. Green flowerpot; 3 pink flowers. Opaque blue ground. "P 1984" cane; basal ring. 115/300.
D: 2½" (6.4 cm.)
Gift of Mr. and Mrs. F. John Barlow, 1984.

1733, 1734
Perthshire Paperweights, Ltd., 1984. Christmas poinsettia and white rose; "P" cane. Wide strawberry diamond-cut polished colorless basal concavity. 19/300. No. 1734 has top and side punties. 18/300.
D: 3" (7.7 cm.) — 1733; D: 2¹⁵⁄₁₆" (7.5 cm.) — 1734
Gift of Mr. and Mrs. F. John Barlow, 1986.

1737
Perthshire Paperweights, Ltd., 1985. 2 pansies surrounded by 2 circles of canes. Cobalt blue ground. Top punty. "P" cane; basal ring. 172/350.
D: 2¹⁵⁄₁₆" (7.4 cm.)
Gift of Mr. and Mrs. F. John Barlow, 1986.

1746
Perthshire Paperweights, Ltd., dated 1986. Floral spray. Blue ground lined with white. "P 1986" cane; basal ring. 140/250.
D: 2¹⁵⁄₁₆" (7.5 cm.)
Gift of Mr. and Mrs. F. John Barlow, 1986.

1728, 1744

1633, 1639

1729, 1735

1649, 1681

1678, 1642

1758, 1682

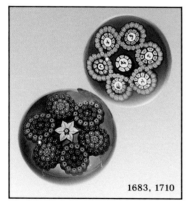

1683, 1710

1706, 1635

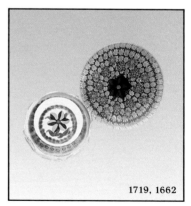

1719, 1662

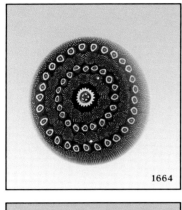

1664

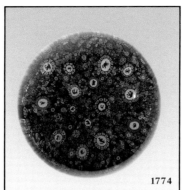

1774

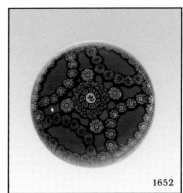

1652

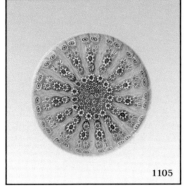

1105

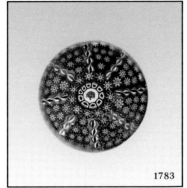

1783

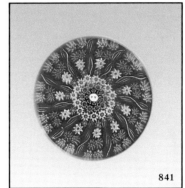

841

1641

1508

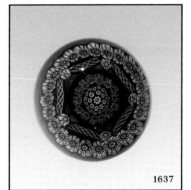

1637

1418

1565

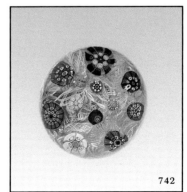

742

1600
Perthshire Paperweights, Ltd., dated 1970. Amethyst dragonfly. Peripheral circle of millefiori canes. Polished concave colorless base signed "P 1970"; basal ring. 500 edition.
D: 2⁹⁄₁₆″ (6.6 cm.)
Gift of Mr. and Mrs. F. John Barlow, 1986.

1635
Perthshire Paperweights, Ltd., dated 1971. Orange pansy, 5 leaves, stem. Upset white filigree ground; peripheral circle of millefiori canes. Wide top punty; 8 side punties. Polished concave colorless base; "P 1971" cane; basal ring. 273/350.
D: 2²³⁄₃₂″ (6.9 cm.)
Gift of Mr. and Mrs. F. John Barlow, 1986.

1639
Perthshire Paperweights, Ltd., dated 1971. "Ryder Golf Cup Commemorative." Crossed blue golf clubs; "USA/GB" compound cane. Peripheral circle of red/white/blue star canes; upset white filigree ground. Polished colorless basal concavity; "P 1971" cane; basal ring. 24/50.
D: 2½″ (6.4 cm.)
Gift of Mr. and Mrs. F. John Barlow, 1986.

1642
Perthshire Paperweights, Ltd., 1972. Miniature. 6-petal pink flower, "P" cane center; 2 leaves; stem. Peripheral circle of canes follow curve of weight to center of polished concave colorless base. 981/1000.
D: 1³¹⁄₃₂″ (5.0 cm.)
Gift of Mr. and Mrs. F. John Barlow, 1986.

1649
Perthshire Paperweights, Ltd., dated 1974. Spaced millefiori canes include "P 1974" signature on blue ground. Smooth base, polished pontil area. 43/500.
D: 2³¹⁄₃₂″ (7.5 cm.)
Gift of Mr. and Mrs. F. John Barlow, 1986.

1662
Perthshire Paperweights, Ltd., 1976. 6-petal blue-striped white flower, "P" cane center, 4 leaves, above ring of millefiori canes. Wide top punty, 8 side punties. Smooth colorless base, polished pontil area. 14/400.
D: 2¹¹⁄₃₂″ (6.0 cm.)
Gift of Mr. and Mrs. F. John Barlow, 1986.

1678
Perthshire Paperweights, Ltd., 1978. Rose/pink/striped white 6-petal flower; compound "P" cane center; pink bud. Peripheral circle of green/white/pink canes drawn to base to form basket. Polished flat colorless pontil area. 335/400.
D: 2⁵⁄₃₂″ (5.8 cm.)
Gift of Mr. and Mrs. F. John Barlow, 1986.

1681
Perthshire Paperweights, Ltd., dated 1979. Central cluster of pink/white/red star canes; ivory/turquoise canes surrounding white/red/blue/green star canes. Blue/white filigree twists form quadrangle, large silhouette cane inside each point. 4 millefiori canes spaced outside quadrangle. Translucent blue ground. Wide top punty; 8 side punties. "P 1979" cane in polished concave base. 48/450.

D: 3⁹⁄₃₂″ (8.3 cm.)
Gift of Mr. and Mrs. F. John Barlow, 1986.

1682
Perthshire Paperweights, Ltd., 1979. Blue/white double overlay; wide top punty, 8 oval side punties. 6-petal shaded rose flower, amethyst/white "P" cane center; 5 leaves form star. Stawberry diamond-cut colorless base. 338/400.
D: 2¼″ (5.7 cm.)
Gift of Mr. and Mrs. F. John Barlow, 1986.

1683
Perthshire Paperweights, Ltd., dated 1979. Double trefoil garland: silhouette cane fills each loop car silhouette in central compound cane. Ruby ground lined with white. Polished colorless base; "P 1979" cane. 119/400.
D: 3⁹⁄₃₂″ (8.3 cm.)
Gift of Mr. and Mrs. F. John Barlow, 1986.

1706
Perthshire Paperweights, Ltd., dated 1981. Miniature. "Royal Wedding Feathers" above date "29.7.81"; upset white filigree cushion bordered by millefiori canes. Wide top punty. Polished colorless basal concavity, "P" cane; basal ring. 282/288.
D: 1³¹⁄₃₂″ (5.0 cm.)
Gift of Mr. and Mrs. F. John Barlow, 1986.

1710
Perthshire Paperweights, Ltd., dated 1982. White 6-petal flower surrounded by circles (3 blue, 3 green). Garnet ground. Polished basal concavity; "P 1982" cane; basal ring. 86/300.
D: 3⅛″ (8.0 cm.)
Gift of Mr. and Mrs. F. John Barlow, 1986.

1719
Perthshire Paperweights, Ltd., dated 1983. Pink/opaque white carpet ground. 8 spaced pink/white canes, 8 spaced pink/green/white canes. Central 5-petal blue flower, 4 leaves, stem. Mottled pink ground. Polished colorless basal concavity; "P 1983" cane; basal ring. 76/100.
D: 3¹⁄₁₆″ (7.7 cm.)
Gift of Mr. and Mrs. F. John Barlow, 1986.

1728
Perthshire Paperweights, Ltd., 1984. Green/black caterpillar on 2 leaves. Wide top punty, 4 clusters of oval side facets. Polished colorless basal concavity reveals pink "P" cane underside leaf; basal ring. 197/300.
D: 2¹¹⁄₁₆″ (6.9 cm.)
Gift of Mr. and Mrs. F. John Barlow, 1986.

1729
Perthshire Paperweights, Ltd., 1984. Flat, blue 5-petal flower, white marking. 5 buds, 6 stems. White latticinio cushion. Polished colorless basal concavity; "P" cane; basal ring. 46/100.
D: 2²⁹⁄₃₂″ (7.4 cm.)
Gift of Mr. and Mrs. F. John Barlow, 1986.

1735
Perthshire Paperweights, Ltd., 1985. Flower: 6 blue petals over 6 pastel blue petals, 3 leaves, 3 stems; white swirled latticinio cushion. Polished colorless basal concavity; "P" cane; basal ring. 199/400.
D: 2⅛″ (5.5 cm.)
Gift of Mr. and Mrs. F. John Barlow, 1986.

1744
Perthshire Paperweights, Ltd., 1986. Aventurine green dragonfly; 3 leaves. Pink "P" cane. Wide top punty; 6 oval side punties, 3 smaller punties near base. Radial-cut, polished colorless basal concavity. 82/300.
D: 2⁹/₁₆″ (6.5 cm.)
Gift of Mr. and Mrs. F. John Barlow, 1986.

1758
Perthshire Paperweights, Ltd., dated 1979. Faceted blue/white double overlay over encased star and panel-cut blue/white double overlay; pink flower, "P" cane center, 6 petals drawn down into center of 5 leaves extending to polished colorless basal concavity; "P 1979" cane; basal ring. Wide top punty, 4 side punties, 8 small ovals between each. One of a kind.
D: 3⅝″ (9.2 cm.)
Gift of Mr. and Mrs. F. John Barlow, 1986.

742
Perthshire Paperweights, Ltd., Crieff, Scotland, 1969. Spaced millefiori canes on scrambled white filigree segments; translucent green ground; smooth flat base.
D: 2¹¹/₁₆″ (6.8 cm.)
Gift of Mr. and Mrs. Clarence A. Peterson, 1969.

841
Perthshire Paperweights, Ltd., 1972. Patterned millefiori: mauve, blue, green, yellow, and turquoise canes alternate with blue/white filigree twists radiating from concentric cluster of white/turquoise florets surrounding white center cane with initials "PT" in black. Cobalt blue ground. Polished concave base encases "P 1972" cane. "PT" commemorates visit of Bergstrom Paperweight Tour.
D: 3″ (7.6 cm.)
Gift of Spink & Sons, Ltd., 1972.

1105
Perthshire Paperweights, Ltd., 1975. Concentric millefiori canes: blue/green/pink/lilac/amber/white, separated by white and pink twists; translucent green ground. Smooth colorless base; pontil mark.
D: 2²¹/₃₂″ (7.6 cm.)
Gift of Mrs. Susan Szekeres, 1975.

1418
Perthshire Paperweights, Ltd., 1976. Millefiori florets and silhouettes (sailboat, mouse, pelican) and cane "P 1976" on pastel blue filigree ground. Smooth colorless base, polished pontil concavity.
D: 2¹⁵/₁₆″ (7.5 cm.)
Gift of Friends of Bergstrom, 1977.

1508
Ink Bottle, stoppered.
Perthshire Paperweights, Ltd., 1982. Spherical colorless glass encases close, millefiori canes on translucent cobalt blue base. Flared neck, ground for stopper. Polished basal concavity. Matching stopper: top punty, 4 punties spaced above 4 side punties. Ground colorless end.
H: 4⁷/₃₂″ (10.7 cm.); D: 3⅝″ (9.2 cm.)
Stopper D: 2⁷/₃₂″ (5.7 cm.); H: 2½″ (6.3 cm.)
Gift of Mr. and Mrs. William L. Liebman, 1983.

1565
Perthshire Paperweights, Ltd., 1971. Spaced millefiori, 2 silhouette canes, "P 1971" cane; upset filigree ground; translucent amethyst. Polished flat base. 230/350.
D: 2¹⁷/₃₂″ (6.5 cm.)
Bequest of J. Howard Gilroy, 1986.

1637
Perthshire Paperweights, Ltd., dated 1971. Patterned millefiori; central compound millefiori cane (amethyst/white/green) surrounded by pink/green/yellow canes. White filigree rods between 5 yellow/white florets form pentagonal motif. Peripheral circle of pink/green/pink canes. Amethyst cushion lined with white. Polished concave colorless base; "P 1971" cane; basal ring. 250 edition.
D: 2²⁷/₃₂″ (7.3 cm.)
Gift of Mr. and Mrs. F. John Barlow, 1986.

1641
Perthshire Paperweights, Ltd., dated 1972. Patterned millefiori: blue/white/red compound center cane within 5 white filigree twist rods alternate with ochre/white canes in pentagonal design. Peripheral circle of pastel turquoise/white canes; amethyst cushion lined with white. Top, 5 side punties. Polished concave colorless base; "P 1972" cane. 251/300.
D: 2⅝″ (6.7 cm.)
Gift of Mr. and Mrs. F. John Barlow, 1986.

1652
Perthshire Paperweights, Ltd., dated 1974. Patterned millefiori garland; flower silhouette within cluster of blue/amethyst/green canes; bright cobalt blue ground lined with white. Polished basal concavity reveals "P 1974" cane. Basal ring. 164/350.
D: 2¹³/₃₂″ (7.5 cm.)
Gift of Mr. and Mrs. F. John Barlow, 1986.

1664
Perthshire Paperweights, Ltd., dated 1976. Green/white "moss" canes (outer row drawn to base) alternate with 2 rows of ruby/white/green florets. Central ruby/white/"arrow" cane. Polished colorless pontil area reveals "P 1976" cane. 95/300.
D: 2³¹/₃₂″ (7.6 cm.)
Gift of Mr. and Mrs. F. John Barlow, 1986.

1774
Perthshire Paperweights, Ltd., dated 1987. Magnum. Close millefiori canes include 15 silhouettes: owl, kangaroo, pelican, elephant, rooster, dog, crab, butterfly, camel, 2 birds, ostrich, desert island, automobile. Mottled translucent green ground. "P 1987" cane in pontil area of polished base. 77/250.
D: 3⅛″ (8.3 cm.)
Gift of Mr. and Mrs. F. John Barlow, 1987.

1783
Perthshire Paperweights, Ltd., 1987. Limited edition made especially for Bergstrom-Mahler Museum Shop. Patterned millefiori: circle of green/white star canes surround compound amber/brown/white center cane with colored silhouette replica of "Old Council Tree" (symbol of early Wisconsin Indian "treaty" tree in Neenah). Mottled green ground. "P" cane centers polished concave base; basal ring.
D: 2¹³/₃₂″ (6.1 cm.)
Museum Purchase, 1987.

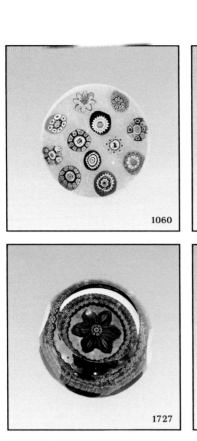

1060

1657, 1663

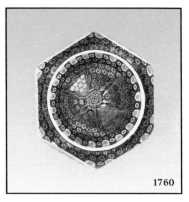

1760

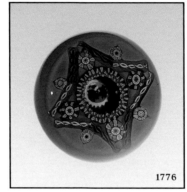

1727

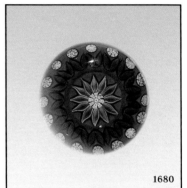

1776

1680

1757

1698

1762

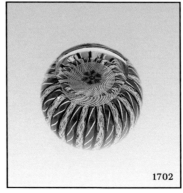

1669

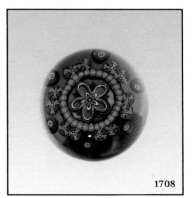

1702

1708

1677

1753

1740

1770

1754

1732

1755

1715

1749

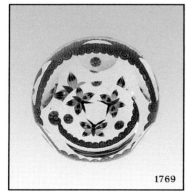

1769

1668

1661

1060
Perthshire Paperweights, Ltd., Crieff, Scotland, 1974.
12 spaced millefiori canes include bear and kangaroo silhouettes and "P 1974" cane; white upset filigree ground.
Polished concave colorless base. 154/350.
D: 2¹³⁄₁₆″ (7.1 cm.)
Museum Purchase, 1974.

1657
Perthshire Paperweights, Ltd., 1975. Patterned millefiori; 5 ochre/turquoise/pink cane clusters surround central compound cane in shades of green with "P" center. Peripheral circle of green/pink canes. Cobalt blue ground, white lining. Polished concave colorless pontil area. 400 edition.
D: 3¹⁄₃₂″ (7.7 cm.)
Gift of Mr. and Mrs. F. John Barlow, 1986.

1663
Perthshire Paperweights, Ltd., dated 1976. Magnum. Hexagonal patterned millefiori and filigree above recessed close millefiori. Cobalt blue ground lined with opaque white. Wide top punty. Polished colorless pontil area reveals "P 1976" cane. 268/300.
D: 3⁹⁄₁₆″ (9.1 cm.)
Gift of Mr. and Mrs. F. John Barlow, 1986.

1669
Perthshire Paperweights, Ltd., dated 1977. 2-layer cushion: star pattern of green and amber millefiori canes on ruby cushion lined with white. Circle of pink and green canes reveal rooster silhouette cane within 2 concentric rings of canes on recessed ground. Polished colorless base reveals "P 1977" cane. 134/350.
D: 2²⁹⁄₃₂″ (7.4 cm.)
Gift of Mr. and Mrs. F. John Barlow, 1986.

1680
Perthshire Paperweights, Ltd., dated 1979. "Sunflower": 12 yellow petals, green/white/blue cane. Center circle of leaves; border of spaced alternating pink/white and green/white canes. Amber ground lined with white. "1979" cane in polished colorless basal concavity. 114/350.
D: 3³⁄₁₆″ (8.1 cm.)
Gift of Mr. and Mrs. F. John Barlow, 1986.

1698
Perthshire Paperweights, Ltd., dated 1981. Veined pink 6-petal flower; stem; 3 leaves; patterned millefiori border; 6 panels of pink/white star canes separated by white/orange/yellow ribbon twists and wedges of blue/white star canes. Mottled amethyst ground. Polished basal concavity; "P 1981" cane; basal ring. 57/250.
D: 3¹⁄₃₂″ (7.7 cm.)
Gift of Mr. and Mrs. F. John Barlow, 1986.

1702
Perthshire Paperweights, Ltd., dated 1981. 6-petal rose-pink flower (5 leaves, stem; fine double swirl latticinio cushion) centers apex of crown motif: green/white/blue striped rods alternate with white filigree twists drawn to base; mottled green core. Wide top punty. Polished colorless basal concavity; "P 1981" cane; basal ring. 41/200.
D: 3³⁄₁₆″ (8.1 cm.)
Gift of Mr. and Mrs. F. John Barlow, 1986.

1708
Perthshire Paperweights, Ltd., dated 1982. 5-petal pink/white flower, compound cane center; 5 leaves encircled by amber/white millefiori canes and spaced magenta/white and cobalt blue/amber patterned millefiori. Ruby ground. Polished basal concavity; "P 1982" cane; basal ring. 300 edition.
D: 2¹⁷⁄₃₂″ (6.5 cm.)
Gift of Mr. and Mrs. F. John Barlow, 1987.

1727
Perthshire Paperweights, Ltd., dated 1984. 6-petal white filigree flower edged with cobalt blue, compound millefiori cane center, within double circle of green/blue/white and amethyst/salmon/white canes. Mottled green ground. Wide top punty; 8 side punties. Polished basal concavity; "P 1984" cane; basal ring. 205/300.
D: 2³¹⁄₃₂″ (7.5 cm.)
Gift of Mr. and Mrs. F. John Barlow, 1986.

1757
Perthshire Paperweights, Ltd., dated 1978. Faceted encased faceted emerald green/white double overlay encases green/white/amethyst concentric millefiori. Thistle center cane, set on mottled green hollow bubble forming mushroom drawn to polished colorless basal concavity; "P 1978" cane; basal ring. One of a kind.
D: 3⁵⁄₁₆″ (8.4 cm.)
Gift of Mr. and Mrs. F. John Barlow, 1986.

1760
Perthshire Paperweights, Ltd., dated 1980. Patterned millefiori. Orange/white filigree twists separate wedges of pink/white, blue/white, and green/white florets. Large central compound pink/white cane. 2 concentric rings of yellow/orange and blue/white florets; outer circle of alternate blue and white staves drawn down to polished colorless basal concavity; "P 1980" cane. One of a kind.
D: 2¹⁵⁄₁₆″ (7.5 cm.)
Gift of Mr. and Mrs. F. John Barlow, 1986.

1762
Perthshire Paperweights, Ltd., dated 1979. Faceted encased diamond-faceted blue/white double overlay encases "Racehorse and Jockey" silhouette cane on pastel blue ground encircled by compound coral-red/white millefiori canes. Wide, medallion-cut top punty; multiple joined ovals near base. Polished colorless basal concavity; "P 1979" cane; basal ring. One of a kind.
D: 3¹¹⁄₁₆″ (9.4 cm.)
Gift of Mr. and Mrs. F. John Barlow, 1986.

1776
Perthshire Paperweights, Ltd., dated 1987. Silhouette of "Horse and Jockey" in large green/white cane — surrounded by 2 rings of blue/white and green/white canes — visible through wide central circle of green/white/pink/blue canes set in blue cushion lined with opaque white. Patterned millefiori quadrant. "P 1987" cane in polished concave colorless base. 66/250.
D: 3⁷⁄₁₆″ (8.8 cm.)
Gift of Mr. and Mrs. F. John Barlow, 1987.

1661
Perthshire Paperweights, Ltd., Crieff, Scotland, 1976. Miniature. Swirl-cut, green/white double overlay; wide top punty, polished colorless base. Butterfly; millefiori cane wings. Chartreuse green body, 2 black eyes, 2 blue antennae. "P" cane under lower wing. 451/500.
D: 2″ (5.1 cm.)
Gift of Mr. and Mrs. F. John Barlow, 1986.

1668
Perthshire Paperweights, Ltd., 1977. Triple overlay: opaque yellow/white/translucent red. Wide top punty; on sides, a row of 8 circular punties above 8 smaller circular punties. 6-petal white flower, dark amethyst edges, "P" cane center; 4 leaves, stem. Radial-cut colorless base. 207/400.
D: 2¹³⁄₁₆″ (7.2 cm.)
Gift of Mr. and Mrs. F. John Barlow, 1986.

1677
Perthshire Paperweights, Ltd., dated 1978. Magnum. Double overlay: blue lined with opaque white. Wide top punty, 7 side punties. Double trefoil garland: pink pastel trefoil overlaps white trefoil, each loop studded with colored bird and flower silhouette canes; "P 1978" center cane. Cobalt blue cushion lined with white. Polished colorless base includes "JD" cane. 119 edition.
D: 3¹⁵⁄₃₂″ (8.7 cm.)
Gift of Mr. and Mrs. F. John Barlow, 1986.

1715
Perthshire Paperweights, Ltd., 1982. Cobalt blue/opaque white double overlay; dome cut flat; sides cut to 6 arched panels with alternate circles and medallions. Bouquet: deep pink central flower, millefiori cane center, 2 pink buds; 2 turquoise flowers, white honeycomb cane centers; 4 stems, 13 leaves. "P" cane. Radial-cut colorless base. 132/300.
D: 2¹⁷⁄₃₂″ (7.1 cm.)
Gift of Mr. and Mrs. F. John Barlow, 1986.

1732
Perthshire Paperweights, Ltd., 1984. Ruby/opaque white double overlay; 5-petal lampwork dark pink rose, 2 brown buds, sepals; 4 stems, 5 leaves, 2 orange leaves; double swirl white latticinio cushion; wide top punty; double row of 12 narrow oval side punties, lower row extending to polished colorless basal concavity with "P" cane. 34/300.
D: 3¹⁄₁₆″ (7.8 cm.)
Gift of Mr. and Mrs. F. John Barlow, 1986.

1740
Perthshire Paperweights, Ltd., 1985. Triple overlay: blue/white/pink; wide top punty; 6 small ovals alternate with 6 larger oval side cuts above 6 circular punties near base. 3 small white-edged, 12-petal cobalt blue flowers; cane centers; 2 half-open buds; 5 stems form floral spray. Amethyst/white "P" cane. Strawberry diamond-cut polished colorless base. 102/250.
D: 3″ (7.7 cm.)
Gift of Mr. and Mrs. F. John Barlow, 1986.

1749
Perthshire Paperweights, Ltd., 1978. Double purple/white double overlay. Wide top punty, 8 oval side punties; edge-cut, 16-point radial star in colorless base. Encased diamond-cut interior double purple/white overlay (thin bubbles) encases sprig of 3 bluebells, 3 stems, 3 leaves. One of a kind.
D: 3⁵⁄₁₆″ (8.4 cm.)
Gift of Mr. and Mrs. F. John Barlow, 1986.

1753
Perthshire Paperweights, Ltd., dated 1982. Magnum. Encased faceted ruby/white double overlay; floral spray: 3-dimensional white/pink flower; white/green flower, white bud, green sepals; yellow/pink flower, bud; pink flower. 8 stems; on large 6-point star-shaped leaf. Wide top punty edged with half ovals; large oval and flute side cutting. Polished colorless base concavity; "P 1982" cane; basal ring. One of a kind.
D: 4″ (10.2 cm.)
Gift of Mr. and Mrs. F. John Barlow, 1986.

1754
Perthshire Paperweights, Ltd., 1982. Blue/white double overlay. Medallion-cut top punty, 8 side ovals, row of 8 smaller ovals near crosscut green base. Garland of 6 5-petal lampwork flowers (2 each: yellow, blue, pink), green centers, 12 leaves, surround opaque yellow "25." Convex translucent mottled green cushion. One of a kind.
D: 3″ (7.7 cm.)
Gift of Mr. and Mrs. F. John Barlow, 1986.

1755
Perthshire Paperweights, Ltd., dated 1982. Encased elaborately faceted purple/white double overlay encases cluster of 4 shaded roses in full bloom, 3 red buds, sepals. 7 leaves; stems. Wide top punty, miter edge cuts form medallion. 2 rows of 8 oval side cuts. Polished colorless basal concavity; "P 1982" cane; basal ring. One of a kind.
D: 3¹⁵⁄₁₆″ (10.0 cm.)
Gift of Mr. and Mrs. F. John Barlow, 1986.

1769
Perthshire Paperweights, Ltd., 1987. 3 butterflies, brown-spotted white wings, brown antennae, translucent cobalt blue body; compound multicolor millefiori cane between each. Peripheral circle of dark pink and green canes include "P" signature. Wide top punty, 6 side punties. Polished concave colorless base. 18/300.
D: 3¹⁄₁₆″ (7.8 cm.)
Gift of Mr. and Mrs. F. John Barlow, 1987.

1770
Perthshire Paperweights, Ltd., 1987. Swirl-cut, red/white double overlay. 3 white "Snowdrop" flowers, stamens, 3 stems, 4 leaves. "P" cane beneath plant. Polished concave colorless base. 189/300.
D: 2⅜″ (6.1 cm.)
Gift of Mr. and Mrs. F. John Barlow, 1987.

1685

924

1739

1676

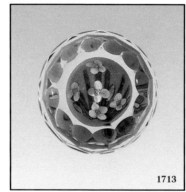

1713

1650

1738

1700

1773

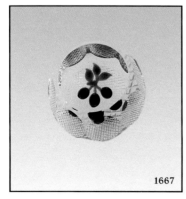

1667

1748

1714

1818

866

1817

1074

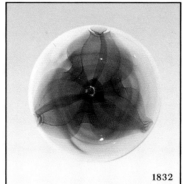

1832

1766

1834

735

1359

1072

1615

1830

Perthshire Paperweights, Ltd., Crieff, Scotland, 1974. Floral bouquet: 5-petal amber/white flower; pink/amber pansy with "P" center cane; 6-petal blue flower; 5 green leaves; 3 stems tied with narrow ochre bow. Above bouquet, a green dragonfly with 2 black eyes, black dots at tips of translucent white lower wings. Large top punty, 5 side punties. Strawberry diamond-cut, concave polished colorless base. 24/300. (Lampwork components surround weight.)
D: 3 1/16″ (7.8 cm.)
Gift of Stuart Drysdale, 1974.
Ref.: Selman, Lawrence, *The Art of the Paperweight,* 1983; p. 64.

1650
Perthshire Paperweights, Ltd., 1974. 6-petal flower (amethyst/white veined petals, amethyst spot on each tip), pink/blue/black/white cane center; 2 white buds, sepals; 5 leaves; 3 stems. "P" cane. Opaque lavender cushion. Smooth colorless base; polished basal concavity. 45/350.
D: 2 27/32″ (7.2 cm.)
Gift of Mr. and Mrs. F. John Barlow, 1986.

1667
Perthshire Paperweights, Ltd., 1977. 3 amethyst plums, black dot blossom ends; 3 stems, branch; 3 leaves. Wide top punty; 2 rows of 8 circular punties on sides; 1 small oval cut signed "P" near strawberry diamond-cut polished base. 188/500.
D: 2 1/8″ (5.4 cm.)
Gift of Mr. and Mrs. F. John Barlow, 1986.

1676
Perthshire Paperweights, Ltd., 1978. Spray bouquet. 3 lampwork flowers: orange/white/chartreuse primrose ("P" cane center); 7-petal blue (white star cane center), and a 7-petal pink flower (honeycomb cane center); 1 yellow bud; 4 stems, 7 leaves. Amethyst ground; smooth base; polished pontil area. 25/350.
D: 3 3/32″ (7.9 cm.)
Gift of Mr. and Mrs. F. John Barlow, 1986.

1685
Perthshire Paperweights, Ltd., 1979. Bouquet: ruby/white primrose, green/white cane center; 3 cobalt blue, 5-petal flowers, white stardust cane center; 1 white/green 6-over-6 petal clematis. 5 stems, 13 leaves. Multicolor "P" cane. Wide top punty; 2 rows of 8 circular side punties; radial-cut colorless base. 79/450.
D: 3 7/32″ (8.2 cm.)
Gift of Mr. and Mrs. F. John Barlow, 1986.

1700
Perthshire Paperweights, Ltd., dated 1981. Lampwork cobalt blue 6-petal flower; compound green/white cane center; green stem, 5 leaves; parallel white filigree rods and mottled translucent amethyst ground. Peripheral circle of blue/white compound florets drawn down to polished colorless basal concavity; "P 1981" cane; basal ring. 97/400.
D: 2 27/32″ (7.4 cm.)
Gift of Mr. and Mrs. F. John Barlow, 1986.

1713
Perthshire Paperweights, Ltd., 1982. Spray of 5 veined pink, 4-petal flowers, 3 pink buds, 7 stems, 5 leaves; "P" cane; translucent finely mottled pastel blue cushion. Wide top punty, allover side facets. Polished colorless basal concavity; basal ring. 60/300.
D: 2 5/8″ (6.7 cm.)
Gift of Mr. and Mrs. F. John Barlow, 1986.

1714
Perthshire Paperweights, Ltd., dated 1982. Translucent ruby overlay, medallion-cut top punty, 2 side rows of 6 circular punties. Garnet red/white pompon, 1 half-open bud; 2 green stems, 4 indented veined green leaves. Garnet red ground. Polished colorless basal concavity; "P 1982" cane; basal ring. 76/300.
D: 2 1/2″ (6.3 cm.)
Gift of Mr. and Mrs. F. John Barlow, 1986.

1738
Perthshire Paperweights, Ltd., 1985. Flower: 7-over-7 pink/white striped petals, the under layer drawn down to base through double tiers of 5 green leaves. Wide top punty, 12 oval side cuts. "P" cane. Polished colorless basal concavity; basal ring. 48/300.
D: 3 5/32″ (8.0 cm.)
Gift of Mr. and Mrs. F. John Barlow, 1986.

1739
Perthshire Paperweights, Ltd., 1985. 4 shaded yellow Scottish Broom flowers, 2 buds, 5 stems, 11 bracts; purple/white "P" cane; emerald green ground. Wide top punty; 16 oval cuts near top; 8 horizontal oval side cuts, 8 cuts near base. Polished basal concavity. 62/350.
D: 2 13/16″ (7.1 cm.)
Gift of Mr. and Mrs. F. John Barlow, 1986.

1748
Perthshire Paperweights, Ltd., 1986. "Golden Dahlia"; "P" star cane center; 4 tiers of shaded amber/white pointed petals drawn down to center of polished colorless basal concavity. Top punty, 5 oval side punties. 88/300.
D: 3 5/16″ (8.4 cm.)
Gift of Mr. and Mrs. F. John Barlow, 1986.

1773
Perthshire Paperweights, Ltd., 1987. Green/red aventurine Hummingbird (white breast, long black beak); 2 cobalt blue flowers with red stamens; 2 stems. Pink "P" cane. Wide top punty, 2 rows of 8 side punties. Concave, strawberry diamond-cut colorless base. 70/300.
D: 2 7/8″ (7.4 cm.)
Gift of Mr. and Mrs. F. John Barlow, 1987.

735
Kent F. Ipsen, Richmond, VA, 1968. Ovoid, transparent pale green glass encases iridescent blue/green inclusions resembling deep sea plants; large elongated central bubble. Rough-ground, small flat base signed "Kent F. Ipsen 1968."
H: 4¹³⁄₁₆″ (12.3 cm.); D: 3⅜″ (8.6 cm.)
Gift of Kent F. Ipsen, 1968.

866
Charles Lotton, Dolton, IL, 1973. Magnum. Greyish glass encases iridized multiple ivy leaves and entwining stems surrounding central "metallic" rock drawn to base. "Lotton 1973" and "#20" inscribed at basal periphery; pontil mark.
D: 5″ (12.8 cm.)
Gift of Leo Kaplan, 1973.
Ref.: *PCA Bulletin,* 1972.

1072
Dominick Labino, Grand Rapids, OH, 1974. Gray-white festoons edged with cadmium yellow, form marbrie motif; translucent amethyst ground. "Labino 1974" signed on curve near polished flat colorless base.
D: 2¹³⁄₁₆″ (7.1 cm.)
Museum Purchase, 1974.

1074
Dominick Labino, 1974. "Emergence in Color." Tapered, tall translucent rose-amethyst "petal" tinged with gold which encloses tear-drop bubble near top and a red-orange "petal," a cobalt blue "petal" and another bubble near center of sculpture. Polished flat colorless base signed "Labino 4-1974."
H: 8⅛″ (20.5 cm.); D: 4⅞″ (12.4 cm.)
Museum Purchase, 1974.

1359
Bottle, stoppered.
Charles Wright, Jacksonville, FL, 1979. Expanded yellow/green/blue loops drawn to colorless footed base; polished flat and signed "C Wright 1979." Tall, symmetrical stopper encases yellow and green looped motif drawn to stopper base; spherical finial.
H: 9¼″ (23.5 cm.); D: 3¹⁵⁄₁₆″ (10 cm.)
Stopper H: 2½″ (6.4 cm.)
Gift of Charles Wright, 1979.

1615
Daum Frères, Nancy, France, 1960s-70s. Ovoid; simulated flowering tree: pink/mauve spatter surrounds upper part of black trunk and branch. Signed "Daum" near periphery of polished flat colorless base.
H: 3⁷⁄₁₆″ (8.7 cm.); D: 2⁵⁄₁₆″ (5.9 cm.)
Bequest of J. Howard Gilroy, 1986.

1766
Brian M. Maytum, Boulder, CO, 1987. Glass sculpture. Twisted, blown magenta/white core encased in spiraled iridescent transparent pale turquoise-blue glass; 4 vertically spaced bubbles. Tall encasing colorless glass cut from flat diamond-shaped apex to 6 panels/ovals near polished flat colorless base signed "Brian Maytum 1987/Daniel McKenna/CSFW090."
H: 11⅝″ (29.6 cm.); D: 3¾″ (9.6 cm.)
Gift of Brian M. Maytum, 1987.

1817
Dominick Labino, dated 1977. Hot glass technique. Iridescent 4 petal linear paisley flower, the petals mottled with predominantly white/yellow/red/black, on iridescent transparent amber cushion. Signed "Labino 2-1977" near polished flat base.
D: 2¹⁵⁄₁₆″ (7.5 cm.)
Gift of Mrs. Virginia Bensley Trowbridge, 1987.

1818
Dominick Labino, dated 1982. Hot glass technique. "Draped Flower." 6 shaded orange/yellow/opaque white fronds radiate from small central bubble. Translucent cobalt blue cushion. Signed "Labino 1982" at periphery of polished flat base.
D: 2¹⁵⁄₁₆″ (7.5 cm.)
Gift of Mrs. Virginia Bensley Trowbridge, 1987.

1830
Charles Lotton, Lynwood, IL, dated 1973. Opaque pastel blue spherical form marbled with darker blue and decorated with 4 spiraled green fronds. Overall iridescent finish. Signed "Lotton 1973" near base; pontil mark.
D: 2²³⁄₃₂″ (6.9 cm.)
Gift of Mrs. Virginia Bensley Trowbridge, 1987.

1832
E. Baker O'Brien, Grand Rapids, OH, 1987. "Trillium"; hot glass technique, using Dominick Labino glass. Ruby and opaline 3-petal flower; dichroic cushion. Signed "Baker 1987 Labino Studio" near periphery of polished flat base.
D: 3³⁄₃₂″ (7.9 cm.)
Gift of Ms E. Baker O'Brien, 1987.

1834
Bottle, stoppered.
Dominick Labino, dated 1967. Blown transparent bluish-green glass with encased freehand petals on 2 sides, copper-brown and opal yellow; bulbous body. Polished concave pontil area signed "Labino 1967 #54A"; polished flat base. Short neck ground for matching spherical stopper; flat cut dome.
Bottle H: 3⅜″ (8.5 cm.); D: 2¹³⁄₁₆″ (7.2 cm.)
Stopper H: 2¹³⁄₁₆″ (7.2 cm.)
Gift of Mrs. Elizabeth S. Labino, 1988.

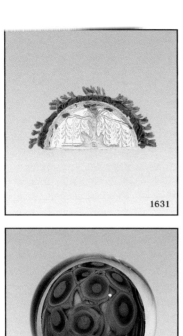

1631

1798

1626

1348

783

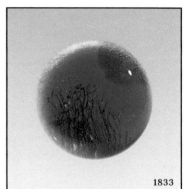

1833

1350

834

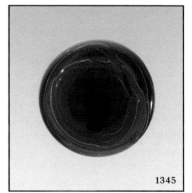

1345

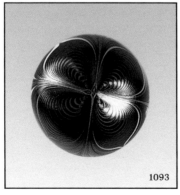

1093

918, 1624, 917

1831

1360, 1361, 1362

1346, 1293, 858

1090, 1091, 1622, 1623

871, 1833

1092, 1619, 1089

1621, 867, 1625

1518

1073

1354

783
Kent Ipsen, Richmond, VA, 1969. Ovoid: mottled, opaque purple bubble drawn to point at base; base signed "Ipsen"; pontil mark.
D: 2⅝" (6.7 cm.)
Gift of Kent Ipsen, 1970.

834
Andre Billeci, Campbell, NY, 1971. Shallow, oval form; pale mauve-colored glass with neodymium-prae-sodymium and silver and blue air inclusions. Polished flat base signed "Andre Billeci"; small pontil concavity.
D: 5⅟₁₆" (12.9 cm.); L: 5⅝₁₆" (14.2 cm.)
Gift of Friends of Bergstrom, 1971.

917
Mark Cantor, San Jose, CA, 1974. Iridized bright orange lily and black stylized vine motif on pastel blue surface. Flat polished base signed "Cantor 2/74."
D: 3⅝₁₆" (8.5 cm.)
Gift of L. H. Selman, 1974.

918
James Lundberg, Davenport, CA, 1973. Festooned green/orange trefoil motif on iridized opaque purple sphere. Flat polished base signed "James Lundberg 12/73."
D: 3¼" (8.2 cm.)
Gift of L. H. Selman, 1974.

1093
Orient & Flume, Chico, CA, 1974. "Threaded and Combed Geometric." Iridescent marbrie-type geometric design, threaded and combed in cobalt blue and gold over white and turquoise. Polished flat base signed "Orient & Flume 515Z 1974."
D: 2¾" (7.0 cm.)
Gift of Jay Gustin, 1975.

1345
William Warehall, Baton Rouge, LA, 1976. Shallow form. Encased translucent dark green glass trailed with rings of pastel brown and blue. Flat rough-ground base signed "Warehall."
D: 3²³⁄₃₂" (9.5 cm.)
Gift of William Warehall, 1978.

1348
Sylvia Vigiletti, Southfield, MI, 1978. "Garden" series. Encased hollow-blown opaque white core trailed with green "stems" and pink-centered brown and beige "flowers." Open center hole in polished flat base; perimeter signed "Sylvia Vigiletti 78."
D: 3⅟₃₂" (7.9 cm.)
Gift of Habatat Galleries, 1978.

1350
Randy Strong, 1977. Encased "crater" motif with exterior iridized blue trailings; polished flat base; perimeter signed "R. Strong 12/77 – 8/7."
D: 3⅜" (8.2 cm.)
Gift of Habatat Galleries, 1978.

1624
Lundberg Studios, Davenport, IA; probably David Salazar; 1975. Iridescent scrolled and festooned gilt and dark blue motif on opaque white core. Polished flat base signed "Lundberg Studios 1975 D.S."
D: 2⅞" (7.3 cm.)
Bequest of J. Howard Gilroy, 1986.

1626
Peter Schiller, Minneapolis, MN, 1986. Frosted sphere; polished angle cut reveals swirled pink/white festooned motif. Frosted flat base signed "Peter Schiller."
D: 2¹³⁄₁₆" (7.2 cm.)
Gift of Peter Schiller, 1986.

1631
Barry Sautner/Douglas B. Merritt, Flemington, NJ, 1985. "Wisteria" Insculpture Diatreta paperweight. Half-circle form. Colorless glass with wisteria shrub insculpture, small bench, pond with waterlilies; diatreta "network": 4-color overlay (amethyst/pink/white/green) cameo-carved and undercut wisteria blossoms and leaves. Signed "1985 VMGS A72 Barry Sautner Doug Merritt 'Wisteria'" in frosted "bark" surface on arch.
H: 1¹¹⁄₁₆" (4.3 cm.); W: 3⅝" (9.3 cm.)
D: 1⅝₁₆" (3.4 cm.)
Gift of Mrs. William L. Liebman in memory of her husband, William L. Liebman, 1986.
Ref.: *PCA Bulletin,* 1982, 1984.

1798
Victor Trabucco, Clarence, NY, 1977. "Bird and Nest." Colorless glass lampwork bird perches on "Y" shape branch; 9 leaves surround nest with 3 eggs; stem end signed "1977/7/125." White marble base.
Commissioned by Paul Jokelson, 1977.
D: 4¹¹⁄₃₂" (11.1 cm.); W: 5⅝₁₆" (13.8 cm.)
Gift of Mrs. Virginia Bensley Trowbridge, 1987.
Ref.: *PCA Bulletin,* 1981, 1987.

1831
Steven Lundberg, Lundberg Studios, dated 1974. Turquoise-blue ground, pink and burgundy "pulled feather" motif on dome; overall iridescent finish. Polished flat base signed near periphery: "Lundberg Studios 3/74/SL." Marbled red core.
D: 3⅝₃₂" (8.0 cm.)
Gift of Mrs. Virginia Bensley Trowbridge, 1987.

1833
Dominick Labino, Grand Rapids, OH, dated 1975. "Moss Scape." Iridescent free-hand motif of grasses and flower-heads on translucent cobalt blue ground. "Labino 1975" signed near periphery of polished flat colorless base.
D: 2⅝" (6.7 cm.)
Gift of Mrs. Elizabeth S. Labino, 1988.

858
Michael Boylen, West Burke, VT, 1972. Blue/amber free-form motif; silver inclusions. Signed "Michael Boylen."
D: 3⅜" (8.6 cm.)
Gift of Michael Boylen, 1973.

867
Charles Lotton, Dolton, IL, 1973. Iridescent blue sphere; scroll design. Signed "Lotton 1973."
D: 3⅛" (8.0 cm.)
Gift of Leo Kaplan, 1973.

871
Dominick Labino, Grand Rapids, OH, 1972. "Moss-scape on Stained Opal"; abstract design on peach ground; free-hand, hot glass technique. Signed "Dominick Labino."
D: 2⁹⁄₁₆" (6.4 cm.)
Gift of Mr. and Mrs. Dominick Labino in memory of Evelyn Campbell Cloak, 1973.

1073
Dominick Labino, 1973. 6-petal stylized yellow tulip free-formed in hot glass. Signed "Labino 1973."
D: 2¹³⁄₁₆" (7.2 cm.)
Museum Purchase, 1974.

1089
Orient & Flume, Chico, CA, 1975. "Blue Iriscene." Iridized motif: blue flower; blue shading to purple stylized leaves, stem; scroll/stripe background design on opaque core. Signed "Orient & Flume 124E 1975."
D: 2¹³⁄₁₆" (7.2 cm.)
Gift of Jay Gustin, 1975.

1090
Orient & Flume, 1975. "Tiger Lily." Iridized motif: 3 lilies; marbled, shiny olive-green opaque core. Signed "Orient & Flume 522Z 1974."
D: 2¾" (7.0 cm.)
Gift of Jay Gustin, 1975.

1091
Orient & Flume, 1975. "Blue Iriscene Geometric." Iridized motif on opaque white core: pale blue/cobalt blue/gold iris-like designs. Signed "Orient & Flume 121 E 1975."
D: 2⅞" (7.3 cm.)
Gift of Jay Gustin, 1975.

1092
Orient & Flume, 1975. "Butterfly" iridized motif on opaque white core; trailed vines on iridescent olive-green surface. Signed "Orient & Flume 127E 1975."
D: 2¹³⁄₁₆" (7.1 cm.)
Gift of Jay Gustin, 1975.

1293
David Huchthausen, Bloomington, IN, 1977. Encased air sculpture motif; iridized black core. Signed "David K. Huchthausen 1977."
D: 3½" (8.9 cm.)
Gift of David Huchthausen, 1977.

1346
William Warehall, Baton Rouge, LA, ca. 1976. Black core; blue/gold/silver iridized leaf designs. Signed "Warehall."
D: 3¹¹⁄₁₆" (9.4 cm.)
Gift of William Warehall, 1978.

1354
Dominick Labino, 1979. "Chambered Nautilus Unchambered." Cut nautilus shell form over white "coral" and green spatter ground which appears dichroic blue in reflected light. Signed "Labino 1979."
D: 2¾" (7.0 cm.)
Gift of Mr. and Mrs. Dominick Labino, 1979.

1360
George Thiewes, South Woodstock, VT, 1979. Ovoid opaque white glass; blue flowers, red centers. Signed "Thiewes '79."
H: 2¹⁷⁄₃₂" (6.4 cm.); D: 2⅛" (5.4 cm.)
Gift of Mr. and Mrs. George Thiewes, Sr., 1979.

1361
George Thiewes, 1978. Silver with red flowers; buckskin ground. Signed "Thiewes '78."
D: 2¼" (5.7 cm.)
Gift of Mr. and Mrs. George Thiewes, Sr., 1979.

1362
George Thiewes, 1979. Copper/green/blue in loop design on "silver" beige ground. Signed "Thiewes '79."
D: 2⁵⁄₃₂" (5.5 cm.)
Gift of Mr. and Mrs. George Thiewes, Sr., 1979.

1518
Victor Trabucco, Clarence, NY, 1981. "Nature in Ice" Series. 2 white daisies, bud, 3 stems, 5 leaves (underside of lowest leaf, signed "VT"), yellow butterfly. Polished top, petal-cut sides, one signed "Trabucco 1981 7/50."
Size: 3¹¹⁄₁₆ x 3³⁄₁₆ x 1⅞" (9.4 x 8.2 x 4.3 cm.)
Gift of Mr. and Mrs. William L. Liebman, 1984.

1619
Orient & Flume, 1975. Iridescent butterfly; flowering plants. Green surface with blue festooning. Signed "Orient & Flume #216 H 1975." Opaque white core.
D: 2²⁷⁄₃₂" (7.2 cm.)
Bequest of J. Howard Gilroy, 1986.

1621
Orient & Flume, 1975. Miniature. Iridescent scrolled and festooned surface decoration on amber-cased opaque white core. Signed "Orient & Flume m3 S 1975."
D: 1²⁷⁄₃₂" (4.5 cm.)
Bequest of J. Howard Gilroy, 1986.

1622
Orient & Flume, 1975. Miniature. Iridescent orange hearts, bronze vines on blue surface. Signed "Orient & Flume m17 H 1975."
D: 1³¹⁄₃₂" (5.0 cm.)
Bequest of J. Howard Gilroy, 1986.

1623
Orient & Flume, 1975. Miniature. Iridescent orange flower, bronze vine, on blue surface. Signed "Orient & Flume m15 H 1975."
D: 1²⁹⁄₃₂" (4.9 cm.)
Bequest of J. Howard Gilroy, 1986.

1625
Charles Lotton, Lynwood, IL, 1972. Iridescent "King Tut" motif. Signed "Lotton 1972."
D: 2⁹⁄₁₆" (6.6 cm.)
Bequest of J. Howard Gilroy, 1986.

1833
See Plate No. 105.

1353

811

1389

1392

919

1388

1387

1369

728

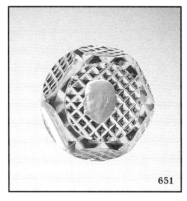

651

1828

636

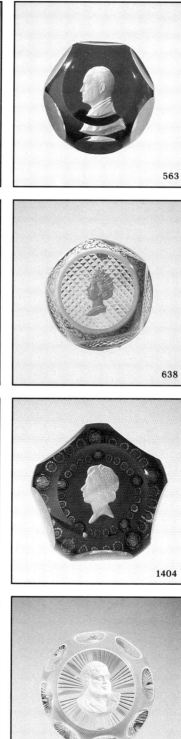
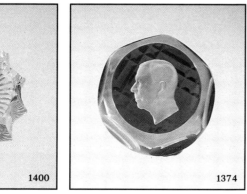

893

634

563

554

564

638

558

556

1404

1400

1374

1382

636
Baccarat, dated 1955. Double overlay: royal blue/opaque white. Sulphide portrait, profile to dexter, of Winston Churchill; "Mar 1953" impressed sulphide edge. Top, 5 side punties. "Baccarat 1955" etched in beveled edge of diamond-cut, colorless base.
D: 3⅛" (7.9 cm.)
No. 652, Pl. 30; Cloak Catalogue, 1969.
Gift of Mr. and Mrs. Ralph S. Johns, 1962.

651
Baccarat, dated 1954. Sulphide portrait, profile to dexter, of Winston Churchill; edge marked "Mar 1953." Top, 6 side punties. "B 1954" etched near waffle-cut, ruby-flashed base.
D: 2¾" (7.0 cm.)
No. 667, Pl. 30; Cloak Catalogue, 1969.
Gift of Mr. and Mrs. Ralph S. Johns, 1962.

728
Cristalleries d'Albret, Vianne, France, 1966. Sulphide bust portrait, front view slightly to dexter, of Christopher Columbus rests on translucent cobalt blue ground. Inscribed "Columbus G.S. 1966" (sculptor, Georges Simon). Large top punty, 6 oval cuts on curve. 3/1000.
D: 2¾" (7.0 cm.)
No. 733, Pl. 32; Cloak Catalogue, 1969.
Gift of Paul Jokelson, 1967.

811
Murano, Italy, 1970. Large circular sulphide plaque commemorates Apollo moon landing. At periphery in semicircle: "E. Aldrin • N. Armstrong • M. Collins," bust portraits below; simulated American flag and date "July 20, 1969." Transparent sapphire blue ground. Flat base cut with 16-point star.
D: 3¾" (9.4 cm.)
Gift of Mrs. C. A. Peterson, 1970.

919
Cristalleries d'Albret, 1973. Sulphide portrait, front view slightly to dexter, of John James Audubon (1785-1851), signed "G. P. J. J. Audubon CA 72" by sculptor Gilbert Poillerat. Large top punty, 8 oval side punties; radial-cut, cerulean blue base. 215/1000.
D: 3⅛" (7.9 cm.)
Gift of Mrs. Fred Leech, 1974.

1353
Saint Louis, 1979. Conceptual sulphide entitled "Amour," by French sculptor Gilbert Poillerat, surrounded by 5 spaced blue flowers (each with white star cane center), green leaves; brilliant opaque pink ground lined with opaque white. Top punty, 5 side punties; wide polished slightly concave colorless base reveals red/white "SL 1979" signature cane. 93/400.
D: 3½₂" (7.8 cm.)
Gift of L. H. Selman, 1979.

1369
Cristalleries d'Albret, 1966. Translucent cobalt blue overlay cut with top and 4 side punties, multiple faceting between each. Sulphide portrait, slightly to dexter, of Christopher Columbus; edge impressed "Columbus G. S. 1966" (sculptor: Georges Simon). Colorless base cut with alternate vertical flutes and miters.
D: 2¹³⁄₁₆" (7.4 cm.)
Gift of George Ackerman, 1979.

1387
Cristalleries d'Albret, dated 1970. Sulphide portrait of Prince Charles, to dexter, edge signed "H.R.H. Prince Charles CA GP 1970." Wide top punty, 7 side punties. Polished, diamond-cut translucent cobalt blue base; pontil area etched "CR. Albret France-" in a circle. 345/1000.
D: 2⅞" (7.5 cm.).
Gift of George Ackerman, 1979.

1388
Cristalleries d'Albret, dated 1970. Translucent cobalt blue overlay; wide top punty; double-star cut between each of 4 side punties. Sulphide portrait of Prince Charles to dexter, edge signed "H.R.H. Prince Charles CA GP 1970." Sunburst miter/flute cut, polished colorless base, ribbed edge; pontil area etched "CR. Albret France-" in circle. 67/200.
D: 3¹⁄₁₆" (7.7 cm.)
Gift of George Ackerman, 1979.

1389
Cristalleries d'Albret, dated 1971. Magnum. Composite sulphide portrait of "The Moon Astronauts" (Edwin E. Aldrin, Jr.; Michael Collins; Neil A. Armstrong; and Alan B. Shepard, Jr.); on edge, /NASA/; "71 G.P." at right. Wide top punty, 8 side punties. Ribbed edge, polished flat transparent cerulean blue base; pontil area etched "CR. Albret France-." 439/1000.
D: 3¹³⁄₁₆" (9.8 cm.)
Gift of George Ackerman, 1979.

1392
Cristalleries d'Albret, dated 1972. Pastel blue/white double overlay; wide top punty; 4 side punties, flute and circular facets. Sulphide portrait of John James Audubon, profile slightly to sinister, edge signed "G.P.J.J. Audubon CA 72." Mitered, rib-edged, polished flat colorless base cut with sunburst miters and flutes; pontil area etched "CR. Albret France-" in circle. 32/1000.
D: 3¹⁄₁₆" (7.9 cm.)
Gift of George Ackerman, 1979.

1828
Cristalleries d'Albret, 1974. Lens-like colorless dome; in bottom of round metal base, a gilt relief sculpture of Sir Winston Churchill (G.P. impressed in shoulder), Big Ben and Houses of Parliament at his right, a red/white/blue British flag to sinister in background. Side of bronze base encircled by double band of tooled decoration. Underside: "Sir Winston Churchill by G. Poillerat/Made in France."
D: 3⅜" (8.6 cm.)
Gift of Mrs. Virginia Bensley Trowbridge, 1987.

554
Baccarat, dated 1953. Sulphide double portrait, profiles to dexter, of Queen Elizabeth II and Prince Philip. Edge of sulphide impressed "G. Poillerat." "Baccarat 1953" etched on beveled edge of fan-cut colorless base.
D: 2⅝" (6.6 cm.)
Bergstrom Bequest, 1958.
EHB acquisition: Unrecorded.
No. 590, Pl. 32; Cloak Catalogue, 1969.

556
Baccarat, dated 1953. Double overlay: blue/opaque white. Sulphide double portrait, profiles to dexter, of Queen Elizabeth II and Prince Philip. Sulphide edge inscribed "G. Poillerat." Top punty, 5 side punties alternate with narrow oval cuts. "Baccarat 1953" etched on beveled edge of diamond-cut colorless base.
D: 3⅛" (7.9 cm.)
Bergstrom Bequest, 1958.
EHB acquisition: Unrecorded.
No. 592, Pl. 30; Cloak Catalogue, 1969.

558
Saint Louis, 1953. Sulphide portrait, profile to dexter, of Queen Elizabeth II on opaque turquoise ground. Pink/white and green/white canes encircle portrait. Top punty, 5 side punties. "Couronnement 2-6-53 Saint Louis — France" etched in circle on polished concave base.
D: 2¾" (7.0 cm.)
Bergstrom Bequest, 1958.
EHB acquisition: Unrecorded.
No. 594, Pl. 32; Cloak Catalogue, 1969.

563
Baccarat, dated 1953. Sulphide portrait, profile to dexter, of Dwight Eisenhower on translucent cobalt blue base. Sulphide edge impressed "547." Top, 5 side punties. Beveled edge of polished flat base etched "Baccarat 1953."
D: 2¾" (7.0 cm.)
Bergstrom Bequest, 1958.
EHB acquisition: Unrecorded.
No. 602, Pl. 31; Cloak Catalogue, 1969.

564
Baccarat, dated 1953. Sulphide double portrait, profiles to dexter, of Queen Elizabeth II and Prince Philip on translucent cobalt blue base. Edge of sulphide impressed "G. Poillerat." 6 side punties; edge of polished flat base etched "Baccarat 1953."
D: 2⅝" (6.6 cm.)
Bergstrom Bequest, 1958.
EHB acquisition: Unrecorded.
No. 603, Pl. 30; Cloak Catalogue, 1969.

634
Baccarat, 1953-59. Double overlay: rose/opaque white. Sulphide portrait, profile to dexter, of Dwight D. Eisenhower. Top punty, 5 side punties spaced between 5 narrow oval facets. Diamond-cut, colorless base.
D: 3⅛" (8.0 cm.)
No. 650, Pl. 31; Cloak Catalogue, 1969.
Gift of Mr. and Mrs. Ralph S. Johns, 1962.

638
Baccarat, 1954-59. Opaque white single overlay, gilt tracery. Sulphide portrait, profile to dexter, of Queen Elizabeth II, sculpted by Gilbert Poillerat, initials "G.P." faintly impressed in sulphide edge. Top, 5 side punties; diamond-cut colorless base.
D: 3⅛" (7.9 cm.)
No. 654, Pl. 32; Cloak Catalogue, 1969.
Gift of Mr. and Mrs. Ralph S. Johns, 1962.

893
Baccarat, 1953. Cobalt blue/white double overlay. Top punty; 5 side punties between 5 flute cuts. Sulphide portrait, profile to dexter, of Dwight D. Eisenhower; shoulder edge marked "39"; strawberry diamond-cut, colorless flat base; signed "B. 1953." 39/178.
D: 3³⁄₃₂" (7.9 cm.)
Mrs. L. E. Kaumheimer Bequest, 1973.

1374
Cristalleries d'Albret, Vianne, France, 1967. Sulphide portrait, to dexter, of Gustaf VI, King of Sweden, edge signed "Gustaf VI Adolf 1967 LH" (Leo Holmgren, sculptor). Sapphire blue base. Top, 6 side punties. Polished, crosscut base etched "CR Albret France." 17/1000.
D: 2¾" (7.0 cm.)
Gift of George Ackerman, 1979.

1382
Cristalleries d'Albret, dated 1969. Red/white double overlay; top punty, 8 side punties; ribbed edge, sunburst-cut polished colorless base, pontil area etched "CR. Albret France-" (in circle). Sulphide portrait of Ernest Hemingway, profile slightly to sinister, edge signed "CA GP 1969." 142/225.
D: 3¹⁄₁₆" (7.8 cm.)
Gift of George Ackerman, 1979.

1400
Cristalleries d'Albret, 1976. Terra cotta cameo portrait of Mahatma Gandhi, slightly to sinister; edge signed "G.P./Gandhi/CA." Wide top punty, 12 side flute facets; star-cut base; polished pontil area etched in circle "CR. Albret France-" 129/500.
D: 2⅞" (7.4 cm.)
Gift of George Ackerman, 1979.

1404
Baccarat, 1977. Silver Jubilee Commemorative. Sulphide profile portrait, to dexter, of Queen Elizabeth II, encircled by 4 green/white/pink star center canes (signifying Her Majesty's children) between each of 5 "Clichy"-type pink/green rose canes. Translucent dark amethyst, slightly concave polished base bears deeply etched Queen's Silver Jubilee 1977 insignia, "150/500" and Baccarat signature. Large top punty, 5 side punties. Portrait modelled by Leslie Durbin CBE MVO.
D: 3¹⁵⁄₃₂" (8.8 cm.)
Gift of David F. Spink, 1980.

1277

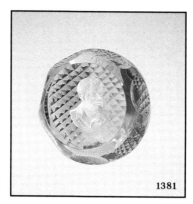

1381

1273

829

828

849

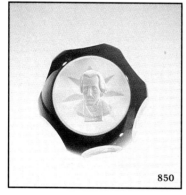

850

642

648

1396

704

696

1030

1373

1352

1401

652

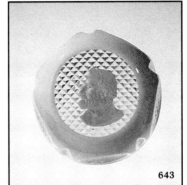

643

736

1376

646

640

1394

1398

642
Baccarat, dated 1954. Double overlay: rose-red/opaque white. Sulphide portrait, profile to sinister, of Thomas Jefferson; edge marked "G.P. 1953" (sculptor Gilbert Poillerat). Large top punty; 5 side punties alternate with 5 pointed oval facets. "Baccarat 1954" etched on beveled edge of crosscut colorless base.
D: 3⅛″ (7.9 cm.)
No. 658, Pl. 31; Cloak Catalogue, 1969.
Gift of Mr. and Mrs. Ralph S. Johns, 1962.

648
Baccarat, dated 1954. Sulphide portrait, profile to sinister, of Thomas Jefferson (marked "G.P. 1953" for French sculptor, Gilbert Poillerat) rests on translucent cranberry-red base; beveled edge etched "Baccarat 1954." Top, 6 side punties.
D: 2¹¹⁄₁₆″ (6.8 cm.)
No. 664, Pl. 31; Cloak Catalogue, 1969.
Gift of Mr. and Mrs. Ralph S. Johns, 1962.

696
Baccarat, 1963. Sulphide bust portrait, slightly to sinister, of John Fitzgerald Kennedy (edge marked "A. David 63") rests on translucent dark red, flanged flat base; underside etched with Baccarat insignia. Top, 5 side punties.
D: 2¾″ (7.0 cm.)
Museum Purchase, 1964.
No. 715, Pl. 30; Cloak Catalogue, 1969.

704
Baccarat, 1964. Double overlay: cobalt blue/opaque white. Sulphide bust portrait, slightly to sinister, of John Fitzgerald Kennedy (edge marked "A. David 63") rests on translucent dark red, slightly footed flat base; underside etched with Baccarat insignia. Top, 5 side punties.
D: 3⅛″ (7.9 cm.)
No. 724, Pl. 30; Cloak Catalogue, 1969.
Gift of Mr. and Mrs. Walter Gray, 1965.

828
Baccarat, 1971. Sulphide bust portrait, front view slightly to dexter, of Herbert Hoover, signed "A. David Paris." Translucent cobalt blue base. Large top punty, 6 side punties. Flanged, polished base etched with Baccarat insignia.
D: 2¾″ (6.9 cm.)
Gift of Andre Vulliet, 1971.

829
Baccarat, 1971. Double overlay: pale blue/opaque white. Sulphide bust portrait, front view slightly to dexter, of Herbert Hoover, signed "A. David Paris." Large top punty (high crown); 5 side punties. Slightly beveled, star-cut and footed polished colorless base etched with Baccarat insignia.
D: 3⅛″ (8.0 cm.)
Gift of Andre Vulliet, 1971.

849
Baccarat, 1972. Sulphide bust portrait, front view slightly to dexter, of Andrew Jackson, signed "A. Jackson" and "M. Renard 1971" (official sculptor for the French Mint). Transparent green ground. Top punty, 6 side punties. Flanged, polished colorless base etched with Baccarat insignia.
D: 2¾″ (7.0 cm.)
Gift of Andre Vulliet, 1973.

850
Baccarat, 1972. Double overlay: deep green/opaque white. Sulphide portrait, front view slightly to dexter, of Andrew Jackson, signed "A. Jackson" and "M. Renard 1971." Large top punty, 6 oval side punties that join flanged colorless base etched with Baccarat insignia. 400 edition.
D: 3⅛″ (8.0 cm.)
Gift of Andre Vulliet, 1973.

1273
Baccarat, 1977. Sulphide portrait, slightly to sinister, of Patrick Henry; edge inscribed "Patrick Henry" and "J. Goy" (French sculptor). Translucent dark green ground. Top punty, 6 side punties; mitered base etched with Baccarat signature.
D: 2²⁷⁄₃₂″ (7.2 cm.)
Gift of Andre Vulliet, 1977.

1277
Baccarat, 1977. Swirl cut translucent blue overlay. Sulphide portrait, slightly to sinister, of Patrick Henry, signed "Patrick Henry" and "J. Goy." Top punty; large star-cut underside of polished base; etched Baccarat signature.
D: 3³⁄₃₂″ (7.9 cm.)
Gift of Andre Vulliet, 1977.

1381
Cristalleries d'Albret, Vianne, France, dated 1969. Sulphide portrait of Ernest Hemingway, profile slightly to sinister, edge signed "Hemingway CA GP 1969." Top, 7 side punties; flute/miter cut transparent red base; polished pontil area etched "CR. Albret France." 3/1000.
D: 2⅞″ (7.4 cm.)
Gift of George Ackerman, 1979.

1396
Cristalleries d'Albret, dated 1974. Vermilion red/white double overlay; wide top punty, 8 side punties. Sulphide front view portrait of John Paul Jones, edge signed "John Paul Jones G.P. 74." Mitered, polished flat sunburst-cut colorless base; pontil area etched "CR. Albret France-" in circle. 59/170.
D: 3¹⁄₁₆″ (7.8 cm.)
Gift of George Ackerman, 1979.

640
Baccarat, dated 1954. Double overlay: blue/opaque white. Sulphide bust portrait, front view slightly to sinister, of Abraham Lincoln; edge marked "G.P. 1953" (Gilbert Poillerat, sculptor). Large top punty, 5 side punties alternate with 5 pointed oval facets. Crosscut colorless base etched "Baccarat 1954" on beveled edge.
D: 3⅛″ (7.9 cm.)
No. 656, Pl. 30; Cloak Catalogue, 1969.
Gift of Mr. and Mrs. Ralph S. Johns, 1962.

643
Baccarat, dated 1955. Double overlay: pale grey/opaque white. Sulphide portrait, profile to dexter, of Robert E. Lee; edge marked "B Mar 1954." Large top punty; 5 side punties alternate with 5 pointed oval facets. "Baccarat 1954" etched on beveled edge of crosscut colorless base.
D: 3⅛″ (7.9 cm.)
No. 659, Pl. 31; Cloak Catalogue, 1969.
Gift of Mr. and Mrs. Ralph S. Johns, 1962.

646
Baccarat, dated 1954. Sulphide bust portrait, front view slightly to sinister, of Abraham Lincoln; edge marked "G.P. 1953" (Gilbert Poillerat, sculptor). Sulphide rests on cloudy translucent amethyst base; "Baccarat 1954" etched on base rim. Top, and 6 side punties.
D: 2⅝″ (6.6 cm.)
No. 662, Pl. 30; Cloak Catalogue, 1969.
Gift of Mr. and Mrs. Ralph S. Johns, 1962.

652
Baccarat, dated 1954. Sulphide portrait, profile to dexter, of Robert E. Lee; edge marked "B Mar 1954." Top, 6 side punties. "Baccarat 1954" etched on bevel edge of crosscut colorless base.
D: 2¾″ (7.0 cm.)
No. 668, Pl. 31; Cloak Catalogue, 1969.
Gift of Mr. and Mrs. Ralph S. Johns, 1962.

736
Cristalleries d'Albret, Vianne, France, 1968. Sulphide portrait, front view slightly to sinister, of Leonardo da Vinci, signed "GP 1968"; translucent deep amber ground. Large top punty, 7 thumbprint cuts on curve; base cut with 16-point star. 921/1000.
D: 2⅞″ (7.3 cm.)
Gift of Paul Jokelson, 1968.

1030
KB, Italy, 1960-70. Magnum. Sulphide portrait of John F. Kennedy, profile to dexter, translucent dark red ground. Polished flat base cut with 16-point star. Paper label: "An original creation by KB — Made in Italy."
D: 3¹³⁄₁₆″ (9.7 cm.)
Gift of Dr. M. J. Caldwell, 1974.

1352
Baccarat, 1979. 22-carat gold sulphide cameo of Dr. Martin Luther King, Jr., slightly to dexter; signed "Joseph Goy 77"; translucent turquoise ground. Top punty, 6 side punties; flanged polished flat base etched with Baccarat signature. 500 edition. Note: This is last edition of sulphide paperweights to be made by Baccarat for the U. S. market.
D: 2¹³⁄₁₆″ (7.1 cm.)
Gift of Andre Vulliet, 1979.

1373
Cristalleries d'Albret, 1967. Transparent emerald green overlay. Double-portrait sulphide of John F. Kennedy, slightly to sinister, and Jacqueline, facing front; shoulder edge impressed "J. F. & J. Kennedy" and "CA G.P." 1967 (Gilbert Poillerat, sculptor). Wide top punty, star and diamond cutting between each of 4 side punties; wide, flat polished colorless base cut with sunburst pattern of 8 flutes alternate with 5 narrow flutes; polished pontil area etched with "CR. Albret France-"; rib-cut edge. 226/300.
D: 3¹⁄₁₆″ (7.3 cm.)
Gift of George Ackerman, 1979.

1376
Cristalleries d'Albret, 1969. Translucent amber overlay, large top punty, 9 small oval side punties. Sulphide portrait, slightly to sinister, of Leonardo da Vinci, edge signed "Leonardo da Vinci G.P. 1969." Basal periphery mitered and vertically cut. Polished colorless base miter- and flute-cut; center etched "CR. Albret France-." 66/200.
D: 3¹⁄₁₆″ (7.8 cm.)
Gift of George Ackerman, 1979.

1394
Cristalleries d'Albret, dated 1973. Transparent amber/white double overlay; wide top punty, 8 side punties. Sulphide bust portrait of Jenny Lind, slightly to sinister; edge signed "Jenny Lind," shoulder signed "GP." Mitered, ribbed polished colorless base cut with sunburst flutes and miters; pontil area faintly etched "CR. Albret France-" in circle. 10/170.
D: 3¹⁄₁₆″ (7.8 cm.)
Gift of George Ackerman, 1979.

1398
Cristalleries d'Albret, dated 1975. Pastel blue/white opaline double overlay; wide top punty, 6 side punties. Sulphide portrait of Charles A. Lindbergh, slightly to dexter, edge signed "C. A. Lindbergh/G.P. 75." Mitered, ribbed colorless base; 6 "airplane" cuts radiate from polished pontil area etched "CR. Albret France-" in circle. 144/200.
D: 3¹⁄₁₆″ (7.9 cm.)
Gift of George Ackerman, 1979.

1401
Cristalleries d'Albret, dated 1976. Terra cotta cameo portrait of Martin Luther King, Jr., slightly to dexter, edge signed "76 Martin Luther King G.P." Wide top punty, 12 side flute facets. Sunburst-cut, lightly frosted base (facets extend to side flutes). Polished pontil area etched in circle, "CR. Albret France-." 148/325.
D: 2¹⁵⁄₁₆″ (7.5 cm.)
Gift of George Ackerman, 1979.
Ref.: *PCA Bulletin,* 1966-67; pp. 19-20.
Selman, L. H. and Linda-Pope: *Paperweights For Collectors,* (Paperweight Press, Santa Cruz, CA, 1975); pp. 114-116.

1397

645

635

798

1378

830

831

1274

1068

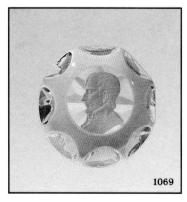

1069

1228

1257

710

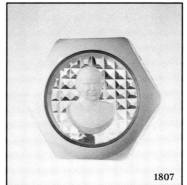

1807

633

1347

1384

1520

847

825

848

1370

1385

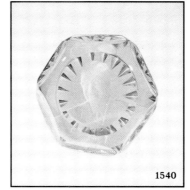

1540

635
Baccarat, dated 1957. Double overlay: green/opaque white. Sulphide bust portrait, front view slightly to sinister, of Martin Luther; edge impressed "Martin Luther 1483-1546 G.P. 1955." Top, 5 side punties. "Baccarat 1957" etched in beveled edge of diamond-cut, colorless base.
D: 3⅛" (7.9 cm.)
No. 651, Pl. 31; Cloak Catalogue, 1969.
Gift of Mr. and Mrs. Ralph S. Johns, 1962.

645
Baccarat, dated 1958. Sulphide bust portrait, front view slightly to sinister, of Martin Luther; edge marked "Luther 1483-1546 G.P. 1955" (Gilbert Poillerat, sculptor). Top, 6 side punties. "Baccarat 1958" etched on beveled edge of waffle-cut, red-flashed flat base.
D: 2¾" (7.0 cm.)
No. 661, Pl. 31; Cloak Catalogue, 1969.
Gift of Mr. and Mrs. Ralph S. Johns, 1962.

798
Cristalleries d'Albret, Vianne, France, 1970. Sulphide bust portrait, front view slightly to dexter, of General Douglas MacArthur signed "GP 1968"; translucent emerald-green ground. Large top punty, 8 thumbprint cuts on curve. Flat base cut with 8 miters forming star, 5 narrow miters between each wider cut. Polished small central basal concavity etched "CR. Albret France-." 24/1500 edition.
D: 3" (7.6 cm.)
Gift of Paul Jokelson, 1970.

830
Baccarat, 1971. Sulphide bust portrait, front view slightly to sinister, of James Monroe, signed by the sculptor Gilbert Poillerat, "B GP 1955." Translucent cranberry-red ground; hexagonally cut top and sides; beveled, flanged polished base etched with Baccarat insignia.
D: 2⅝" (6.6 cm.)
Gift of Andre Vulliet, 1971.

831
Baccarat, 1971. High-crowned weight flashed with transparent apple-green. Top punty, double star cuts alternate between 4 side punties. Sulphide bust portrait, slightly to sinister, of James Monroe, signed "B GP 1955" by sculptor Gilbert Poillerat. Flanged colorless base cut with 24-point star.
D: 3⅛" (7.9 cm.)
Gift of Andre Vulliet, 1971.

1068
Baccarat, 1974. Sulphide bust portrait, profile to dexter, of General Bonaparte, who later became Napoleon I; edge of cameo signed by sculptor Jean Goy. Garnet-red ground, polished base etched with Baccarat insignia and date "1974." Top and 6 side punties. 2400 edition.
D: 2¾" (7.0 cm.)
Gift of Andre Vulliet, 1974.

1069
Baccarat, dated 1974. Double overlay: yellow/opaque white. Sulphide bust portrait, profile to dexter, of General Bonaparte, later named Napoleon I. Cameo signed by sculptor Jean Goy. Top and 8 oval side punties; 8-point star-cut, polished colorless base etched with Baccart insignia and "1974." 400 edition.
D: 3⅛" (7.9 cm.)
Gift of Andre Vulliet, 1974.

1228
Baccarat, 1976. Double overlay, jade green over opaque white, top punty, 5 side punties alternate with 5 oval cuts. Sulphide portrait, front view slightly to dexter, of Thomas Paine by sculptor Jean Goy, signed "J. Goy 1975"; colorless ground; wide star-cut polished mitered flat base etched with Baccarat signature. 400 edition.
D: 3³⁄₃₂" (7.9 cm.)
Gift of Andre Vulliet, 1976.

1257
Baccarat, 1976. Sulphide portrait of Thomas Paine, front view slightly to dexter, edge signed "Thomas Paine" and "J. Goy 1975"; mitered blue opaline base, polished flat and etched with Baccarat signature. 2,000 edition.
D: 2⅞" (7.3 cm.)
Gift of Andre Vulliet, 1976.

1274
Baccarat, 1976. Magnum. Oval double overlay: rose-red/white opaline. Sulphide replica by sculptor Jean Goy of Mt. Rushmore Monument; translucent dark blue ground. Top and 8 side punties. Mitered base etched with Baccarat signature, "549." 1000 edition. Dated 1976.
D: 3½" (8.9 cm.); L: 4¼" (10.8 cm.)
Gift of Andre Vulliet, 1977.

1378
Cristalleries d'Albret, 1968. Translucent lime-green overlay; large top punty, 4 side punties alternate with facets. Sulphide portrait, profile slightly to dexter, of General Douglas MacArthur, edge signed "G.P. 1968." Edge flute and miter-cut; polished colorless base; center etched "CR. Albret France-." 54/225.
D: 3" (7.7 cm.)
Gift of George Ackerman, 1979.

1397
Cristalleries d'Albret, dated 1975. Sulphide portrait of Charles A. Lindbergh, slightly to dexter, edge signed "C. A. Lindbergh/G.P. 75." Wide top punty, 6 side punties. Polished cerulean blue base. 6 "airplane" cuts surround pontil area etched "CR. Albret France-" in a circle. 346/415.
D: 2²³⁄₃₂" (7.0 cm.)
Gift of George Ackerman, 1979.

633
Baccarat, 1960. Sulphide bust portrait, profile to dexter, of Pope Pius XII; sulphide edge impressed "A. David 1959." Top, 6 side punties. Star-cut, ruby-flashed, concave base etched with Baccarat insignia.
D: 2¹³⁄₁₆" (7.2 cm.)
Museum Purchase, 1960.
No. 669, Pl. 31; Cloak Catalogue, 1969.

710
Baccarat, 1966-67. Double overlay: yellow/opaque white. Sulphide bust portrait, profile to dexter, of Pope John XXIII (edge marked "A. David Paris 1964"), which rests on mitered transparent ruby-red shallow foot. Six-lobed rosette faceting on crown, 6 oval cuts near base etched with Baccarat insignia.
D: 3⅛" (7.9 cm.)
Museum Purchase, 1967.
No. 742, Pl. 32; Cloak Catalogue, 1969.

825
Cristalleries d'Albret, Vianne, France, 1970. Translucent amethyst overlay. Sulphide bust portrait, profile to sinister, of Franklin Delano Roosevelt, signed "G.S. 1969" (sculptor Georges Simon). Wide top punty, 4 side punties each alternated with two 9-point facets. 40-point star encircled by miter cuts in polished flat colorless base. 165/300.
D: 2⅞" (7.3 cm.)
Gift of Mr. and Mrs. Ralph S. Johns, 1971.

847
Baccarat, 1971. Sulphide bust portrait, front view to sinister, of Eleanor Roosevelt on thin, translucent deep amethyst ground. Sulphide (the last designed by sculptor Albert David) is etched "DAVID 1971" on base. Large top punty, 6 smaller side punties; sunburst-cut, colorless flanged base etched with Baccarat insignia.
D: 2¾" (7.0 cm.)
Gift of Andre Vulliet, 1973.

848
Baccarat, 1971. Double overlay: amethyst/opaque white. Sulphide bust portrait, front view to sinister, of Eleanor Roosevelt, set deep in weight. Cameo base signed "DAVID 1971" by sculptor Albert David. Top punty, 5 side punties. Star-cut, flanged polished colorless base etched with Baccarat insignia.
D: 3" (7.6 cm.)
Gift of Andre Vulliet, 1973.

1347
Jean Hartwig, Lorris, France, 1977. Sulphide bust portrait, front view slightly to sinister, of Elvis Presley, inscribed "1935 1977JH"; translucent cerulean blue ground. Multi-faceted top, sides, and perimeter of hexagonal concave base signed "Hartwig Jean France 1977." 8/150.
D: 2⅝" (6.8 cm.)
Gift of Ms Jean Hartwig, 1978.

1370
Cristalleries d'Albret, Vianne, France, 1967. Sulphide profile, to sinister, of Franklin Delano Roosevelt, edge signed "F. D. Roosevelt/G.S. 1967." Translucent amethyst base, cross-cut. 1430/2000.
D: 2²⁵⁄₃₂" (7.1 cm.)
Gift of George Ackerman, 1979.

1384
Cristalleries d'Albret, dated 1969. Grey/white double overlay; wide top punty, 8 side punties; polished colorless base cut with alternating miters and flutes; pontil area etched (in circle) "CR. Albret France-." Sulphide portrait of Paul Revere, front view; edge signed "CA.GP 1969." 6/200.
D: 3¹⁄₁₆" (7.8 cm.)
Gift of George Ackerman, 1979.

1385
Cristalleries d'Albret, dated 1969. Sulphide portrait of Albert Schweitzer, front view slightly to sinister, edge signed "A. Schweitzer. CA GP 1969." Wide top punty, 7 side punties. Polished, diamond-cut translucent cobalt blue base; pontil area etched, in circle, "CR. Albret France-." 63/1000.
D: 2¹³⁄₁₆" (7.2 cm.)
Gift of George Ackerman, 1979.

1520
River Shore, Ltd. (American), ca. 1979. Sulphide likeness by Roger Brown of Norman Rockwell's "Triple Self-Portrait," signed and dated. Sèvres lead crystal; flat cut top, 5 side punties; mitered translucent turquoise-green base cut with 24-point star and etched: "Rockwell's Triple Self-Portrait by Roger J. Brown © 1979 River Shore, Ltd. 0497/2500."
D: 2¾" (7.0 cm.)
Gift of Mrs. James T. Henry, 1985.

1540
Baccarat, 1973. Sulphide portrait, to dexter, of Harry S. Truman on edge-cut, flanged translucent amber base. Top, 6 side punties. Polished flat base etched with Baccarat insignia.
D: 2²⁵⁄₃₂" (7.1 cm.)
Bequest of J. Howard Gilroy, 1986.

1807
Saint Louis, dated 1981. Opaque white overlay; wide top punty and 6 side punties edged in gilt. Sulphide portrait of Pope John Paul II, slightly to dexter, shoulder edge marked "G.P. Jean-Paul II." Diamond-cut colorless base, "SL 1981" in gilt near edge. 11/300.
D: 3⅛" (8.0 cm.)
Gift of Mrs. Virginia Bensley Trowbridge, 1987.

GLOSSARY OF GLASS PAPERWEIGHT TERMINOLOGY

By Geraldine J. Casper

Anchor Cane. (632)
Simplified "anchor" silhouette.

Arrow Cane. (208)
Arrowhead with precise point.

Aventurine. (1125)
Translucent glass with suspended flecks of copper (gold-stone) in imitation of aventurine quartz; also, iron oxide (red aventurine) or chromic oxide (green aventurine). First recorded in Murano, early 17th century.

See red aventurine snake by Paul Ysart, No. 1078.

The grounds for No. 1125 and for No. 487 are actually "metallic green."

Basal Ring.
Flat (frosted or polished) circular surface surrounding pontil area. See "Pontil."

Base.
Bottom of paperweight.

Basket. (217, 93)
(1) Cone-shaped, spiral latticinio ground on which motif rests. (2) Stave (flat) rods surrounding close or concentric millefiori motifs, characteristic of Clichy.

Bouquet. (230, 338)
Two or more stylized or "natural" flowers in (1) flat or (2) upright arrangement.

Cameo Incrustation. (197)
A porcelaneous medallion in relief (cameo) encased in glass. Also "crystallo ceramie" (English) and "sulfure" (French), commonly called "sulphide."

Cane.
Segment or slice of glass rod: colorless, monochrome, millefiori, filigree, or silhouette — the design extending end-to-end.

Carpet Ground. (136)
Closely packed identical canes, sometimes in combination with single millefiori apex cane (No. 478), spaced florets and silhouettes (Nos. 136 and 158), or garland pattern (No. 95). Also "moquette" (French).

Chequer. (477)
Individual millefiori canes set within framework of straight sections of filigree or ribbon twist rods.

Close Millefiori. (430)
Motif of closely set multiple slices or segments of various millefiori canes.

Concentric. (484)
Millefiori canes and/or florets arranged in contiguous circles, sometimes within stave basket or in mushroom motif.

632

208

1125

217

93

230

338

197

136

477

430

484

Crimp. (GE-2)
Metal tool for shaping three-dimensional flowers, particularly "Millville" type roses.

Crown. (1159)
Refers to colorless dome of a paperweight and also to motif in which ribbon twists and/or spiraled filigree rods radiate from central cane or floret at apex, converging at base. Crown weights are usually hollow.

Crystal.
Transparent colorless glass resembling rock crystal. By current standards, "crystal" must contain at least 24% lead oxide.

Cushion. (185)
Convex-shaped ground.

Date. (124, 142, 149, 214, 348, 1106, 1107, 1299)
About one-third of antique Baccarat millefiori paperweights include the factory initial above the year in red, blue, or green in linked white canes (1846-1849, the latter rare with the "B"). The years 1847 and 1848 are most common.

In Cristalleries de Saint-Louis paperweights and some related items, the initials "SL" precede years 1845 through 1849, usually black, but may be blue or red. The year, however, is sometimes omitted. "SL 1848" is found most often. Fewer antique Saint Louis products than those by Baccarat are signed and dated.

Clichy millefiori paperweights and related items may include one or more "C" initial canes. Of three different "C" elements, one is without serif. A full "CLICHY" signature is rare, and a dated Clichy weight is as yet undocumented.

Millefiori paperweights (No. 22) and inkwells of English origin, dated "1848," have been traced to John Walsh-Walsh, Ltd., Birmingham, 1930s. (Ref.: John Smith, "The Myth of Whitefriars," 1987 PCA BULLETIN, pp. 4-6.) Whitefriars, Ltd., Wealdstone, England, produced similar *undated* items between the 1930s and 1980, when the glasshouse closed.

"1852" (sometimes in reverse), white numerals/blue canes seen most often, appears in Boston & Sandwich and New England Glass Co. scrambled millefiori weights.

Spurious 19th century dates could be special-ordered for early 20th century Baccarat pansy and patterned millefiori paperweights. (Ref.: Guillaume Chaumeil, "Short History of Baccarat Crystal Paperweights," 1973 PCA BULLETIN, p. 36.) Fake 19th century black dates in serrated oblong white plaques have appeared in weights of various other origins, particularly those made in Murano after 1952.

Most contemporary examples by leading makers and factories bear an etched basal identification and/or an encased signature/ date cane, or are signed with a diamond-point pen near base.

Facet. (400)
Wheel-cut flat or concave decoration, usually exterior, in one or more styles. See also "Printy."

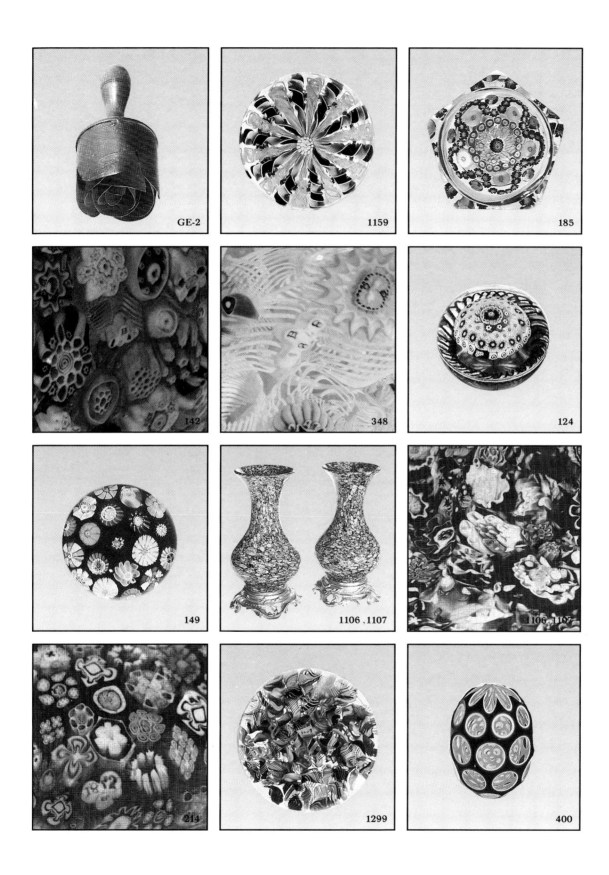

GE-2

1159

185

142

348

124

149

1106 , 1107

1106 , 1107

214

1299

400

Filigree. (440)
A glass rod enclosing fine threads of spiraled or twisted opaque white or colored glass. Also referred to as "lace," particularly when used as a ground.

Flash. (1528)
A thinly applied exterior layer of translucent colored glass for overlay or basal decoration (amber, red, blue, green, or amethyst).

Floret. (449)
Flower-like patterns in glass rods cut crosswise. Also "fleurette."

Garland. (95)
A chain pattern of florets, often looped and interlaced.

Ground.
Background for motif, such as color, carpet, jasper, latticinio, moss, filigree, upset filigree, etc. (See Nos. 1125, 136)

Jasper. (263)
Finely crushed glass particles of two or more colors used as a ground.

Lampwork. (67)
A glassworking technique that employs the direct flame of a torch; used for shaping individual parts of flora and fauna to be encased in paperweight.

Latticinio. (369)
Single or double spiral of flat opaque white or colored glass threads that radiate from center of ground or basket with "lattice" effect.

Macédoine. (530)
Segments of millefiori and/or filigree canes in random arrangement; also called "scrambled."

Marbrie. (467)
Festooned decoration in two or more colors, usually on opaque white globular ground; encased.

Millefiori. (142)
Decorative glass canes most often of floret type. Derived from Italian term for "thousand flowers" (mille fleurs in French).

Moss.
Green rods with or without white stars sometimes forming a ground resembling moss-like carpet.

Mushroom. (137)
Millefiori rods, tufted at top, in convex close or concentric arrangement, the ends drawn down to form sheaf; usually encircled by torsade at base.

Overlay. (96)
Colorless glass cased with one or more layers of opaque and/or translucent colored glass. Various types of faceting are used to reveal paperweight motif: millefiori or upright bouquet. Saint Louis overlays are generally faceted and then encased in colorless glass.

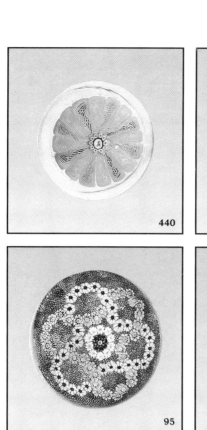

440

1528

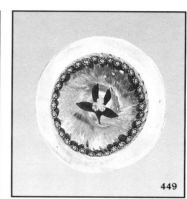

449

95

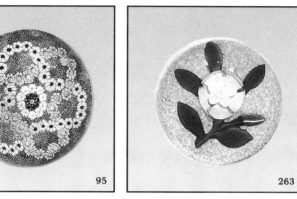

263

67

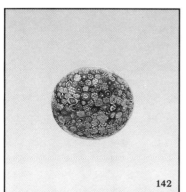

369

1306

467

142

137

96

Paperweight Terms.
Letter weight; press-papers; presse-papiers (French); fermacarte (Italian); briefbeschwerer (German).

Pastry Mold Cane. (147)
Floret, usually larger in size, that flares toward its base.

Pedestal.
A paperweight mounted on flared stem; footed. Also "piédouche" (French).

Pinchbeck. (504)
Foil-covered, relief-modeled motif set under thick lens-like dome glued to circular base of marble, pewter or wood. "Pinchbeck" derives from an inexpensive gold alloy of copper and zinc invented by Christopher Pinchbeck (1670-1732), London watchmaker.

Printy. (318)
British term for concave or flat circular cutting used to reveal motif in color-cased weights; also called "punty" or "window."

Pontil.
A long, solid metal tool about one inch in diameter used for gathering from the furnace molten glass and working it. Roughness that results when pontil rod is removed from finished object is called a "pontil mark." After annealing the glass, this roughness is most often ground away.

Rod.
Single monochrome design element or cane.

Silhouette. (1234)
Cane with figural image in cross-section; used in 19th century Italian, Bohemian, Baccarat, Saint Louis, Boston & Sandwich, New England Glass Company, and certain 20th century weights.

Swirl. (147)
Rods of two or more alternating colors spiraled from floret at apex.

Sulphide.
Common term for "Cameo Incrustation." A ceramic cameo or medallion encased in glass.

Torsade. (448, 137)
A coil, or "cordon," usually colored, that surrounds spiraled or twisted opaque white filigree and encircles base of motif (mushroom or upright bouquet). Most often seen in antique Baccarat, Saint Louis, and Bacchus weights.

Baccarat and Bohemian torsades, filigree, and ribbon twists spiral to left. Those by Bacchus, Boston & Sandwich, Clichy, New England Glass Company, and Saint Louis characteristically spiral to right. A rare Saint Louis crown weight (No. 371) includes twists in both directions, as do weights of Venetian and Val St. Lambert origin.

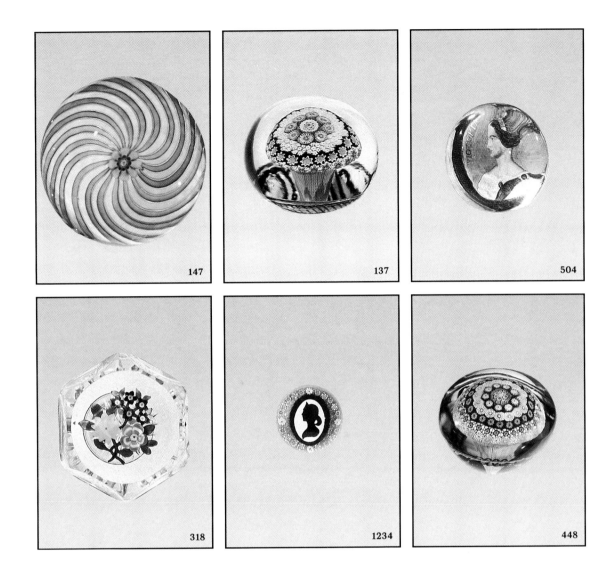

147

137

504

318

1234

448

NUMERICAL INDEX

PAPER WGT. NO.	PLATE NO.	PAPER WGT. NO.	PLATE NO.	PAPER WGT. NO.	PLATE NO.	PAPER WGT. NO.	PLATE NO.	PAPER WGT. NO.	PLATE NO.	PAPER WGT. NO.	PLATE NO.	PAPER WGT. NO.	PLATE NO.
1	69	50	77	100	31	146	36	188	17	233	32	282	25
2	74	51	38	101	76	147	33	189	11	234	6	283	5
3	10	53	9	103	9	148	11	190	12	235	35	284	39
4	27	54	18	104	79	149	15	191	63	236	49	285	96
5	37	56	9	105	13	150	48	192	64	237	69	286	68
6	35	57	8	106	7	151	14	193	17	239	60	287	67
7	58	58	51	107	14	152	74	194	31	240	60	289	35
8	48	59	27	108	59	153	68	195	58	241	54	295	69
9	15	60	27	110	66	154	7	196	33	242	39	296	69
10	20	61	82	111	54	155	18	197	6	243	53	297	34
11	13	62	55	112	16	156	61	198	42	244	59	298	94
12	43	65	77	113	57	157	55	199	21	245	69	299	71
13	52	66	16	114	20	158	23	200	62	246	6	300	70
14	80	67	51	116	77	159	30	201	7	247	20	301	70
15	69	68	13	117	48	160	14	202	52	248	21	302	60
16	70	69	54	118	58	161	56	203	18	249	69	303	44
19	73	70	32	119	47	162	44	204	28	250	69	304	72
20	38	71	19	120	81	163	73	205	38	252	42	305	68
21	42	72	45	121	52	164	81	207	65	253	78	306	30
22	14	73	19	122	84	165	15	208	16	254	68	307	66
25	66	74	9	123	23	166	8	209	40	255	44	308	46
27	74	76	42	124	21	167	58	210	44	256	58	309	96
28	72	77	78	125	1	168	31	211	17	257	51	311	5
29	60	78	80	126	22	169	53	212	65	258	5	312	48
32	74	79	70	127	50	170	13	213	8	259	11	313	2
33	74	80	7	128	51	171	53	214	63, 64	260	53	314	49
34	70	82	11	130	56	172	40	215	59	261	7	315	1
35	82	84	84	131	6	173	7	216	56	263	43	316	66
36	73	85	18	132	23	174	8	217	55	264	43	317	39
37	16	86	74	133	32	175	57	218	51	265	68	318	51
38	84	87	56	134	17	176	41	219	24	266	68	319	35
39	75	88	39	135	49	177	6	220	45	268	79	320	71
40	75	90	18	136	23	178	8	221	44	269	85	321	71
41	75	91	18	137	20	179	45	222	44	271	84	322	1
42	74	92	57	138	56	180	15	223	72	272	80	323	1
43	60	93	13	139	40	181	22	224	74	274	65	324	2
44	19	94	59	140	51	182	52	227	70	275	52	325	5
45	41	95	17	141	40	183	63	228	47	276	55	326	2
46	9	96	30	142	10	184	29	229	54	277	50	327	3
47	40	97	39	143	22	185	18	230	53	279	2	328	70
48	77	98	24	144	21, 65	186	61	231	51	280	58	330	68
49	77	99	55	145	23	187	45	232	60	281	54	331	11

PAPER WGT. NO.	PLATE NO.	PAPER WGT. NO.	PLATE NO.	PAPER WGT. NO.	PLATE NO.	PAPER WGT. NO.	PLATE NO.	PAPER WGT. NO.	PLATE NO.	PAPER WGT. NO.	PLATE NO.	PAPER WGT. NO.	PLATE NO.
332	4	386	39	440	35	501	62	563	108	635	111	711	45
334	35	387	36	441	20	502	29	564	108	636	107	712	81
335	80	388	69	442	57	503	26	567	67	637	4	713	82
336	80	389	69	443	61	504	61	568	70	638	108	715	79
337	59	390	77	444	74	505	79	569	65, 70	640	110	716	82
338	54	391	46	445	31	506	61	571	76	642	109	719	95
339	37	392	86	446	11	507	89	572	77	643	110	720	84
340	24	393	67	447	22	508	51	573	77	645	111	725	95
341	7	394	53, 67	448	20	509	50	574	77	646	110	726	95
342	7	395	82	449	52	510	43	575	63	647	3	727	96
343	72	396	59	451	7	511	61	576	63	648	109	728	107
344	72	397	96	452	52	512	74	577	63	649	4	729	88
345	72	398	76	456	4	513	15	579	76	651	107	731	78
346	41	399	12	457	4	514	72	580	76	652	110	733	56
347	40	400	32	458	17	515	58	581	68	655	89	734	13
348	63, 64	401	61	459	16	516	96	582	68	656	81	735	104
349	15	402	56	460	6	517	19	583	71	670	88	736	110
351	78	403	53	461	61	518	26	584	71	671	86	737	45
352	70	404	40	463	57	519	72	585	3	672	89	738	91
353	15	405	70	464	79	520	78	586	2	673	45	739	92
354	68	406	15	465	7	521	74	591	70	674	45	740	9
355	68	407	2	466	36	523	50	592	3	675	44	741	89
356	79	408	7	467	34	524	9	595	76	676	89	742	100
357	47	409	16	468	10	525	35	596	76	677	86	744	5
358	70	410	3	469	34	526	42	597	76	678	44	745	34
359	70	411	3	470	30	527	8	598	70	679	89	746	8
360	66	412	68	471	43, 11	528	77	601	70	680	89	747	82
361	66	413	3	473	62	529	57	602	70	681	89	751	83
362	70	414	24	474	20	530	67	603	70	682	89	753	84
363	26	415	2	475	28	531	61	604	70	684	89	754	82
365	1	416	48	476	29	532	28	605	72	685	89	758	84
366	42	418	83	477	25	533	28	607	72	686	95	759	85
367	48	419	31	478	20	534	5	609	71	687	92	760	78
368	5	420	1	480	22	535	62	610	80	688	95	761	79
369	39	422	81	481	46	536	2	612	71	689	92	762	79
370	33	423	72	482	6	537	45	613	72	690	85	764	83
371	36	424	22	484	14	540	82	616	72	691	10	767	87
372	21	425	56	485	38	544	6	617	71	692	32	769	86
373	44	426	42	486	47	545	95	621	71	693	31	770	88
374	44	427	57	487	41	546	33	622	71	694	45	771	11
375	44	428	13	489	68	548	81	624	71	696	109	772	93
376	4	429	12	490	65, 66	549	84	625	71	697	80	773	82
377	4	430	11	491	11	550	78	626	57	699	80	774	80
378	44	431	61	492	73	552	82	627	57	700	90	780	55
379	26	433	77	493	61	553	79	628	57	701	45	781	21
380	66	434	39	494	24	554	108	629	77	702	45	782	54
381	48	435	21	495	85	555	50	630	57	703	45	783	105
382	41	436	8	496	5	556	108	631	57	704	109	784	51
383	58	437	9	497	46	558	108	632	52	705	8	790	83
384	52	438	81	498	71	559	7	633	112	709	85	793	93
385	48	439	17	499	62	562	74	634	108	710	112	795	32

PAPER WGT. NO.	PLATE NO.	PAPER WGT. NO.	PLATE NO.	PAPER WGT. NO.	PLATE NO.	PAPER WGT. NO.	PLATE NO.	PAPER WGT. NO.	PLATE NO.	PAPER WGT. NO.	PLATE NO.	PAPER WGT. NO.	PLATE NO.
797	92	881	48	1018	27	1128	53	1193	37	1286	6	1367	70
798	111	882	25	1020	83	1129	40	1194	56	1287	10	1369	107
799	73	883	19	1021	83	1130	53	1197	41	1288	48	1370	112
801	87	885	33	1029	83	1131	50	1199	11	1289	8	1373	110
802	88	886	33	1030	110	1132	49	1201	16	1290	39	1374	108
810	69	889	55	1038	84	1133	2	1202	70	1291	32	1376	110
811	107	890	40	1047	81	1134	6	1207	69	1292	83	1378	111
813	69	892	51	1049	83	1135	55	1208	3	1293	106	1381	109
814	81	893	108	1052	83	1136	15	1209	5	1295	75	1382	108
819	80	897	41	1060	101	1137	40	1214	85	1296	76	1384	112
820	96	901	89	1061	79	1138	16	1216	94	1298	73	1385	112
821	61	902	88	1062	88	1139	54	1218	87	1299	27	1387	107
822	89	903	88	1063	57	1140	56	1219	93	1300	27	1388	107
823	37	904	89	1064	57	1142	50	1220	94	1301	52	1389	107
824	17	905	89	1065	86	1143	49	1221	93	1302	66	1392	107
825	112	906	88	1066	77	1144	46	1223	87	1303	69	1394	110
827	93	907	89	1068	111	1145	42	1228	111	1304	54	1396	109
828	109	908	95	1069	111	1146	49	1229	86	1305	18	1397	111
829	109	910	84	1072	104	1152	55	1230	73	1306	27	1398	110
830	111	912	84	1073	106	1153	40	1231	91	1307	43	1400	108
831	111	914	83	1074	104	1154	95	1232	91	1308	38	1401	110
833	85	915	91	1076	85	1155	49	1233	76	1310	72	1402	68
834	105	917	105	1078	95	1156	58	1234	88	1311	69	1404	108
835	53	918	105	1079	91	1157	49	1235	96	1313	60	1406	34
837	13	919	107	1082	14	1158	54, 67	1244	89	1314	60	1411	96
838	75	924	103	1085	75	1159	36	1245	90	1315	75	1415	78
839	87	927	46	1089	106	1161	39	1246	90	1316	73	1418	100
841	100	929	80	1090	106	1162	15	1247	89	1317	57	1424	84
844	81	931	83	1091	106	1164	58	1248	90	1319	76	1426	83
845	83	933	45	1092	106	1165	40	1249	89	1328	60	1427	69
847	112	934	79	1093	105	1166	20	1253	75	1329	75	1430	56
848	112	937	95	1095	33	1169	55	1254	93	1332	19	1431	2
849	109	940	85	1099	80	1170	50	1255	93	1336	88	1432	48
850	109	946	75	1100	80	1172	54	1257	111	1340	87	1433	75
853	93	947	83	1103	87	1173	50	1258	18	1341	57	1438	80
854	93	948	57	1105	100	1175	15	1262	78	1345	105	1449	95
855	86	952	88	1106	64	1176	21	1263	75	1346	106	1454	35
858	106	957	73	1107	64	1177	60	1266	75	1347	112	1458	38
859	58	962	87	1110	74	1178	50	1269	73	1348	105	1459	61
864	45	963	83	1112	37	1179	50	1270	81	1349	96	1460	96
866	104	964	83	1113	37	1181	25	1272	26	1350	105	1463	96
867	106	975	83	1114	39	1182	27	1273	109	1352	110	1464	91
868	69	976	82	1115	32	1183	16	1274	111	1353	107	1467	92
870	49	979	83	1117	54	1184	17	1275	43	1354	106	1468	23
871	106	981	78	1119	53	1186	8	1276	73	1355	73	1469	94
872	35	982	78	1121	49	1187	27	1277	109	1356	75	1470	87
873	41	987	53	1122	51	1188	25	1281	21	1357	93	1471	87
874	41	997	83	1123	8	1189	43	1282	60	1359	104	1472	76
875	52	999	83	1124	58	1190	12	1283	49	1360	106	1473	76
876	16	1004	32	1125	41	1191	41	1284	27	1361	106	1474	76
878	15	1010	82	1127	48	1192	39	1285	6	1362	106	1475	85

PAPER WGT. NO.	PLATE NO.	PAPER WGT. NO.	PLATE NO.	PAPER WGT. NO.	PLATE NO.	PAPER WGT. NO.	PLATE NO.	PAPER WGT. NO.	PLATE NO.
1476	76	1564	80	1653	97	1718	97	1785	92
1478	94	1565	100	1654	98	1719	99	1786	1
1483	94	1577	83	1655	98	1720	97	1787	25
1487	93	1581	83	1657	101	1721	97	1788	19
1489	90	1584	90	1660	97	1723	97	1789	16
1490	91	1585	90	1661	102	1725	98	1790	13
1491	30	1586	92	1662	99	1726	98	1791	46
1492	86	1588	46	1663	101	1727	101	1792	46
1493	91	1589	96	1664	100	1728	99	1794	81
1494	90	1590	88	1665	98	1729	99	1795	92
1495	91	1591	88	1666	97	1730	97	1797	94
1497	91	1593	89	1667	103	1732	102	1798	105
1498	94	1594	93	1668	102	1733	98	1799	19
1499	88	1595	91	1669	101	1734	98	1800	94
1505	86	1597	91	1671	97	1735	99	1801	94
1506	14	1599	75	1672	98	1736	97	1803	92
1507	91	1600	83	1673	97	1737	98	1804	55
1508	100	1603	88	1674	98	1738	103	1805	96
1509	85	1604	88	1675	98	1739	103	1807	112
1510	41	1605	78	1676	103	1740	102	1813	91
1511	72	1609	46	1677	102	1742	11	1814	92
1512	85	1611	95	1678	99	1744	99	1815	90
1513	71	1612	94	1679	98	1745	94	1816	90
1515	30	1615	104	1680	101	1746	98	1817	104
1516	86	1618	76	1681	99	1748	103	1818	104
1517	91	1619	106	1682	99	1749	102	1823	66
1518	106	1621	106	1683	99	1753	102	1824	71
1519	5	1622	106	1685	103	1754	102	1825	88
1520	112	1623	106	1686	98	1755	102	1826	85
1521	72	1624	105	1687	98	1756	94	1827	14
1522	84	1625	106	1688	98	1757	101	1828	107
1523	42	1626	105	1689	97	1758	99	1829	32
1526	89	1627	90	1690	55	1759	97	1830	104
1528	29	1628	91	1692	98	1760	101	1831	105
1529	90	1630	56	1696	98	1761	55	1832	104
1531	11	1631	105	1697	97	1762	101	1833	105,106
1532	32	1632	36	1698	101	1763	3	1834	104
1535	86	1633	99	1700	103	1765	52	GE-1	79
1538	14	1634	97	1702	101	1766	104	GE-2	46
1540	112	1635	99	1704	88	1767	10	GG-18	5
1543	93	1636	97	1705	75	1769	102	GG-142	9
1544	32	1637	100	1706	99	1770	102		
1545	87	1638	98	1707	98	1773	103		
1547	75	1639	99	1708	101	1774	100		
1555	77	1641	100	1710	99	1776	101		
1556	77	1642	99	1711	88	1777	46		
1557	87	1643	98	1713	103	1779	85		
1558	16	1647	97	1714	103	1780	93		
1559	92	1649	99	1715	102	1781	68		
1561	86	1650	103	1716	98	1783	100		
1563	84	1652	100	1717	11	1784	60		

SUGGESTIONS FOR NEW COLLECTORS

Distinguishing characteristics of certain origins become more readily apparent as the collector gains experience.

What at first may appear to be a confusing maze of patterns assumes increasing definition on further scrutiny:

- quality of glass
- profile and shape
- placement of design in the weight
- millefiori cane or floral types and arrangements
- ground — color, filigree, latticinio, jasper, or aventurine
- style of faceting
- pontil area in base
- signature, date, or paper label
- documented prototype
- fluorescence as a tool

Care of Paperweights

- Avoid scratching glass surface; protect from diamond-ring damage while handling.
- Display on clean surface with space between each weight; glass bruises other glass.
- Store individually in a padded box, never loosely in a drawer!
- *On padded surface,* clean glass at least annually with very mild detergent or just plain cool water. Avoid abrasives. Rinse with cool damp soft cloth.
- If surface is iridescent, avoid commercial cleaning solutions.
- ALWAYS support base of weight for added security during handling.
- Avoid sudden changes of temperature.